Black Robes Enter Coyote's World

Chief Charlo and Father De Smet in the Rocky Mountains

SALLY THOMPSON

Foreword by Myrna Adams Dumontier and Greg Dumontier

University of Nebraska Press | Lincoln

Manufactured in the United States of America

The University of Nebraska Press is part of a land-grant institution with campuses and programs on the past, present, and future homelands of the Pawnee, Ponca, Otoe-Missouria, Omaha, Dakota, Lakota, Kaw, Cheyenne, and Arapaho Peoples, as well as those of the relocated Ho-Chunk, Sac and Fox, and Iowa Peoples.

♾

Library of Congress Cataloging-in-Publication Data
Names: Thompson, Sally (Sally N.), author. | Dumontier, Myrna Adams, writer of foreword. | Dumontier, Greg, writer of foreword.
Title: Black Robes enter Coyote's world: Chief Charlo and Father De Smet in the Rocky Mountains / Sally Thompson; foreword by Myrna Adams Dumontier and Greg Dumontier.
Description: Lincoln: University of Nebraska Press, [2024]. | Includes bibliographical references and index.
Identifiers: LCCN 2024010227
ISBN 9781496239617 (hardback)
ISBN 9781496241719 (epub)
ISBN 9781496241726 (pdf)
Subjects: LCSH: Charlo, Salish chief, 1831–1910. | Smet, Pierre-Jean de, 1801–1873. | Salish Indians—History—19th century. | Salish Indians—Biography. | BISAC: HISTORY / Indigenous Peoples in the Americas | LCGFT: Biographies.
Classification: LCC E99.S2 T523 2024 | DDC 978.6004/979435092 [B]—dc23/eng/20240718
LC record available at https://lccn.loc.gov/2024010227

Set in Merope (Charles Ellertson) by A. Shahan.

To the Séliš People

May your grandchildren's grandchildren experience a supportive community of people, both Native and non-Native, working together to help sustain the beautiful, interconnected life of this Rocky Mountain world.

With much gratitude

Contents

Illustrations

Figures

Maps

Foreword

Myrna Adams Dumontier and Greg Dumontier

As descendants of the Bitterroot Salish people and present-day enrolled members of the Confederated Salish and Kootenai Tribes, we welcome the arrival of this book by Dr. Sally Thompson. *Black Robes Enter Coyote's World* brings forward an important time in our long history that is unfortunately misunderstood and all too often has been misrepresented by accounts that are poorly researched. We appreciate Sally's sympathetic view of what Salish people have endured throughout the difficult decades during the life of Chief Charlo. With the many intimate details brought forward here, many in our own tribal community will gain a clearer understanding of who they are and where they come from. We hope our neighbors, too, will read these words.

Although Sally is not from our Salish world, she has done an admirable job in telling this story in a responsible way. The book integrates records of firsthand experiences with our ancestors by European missionaries and later surveyors and settlers and presents the experiences from a viewpoint that is sensitive to the Salish.

That said, no outsider could ever fully grasp how we understand the world without first experiencing it as we have. We dwell in deep and active relationship with the gifts of creation in and around western Montana and the buffalo plains across the Continental Divide. After thousands of years, we know these lands in ways those from other lands cannot grasp. Through the respectful treatment of our culture and history presented in this book, the reader will gain insights into many important aspects of our world. This writing is both welcomed and needed, but it is not the whole story. We hope this book creates a hunger to learn more instead of a belief that a full understanding has been established. Our way of knowing can be like a breeze that cleanses the air or like a sip of water on a hot day. Much remains to be discovered.

Preface

Thirty years ago, when I first heard the phrase "our covenant with the Creator" from an elder at Taos Pueblo, I have wondered about its implications. I have since learned this concept isn't restricted to Taos, or to the Puebloan people of the Southwest, but rather it is universal among Indigenous people. This ongoing covenant shapes a different way of being in the world than the one I and other descendants of Christian European colonists have known since severing ties with our original homelands.

The magnitude of the underlying differences began to sink in during the early 1990s while I was conducting a Traditional Cultural Properties study in the homeland of the Pikunni (Blackfeet). The regulatory concepts within which I was to work failed to grasp their way of knowing. The government wanted them to identify particular "sites" and to draw lines around such discrete places of importance as if the places in between didn't matter. One world didn't translate into the other, resulting in regulations that were at odds with the holistic way Blackfeet know places. They couldn't do it. Theirs is a spiritual reality while the government's is material, measurable, and separable. If we were considering the human body instead of a natural area, the process would have us protect the organs while assuming everything else to be less important and therefore unworthy of protection, making it subject to exploitation.

The idea for this book came to me during my second reading of Jesuit missionary Pierre-Jean De Smet's Kootenai Country journal. The first time I read his account, I was absorbed with tracking his route through an area I know well. Questions did not emerge until later, when I reread his description after working with Kootenai people on the book *People before the Park* (2014). I wondered why De Smet, with no apparent motivating interest, reported on minerals, stands of timber, and grazing lands for future development as he traveled along. After all, these were Indian lands when the vast Oregon Country was not yet within the jurisdiction of the United States. Why would a Jesuit missionary be so focused on potential settlement locations for American immigrants? More to the point, why are Euro-Americans and Native Americans so fundamentally different in the ways they relate to land and nature?

My desire to bring to light the distinctions between the Indigenous and Euro-American worlds is driven by despair with our present global climate crisis and my recognition of our great need for wise guidance. I chose to focus on the Bitterroot Salish because I have spent more than four decades living in and developing a relationship with their homeland. Also, these were the lands and people with whom the Missouri Jesuits first established a relationship and about which Father De Smet wrote the most and cared most deeply. Finally, I believe the Salish story deserves more attention. Always a welcoming and generous people, time and again, through the difficult decades of the nineteenth century—at a time when warfare was the more common choice in the region—they opted for diplomacy.

The historical narrative of the West has tended toward tales of war. Americans love to read about the heyday of the Plains Indians, of Sitting Bull and Crazy Horse, and of the flight of Chief Joseph and the Nez Perce from the U.S. Army. To write such history as the one told in such narratives is having to rely on piecemeal and generally biased sources. Much of the work is filling in the blanks. Little is available to read about tribal communities that made other choices and about the pitiful and unglamorous period after reservations were established. But to ignore this part of the story is to fail to grapple with the reality of what happened to Native people and all the other living beings with the imposition of Manifest Destiny all across this land. This was more than a concept. This very European idea—the inevitable taking of lands from Indians—has had weighty ramifications, the consequences of which continue today. No matter where you live in North America, this story has been repeated.

What is astonishing about this story of America is that Indian people are still here, and they have managed to retain their fundamental values—those qualities that make them who they are. This book explores the heart and the roots of the remarkable resiliency of Indian people through the history of the Bitterroot Salish.

Acknowledgments

I struggle to know where to begin in the accounting of how this book came to be and to remember all those who helped me along the way. In a way it all started in 1997, when the Confederated Salish and Kootenai Tribes contracted with me to provide litigation support as an anthropological expert for an off-reservation treaty rights investigation of the upper Clark Fork River. My first tasks were to read all the original source material I could find about the area and its Native inhabitants and to learn their oral history and stories about the area. A team of elders assisted with my education, and members of their culture committee joined me for investigative field trips along the river. Their cultural memories of families checking the sloughs to see which tributaries had healthy fish populations connected them back to the time before the Anaconda Company, when the Clark Fork was a life giver, not something that needed remediation. This project was life changing for me. For one thing, this was the first time I read the writings of the Black Robes of the Rocky Mountain Mission and other early written accounts of the area. More important, I came to know my own place more deeply. After nearly two decades in Missoula, I started to fathom the rhythms of life in western Montana and to feel more rooted in my adopted homeland.

In 2002–3 I served on a committee to plan a cross-cultural conference in anticipation of the Lewis and Clark Bicentennial. At that time and over the next several years, I met a number of Bitterroot Salish descendants and had the opportunity to hear their stories and their concerns about the land, the state of their language, and their grandchildren. I want to especially thank Arleen Adams for her generous spirit and kindness to me at that time. She and other participants added human faces and deep histories to what I had learned from archives.

Over the next few years, four archivists and an old friend made a significant contribution to this book. My visits to Gonzaga University in Spokane and the Jesuit Archives in St. Louis were always met with a kind welcome and productive interaction by David Kingma at Gonzaga and by Nancy Mertz and later David Miros in St. Louis. I am grateful for their knowledgeable and generous assistance.

In 2005 Kingma played an outsized role in getting me into the inner sanctum of the Jesuit Archives in Vatican City (Archivum Romanum Societatis Iesu [ARSI]). My daughter Sarah and I had the opportunity to travel there to meet up with my other daughter, Ingrid, who was studying in Milan. We three were to spend part of the Christmas holiday in Rome. When I mentioned the trip to Dave, he replied that I really should go to the Jesuit Archives and that it would be a shame to miss seeing them. I was reluctant to work on this family vacation, but after receiving beautiful photos in the mail, with cautions about missed opportunities, I conceded. There, in the Jesuit enclave just a block from the Vatican, I landed in a treasure trove of documents from the Rocky Mountain Missions.

Back in Missoula, my friend and University of Montana colleague Gay Allison arranged for a small grant from EPSCOR for me to return to Rome that spring to organize relevant documents for scanning so that I could continue the research. Then that fall in St. Louis for the final event of the Lewis and Clark Bicentennial commemoration, I stopped in to visit with Gregory Pass, director of St. Louis University's Vatican Film Library, who suggested we visit the library's Special Collections. A short while later I was presented with an unprocessed box of "DeSmetiana" containing an illustrated field journal of De Smet's journey into the mountains from Vancouver, following the Clark Fork River to the Mission, Missoula, and Bitterroot Valleys in the winter of 1858–59. The sum of documents acquired through these opportunities forms the basis of the story told in this book. I remember each of these colleagues with deep gratitude.

My two daughters weren't the only ones to weather life with a research fanatic. My son Tim was subjected as well. The worst time was when we were headed to Kalamazoo for Sarah's college graduation and I couldn't resist making use of a few hours' layover in the Twin Cities with a stop at the Minnesota Historical Society. Neither of us will forget waiting for the taxi that never arrived, nearly causing us to miss our flight. My apologies to all three tolerant offspring for all inconveniences caused and heartfelt appreciation to each of you for your loving support.

A family reunion in Durango, Colorado, in 2010 led to a serendipitous connection with Dirk Behrens, a historian from Belgium. Dirk gave me the idea of traveling to Belgium to visit archives and places of importance to Father De Smet. Two years later he, along with his wife, Els, hosted me (and Ingrid) at their home in Ostend following our visits to the Catholic University archives in Leuven; then we went on to the Stedelijke Musea in Dendermonde, where the director, Aimé Stroobants, kindly escorted us on a De Smet tour in his hometown. Jackie Peterson, who a few years before had launched the notable exhibit and book *Sacred Encounters*, provided contacts to enhance the trip. I marvel at so much kindness and generosity.

Fast forward to 2016, when I applied for and was granted a fellowship from the Montana Committee for the Humanities (now Humanities Montana), at the time led by Ken Egan. The fellowship awarded by this crucial Montana organization was pivotal. It gave me a much needed nudge to prioritize work on this book project. I remain humbled by and grateful for the committee's support.

I want to thank University of Nebraska Press acquisitions editor Matt Bokovoy and the two reviewers who took me to task for sloppy citations and a cumbersome storyline. Their suggestions for improvements resulted in a more cohesive story, with more reliable quotes and citations. Anonymity allowed them to provide this critical input, which friends had sidestepped. Although I had a few moments of despair at the thought of a major rewrite, it soon became clear that they had shaped a much better and more readable book than what they had read.

A number of archivists helped bring about this amply illustrated narrative, especially Dave Miros and Ann Knake at the Jesuit Archives and Research Center (JARC), Henria Aton at the Archive of the Jesuits in Canada (Archives des jésuites au Canada), and Mark Fritch at the University of Montana. I also want to thank Bill Whittaker, Iowa Office of the State Archaeologist; Alessandro Pezzati at the University of Pennsylvania Museum; and Charles Doran at the Princeton University Library. I also want to thank Blake Norton, director of the Cultural Heritage Center of the Citizen Potawatomi Nation, for his generous help. Maps were skillfully prepared by Hannah Shafer.

Thoughtful colleagues, friends, and experts in various fields have commented on various drafts and through many titles. Others helped me work through the phases of finding a publisher. Some simply encouraged me with various kinds of support through these long years. My appreciation for their kindness and generosity knows no bounds. I hold deep gratitude for each and every one: Francis Auld, Dirk Behrens, Bob Bigart, Violet Birdstone, Kim Briggeman, Ted Catton, Rosemary Caye, Mark Connell, Nancy Connell, Sara Dant, Anita Doyle, Ken Egan, Bill Farr, Dan Flores, Gwen Florio, Joyce Hocker, Minette Johnson, Bob Knight, Thea Koehler, Brian Matz, Sally Muller, Susan O'Connor, Neva Oliver, Marvie Redmond, Roly Redmond, Darnell Rides At The Door, Marina Ritchie, Jenny Rohrer, Bryony Schwan, Sandra Scofield, Annick Smith, Julie Stevenson, Mary Stranahan, David Suwalsky, and Sara Wilcox.

Important support came my way through participation in a small writing group with Beth Judy and Donna Erickson. The thoughtful, perceptive input provided by these talented authors, chapter by chapter, kept me on track and on my toes. Their continuing support throughout the process is a great gift in my life.

Three individuals stand out above the rest for their dedicated and ongoing assistance. First, early in the process I met George Capps, an entrepreneur and scholar from St. Louis. Although he is much younger than I, his knowledge of the Rocky Mountain Mission Jesuits, fur traders, and Salish leaders dwarfs what I have acquired over the decades. His careful reading of multiple drafts of this work has saved me from some embarrassing errors. More essential, though, has been his willingness to share carefully compiled information about individuals in the story, specifically people of the Bitterroot Salish community and Iroquois fur trappers who settled among them. This contribution lies at the core of what allowed me to tell a close-up story, with fleshed-out individuals. Thank you, George. May your generosity return to you manyfold!

Second, friend, neighbor, and talented writer Peter Stark volunteered to read through the manuscript not once but twice, each time making substantive suggestions that resulted in a much improved narrative.

During the COVID year, he and his wife, Amy Ragsdale, would gather with me around one of our campfires to share their experiences of the publishing world. They helped assist me through each phase of the process. Much gratitude to them both!

Third, the person who kept me on track throughout the prolonged process of writing and encouraged me during periods of doubt was my husband, John Weaver. For several years, whenever we drove anywhere for more than half an hour, he would listen to me read aloud from drafts of chapters. On countless occasions, brushing aside frustration over hikes not taken due to the seemingly endless writing odyssey, he brought his fine mind and keen understanding into the moment to help me remember the big picture. Time and again he encouraged me to bring my best work forward. I treasure these gifts.

Once a solid draft of the manuscript was ready for review, I asked Johnny Arlee, Mary Jane Charlo, Myrna Adams Dumontier, Greg Dumontier, and Lucy Vanderburg—all Bitterroot Salish descendants—to read and comment on what I had written. I knew that this was a risky move but one that had to be taken. This book addresses history during a pivotal time in the lives of their grandparents, and I needed their blessing to move forward. As Myrna and Greg express in the foreword, each of them appreciated what they read and encouraged me to proceed. Their affirming words make the long years of work worth every effort. I hope this book helps build better relationships through greater understanding.

Finally, I would like to express my gratitude to the PROP Foundation, Missoula, for helping to cover costs of image acquisition and indexing.

Black Robes Enter Coyote's World

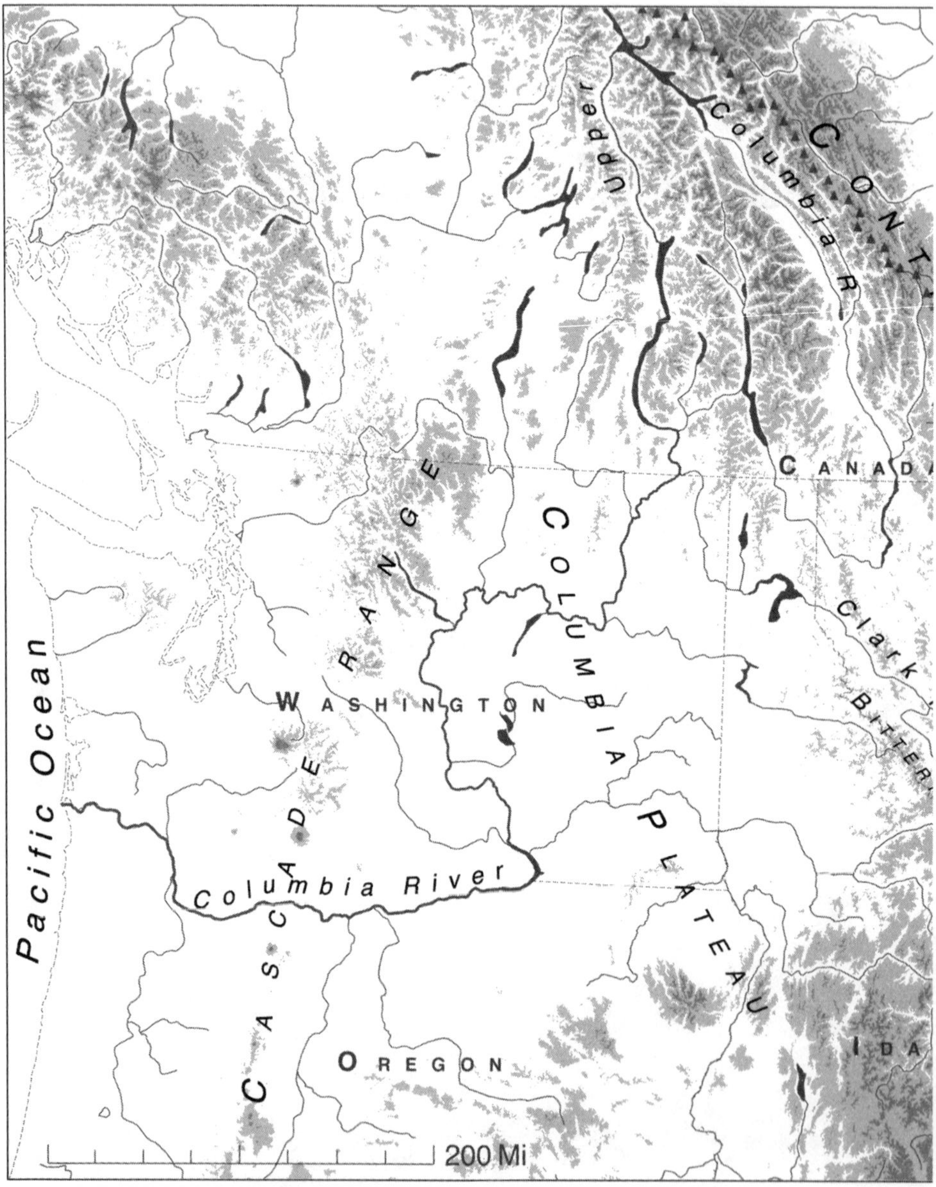

MAP 1. Overview map. Hannah Shafer, cartographer.

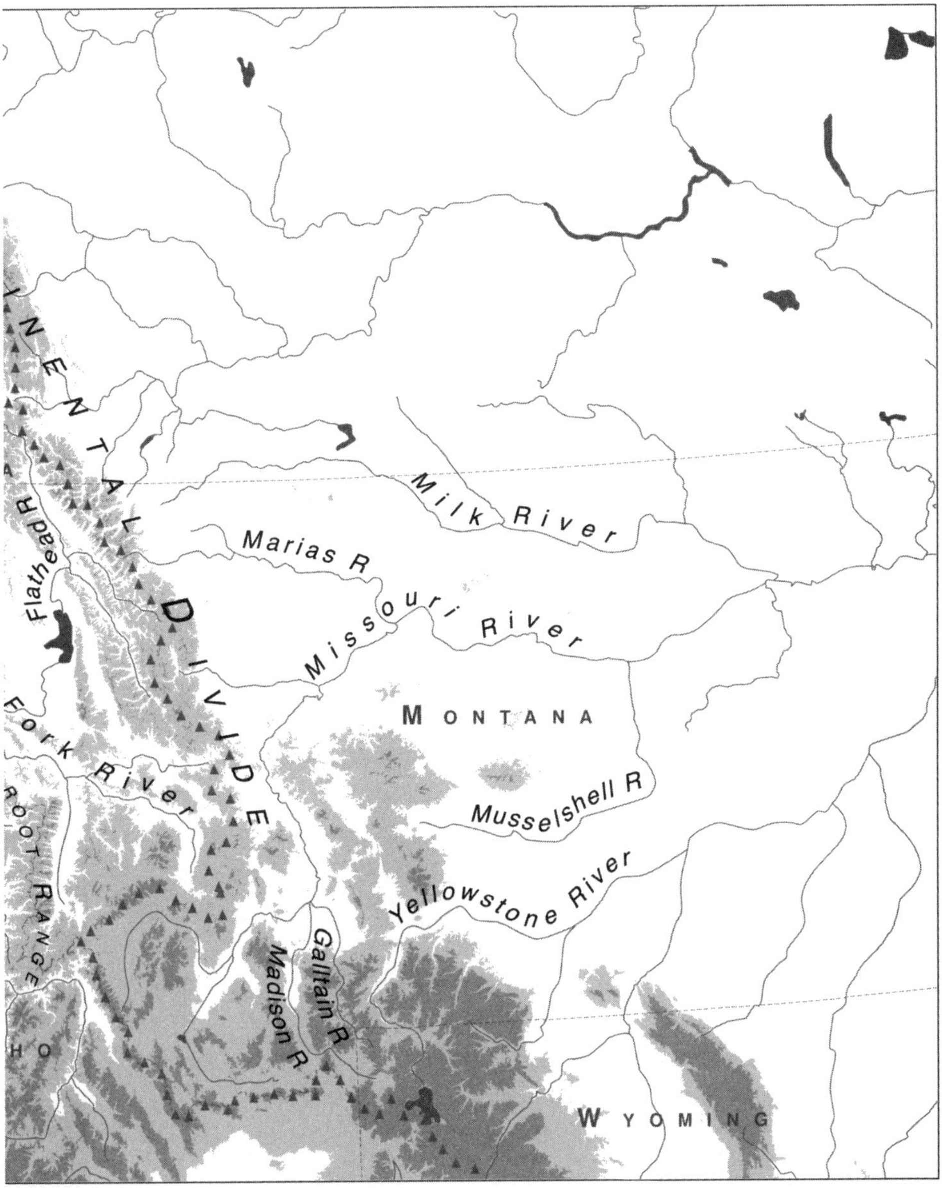
Milk River
Marias R
Missouri River
Flathead R
Fork River
ROOT RANGE
MONTANA
Musselshell R
Yellowstone River
Madison R
Gallitain R
WYOMING
HO
INENTAL DIVIDE

Introduction

Midstream Moment

> Each of us is responsible for how we see, and how we see determines what we see. Seeing is not merely a physical act: the heart of vision is shaped by the soul.
>
> —John O'Donohue, *The Invisible Embrace*

Bitterroot Valley, Montana Territory, 1876. On a cold day in February in the year of the nation's centennial, the mood among those gathered at the Place of Wide Cottonwoods was far from celebratory. The Native people of the Bitterroot Valley were there to learn from their chief, "Claw of the Small Grizzly," about the latest threat to their well-being. Chief Charlo, as he was known in the white world, wanted his impoverished people to understand the property taxes about to be levied against them by the Missoula County Commission.

On that crisp morning, heart as cold as the air, Charlo looked into the faces of his people and then to the snowy peaks beyond and took courage. He began, and his words were harsh: "Yes, my people, the white man wants us to pay him." Charlo's voice carried through the hushed crowd.[1] "[The white man] says we must pay him—pay him for our own—for the things we have from our God and our forefathers; for things he never owned and never gave us." The chief thought back to the day that the white man first stepped foot onto their treasured homeland, reminding those gathered there of their shared history.

"More than seven times ten winters have snowed and melted," Charlo called out, referring to the time since the Lewis and Clark expedition had arrived among them. His grandfather Three Eagles had been chief then, and he had taken pity on the poverty of these hungry, pale-faced travelers. Charlo's father, Many Horses, known to the whites as Victor, had been a young teenager then and told his son stories of that time. The Salish had fed these travelers, changed out their broken-down horses, and showed them the pathways through their lands. Without Salish help the famous explorers would likely have failed in their attempt to cross the snowy Bitterroot Mountains in September 1805.

When Charlo was about ten years old, thirty-six winters after that first encounter, the Salish had welcomed into their midst the first Jesuit priests, led by Pierre-Jean De Smet. These "Black Robes" had established St. Mary's Mission not far from the very place where Charlo was addressing new threats to his people's existence. The mission was where they had learned stories of the Bible when they were children. Charlo's father had become head of the first Christian men's society.

The Jesuits had arrived at a pivotal time in Salish history, before the Place of Wide Cottonwoods became Stevensville, before boundary lines defined property, and before the buffalo were gone. The missionaries had built the first fences and planted crops of Europe—alongside a fear of the devil. They had imposed a very European world onto an ancient Salish landscape and onto the people themselves. They would be transformed through baptism, Christian teaching, and general education in the ways of civilization. The missionaries had worked to replace Salish stories with those of the Bible, not understanding that the traditional stories reflected the lived experience of their ancestors and themselves in that very place they still called home. The abstract world of the priests could never fully replace this cultural biography.

It was this disconnect between worlds that set into motion the despairing speech of Chief Charlo three decades after De Smet had left the area. Since first contact, the Salish people had shown kindness to white visitors—explorers, fur traders and trappers, missionaries, railroad surveyors, and treaty makers—but their efforts had not served them well. In 1855 Charlo's father and other leaders signed a poorly understood treaty in which they ceded the majority of their vast homeland to the U.S. government. Each side, Indian and white, had its own understanding of the document to which the representatives affixed their marks. The Indians were promised monetary compensation, along with goods and services, in exchange for their agreement to open their lands to others. The U.S. government expected the Indians to move to the Flathead Reservation, some sixty miles to the north, after loose ends regarding the Bitterroot Valley were resolved. Some of the people did move, especially those drawn there by the new mission of St. Ignatius, but many, led by Victor, refused to leave the place where their ancestors were buried.

By 1876 those Salish families who remained in the Bitterroot Valley were suffering. They had received little of what had been promised in the treaty. Their small farms were insufficient to provide for their needs, and each year the buffalo were harder to find. The very survival of these people, who had never lifted a hand against a white man, had become tenuous. These were the circumstances that led to Charlo's speech.

After he concluded his overview of the Salish history with Euro-Americans, his thoughts took a different turn. Every white person gathered there must have been astonished to hear what came next. The white man "is his own snake," the chief declared, "which he says stole on his mother in her own country to lie to her." Although the translation reported in the *Weekly Missoulian* newspaper begs clarification, the words clearly alluded to Eve and the snake. Charlo went on to say that these Europeans, based on their own story, believed "that man was rejected and cast off," in reference to the casting out of the first people from the Garden of Eden. The perceptive Salish chief had come to believe that the meanness and greed he experienced among Euro-Americans were rooted in their own creation story. These cast out, "fallen" people—orphans from another land, with no sense of rooted belonging—had needs that could never be filled.

"Why did we not reject him [the white man] forever?" Charlo asked, and his question triggered heartbreaking memories for all the people gathered under that overcast sky. They remembered dead relatives, broken promises, and lost lands. Now this taxation, if levied, might force them from their homeland and the graves of their ancestors.

The angry leader understood the consequences if taxes were levied. The Salish people would lose what little livestock they had, and the losses would be catastrophic. Their horses took them to food, especially to buffalo, and their cattle provided a safety net when they returned from buffalo hunting empty-handed, an increasingly frequent outcome.

Concluding, the chief reminded his people about what truly mattered: their own laws, which were established by the Creator at the beginning of time. They should remember that the white man's laws never gave them "a blade nor a tree, nor a duck, nor a grouse, nor a trout." Charlo then made clear his position on the white man's notion to tax the Salish: "We owe him nothing; he owes us more than he will pay."

⟩⟩⟩

We are all shaped by the world of our experience and the beliefs introduced to us in childhood and refined through the years. The resultant views literally shape what we can see. Euro-Americans and Native Americans may have occupied the same spaces but have lived in different worlds. To read American history is to know only one version of the past. In western Montana the records of explorers, fur traders, missionaries, surveyors, and early settlers reflect their own interests and biases, and relatively few records of the Native perspective have survived. The writers of this history have directed our eyes toward what *they* see and believe, essentially a story of European superiority.

The ancient wisdom of the Indigenous people of North America has essentially been ignored by colonists since the time of their arrival. Vast oral libraries of knowledge have been lost through disease and warfare, and what remains in the written record has been distorted through the eyes of the beholders, those who have held the pen. Even the European side of the story is more complicated than the one most often crafted, and the Indian side has been presented like a footnote.

With the arrival of light-skinned people from across the sea, Native people watched their relations be annihilated and their beloved lands whittled away through tricks and treaties. In what to Indigenous people must have seemed like a quick blink of an eye, the ancient living systems that had sustained them since time immemorial were reduced to mere remnants. At times they too participated in the destruction of natural bounty. Ultimately many accepted the ways of the white people or faced annihilation in this American holocaust. Early in the twentieth century, so bleak were the reports from Indian Country that photographers Edward Curtis and Rodman Wanamaker both focused on creating visual records of the "noble, though vanishing race" before the people native to the land were gone. What is astonishing about this story is that despite overwhelming odds and indescribable abuses, Native people of America *are still here*.

Imbedded within American history is a story of two distinctive options for how to live in this world. Rarely are both perspectives so well documented in one distinctive place as in the Bitterroot Valley and the larger Salish homeland. This unusual history allows us to look back and consider the consequences of the different ways of being. We have Father De Smet's detailed narratives and those of his fellow missionaries and other white observers to be considered alongside intact tribal memories. Contrasting these historical sources provides a lens focused on two ways of life, played out in real places among real people, not just philosophically. De Smet's writings provide the means to consider the larger context of westward expansion into the interior Rocky Mountains, and Chief Charlo's speech provides exceptional entry into a world rarely noted, along with his thoughts on the essential relational differences between Euro-Americans and Native Americans. For other reasons as well, this story of a valley in what is now western Montana, told through the different vantage points of Jesuit missionaries and Salish leaders, holds exceptional possibility for piercing the veil between the worlds. The bicultural historical record of the intertwined lives of Chief Charlo and Father De Smet provides a particularly rich story from which to consider the future as well as the past.

The valleys of western Montana and north Idaho and adjacent parts of Canada are still inhabited by their original occupants, and for this reason history was not so long ago. The timeless worlds of the Salish (Séliš), their Pend d'Oreille (Ql'ispé) relatives, and neighboring Kootenai (Ktunaxa) tribes continued well into the nineteenth century because they were some of the last lands to be settled by Euro-Americans. And today, despite their many losses, these tribal nations continue to be grounded in their original worldview in this place they still call home.

De Smet's travels—from Europe to America, then from a plantation in Maryland to a Catholic novitiate near St. Louis, and finally to the Rocky Mountains—provide a thread for us to follow a European worldview carried to a new continent. With interests reaching far beyond saving souls, De Smet's writings provide glimpses into the unfolding history and geography, the changing demographics, and his own attitudes carried from his land across the Atlantic to this homeland of others.

Father De Smet's writings and those of his fellow Jesuits have generally been taken at face value. They were there, after all, in the Wild West, recording their written and visual observations. But the record needs to be reexamined. The backgrounds and worldview of the missionaries differed significantly from those of the native inhabitants. De Smet's were shaped along the shores of a shipping hub in Dendermonde, Belgium, during the Napoleonic Wars at the beginning of the Industrial Revolution. His world in no way prepared him to fathom the full picture of life in Indian Country. The Jesuits described the particular trees but not the forest. We don't need to question the truth of their words, only their points of view.

Wisdom resides in ancient places and can be gleaned from this story of the braided cultural streams that merged—for a time—at the Place of Wide Cottonwoods in the Bitterroot Valley. This is not a call to go back to the old ways that Native Americans lived before Pilgrims arrived on these shores. The rest of us cannot simply adopt Indian ways of being, and even if we could, there is no "back" to go to. Instead this is a call to reconsider attitudes and beliefs about the nature of the living world and our relationship to it.

The contents of this nineteenth-century narrative flow through millennia—from the last ice age to the present, from close-up to big view—sweeping across a beloved homeland in order to understand foundational influences on our systems of belief. There is an essential wisdom in the old ways. As the shifting streams approach the delta, we catch glimpses of the flash-flood impacts of our lifeways and seek out the small, healthy channels that carry hope for restoration before the waters reach the sea.

Part 1. Merging Streams, 1790–1840

Nature is, above all, profligate. . . . Nature is a spendthrift, lavish in her economy, infinitely inventive, but failing to keep books—a penny spent or a penny saved.

—Henry Beston, *Outermost House*

1. Separate Worlds

Young Charlo (1830–40)

Little is known about the boy who would become known as Chief Charlo of the Salish (Séliš) Nation. Depending on the time of year of his birth, his people could have been settled into their winter village in the Bitterroot Valley at Łq éł mlš, the Place of Wide Cottonwoods, or they could be fishing for bull trout and digging roots in the Missoula Valley, or perhaps they were on the buffalo plains or someplace in between. Their village leader would have determined such details with the help of the men and women of the community. Their decisions would reflect the unfolding world around them—especially the stage of plant cycles and the flow of the rivers.

Charlo's mother, Kahkahpee, might have excused herself from the traveling camp while she brought her son into the world, then caught up with her people a day or two later, with her infant bathed and swaddled in deerskin and carried in a cradleboard. She might have given him a name related to the first object she saw after he emerged.

Kahkahpee and her older sister were both married to Lodge Pole, the son of the deceased head chief, Three Eagles. It was not uncommon for men to take second wives during this age of warfare, when so many women had no one to hunt for them. Charlo's father was a brave man and a good provider, much admired in the community. Although the spirit helper he acquired when he was young was but a small rabbit, its protection had served Lodge Pole well. He had gained the support of this humble creature after saving one such animal from an attacking hawk.[1] Even though rabbits are extremely vulnerable to predation,

Lodge Pole was known to have escaped from many life-threatening situations with the aid of this spirit ally.[2]

Mothering included bathing baby Charlo in the stream each morning before dawn. When Kahkahpee brought him back to the lodge, she would lay him down on a soft robe so his arms and legs would be free to move all around—something not possible in the cradleboard. Massaging arms, legs, hands, and feet was an important part of taking care of babies. Ointments would be rubbed into his skin that carried power to make him brave and a good hunter. Often a sibling or cousin or a young girl would help attend to his needs by singing and playing with baby Charlo until sleep overtook him.

Raising children was a community affair. Newborns were lavished with gifts, especially by grandparents. A young colt was the most cherished gift.[3] Charlo's grandfather Three Eagles had already died, but the boy had others in the community to fulfill this role. In this Salish village there was no distinction between grandparents and grand-aunts and grand-uncles. All of these relatives were the immediate family.

The world into which the future chief was born was surprisingly cosmopolitan, given the relative isolation of his homeland from more populous hubs. In addition to his own people, the Salish, his world was shared with men and women from many of the neighboring tribes: their relatives—the Ql'ispé (Kalispels; Upper and Lower Pend d'Oreille), Nimiipuu (Nez Perce), Apsáalooke (Crows), Ktunaxa (Kootenais), and Agaidika (Lemhi Shoshones)—and even their enemies, the Pikunni (Blackfeet). Others, like the Mohawks, Shawnees, and Hurons, came from faraway places not long before the boy entered the world.[4] *Suyapis* (white men) too were part of Charlo's childhood. From the time of Three Eagles, the Salish chiefs had welcomed these men from many places to settle among them.

Since the Canadian fur trade had armed the Blackfeet, before the first white men passed through the Salish country, the people had suffered. The power dynamic shifted when Lodge Pole was a young man and Canadian fur trader David Thompson's people brought guns to trade.[5] After that they could fend off attacks and stand up to their enemies. They no longer felt like hunted sheep, but they lost as many or more people in battle than before. The influx of Iroquois and French Canadian trappers added to their numbers of fighting men.

Trappers and traders arrived in the region about two decades before Charlo entered the world. The Salish often traveled with these white men, who helped with their defense, and beaver trapping became part of the seasonal round for some of the Salish. The fur companies provided guns and ammunition and other trade goods in exchange for pelts. The people replaced their own creations with more durable options like kettles and knives and beads, and they acquired adornments, like tinkling bells, pleasing to the eye or ear. Women's work was made easier by these ready-made objects while at the same time the women took on additional work to gain the benefits that came through trade. They prepared the hides that men traded for ammunition and plugs of tobacco for themselves, and for their wives, household goods, beads, and other ready-mades were acquired.

New technology swept away the old. Many traditions of the Salish had faded into memory by the time of Charlo's birth. Rarely did his people stop at their traditional stone-gathering places for materials to make tools. Only the older men remembered how to chip the stone to create the particular shape and thinness of an arrow or lance point. With long-lasting, ready-made metal tools available, they didn't need to.

Along with kettles and iron blades came the medicine powers the Iroquois trappers spoke of and the prayers they chanted from their little books. Head chief Face-Raised-Up Grizzly—a man Charlo referred to as "uncle"—was drawn by this way of communicating with the spirit world and intrigued by what Grand Ignace and other Iroquois believers told him of men who wore black robes.[6] These must be the same people that Shining Shirt, the Pend d'Oreille medicine man, proclaimed would be coming.[7]

After the First Roots Ceremony in the springtime when Charlo was still an infant in his cradleboard, his people traveled south to the Snake River plain for hunting buffalo bulls, highly valued especially for their hides.[8] They killed only bulls at this time of the year because "the cows already have calves or soon will have them."[9] They gathered foods in the mountains before returning to their main village.

In early fall Face-Raised-Up Grizzly led his people to hunt buffalo cows in the Jefferson River Valley, in the vicinity of present-day Dillon, Montana.[10] The people would feast on fresh meat and then the women would dry what remained for winter stores and prepare the supple hides. Depending on how much they had and how burdened their horses were, they would either head home by a direct route or extend the fall hunting season into the mountains for elk, sheep, or deer. Women gathered the last fruits as they headed back toward the Bitterroot Valley.

The next spring, when Charlo would have been toddling, the Salish might have set up their camp at the mouth of Rattlesnake Creek in what is now Missoula, at the place they called Nłʔay, Place of the Small Bull Trout. The women would dig bitterroot while the men fished and their horses fattened up on the emergent spring grasses.

In the spring of Charlo's second year, the Salish met up with trader Warren Ferris, who supplied them with ammunition, tobacco, and other desired items and invited Face-Raised-Up Grizzly to bring his people to the annual rendezvous at Pierre's Hole, just northwest of the Tetons. These jamborees began in 1825 as a place where fur trappers, their suppliers, and buyers could meet to exchange goods and celebrate the end of the season. The chief had enjoyed himself at the gatherings he had attended, so he agreed. The Salish camp proceeded southward from the Beaverhead Valley to the high basin at the headwaters of the Teton River, on the sunset side of the towering Teton Mountains.[11] Once lodges were up and ready and families were settled into their spaces at the edge of the great gathering place, Chief Face-Raised-Up Grizzly, astride his well-trained horse, made his rounds. He went lodge to lodge, reminding his people about his expectations regarding their behavior while attending the rendezvous. Wearing his black stovepipe hat adorned by four red feathers, he delivered a "moral lecture" each day.[12]

The Salish chief "was a great favorite with all white men, and received generous presents from all the various companies," according to Ferris, who reported that the old chief responded with generosity and gratitude and then offered an earnest prayer to the Great Spirit that the white men would be protected in all they did.[13] Face-Raised-Up Grizzly was an inspiration to all those who knew him and a model for how a young Salish boy should grow up to be.

Charlo would have learned to ride a horse as soon he could sit up and hold on. At the big gathering of mountain men and Indians, the four-year-old might have marveled at the sight of their war chief Insula, Standing Head-Feathers, jumping onto the bare back of a wild mustang with nothing to hold onto except the mane, then coaxing the horse into trusting him.[14] Men earned the respect of others when they could influence animals like that. Many of the boys imagined themselves able to settle a wild horse so easily when they were older. They would need to hone their skills well if they were to survive the battles, skirmishes, and horse raids their people endured.

When children were old enough to be playing together, they were watched by an adult male appointed by the chief to keep them in check. This man would be one known for "his kindness and affection for children." His responsibilities were to keep them from getting underfoot, "away from sacred objects or places," and safe from harm.[15] The son of Lodge Pole and Kahkahpee, along with his peers, learned games that taught practical skills needed to survive in their world. The hoop-and-dart game taught him to aim and time the release of an arrow to pierce a rolling hoop, and he developed intuition and powers of perception by watching his family members while they played "hands," the stick game. In the summer of 1834 Charlo might have found himself mesmerized by the way old Sinsipee, the medicine woman, played the game.[16] She would lead the singing for her team, and with her strong powers, her team usually won. The other team rarely guessed which hand held the marked bone.

As young Charlo grew, he learned to snare small animals to help feed his family. He learned to fish and to know what materials made the strongest bows and straightest arrows and fishing spears. He learned what to look for in a good buffalo horse and how to stay astride no matter what direction his horse might jump. His aim grew ever more true. In camp this serious boy learned the prayers taught to his people by some of the Iroquois.

The year when Charlo turned six, he and his family had quite a scare. That summer, just before the rendezvous began on the Green River, on the east side of the Tetons, his mother and her sister were feeling very anxious. Lodge Pole was late returning from an excursion with a small

FIG. 1. "Jeux des petits sauvages" (Games of the children). Nicolas Point Missionary Drawings Collection, JA-IX-C-9-093, Jesuit Archives and Research Center.

group of mountain men to learn what had become of the supply train from St. Louis. They were attacked twice by Crow Indians who stole their horses, leaving Lodge Pole and the others to return the slow way, with one tired foot in front of the other.[17]

The next spring, the family was in the root-gathering camp in the Bitterroot Valley when a Protestant minister named William Gray came through. When the white man "gathered the Indians . . . and sang some hymns," Charlo might have sensed that his father was not impressed. He wasn't alone.[18] Gray was not what the Salish were waiting for. Perhaps he did not speak from the heart, and he was not what their prophet had foretold.

In the winter lodge the boy heard stories of his ancestors and the Animal People. Close to the time of the longest night, the community participated in medicine dances introduced to them by the religious leader Shining Shirt.[19] He foretold the coming of the Black Robes, among other prophecies that came to him through a mysterious voice when he was in a deep meditative state.[20] Shining Shirt was also a successful war leader, due in part, he believed, to a little, supernaturally charged metal talisman he carried with him. He claimed that those who bit into the metal before engaging in battle would be protected from arrows or shells.

Learning was by doing. Charlo followed the example of older boys and men in this close-knit community. Boys started on their road to manhood with small chores, then gained more responsibility as they were able. They came to know how to live, what to eat, how to find water and food, how to find their way, and how to get along with others. They looked forward to the time that they would have the chance to gain a spirit helper and wondered if their courage would sustain them through this test. As the son of a chief's son and nephew of the head chief, Charlo learned by example to take care of those in need.[21] Generosity was emphasized. Sharing with others was expected. It didn't matter who shot what on a buffalo hunt; everyone would eat and have dried meat for later. By the time Charlo was ten, he was a capable, contributing member of his community. That would be the year that he saw his first Black Robe.

Iroquois Trappers (1814–25)

Three Iroquois men—Pierre Gauché, Petit Ignace, and Grand Ignace—are essential elements in this story of Chief Charlo and Father De Smet. They are the bridge between the two. All three had settled into life with the Salish before Charlo was born, having traveled from their Mohawk villages on the St. Lawrence River to the Rocky Mountains as voyageurs with the fur trade some years before.

Pierre Gauché carried the surname Kassawessa (Gahsaweta, meaning Chalk/Lime). He came from Akwesasne, "Land Where the Partridge Drums," a remote village with the mission of St. Regis, situated more than one hundred miles southwest of Montreal.[22] From there, Pierre and his group came west with the North West Company (NWC) in 1817. After reaching the southern headwaters of the Columbia River in 1819, the company put his group to work in the Snake River Country of what is now Idaho. The work was not to Pierre's liking. He deserted and disappeared from history for a couple of years. When he reemerged in 1822, he rejoined the Snake Country Expedition under the Hudson's Bay Company (HBC).

In 1821 the HBC had implemented the Snake River Brigades, a kind of scorched-earth plan concocted to discourage Americans from trapping in the Oregon Country. This was territory the British thought of as their own since they had raised their flag at Fort George (formerly the American commercial establishment of Astoria) in 1812. These large brigades would kill every fur-bearing animal they could find across a wide swath of earth and river. Their intention was that HBC would leave the Snake River Country so devoid of commercially lucrative life that the Americans would not risk venturing across. Working conditions were terrible, and again Pierre deserted and disappeared.

The HBC thought its wayward employee had died in a snowstorm, but Pierre—also known as Gauché or Pierre Lefthand—was one of two ragged Iroquois who turned up at Fort Atkinson in Nebraska in July 1823.[23] He and his companion had been attacked during the winter by Crows, who kidnapped a woman and two children who were with them. These two were the only ones to embark on the dangerous journey across enemy country to seek assistance in recovering those who had been taken. They endured "many bloody encounters with the Indians" on their journey to Fort Atkinson, twenty miles north and across the Missouri from Council Bluffs.[24]

History has lost details of how Pierre came to live among the Salish, but it is likely due to his having a Salish wife. Within her community he helped spread the word about the religion of the Black Robes.[25] His story picks up again in 1839, when he finds himself back on the lower Missouri at Council Bluffs and helps to weave this intertwined story together.

Another Mohawk, known as Ignace Chapped Lips, came to the Rocky Mountains with Pierre. Presumably he also came from the village of Akwasasne.[26] He married a Salish woman named Louise, and together they had two daughters. We know little else about Petit Ignace's life until 1839, when he and Pierre arrived at Council Bluffs. Ignace was known to history as "Petit Ignace" or, as the Salish pronounced the name, "Eneas." He was called Petit Ignace to distinguish him from the better-known "Grand Ignace."

Ignace Perthuis, or Grand Ignace, was the best known of the Mohawk émigrés.[27] He was born in 1799 to a Mohawk mother and a father of

Mohawk and French ancestry at Kahnawak, a Mohawk village just west of Montreal. His parents were dedicated Catholics, as had been many generations before them. Ignace, who became known as Grand Ignace, began assisting the Jesuit missionaries at his village church after he made his first Communion when he was a boy of eleven. His ancestors had fought in the French and Indian Wars (1754–63), and war again crept into their lives with the War of 1812, when Ignace reached his teen years. The great Shawnee chief Tecumseh was killed in battle when the boy was fourteen, and the war ended in the Great Lakes arena a year later. With the defeat of the Indians and then their British allies by American forces, the future for Indian people in the region looked dismal. Ignace signed on for a short-term job ferrying supplies by canoe for the British government, and when that responsibility ended, he went to work as a river man for the fur companies. News of a group of men from related villages heading west caught his ear, and he made ready to join them. With three years' experience working on the rivers, he confidently joined the NWC with sixteen other trappers and headed west.[28]

The group was known as Martin's band, named for its leader, Martin Tsiniaquin, the eldest and most experienced of these mostly related travelers. Late in 1818 nineteen-year-old Ignace Perthuis and the others signed four-year contracts with NWC to serve as trappers west of the Rockies, and they departed. They traveled slowly, trapping as they went. Nine months later they reached Fort Edmonton, then crossed the Continental Divide in 1820, and made their way to Fort Spokane, their new base of operations. During this time they began to know people from the local Indian communities who would venture to the fort to trade furs and leather for cloth and kettles and such. Some of the Iroquois trappers would find wives among the Salish, Pend d'Oreille, Kootenais, and other tribes of the area, whose leaders would welcome the Iroquois with open arms. Their presence would bolster the critically low number of healthy grown men in these villages due to the twin horrors of epidemic disease and well-armed enemies.

In December 1822, when these trappers completed their terms of service, many of them went to work as freemen for the HBC. Grand Ignace and his compatriots, like Pierre and presumably Petit Ignace, participated in the miserable Snake River brigades, along with their families, if they had them. Unlike the wives of their British bosses, Indian women did not stay "back home" while their husbands were traveling because home was wherever they were, not a fixed location. They traveled together. Living was mobile, not stagnant. The women tended their camps and prepared food, just as they would under any other circumstances.

Working conditions were dreadful, and the HBC kept the men in a cycle of debt that bound them perpetually to the company, regardless of their status as "freemen." In February 1825 one of the Iroquois was accidentally shot and killed by his Kalispel wife, Sinshe. Right after the burial Grand Ignace stepped up to marry the widow. Whatever the reasons, a primary one must have been that he would become provider for her and her little son La Mousse. Someone needed to take them in. Sinshe turned out to be a dedicated wife and mother and a truly remarkable woman.[29] Sometime before the end of the year, she gave birth to another son called Saxa, who would come to play an important role in a rapidly changing world. The following year, conditions for the brigade were so terrible that Ignace and twenty-two other trappers decided they had had enough. Having no allegiance to the British, they absconded from the HBC and shifted their business to American traders.

Around that time, Ignace Perthuis, Sinshe, five-year-old La Mousse, and baby Saxa settled among the Bitterroot Salish. This remarkable Mohawk man was admired among these people for his virtuous behavior and his religious beliefs. He taught his adopted people to make the Sign of the Cross, to recite the Lord's Prayer, and to honor the Sabbath, but he never presumed to be their priest. His role was more that of a harbinger, like that of John the Baptist before the arrival of Jesus. The spiritual medicine of the Black Robes could help protect the Salish in these terrible times. Ignace's stories echoed Salish prophecies, especially the one that anticipated the future arrival of a black-robed teacher.[30]

The decision to leave the HBC, in a roundabout way, led to the circumstances that would materialize some thirteen years in the future as an answer to prayers for many people, including these Iroquois trappers, the beleaguered Salish community, and a Belgian Jesuit. By participating in the American system, their sphere of operation shifted from Hudson's Bay to the trade center of St. Louis and to the newly minted

Rocky Mountain Rendezvous. It might have been at a rendezvous that Ignace Perthuis and his compatriots learned about the presence of "black-robed teachers" in St. Louis.

How Peter-Jan De Smet Came to the Rockies (1801–21)

Peter-Jan De Smet, the seventh child of a wealthy sixty-five-year-old Flemish merchant, found himself as a missionary to Indians in the Rocky Mountains of North America through a string of unanticipated opportunities, like stepping stones across a river. De Smet's stones took him from Belgium to Maryland, then across the continent to Missouri, and on to his first position as a missionary among displaced Prairie Potawatomi Indians in Iowa. There he had a strange encounter that would ultimately lead him to the life for which he must have felt destined.

De Smet was born in the beautiful East Flanders town of Dendermonde, moments before the birth of his twin sister, in January 1801, the year Thomas Jefferson became president of the United States. Three years later Jefferson would initiate the transcontinental military expedition across the Rocky Mountains in the area that would become De Smet's base of operations thirty-five years in the future.

Like Charlo and the Mohawk trappers, Peter grew up during a time of war, when Napoleon's reach caused Belgium to be ping-ponged among monarchies and religions. The future Jesuit's childhood was colored by the sights and sounds of soldiers. When a neighbor opened the shutters on an upstairs window to encourage a breeze on a summer morning, she might have seen the neighborhood gang in the street below, with De Smet, the ringleader, directing the antics. His nickname of "Samson" suggests a young man of great strength. Although only 5 feet 7 inches tall, he was heavy, built like a bull, and loved rough-and-tumble sports. "[He] was a kind of Hercules, a terror to his school-fellow, impetuous in the extreme, disputatious," according to one of his sisters.[31] A terror? Impetuous and disputatious? Not exactly qualities that we might have expected for a future priest who was famous for his peacemaking skills. The sister also remembered that Peter was drawn to water, either floating in it or sitting along the bank of the Scheldt River, near the family home at the confluence with the Dender. Perhaps, as some have surmised, his attention was on the boats, "with wistful fancies of the great world beyond."[32] The mighty Scheldt was probably the closest he could come to the wild, as he watched the river change through the seasons. Perhaps something there spoke to an ineffable longing in the boy. Even then his aging father worried about what the future would hold for his young son. He is remembered as having believed that Peter would become "a soldier or a great traveller" and hoped God would protect him.[33]

How Peter's interest in American Indians originated is unknown. He and friends might have snuck off for a traveling show featuring a Native American. Europeans had long been fascinated with curiosities from other lands, including people of different skin color. Exotic "red men" were brought to Europe as marvels as soon as encounters began. Perhaps books in the family library led to an interest. From soon after first contact, Europeans wrote descriptions of particular tribes or regions, along with speculations about their origins. A common thread was to affirm European superiority over these natural men, "savages." *The Adventures of Colonel Daniel Boone* might have been in the De Smet household. First published in 1784, this popular biography, based on interviews with the famous frontiersman, was translated into both French and German. It is possible that the family acquired a copy of Nicholas Biddle's narrative of the Lewis and Clark expedition, published in 1814, a book that rapidly gained a wide audience on both continents.

One book likely to have been in De Smet's sphere was Adriaen van der Donck's *A Description of New Netherland*, 1652, written in Dutch, describing tribes around New York. A common belief in works such as this was that American Indians were descendants of the ten lost tribes of Israel. American Indian religions were presented in these books as inferior; their lives could be improved only with the introduction of Christianity as part of their conversion toward becoming civilized.

The De Smet household library may have included the works of Father Pierre De Charlevoix, S.J. on the history and geography of New France. Charlevoix spent the years between 1705 and 1709 in Quebec for part of his Jesuit training. In 1720, back in France, he received a commission from the French crown to return to New France to conduct some survey work. While in Quebec, he was assigned the duty of finding a route to the "Western Sea" while giving "the impression of being no more than a traveler or missionary."[34] He was equipped with only two canoes, eight voyagers, and trade goods. From Quebec they traveled southwestward, up the St. Lawrence River, and then, instead of continuing westward, they traveled down the Mississippi to its mouth. Charlevoix's report of findings recommended the Missouri as the route to the Pacific, which he suspected was not too far away. Some of his popular journals about Indians he met along the way may have found their way into the De Smet household and triggered young De Smet's fascination. No doubt the boy was exposed to these ideas either at home or at one of his many schools.

Peter attended four different schools in seven years. At thirteen he was sent to a Catholic boarding school near Ghent because his father was worried about his restlessness and his lack of direction. The young De Smet moved from one school to another over the next couple of years, possibly dismissed for poor performance, or, with his "disputatious" inclinations, perhaps he was expelled for fighting. His brother Francis explained Peter's frequent moves as a reflection of his inability "to settle down anywhere long."[35] Whatever the cause, the haze of ash that darkened the sky after the massive 1816 eruption of Indonesia's Mount Tambora could only have added to Peter's aimlessness. About a year later De Smet finally settled down, as did the ash. His fourth school, twenty miles from home at the junior seminary in Mechelen, seems to have been a good fit. There he was reported to be a solid student, known as a writer.

No mention of an interest in the priesthood appears in the limited record of Peter's school years. His youthful inclinations seem to have been directed elsewhere until a fateful day in 1821, when Charles Nerinckx, a Belgian Catholic missionary to America, became known to the impressionable young De Smet.

The Jesuit order was just beginning to make a comeback in 1815, following a period known as the Suppression. The order had been abolished by papal order in 1773, but the ban was lifted in 1814. The restoration of the Jesuit order was tied closely to a need for teachers in Europe. Scholarship had long been a focus of the Jesuits but not of many other orders. Although they were needed, their resurgence was not universally welcomed. Other Catholic orders resented their power and influence, and the reappearance of Jesuits was not to the liking of at least some of America's founding fathers. John Adams wrote to Thomas Jefferson expressing his concern about the "restoration" of the Society of Jesus, "a body of men who merited damnation on earth and in Hell. . . . Shall we not have regular swarms of them here, in as many disguises as only a king of the gipsies can assume, dressed as printers, publishers, writers and schoolmasters?" He went on to acknowledge that the nation's "system of religious toleration" compelled the United States "to offer them an asylum."[36] America wasn't alone in its prejudice, as Nerinckx, the "Apostle of Kentucky," well understood.

Although not a Jesuit himself, Nerinckx agreed to recruit novices for work in America. He had succeeded in recruiting a batch of eager young Belgians in 1817 and agreed to return again three years later. When he embarked on this second recruitment venture—the one that would prove pivotal for the young De Smet—he was well aware of the dangers that awaited him under King William I of the Netherlands. This self-proclaimed post-Napoleonic ruler, a Calvinist, was particularly hostile toward Catholic mission work abroad. So the sixty-year-old Nerinckx, traveling incognito, stayed with friends and moved frequently to avoid discovery. He carried with him a letter from one of the novices in America to a friend, a zealous potential recruit, Judocus Van Assche, who had wanted to join Nerinckx in 1817 but had been too young at the time. The recruiter managed to deliver the letter to the young man's parents at their home near Mechelen, and they got word to their son, a student at the Mechelen junior seminary.

A few months later Van Assche and a friend from the senior seminary managed to find the elusive Nerinckx in Dendermonde. The stealthy priest told them about his life in America, about serving the poor since 1804, and he spoke of the fledgling work of the Jesuits. The young men, impressed by his strong faith and his physical strength, were eager to join. But, Nerinckx cautioned, his situation was far too dangerous for him to be openly recruiting. If discovered, he would be arrested and likely imprisoned. If they were clear as to their calling, however, the ship they would take to America would be sailing in the spring, probably in May. Word would be sent. They should speak of this to no one.

The two young men went back to school and waited. It was difficult to stay focused on their studies when such an adventure awaited. Van Assche's housemates must have wondered about his changed countenance, and apparently he was unable to stay quiet about his plans. Word of Nerinckx's presence was murmured quietly from one young man to another, and by the time spring rolled around, nine of them, including the impetuous De Smet, were committed to pledge their lives to missionary work in America.

Their excitement and anxiety grew as they waited for word of departure. The linden trees bloomed, casting their lemon peel and honey scent across the land. May passed, then June. Finally word was whispered in July in Mechelen from a wealthy tobacco merchant who spoke for Nerinckx that the ship would leave Amsterdam in August. They should travel in separate groups with just what they were wearing and tell no one of their plans, not even their parents. The disdain of the government for Catholic missionaries would thwart their plan if discovered. De Smet's group of four made its way through the lowlands to Antwerp. Tension filled the carriage as the boys approached the city. Traveling without passports, they could not enter the city legally. The plan was to exit the carriage before the city gates, then to join the locals entering the city by foot. With all the nonchalance they could muster, they crossed through the gates without notice.

The zealous young men traveled on to Amsterdam, where they remained cautious. No city official intervened with their plans, but Charles De Smet, Peter's older brother, nearly did. It is remarkable that, having no clue where to look for his wayward brother, Charles literally ran into Peter and his companions while they were crossing a busy bridge. Despite the purpose of the errand his father had sent him on—to retrieve his brother—Charles came to understand Peter's commitment. Not only did he send him off with his blessing, but he also provided some needed funds. With each day in Amsterdam their risk of discovery grew, so the young men moved on from the city, weathering a difficult trip in a small boat across the Zuyder Zee to the island of Texel. Finally, after a seemingly endless wait, they learned that the ship that would take them to America was arriving. The name of this ship, the *Columbia*, foreshadowed De Smet's future in the American Northwest. Once aboard, Nerinckx, still traveling incognito, emerged from secret quarters. Apparently none of the recruits except the original two had ever laid eyes on the Apostle of Kentucky before that day.

We know nothing about conversations during their mythic forty-day journey across the Atlantic to Philadelphia. From that bustling city they continued by boat to Baltimore, then by carriage they ventured on to the nation's capital and Georgetown College, the birthplace of Jesuit education in America. The restless young De Smet had finally found his calling. It was a calling to serve God and also for adventure and a way to make his mark, and it was a way out of the constrained life in Dendermonde. His mother had recently died, leaving him without her moderating influence, and his eighty-five-year-old father had never really understood him. It was time to chart his own course.

Despite the many volumes he would fill from his years in America, De Smet never wrote about the epic moment when he set the course for the rest of his life with one grand decision: to follow Nerinckx across the Atlantic. He had taken a bold step into the future. Two decades would pass before this Belgian lowlander reached the Rocky Mountains, where he would become the famous Black Robe. His route was circuitous, or perhaps zig-zag, and it wasn't always clear if he would succeed. Indecision and illness plagued him. He was bold, yet impetuous. Unsettled. The characteristics from childhood remembered by his siblings followed him across the sea. Courage and patience were the two qualities most needed for a missionary on the frontier.[37] De Smet certainly showed courage. His patience had yet to be tested.

Peter De Smet represented the third hank that came together to weave this braided history of the Salish, the Iroquois, and the Jesuits. Without all three components—alongside the timing of some pivotal U.S. policy decisions regarding Native Americans—the story told here would almost assuredly not have happened. The moment of convergence occurred at the base of a bluff on the Missouri River in September 1839, setting into motion circumstances that would dramatically alter the Salish world. To understand this moment in history, we first need to know how De Smet, the twenty-year-old Jesuit novitiate, found his way to Council Bluffs, Iowa.

2. Westward Ho

De Smet Arrives in America (1821)

By the time De Smet landed in Philadelphia in late September 1821, the Eastern seaboard had been transformed to reflect European—and particularly Puritan English—values. On the lands where hundreds of thousands of Native peoples had lived just before European settlers arrived now lived over eight million Euro-Americans and some one million West African slaves. Native populations had been decimated. To a large extent, what disease hadn't taken, white men had.[1] Land ownership throughout the new Euro-America had shifted from the natural rights of the Native inhabitants to the freshly applied concept of civil rights for those who "improved" the land.

De Smet entered an America where Catholics were not very welcome. Just a month or so before the Belgian recruits had boarded the *Columbia*, John Adams had again written to Thomas Jefferson regarding his concern. In the letter he posed the question, "Can a free government possibly exist with the Roman Catholic religion?"[2] When times are tough, someone is always to blame. People tend to strengthen their camps of "us" and "them." Protestant Philadelphia, where De Smet first landed, was no exception.

The home of Independence Hall, the Liberty Bell, and the American Philosophical Society had been hit hard by the depression following the War of 1812. Where previously a textile industry had boomed, unemployment reached 10 percent. The Panic of 1819 led to an economic collapse that lasted more than two years. Monetary policy of the central bank was at the core of this financial crisis, compounded by land speculation and the excessive printing of paper money. The city's Calvinist elite launched the "Society for the Promotion of Public Economy" to investigate the situation. Indigence, they reported, was due to a number of factors, including low wages for women, the influx of poor foreigners, and a downturn in manufacturing. Long, cold winters added to the suffering and made people vulnerable to illness. At the root of the problem, though, the society members concluded, was intemperance, a moral failing. They concluded that two types of poor people were involved: paupers and the worthy poor. While the worthy poor were victims of regrettable circumstances, paupers were lazy, profligate idlers who preferred to live off the good will of others, public or private, rather than work.[3] This might have been one of the first English-American studies based in ethnic profiling.

On their journey from Philadelphia to their destination in Maryland, De Smet and his cohort would see various expressions of slavery and poverty juxtaposed against a building boom befitting of this abundant land. The young Belgians settled into their routine as Jesuit novices at White Marsh, a secluded two-thousand-acre plantation situated on a back road between Georgetown and Annapolis. White Marsh was an important hub of Catholic life, "sort of a Catholic capital of the United States in the first years of [the country's] independence."[4] Slave laborers worked the surrounding fields. Although Catholics remained on the outside of American politics, wheels were turning that would soon influence the direction of future work for these young Jesuits in collaboration with the expanding United States.

When Peter De Smet stepped onto American soil in 1821, he could not have set about to become a missionary to Indians in the West. Plans were emerging for such a possibility, but at the time no system was in place for him to do that. President James Monroe and his cabinet were designing the set for a dramatic production, where the exploitation of vast natural resources beyond the Mississippi would fuel the staggering economy.

Early in his presidency Monroe had found himself challenged by the fact that tribes, by treaty and precedent, were considered sovereign nations. While he and his cabinet contemplated schemes to legally acquire Indian lands, the president assured tribal leaders of their rights: "As long as water flows, or grass grows upon the earth, or the sun rises

FIG. 2. Young De Smet. From Chittenden and Richardson, *Life, Letters and Travels of Father Pierre-Jean De Smet, S.J., 1801–1873*, 1:150.

to show your pathway, or you kindle your camp fires," he told the western Cherokees, "so long shall you be protected by this Government, and never again removed from your present habitations."[5]

As part of his first message to Congress in 1817, President Monroe explained why tribes would have to change from their communal forms of living: "The hunter state can exist only in the vast uncultivated desert. It yields to the more dense and compact form and great force of civilized population." It was time this hunter state should yield. His rationale was that "the earth was given to mankind to support the greatest number of which it is capable, and no tribe of people have a right to withhold from the wants of others more than is necessary for their own support and comfort." American values were taking a particular form with regard to property and possession reflective of the colonial values of England.

To encourage westward expansion, credit was dispensed with a loose hand, heedless of the financial disaster that awaited. After two years of economic freefall, Congress passed a recovery act in 1821, and the westward-bound wheels once again started turning. This was the America of De Smet's arrival. The nation looked toward its vast natural resources to grow the economy. First, though, borders between the United States and its neighbors needed to be settled. The Treaty of 1818 established the border with Canada at the 49th parallel from the Atlantic Coast to the Continental Divide. The parties were unable to reach an agreement regarding the boundary in the Oregon Country, west of the Divide, so the United States and Britain agreed to joint occupancy of those lands between the Spanish territories at 42 degrees and the Russian territories at 54 degrees latitude. So far removed from the focus of American life, the far northwest could wait. Maybe its remoteness is what drew Martin's band of Iroquois trappers west during this time.

A treaty with Spain in 1819 resolved questions of possession and possibility along the southern border all the way to the Pacific Coast. Spain gave Florida to the United States in exchange for precluding any American claim to Texas, and the United States agreed that Spain would control all lands south of the 42nd parallel west of the Continental Divide along with Texas. With boundaries clarified, President Monroe started working on his famous foreign policy doctrine. The aspect most relevant to westward expansion was the declaration that any European attempt to recolonize the Americas would be considered a hostile act toward the United States, and a declaration of war would follow. Everything was in place for American expansion. St. Louis, the westernmost capital, so well positioned at the hub of the big rivers, could serve as the launching place.

President Monroe Sets the Stage (1817–22)

Since the days of General Washington, Indian men on the expanding American frontier had fought to defend their homelands. When Martin's band members decided to follow the beaver trade west, they had experienced decades of war and displacement. These young men would go west to the Columbia headwaters country, beyond the reach of their troubles. Decisions were being made in Washington that would eventually reach beyond the Mississippi and even to the tribal nations of the remote mountains beyond the Missouri, even to the remote headwater streams of the Columbia. The Salish people would fall within this reach.

During President Monroe's tenure, Indian affairs were under the purview of his secretary of war, John C. Calhoun. This ardent supporter of slavery conceptualized a significant shift in Indian policy that he presented in his report to Congress in 1818.[6] In it he asserted that Indians

FIG. 3. Map of North America, with the contiguous British and Spanish possessions. Library of Congress, https://www.loc.gov/item/96686680.

had become overly dependent on trade with the "civilized" world for their survival. They had lost their independence and were now helpless. Congress should stop considering Indian tribes as nations, and Indians must conform to the nation's laws and become civilized. Indians needed to live like white people.

Calhoun created the Office of Indian Affairs without congressional authorization.[7] He simply filled a vacant clerkship in the War Department and directed all matters relating to Indians through that office. It worked. That office oversaw the four regional superintendents of Indian affairs and held sway over the political decisions regarding Native Americans.

President Monroe appointed William Clark as the first superintendent of Indian affairs for the Louisiana Territory. No white man had more experience in Indian Country than Clark. He had lived in St. Louis since the end of the expedition for which he and Meriwether Lewis were famous. There he had served as U.S. agent for Indian affairs, responsible for licensing traders and overseeing posts, forts, and factories in Indian Country, as established under the 1793 Trade and Intercourse Act. As superintendent, Clark's responsibilities included oversight of Indians as well as those who worked in or traveled through Indian Country. He issued licenses to the growing number of traders, granted passports to travelers, intervened in cases of hostilities between tribes, and directed a military force to arrest lawbreakers and to remove unauthorized persons. He did all of this in addition to conducting treaty councils and overseeing the distribution of annuities after a treaty was ratified.[8] This treaty work wasn't new for him. Since 1815 he had negotiated thirty-seven treaties, about 10 percent of the total number of ratified treaties between American Indians and the United States at the time.[9]

Long a fan of American expansionism, Clark was a good choice for the team of Monroe and Calhoun. He agreed with their principles that Indians must surrender their lands and acculturate and that they needed to recognize the authority of the U.S. government. That said, because of his years of experience, he also recognized their nationhood, their unique languages, cultures, and histories, and he worked to negotiate treaties that would protect them from alcohol and other negative influences from Euro-Americans. These same treaties, though, removed people from their ancestral lands and imposed European-style education on their children, all with the goal to eradicate their traditional lifestyles and religious beliefs.[10] Like Calhoun, Clark assembled artifacts for a museum and had portraits painted of Indian leaders as part of his attempt to preserve their cultures or at least some facsimile of their lives.

Calhoun articulated an aggressive plan to acquire more land for the citizens of the United States. He recommended the removal of the "civilized" tribes of the southeast—the Cherokees, Choctaws, Creeks, Chickasaws, and Seminoles—to west of the Mississippi, and Monroe authorized General Andrew Jackson to make it happen. "By a proper combination of force and persuasion, of punishment and rewards," he told Congress, the United States could establish firmer control over Indian tribes. Indians should be persuaded to own land as individuals, with fee simple titles.[11] The traditional communal approach to land ownership would end, creating a surplus of former Indian lands to be made available for others. As these federal officials looked beyond land acquisition, they believed that to be successful, the Indian occupants of these lands would have to be both assimilated and acculturated. This is where the missionaries entered the story.[12]

Changing the way people think would require control of their education. Congress would need to allocate funds to build schools. These schools should teach subjects most applicable to the goals of transforming their lifeways: agronomy, homemaking, Christianity, and citizenship. In 1819, as part of the Indian Civilization Act, Congress authorized a "civilizing fund," essentially to make Indians like white people through education. Attendance by Indian children for such education would be compulsory. An annual budget of $10,000 was approved. Recognizing that this sum would fall far short of the vision, Calhoun turned to American missionary societies for their help. When the Pawnee leader Sharitarish heard of President Monroe's plan to send Christian missionaries to Indian Country to teach skills in agriculture and other forms of learning, he voiced his clear objection: "We have everything we want," he told the president. "We have plenty of land, if you will keep your people off it."[13] His concerns were echoed all the way to the Pacific.

In this pregnant moment in American history—just before Peter De Smet boarded a ship bound for his new world, as Iroquois paddlers headed upriver toward the Rockies, when the HBC sought control of the old Oregon Country, and around the time that an exceptional young Salish brave gained the name Bear Tracks (also called Bear Track)—a marriage of strange bedfellows was about to be consummated.

When One Door Closes (1823)

At the same that time Monroe was misleading Indians about their future, the Jesuits of Maryland were struggling to survive. Their work was doubly challenged by strong anti-Catholic sentiment and financial troubles due to the decline in tobacco production. They sold off most of the enslaved people who had worked their tobacco fields, but the profits were not enough to save them. The novitiate at White Marsh would have to close. This news would have been a disaster for De Smet and his fellow students and administrators if it weren't for the new Indian policies of the Monroe administration. As the government signed treaties promising services to Native communities in exchange for land, it needed help, and it found the perfect partners in the reemerging but financially strapped Jesuits. In late March 1823 the Jesuits signed a letter of intent to evangelize the Indian tribes of Missouri and Louisiana country.[14] They would build a new center in Florissant, Missouri. The land and building expenses for this purpose would be provided by the Catholic Church.

That same year Chief Justice John Marshall wrote an opinion about a landmark decision regarding the purchase of lands from Native Americans. In the *Johnson v. M'Intosh* case the Supreme Court decided against the rights of private citizens to purchase land directly from Indians. Marshall applied the 1493 Papal Bull, the "Doctrine of Discovery," which states that "the Catholic faith and the Christian religion be exalted and be everywhere increased and spread, that the health of souls be cared for and that barbarous nations be overthrown and brought to the faith itself." Justice Marshall applied the basis for this edict to the United States, giving the government legal justification for seizure of Indian land.[15] The Jesuits were on the crest of a Euro-American wave to replace the lifeways and beliefs of Native peoples with those of Europeans, principally the English, in order to clear the way for Euro-American expansion.

Just after Easter in 1823, eleven poverty-stricken Jesuits, accompanied by three enslaved couples, left White Marsh and headed for Missouri.[16]

Their travel was by wagon from Baltimore to Wheeling, a hub on the Ohio River, along the partially completed National Road. There they exchanged wagons for two flatboats and picked up a copy of *The River-man's Guide to the Ohio River* since none of them had boating experience. They trusted they would manage with the help of the Almighty.

Thomas Jefferson loved the Ohio, with its "current gentle and waters clear." He believed this principal corridor for westward expansion to be "the most beautiful river on earth."[17] With their rafts lashed together, the Jesuit travelers launched into the fast-flowing springtime flow of the mighty Ohio River. They witnessed fledgling towns of white settlers along the river where once had stood villages of wigwams. Native people had receded into the background. The fast waters carried the faithful travelers quickly through the traditional territories of the Shawnee and Miami, but these Algonquian-speaking tribes had been pressured westward by Iroquois a century before. The Iroquois nation of Seneca had given the river its name: Ohi:yo', translated as "Good River" or "Beautiful River."[18] In 1789 the newly minted United States of America provided funds to Iroquois nations who had been loyal to the colonists for the purchase of the former Shawnee and Miami lands.[19] White settlers moved in following the Northwest Indian War (1786–95), taking the prime agricultural lands. Each wave of disruption interrupted complex systems of trade and communication all along the river corridor and its tributaries.

The missionaries' destination of St. Louis, a settlement of over ten thousand people, was incorporated as a city the same year De Smet arrived in America, but the river hub had been a cultural center for at least a thousand years. The warm climatic episode that led Norse families to settle in Greenland around 1000 BCE also provided conditions to support a northward spread of farming practices from Mexico. This was the time of Cahokia, which at its peak reached a population of forty thousand. Cahokia was one of the largest settlements in America at the time, along with the complex of communities at Chaco Canyon in the American Southwest. Cahokia was a sophisticated, stratified society, engaged in long-distance trade in every direction, including obsidian from Yellowstone, raw copper from the Great Lakes, and shells from the Gulf of Mexico. Residents smelted copper, grew a variety of crops, and constructed an astronomical observatory and ceremonial center, a "woodhenge." Cahokia declined when the colder climate of the Little Ice Age impacted the occupants' ability to grow food. They were forced to spread out in smaller groups of Illinoian peoples, seeking new lands where they could fend for themselves.[20]

Nearly six centuries after Cahokia's decline, the U.S. population was skyrocketing. The 1830 census counted over ten million Euro-Americans and two million African slaves. The Native American population east of the Mississippi had fallen to just over one hundred thousand souls. Pressure was steadily mounting for the United States to secure more land for white farmers, and when Andrew Jackson became president, he prioritized relocating Indians. With the passage of the 1830 Indian Removal Act, the president was enabled to legally force tribes out of their homelands east of the Mississippi and remove them to lands beyond the river, whatever their preferences and no matter how long their ancestors had occupied their traditional territories.

White colonists saw no reason to learn from these people, whose ancestors had survived through droughts, storms, plagues, and unusual winters since time immemorial. Even the knowledge of tribes considered "civilized" by Europeans, such as the Cherokees—admired for their sophisticated systems of governance, trading practices, and natural dignity—was essentially ignored. When it came to land, it mattered not whether tribal people had adopted the practices of the colonists, including written constitutions and Christianity. Tens of thousands of Native people were forced to move, some at the points of bayonets. The most famous story of this era is that of the 1838 Cherokees' Trail of Tears, when they were forced to march to Oklahoma after gold was discovered in their Georgia homeland. Theirs was just one of many trails of tears during that decade of American history, as an eager young De Smet would soon learn.

Illness and Indecision for a Wavering Jesuit (1827–37)

De Smet's first eleven years in America, from 1821 until 1832, were spent in Jesuit training, first in Maryland, where he and his classmates studied Latin, poetry, rhetoric, and logic, and then in Florissant, Missouri (outside of St. Louis), where they completed studies in philosophy,

FIG. 4. St. Regis Indian Seminary at Florissant. From Chittenden and Richardson, *Life, Letters and Travels of Father Pierre-Jean De Smet, S.J., 1801–1873*, 1:6.

metaphysics, natural philosophy, and theology. His first exposure to Indians occurred there in 1824, when he served as one of the teachers at the St. Regis School, one of the first Indian boarding schools in the nation, built under the auspices of the Civilization Fund Act.[21] Although the two-story log structure was built large enough for forty pupils, only two Sauk and three Iowa boys attended during the first year. Two years later De Smet was the lone teacher of some thirty Indian boys, instructing them in writing and English and attempting to convert them to agriculturalists as well as Catholics.[22] Within their communities, however, farming work belonged to the women, so the boys resisted participating.

Ordained in September 1827, De Smet entered his last stage of training, the tertianship, in January 1828, just before his twenty-seventh birthday. The young Jesuits followed a strict daily regimen of prayer and study, and they were expected to contribute two hours of manual labor each day, adding their labors to those of the slaves. De Smet was just three months shy of completing his long years of training when, in 1830, the program ended abruptly. The Indian school for boys closed, and De Smet was reassigned to St. Louis College. He would continue his tertianship in St. Louis while teaching English, in addition to serving as the college treasurer. But as Gilbert Garraghan relates in his history of the Jesuits of the Middle United States, De Smet's journey toward missionary life would take years, not months, to complete.[23]

Along his sputtering, stochastic path to become a missionary to the Indians, De Smet was waylaid by "a cutaneous malady"—maybe eczema—in March 1832, and it caused him to seek permission to return to Europe to recover. Some of his cohorts were seriously stymied by his request. Why was Peter being sent home, questioned a fellow Belgian, since his ailment wasn't getting in the way of his service? Besides, his absence would leave a substantial gap. After all, even with his skin condition, De Smet was, as his disgruntled colleague put it, "the most robust of all our men here."[24] His request to leave made the Father General question his charge's "steadiness in his calling as a Jesuit," and one of his superiors reported that De Smet appeared to "be restless and in a somewhat unsettled state of mind as to his future."[25] Was he wavering in his commitment and using his health as a way to reconsider?

When De Smet finally left for Europe in September 1833, the very month he had been scheduled to take final vows, he was in despair, and, by his own admission, he was shedding many a tear. By the time he arrived in Paris in December, he had already petitioned to return to St. Louis. In his letter of request he claimed his departure had been involuntary. Students of history are left to imagine what really happened. Something was going on that never fully made its way into the written record.

In Belgium an unsteady De Smet engaged in fundraising for the Missouri Mission while waiting for permission to return to America. Permission was received in September 1834, and at the end of October, in stormy weather, he boarded a ship bound for America. Like a Homeric saga, the notorious fickle hand intervened again. Soon after leaving the port of Antwerp and reaching the North Sea, De Smet became so ill that the captain put him ashore on the coast of England to consult a doctor. Three days later the ship sailed without him because the English doctors, unsure of his health, determined him unfit to travel. Faced with being a burden to the Society of Jesus, he made the painful decision to petition the superior to release him. He was thirty-four years old, and his dream was evaporating. If this was his dark night of the soul, he left no written reflections about it.

When word arrived in May 1835 that his petition to leave the order had been accepted, he wept again, regretting that he had ever made the request. A moment of discouragement caused by his illness had led him to make what he considered to be such a "stupid" decision. Once again, his impetuous actions had led to indecision and despair. His friends back in St. Louis, understanding his need for intellectual stimulation and his fascination with the natural world, sent him minerals, fossils, and other curiosities and kept him aware of news from home. He might have learned of the new Kickapoo Mission with an Indian school established in 1836 on the west bank of the Missouri, upstream from St. Louis, and he longed to be there.

Although he was no longer affiliated with the Jesuits, De Smet remained a priest and continued to fundraise for the Missouri Mission. So successful was he that his name topped the register of donors at St. Louis University in 1836. In Dendermonde, his hometown, he found work in an orphanage and a nunnery. One of the sisters wrote that De Smet always asked for their prayers for his health to be restored so he could "return to the Indians."[26] This was a curious request since he hadn't yet worked with "the Indians" except for the short time teaching the boys in Florissant. Apparently his dream of working with Native tribes of America had not lost its allure. Had he stayed in Missouri, he might have met Grand Ignace, the Iroquois, and his sons in the fall of 1835, when they petitioned the Jesuits to send a missionary among the Salish Indians in the Rocky Mountains.

3. Like Braided Streams

The Search for Black Robes (1831–39)

During the summer of 1831, when De Smet was floundering in his Jesuit training, baby Charlo's people were hunting buffalo with a band of Nez Perce in the vicinity of what is now Monida Pass between Dillon, Montana, and Idaho Falls.[1] In that camp elders of the two tribes concocted a plan to send a delegation to St. Louis to investigate the legendary Black Robes reported to be residing there. A powerful religious wave was washing through the interior mountain tribes of the region, and Salish leaders did not want their people to be left out. They had already been influenced by Grand Ignace and other Iroquois about the powers of the black robed men, and the newly minted preacher Spokane Garry and his father were attracting followers as well. Some years before, Garry and a few other boys from the mountain tribes had been sent by Hudson's Bay traders to the Red River Missionary School at Fort Garry, near Winnipeg, to learn the Anglican faith. Garry, with the help of his father, was beginning to attract a large following. Across the region people were eager to hear his preaching, listen to him read from a book, and obtain the agricultural knowledge he had acquired among the Canadians.

Beyond the desire for the respect that came with new ideas, the Salish and Nez Perce leaders of this camp were aware of the great need for stronger spiritual power to protect them against all the negative forces confronting them. Not only had diseases taken a great toll on their communities, but they had also suffered from battle after battle with the Blackfeet and other tribes over their right to hunt on the bison plains. Many widows lived in the villages, having lost their men to this endless war. All anyone had to do was to look around. The people were suffering, and their survival was in question.

The first St. Louis delegation was led by Martin Tsiniaquin, of the Mohawk Nation, one of the five tribes of the Iroquois Confederacy.[2] The group would meet up with the American Fur Company's caravan at the conclusion of the Green River Rendezvous and travel to St Louis together, following what would become known as the Oregon Trail. The end of the trail was a place called Chouteau's Town or Westport at what is now modern-day Kansas City, Missouri, where some Iroquois had settled after retiring from the fur trade. One of these men was Gabriel Prudhomme Sr., a Frenchman with whom Grand Ignace and Martin had worked in the Snake River Brigades. Prudhomme, with his Cree wife, Josephine, and five children, had settled into this community that February.

When Martin and his party arrived in Westport, several of the party were ailing. They would have to rest before proceeding down the Missouri. While there, no doubt, the men enjoyed catching up on news from their old friends, but some of their ailing traveling companions were too ill to continue the journey. Cryptic and scattered evidence suggests that Martin was one of those who was unable to go on.[3] A demoralized, downsized crew of men made the journey without their leader to translate for them. Their first stop was with William Clark, whom the elder Nez Perce delegates remembered well from his time spent in their village in 1805 and 1806. Clark took a great interest in their story and arranged for them to meet with both Catholic and Protestant representatives to present their case for missionaries to join them. De Smet was in St. Louis at the time, focused on completing his Jesuit training. He would have loved to hear their story and would have looked for any means possible to accommodate the delegates' request, but at that time no one would have thought to ask his opinion about the matter.

Both meetings with church representatives were unsuccessful in the minds of the delegates because neither religious organization accepted their invitation. Of the two, the Protestants expressed more enthusiasm. The Jesuits' qualified response was that a priest would be sent as soon as possible. Realistically, though, at that time the Jesuits were fully invested in their efforts to establish a mission among the Kickapoo, and they had no personnel to spare, not to mention no funds to support such an undertaking. The Protestants expressed their commitment to explore possibilities.

To add to the disappointment, two members of the party, both Nez Perce, died from their illnesses and were buried in St. Louis, and another member, Salish, died shortly after the survivors headed back upriver.[4] A fourth was killed by Blackfeet before returning home. The disheartened remaining members learned good news and bad when they reached Westport.[5] They must have been elated to find that a couple of the Salish members of the original group had survived but shocked to learn that forty-year-old Gabriel Prudhomme Sr. was dead—reportedly killed in a barroom brawl in November, although questions lingered. Josephine, pregnant with her sixth child, faced a grim future.[6] Fourteen-year-old Gabriel Jr., the oldest child, would need to step up. When the road was clear in the spring of 1832, the survivors began their long journey toward home. They traveled in a group led by Andrew Drips of the American Fur Company, bound for the Green River Rendezvous.

The pilgrimage to St. Louis had not been in vain. The Protestants with whom they had met were considering how to capitalize on the proposed opportunities. Since their meeting in St. Louis, they had published a call for missionaries in eastern newspapers, and two Methodists had responded. In New York Jason Lee and his nephew Daniel decided to attend the 1834 fur trade rendezvous to explore the possibilities. Among the various tribal leaders they met were Grand Ignace and his Salish companion Insula, the Little Chief. The Lees, however, did not accept their invitation to accompany them home. They chose, instead, the Willamette Valley, where they would build a mission school for Indian boys in the comfort of a growing white population.

A year later Presbyterian ministers Marcus Whitman and Samuel Parker attended the rendezvous, where they also met Insula and Grand Ignace. Despite Little Chief's "open honesty and friendly disposition," which made him a favorite among fur trappers and traders, nothing came of this meeting, perhaps because Grand Ignace was set on getting Black Robes rather than any failing on the part of Insula to attract the Protestants to Salish Country.[7] When the trading ended, the influential Catholic Mohawk headed toward St. Louis from the Green River Rendezvous with his ten-year-old son Saxa and fourteen-year-old stepson La Mousse.

Ignace and his sons arrived at the fledgling St. Louis University on December 2, 1835. There they met with Father Ferdinand Helias. Helias described Ignace as "very tall of stature and of grave, modest, and refined deportment," befitting the title "Grand." The priest was impressed by the boys' comportment and described them as "of handsome figure and very intelligent."[8] Ignace made his confession and requested for his sons to be baptized. Father Helias agreed and proceeded to instruct the boys in the essential knowledge, speaking French while Ignace translated the teachings into Salish. Saxa was baptized Francis Xavier and La Mousse as Charles. Following the ceremony, Ignace shared his own story, focusing on the principal reason for his visit. He told Helias about the seven tribes of the Columbia headwater country—combined population of six thousand—who had asked him to bring a Black Robe to them.[9] He also hoped that the boys might stay at the college and offered a dollar to enroll Saxa and La Mousse. His request was denied because the rector "did not think himself authorized to grant this favor."[10] Despite the positive time spent together, neither of Ignace's requests were fulfilled.

With heavy heart, father and newly baptized sons headed back to the Iroquois settlement at Westport, where they would winter. Ignace found a boarding school where the boys could learn English and brush up on their French, while their father enjoyed time with his fellow Iroquois veterans of the fur trade. When he departed for the Rocky Mountains in the spring of 1836, he left François Saxa and Charles Lamoose at their school for another year to further their education.[11] The education would serve them well as future interpreters for chiefs, missionaries, traders, and government officials. Both boys would grow up to become important members of Salish society.

Grand Ignace might have traveled back to the Oregon Country alongside two Presbyterian couples that spring. The Whitmans had been joined by the Spaldings to establish missions in that remote part of the continent. While in St. Louis, these Protestants had attended High Mass at the new cathedral. Eliza Spalding later reported that "witnessing their heartless forms and ceremonies, induced us soon to leave, rejoicing that we have never been left to embrace such delusions."[12]

Her animosity would never wane. This zealot would eventually create a device for teaching religious history to the Nez Perce that nearly equated the pope with Satan himself. News of their arrival in Oregon Country might have aroused De Smet's competitive instincts and catapulted him back across the ocean the following year.

At the 1837 Green River Rendezvous, when Bitterroot Salish leader Tjolizhitzay, or Big Face, was told of an opportunity to have his own children learn about the spiritual ways of white men, he leaned toward the possibility. Big Face had always been drawn to what Grand Ignace had shared about the teachings of his youth. An escort materialized in the form of William Gray, an assistant to various Presbyterian missionaries in the Oregon Country. He was already escorting the young son of Francis Ermatinger, the HBC factor at Fort Hall, to a boarding school in the states and offered to place the chief's children as well.[13] Despite significant trepidation about Gray's limited experience and seeming lack of caution, the chief let his desires cloud his better judgment and agreed to send his sons along. He hoped his sons would bring back powerful medicine ways to the Salish as had Garry to the Spokanes. Grand Ignace, who needed to retrieve his own sons in Westport, would accompany them. Big Face sent them off and never saw them again. Lakota warriors slaughtered the Indians in that traveling party in a beautiful valley along the North Platte River called Ash Hollow, near today's Ogallala, Nebraska. They spared the lives of Gray and the other white men, fearing reprisal from the U.S. military. Ignace, a mixed-blood wearing the clothing of a white man, could have passed but chose instead to stand and fight with the Indians in the group.

Upon hearing the news of her husband's death, Sinshe headed south to retrieve her sons.[14] The reunited family remained in Westport for the winter and returned to the Rockies in the spring of 1838, just a few months before De Smet arrived at Council Bluffs for his first missionary assignment. After her remarkable and harrowing journey, Sinshe became known as "Blanket Feet."[15] Having worn through her moccasins, this brave woman wrapped her bloody feet in scraps of blanket to continue her journey.[16]

Despite three failed attempts, including the one that caused the death of his sons, Big Face chose to send a fourth delegation. In the spring of 1839 he sent Pierre Gauché and Petit Ignace to St. Louis to try, once again, to secure the spiritual power of the Black Robes.[17]

De Smet Returns to the Jesuits (1837–38)

In the summer of 1837, when Grand Ignace and the sons of Big Face were killed in Sioux Country, De Smet's health was much improved. After three and a half years in Europe, he planned to return to Missouri to be readmitted to the Society of Jesus. Incredibly, though, illness intervened again while he was in Paris on route to Le Havre. He became so ill that two doctors declared it unsafe for him to travel, perhaps fatally so. What the illness was, or why it vanished as mysteriously as it had arrived, is not known. The crisis passed, and the recovered priest returned to his beloved America in late November with a new batch of recruits.

Back in St. Louis, at last, De Smet appears to have buckled down and accomplished what was expected of him in his final novitiate. Perhaps the unpredictable Belgian's wildly successful fundraising efforts helped improve the attitude of his superiors toward him. It is ironic that during his time in Europe, which to him seemed like years of exile, he helped save the Missouri Province from bankruptcy.

In May 1838 the returnee was permitted to take his vows. Rather than first vows, though, these were "vows of devotion" only, where the individual is bound to the Society of Jesus but no reciprocal obligation is assumed by the society for the individual.[18] Did the Jesuits still have doubts about him? Doubts may explain why the talented thirty-seven-year-old Belgian was not on the short list for the team to establish a mission among the Potawatomi at Council Bluffs, upriver on the Missouri. He was a last-minute replacement. Regardless of particulars, he had gained his chance at long last, nearly seventeen years after first stepping foot on American soil, to work as a missionary among Indians.

Father De Smet carried a model for a successful mission in his mind based on the seventeenth-century Jesuit program among the Guarani Indians of Paraguay. There, he had learned, the missionaries had established a system of "reductions," an idyllic precursor to reservations, where the local Natives gave up their mobile lifeways to settle into agricultural communities centered around Catholic missions. The priests and brothers of these reductions attempted to protect the Indians from attacks by neighboring tribes and by Portuguese and Spanish slave traders. Although ultimately these Jesuits were expelled from Portuguese and Spanish lands in the region, Catholics still consider this Jesuit experiment as one of their most successful missions.[19] On a visit to Paraguay in 2015, Pope Francis called it "one of the most important experiences of evangelization and social organization in history."[20] De Smet imagined himself establishing just such a program as he set out for his first missionary work.

Potawatomi Mission (1838–39)

Around the time Sinshe and her boys returned home from Missouri, when Charlo was about eight years old, Father De Smet was struggling in his first posting as a missionary to Indians. He began his career in a Potawatomi refugee camp, among people who could have related to the Hebrews, having had to move time and again, with great suffering and loss all along the way. Since the time of the French and Indian Wars they had sided with the losers, first the French against the British and then the British against the Americans. Each outcome had moved them westward, grieving losses in homeland and relatives. Under regulations of the Indian Removal Act of 1830, the Prairie Potawatomi—Mshkodésik, "People of the Small Prairie"—had ended up at Council Bluffs on the Iowa side of the Missouri River in late May 1838. De Smet's first sight of them was from shipboard, when seemingly all two thousand of them, dressed in their finest, were gathered for the steamboat's arrival. Thinking the people had gathered there to welcome the Jesuit fathers and brothers, he soon realized the Potawatomi were focused on food and supplies and made no effort to greet the missionaries.

The principal task of these Jesuits, as federally subsidized missionaries to the Indians, was to implement the twin principles of conversion, Christianity and civilization, yoked together like a pair of oxen.[21] The missionaries' strategy for transforming tribes into sedentary farmers was threefold, as documented by one of De Smet's colleagues, Father Nicholas Point. First, they would slowly "substitute the fruits of agriculture for those of the chase." Second, "the innocent pleasures of the fireside" would replace "those offered by the varied life of a hunter." Third, and most important, "religion had to assume an important position in their lives"—Catholic of course.[22] They began their work with a clear vision and understanding that the European way of life was the only viable path forward for the Indians in this rapidly changing world, where the frontier of white encroachment expanded and grew like the spring thaw. But vision and implementation are two very different things, and conversion was no simple task.

The two Belgian missionaries at Council Bluffs had received no education about the Potawatomi prior to their arrival. Their unfamiliarity with the language and their limited grasp of the Indians' lifeways and beliefs severely limited their ability to establish relationships. Because they did not speak the language, the missionaries were unable to understand how differently the Potawatomi language reflected their reality. Indo-European languages have significant differences from Native languages that make direct translation impossible. European languages, especially English, trap things within static categories—person, place, or thing. Languages of Native America—whether Algonquian, Salish, Kootenai, or any of the other thirty language families of North America—favor verbs, reflecting a world where everything is fluid, moving, alive, and connected.[23]

The main settlement, called "Caldwell's Village" by the soldiers from Fort Leavenworth, was situated some four miles from the landing on the Missouri. The chief there, a mixed-blood Irish Potawatomi named Billy Caldwell, offered the missionaries the use of four fourteen-foot-square, poorly constructed, mice- and mosquito-infested cabins the soldiers had built the year before. When the priests arrived, only two individuals of the thirty families who lived there shook hands with them. Very few of them had been baptized or seemed interested. The more conservative families lived farther removed from the center where they had more potential to live in a traditional manner, focused on the gifts of each season, in the rhythmic cycles of nature.[24] The village of the head chief, Potagojecs, "Pile of Lead," was eight miles beyond Caldwell's camp.[25] Potagojecs hoped distance would protect his people from the influences of river traffic with its alcohol and rough, disrespectful traders and trappers.

With limitations of language and worldview, De Smet experienced many obstacles to converting these people to either Catholicism or

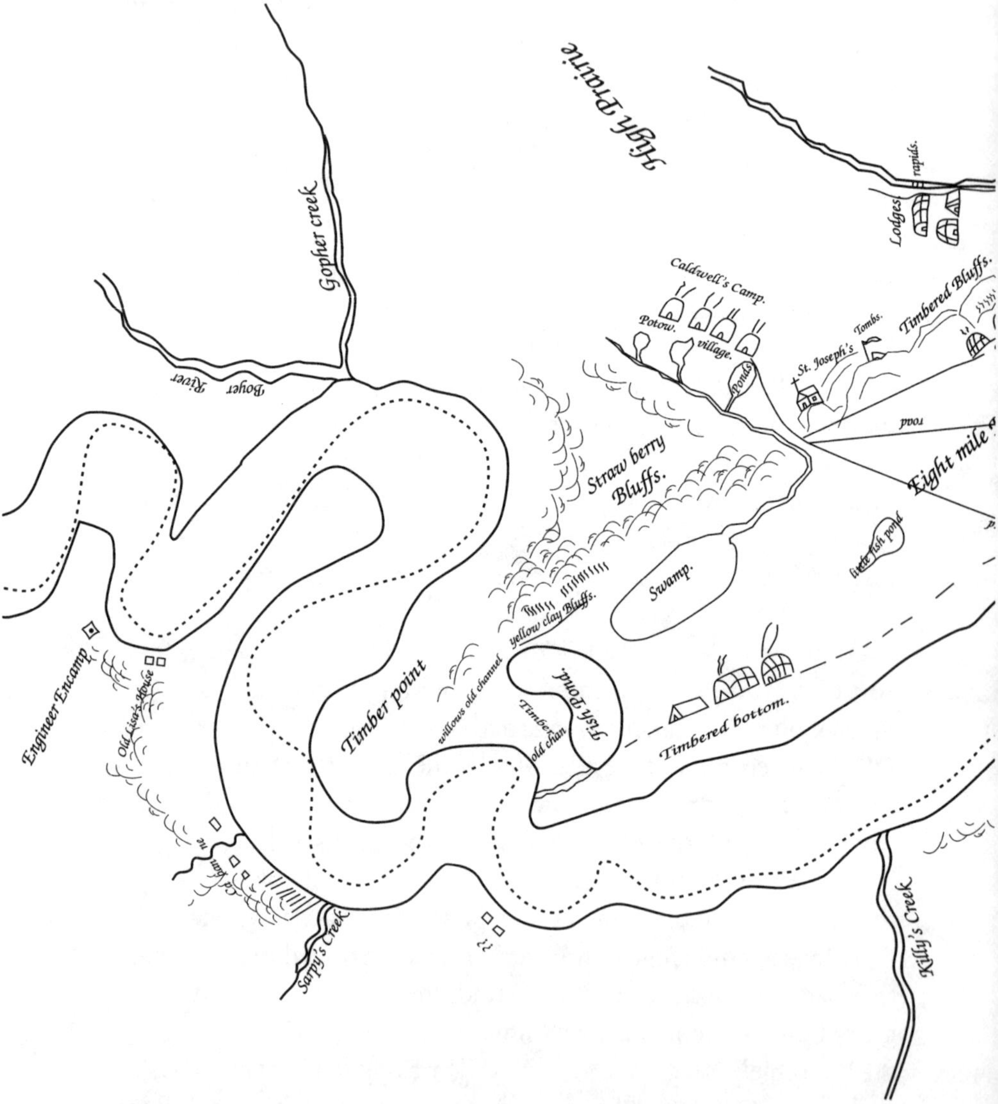

MAP 2. Rendering of De Smet's map of Potawatomi villages at Council Bluffs. By and courtesy of William Whitaker.

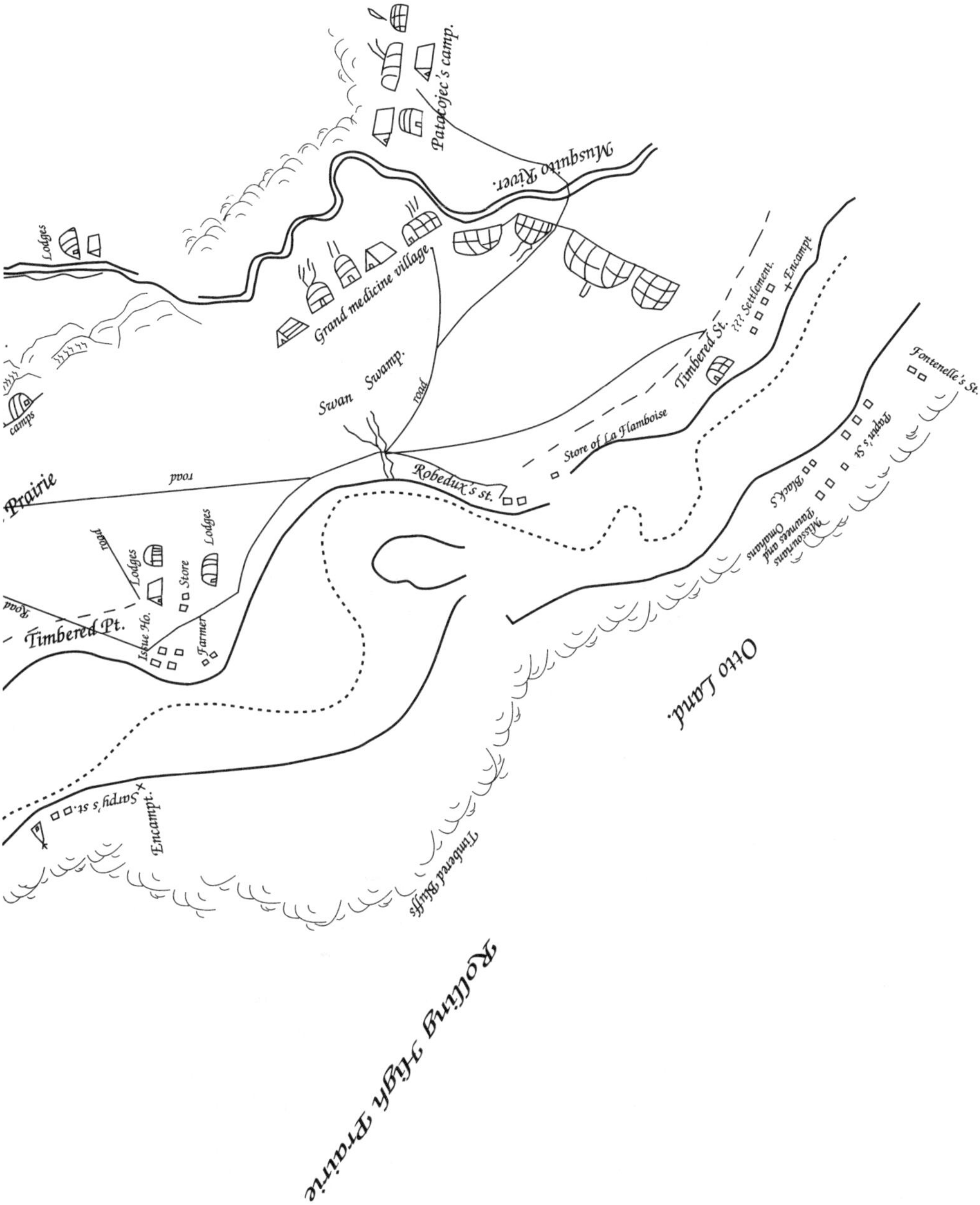

Patacojec's camp.
Musquito River.
Lodges
Grand medicine village
camps
Swan Swamp.
road
Prairie
road
Timbered St.
??? Settlement.
Encampt
Store of La Flamboise
Robedux's st.
Fontenelle's St.
Papin's St.
Black's
Missourians Pawnees and Omahans
road
Lodges
Store
Lodges
Road
Timbered Pt.
Issue Ho.
Farmer
Otto Land.
Sarpy's st.
Encampt.
Timbered Bluffs
Rolling High Prairie

civilization. He judged their "inclination to a wandering life [to be] so strong that they become melancholy and morose if they stay three months in the same place."[26] Their land base was not large enough to support a sustainable life of hunting and gathering, supplemented by crops, and the U.S. government was not providing the rations guaranteed by treaty.

Father De Smet slowly got to know the people in the scattered villages, more in service as a healer than a priest. For the Indians the roles were one and the same. People with strong medicine from the spirit realm served in both capacities. The people turned to De Smet for physical healing since he was a spiritual leader, a position that, in their world, included the practice of medicine, and they hoped especially for his help with new diseases brought by the Europeans. He stepped into the role to the best of his ability. When the family of a gravely ill child opposed the priest's religious teaching, he relied on his medicine vials and a little sleight-of-hand. He would rub the child with a dose of camphor, then add baptismal water and baptize the child without the parents suspecting a thing. He felt justified in the deceit because, in his mind, through baptism he was opening the gates of heaven for this innocent child. He felt that he outwitted the devil through this clever ploy, saving many a soul this way.[27]

After the priests had been among the Potawatomi for three months, only twenty adults were partaking of communion at the small mission house the Jesuits had built in honor of St. Joseph. Given that the population was close to two thousand residents, these results were paltry, even pitiful. The priests focused their attention on establishing a school to teach Indian children the Euro-American belief system and ways of living, as part of their arrangement with the federal government. The United States had promised the people, by treaty, an appropriation to be used for education and the encouragement of domestic skills, and the Jesuits worked to make this happen. The biggest challenge was to get parents to let their boys attend. As summer turned to fall, thirty boys were attending the little mission school.

The Jesuits were surprised by the tenacious memories of these children. Some of the boys could recite their lessons after two hearings. Had the priests spent more time with Native people, they would have observed the distinctive ways that oral cultures learn. Listening is what they have been trained to do from early childhood. Whether they were hearing the voices of elders telling the stories of their people or moving quietly through woods as they tracked animals, they had learned to listen. The living, breathing world captured all their senses and their feelings as well, creating ideal conditions for learning and remembering. Reading, by contrast, was remote and abstract.

De Smet reported to his superiors that the boys "studied from morning to night, sang hymns, recited the rosary, and assisted at religious instructions twice a day." After several months of this kind of learning, De Smet reported that these children "were changed into entirely new beings."[28] For the priests there would have been no question that this was a good thing. How the boys and their families felt about it is unknown.

The missionaries came to recognize two faces of the Potawatomi: drunk and sober. When they were sober, De Smet was impressed by the "profound peace in which they live," which he believed was the result of "letting every man do what seems to him good." They were dignified. De Smet's superior, another Belgian, noted that the Indians "never got out of temper in conversation or argued or interrupted others or obtruded themselves into other people's affairs." Quarreling was virtually unknown until alcohol was consumed, and then "all good qualities vanish." Even drunk, though, their language contained few ways to express disdain for another. When angered, the most injurious term they had for a nemesis was "dog," and "[they had] no expression to blaspheme the name of the Lord."[29] In this way and others, their language shaped and reflected a very different reality from the one the Belgians knew.

Food was scarce after the first long, cold winter, with only acorns available to sustain the people, along with a measly supply of roots the women had gathered the previous spring. Indians and Jesuits alike suffered. Rampant abuse of alcohol made many in the community seem beyond the reach of redemption. De Smet grew increasingly frustrated by the devastating impact of alcohol whenever a supply boat arrived. Soldiers at the checkpoint of Fort Leavenworth were failing to do their job. The fort had been established in 1831 for the purpose of preventing alcohol from making its way upriver. A furious De Smet wrote letters to President Van Buren's secretary of war, demanding prohibition. De Smet's superiors toned down his letters to protect the paltry sum they received for their missionary work among the Indians. The problem only grew. Had William Clark still been alive, perhaps he would have worked to better control the traders, but he died soon after providing the passports for the Jesuits to travel to Council Bluffs the previous year. His replacement, Joshua Pilcher, as president of the Missouri Fur Company, had little motivation to change the practices in effect since they bolstered the trade.

On April 20, 1839, in the Potawatomi's Month of the Young Rabbits, all the community members headed to the river to witness the arrival of the long-awaited supply boat, bringing clothing and provisions for the year, along with sacred objects for the chapel. They got there just in time to witness the boat's sinking, with all its treasures. Jumping into the chaos, De Smet managed to save a saw and a plow for the mission, along with wine for the Mass, and for himself, only a much-needed pair of boots. All the food from the boat sank to the bottom of the river.[30] Despair settled in all around. The people sought food wherever they could, but two thousand people living within a relatively contained area had seriously depleted nature's gifts.

Yankton Diversion (Spring 1839)

To cure the despair that beset him after the supply boat's demise, the restless De Smet concocted a trip. The purpose, he explained, was to proselytize among the Yanktons and to encourage peace between this western Dakota tribe and the Potawatomi.[31] At the end of April 1839, just nine days after the boat debacle, De Smet boarded the American Fur Company steamer to go up the Missouri. Maybe he had received word that his acquaintance Joseph Nicollet, the famous French surveyor, would be on board.

Nicollet (1786–1843), head of the newly created Corps of Topographical Engineers, had spent time in the library at St. Louis University and had helped the Jesuits gain permission from the federal government for the school at Council Bluffs.[32] He and his young assistant, John C. Fremont, were completing a survey of the Mississippi and its tributaries. German botanist Charles A. Geyer was also aboard. This esteemed group took every opportunity during the twelve-day journey to explore land along the way. Nicollet took De Smet under his wing and taught him rudimentary mapping skills, and Geyer shared his plant knowledge, especially regarding the plants that were edible. What a wonderful respite this was for De Smet, away from the oppressive concerns of the mission. Traipsing around the countryside and learning about plants, survey techniques, natural history, geology, and geography awakened in him a passion for exploring. The tools he was given by the surveyor—a barometer, compass, thermometers, and an inclinometer (an instrument designed to calculate the height of landmarks)—soon became some of his most precious possessions. De Smet's readings contributed to Nicollet's Missouri River survey results.[33] The missionary could not have imagined it at the time, but over the next six years he would map much of the Oregon Country, comprising the modern-day states of Oregon, Washington, north Idaho, western Montana, and adjacent parts of Canada. The Belgian priest had become a fledgling cartographer.

De Smet's peace mission was successful as well, at least for the time being. He convinced some of the Yanktons to make presents for the children of those they had killed among the Potawatomi. Some of them agreed, and they also consented to visit Council Bluffs and smoke the peace pipe with the Potawatomi. As many treaty negotiators learn, though, just because some people agree to the terms does not mean that peace has been achieved or could be maintained. The old men would sign treaties while acknowledging that the young men had minds of their own.

After a pipe ceremony given in his honor by the Yanktons, De Smet chose to return to Council Bluffs by dugout canoe. He camped at night on sandbars, sleeping atop a buffalo robe, and relished the experience of fresh air under the fathomless night sky. This Belgian was embracing the wild that had called to him since childhood. Instead of the tame Dender, with its manicured banks, he was immersed in the erratic, channel-shifting Missouri River and the vast buffalo plains through which it meandered.

De Smet returned to Council Bluffs to find that the excesses of liquor had not abated; if anything, they had grown, and the priest despaired.

In a letter to a friend he shared the horrors of life at Council Bluffs. He likened the arrival of the supply boat to the landing of "fifty large canons [that were] ready charged with the most murderous grapeshot," bringing horror to their daily lives, beyond anything the Belgian priests had ever imagined.[34]

After the liquor had been consumed and its imbibers had sobered up, they enjoyed a pleasant break until another supply ship arrived in early August. De Smet wrote to his superior of the terrible state of things. So tragic was the situation, De Smet lamented, no matter the extent of their efforts to the contrary, that the missionaries could not reverse "so many eviles and obstacles."[35] He must have struggled emotionally with what could only be considered a significant failure.

By early September De Smet reached the conclusion that the Prairie Potawatomi were too far gone to be helped. More than one hundred people had been killed in the community during his time there. After so many fantasies about working among the uncorrupted innocents, he realized that his Paraguayan model would never be possible at Council Bluffs. His disappointment was so great that a kind of energetic paralysis set in.

If he were honest, though, things weren't that much worse than they had been during the previous summer. He was the one who had changed, ever since his trip up the Missouri. He had experienced the prairie in all its open glory and had met Indians still living free, and he had loved it. His taste of freedom made everything at St. Joseph's Mission seem bleaker than before. Understanding that he would never be able to accomplish his missionary dream among the Potawatomi, he prayed for a new flock in greener pastures.

A Chance Encounter (Fall 1839)

Some people believe prayers are answered as soon as they're offered. If De Smet had doubted that possibility before, he might have changed his mind in mid-September 1839, when two Catholic Iroquois pulled their canoe ashore. Stopping to resupply on route to St. Louis, they could not believe their good fortune when they saw a black-robed priest striding toward them. The delight was mutual, and the two men, Ignace Chapped Lips and Pierre Kassawessa (or Chalk), ended up spending several weeks in the village sharing stories with the welcoming and enthusiastic priest.[36]

De Smet learned a great deal about the lives of these fascinating multilingual Mohawk travelers, from their beginnings on the St. Lawrence River, through their lives as trappers, to the Native people they had settled among and whom they called Flatheads. Not many of the original group of Iroquois immigrants who had settled in the Rocky Mountains remained with the tribal communities.[37] Some of them had settled in Westport after retiring from the HBC.

The travelers gladly shared with De Smet details of their adopted homeland and of the various tribes of that region and their relationships. The missionary had some background about these Indian nations through William Clark and the records of the Lewis and Clark expedition. His malaise turned to fascination through the stories they told. The Flatheads, they explained, are more accurately called Séliš (Salish), and they don't have flat heads. They speak the Salish language along with their relatives, a band of the Ql'ispé (Kalispel), whom the Frenchmen call Pend d'Oreille, referring to the shell earrings worn by both their men and their women. The French name stuck on the upriver group but not the lower.

Much to De Smet's delight, Pierre and Ignace and their Salish wives were raising their children in the ways of the Church. Their families had been Catholic for generations. Back home in Quebec, they had grown up in a mission village where Catholicism had defined the rhythm of their lives. French Jesuits had been operating missions among all five of the Iroquois nations—Mohawk, Oneida, Onondaga, Cayuga, and Seneca—for nearly two centuries. Back then, the men told De Smet, as the growing numbers of white colonists overwhelmed the Native people, the world as they knew it was vanishing. For some of them, the priests and their teachings became important stabilizing factors.

Growing tension between French immigrants and the Iroquois spread to the missions, and soon after the Christian calendar turned to the eighteenth century, the missions began to close, one by one, including one on the Mohawk River. With the Black Robes gone and with troubles brewing in upper New York, some of the Christian Mohawks of that village removed themselves upstream from the fur-trade center of Montreal. They named this new village on the St. Lawrence River Kahnawake, "at the rapids," after their home village. The men worked in the fur trade, as their fathers had done before them. Eventually the Jesuits were able to establish a mission at Kahnawake. That was the place where Grand Ignace had grown up.

By the late 1750s, as the tensions of the French and Indian Wars escalated, the non-Native population was growing disproportionately. The people of Kahnawake found it difficult to make a living. The animals on which they depended for their livelihood, including those they trapped for fur, were becoming scarce, and their land was becoming depleted. Elders were alarmed by the behavior of their young people whenever traders brought rum to the village. Some of the village leaders—both men and women—decided to move farther west, away from these destructive influences. Thirty families from Kahnawake moved upriver to create a new settlement where several small rivers converged with the St. Lawrence River, just south of the line that would soon separate the United States from Canada. They called the place Akwesasne. Jesuits went along and founded the St. Regis Mission there in 1755. Ignace and Pierre had grown up in that environment.

De Smet felt a kinship with these travelers who were so keyed into the landscape. They oriented the priest to the geography between the Missouri and the place where they lived, deep in the Rockies. He could not hear enough of their stories about the Flatheads and Nez Perce and their battles with the Blackfeet on the bison plains. De Smet's world, too, had been shaped by warfare. As a boy, he had often coaxed his neighborhood gang to rally the troops in mock attempts to overthrow the army. Twenty-five years later, although tempered, he remained drawn to adventure and the intrigues of war, subjects that would soon fill the pages of his own books.

The more the visitors told De Smet of their histories and their lives among the Salish in the Rocky Mountains, the more the priest began to imagine a future there. He could hardly believe his ears when they revealed to him the primary purpose of their travels. Salish chief Big Face had sent them on this journey specifically in order to engage a Black Robe to come and live among them. They explained about earlier delegations to St. Louis and the tragic deaths of Grand Ignace and the chief's sons. Big Face was counting on Petit Ignace and Pierre, the fourth delegation, to succeed where the first three had failed.

Peter-Jan De Smet, restless and always dreaming of greener pastures, could barely contain his excitement. The unsullied mountain world of the Salish people must be his calling. With the ground already prepared for Christian life by these Iroquois, he would be able to nurture the seeds of Catholicism among innocents, as his religious forebears had done before the Suppression. With this opportunity he might help restore dignity to the reputation of the great Jesuit order.

In that fall of 1839, from a bluff overlooking the yellow line of cottonwoods along the Missouri River, the Jesuit might have pondered the changing world the Mohawk ancestors of the two emissaries had endured. It may have been the prophecies that had spread across the plateau in the preceding years that were in part what motivated the Iroquois and their Salish hosts to seek the establishment of a mission. A mission, like Kahnawake, according to fur-trade scholar George Capps, "could help the local people navigate the changes to come. [It] could serve as a place where the Indians could preserve some sense of indigenous identity and culture even while adapting to and partially integrating themselves into a new system and worldview."[38]

As had happened in the takeover of "New England" and Quebec in the seventeenth and eighteenth centuries, droves of white settlers would find their way to the remote valleys of the Rocky Mountains—just as they had to Kahnawake—and they would deplete the resources upon which the Salish depended as surely as they would ply their liquor. But where the Mohawks, back then, had options for where they could move to avoid these influences, the Salish, by the 1860s, would be surrounded. There would be nowhere left to turn.

4. Prayer and Possibility

Escape Plan Materializes (Winter 1839–40)

On October 20, 1839, the two Iroquois emissaries said their adieus to their gracious host, climbed back into their canoe, and headed downriver. Father De Smet sent them off with a letter of introduction to Father Verhaegen, a Belgian who had been at the Mechlen Seminary and had traveled to America with De Smet in 1821. In St. Louis the unusual envoys told their story to Bishop Rosati and Father Verhaegen, impressing these church leaders with their understanding of the Christian faith and with their ability to express it in French. One of them had a "little printed book in his own language," and from this Mohawk hymnal he sang "a number of sacred songs."[1] After they had made their confessions and received Holy Communion in the cathedral, Bishop Rosati confirmed the two visitors. The bishop sent them off with a promise that two priests would visit them in the spring.

The following day, with their assignment completed, the two men left for the Kickapoo Mission, north of Westport, where Ignace would spend the winter waiting for the springtime arrival of the promised Black Robes. Pierre immediately started for home. He and a Nez Perce companion risked a perilous journey to reach the Flatheads in time to arrange a welcome for Ignace and the priests at the next summer rendezvous.

Father De Smet went about his daily work at the mission, but his mind, like a caged rabbit, jumped from spot to spot, trying to find a comfortable landing place. He longed to go far away from the corruption of white opportunists on the frontier. Anxious to learn the outcome of the Iroquois' meetings in St. Louis, he wanted to know what the bishop had decided about sending missionaries to the Flathead Indians. He watched the river for the arrival of a mail boat. What a shame it would be to let the Protestants acquire all the best opportunities to work among untarnished innocents.

December's monotony was interrupted by the welcome arrival of a Yankton delegation of forty warriors. They had come to smoke the pipe of peace with the Potawatomi, as they had promised De Smet back in August. These former enemies stayed several days. They even joined in the singing of carols with the mission community. The apparent success of Father De Smet's efforts marked the beginning of his career as a peacemaker among the Indians.[2]

The joy of the Yanktons' visit soon faded as the dreary monotony of winter at Council Bluffs wore on. While waiting for word from St. Louis, the anxious priest continued his fundraising outreach. He was able to present a strong case for support of the Indian missions, and through his correspondence he developed a wide audience for both fundraising and creative prose. Sometime late that winter De Smet began to concoct a plan—or maybe a plan began to concoct itself—and it emerged suddenly with one impetuous move.

In mid-December De Smet sent a letter, by courier, to Father DeVos in St. Louis about a critical shortage of food and supplies at the Potawatomi Mission and volunteered to travel to St. Louis to discuss the matter with his superiors and to pick up supplies.[3] Also, he noted, he needed medical attention. None of this rash behavior was out of character. Since childhood, according to his older sister, he had always been "impetuous in the extreme."[4] Without waiting for an answer, the impatient priest and one companion set out in February 1840, in the dead of winter, on an overland journey of over four hundred miles, "first on foot, then on horseback, and at times in a cart."[5] His superiors must have been shocked by the sight of their ever-challenging compatriot when he finally arrived in St. Louis on February 20. He was in terrible condition, especially his lungs. Doctors prescribed complete bed rest.

Why had the missionary undertaken such a potentially dangerous journey? Perhaps he made the trip because he had learned that his superiors had selected two priests to travel to the Flathead country, and he needed to plead his case. Or maybe he had had no advance warning but could not contain his wondering any longer, so he conjured up his trip simply to get an update on the plan to send missionaries into the mountains. What angst he must have suffered to learn that he had not been selected to forge the way into the mountain tribes. Instead he was to return to Council Bluffs with supplies for the needy mission.

He headed back up the river while he struggled with his fate. At no time must his vow of obedience have been harder to accept. Soon after his arrival, though, he was notified by messenger that his superiors had changed their minds. De Smet would be the one, after all, to travel to the Rocky Mountains. The headstrong priest was elated. He thanked his God for this opportunity, knowing that neither the U.S. government nor the Jesuits would have thought to leapfrog over so many tribes to set up a mission program in the Rocky Mountains, some sixteen hundred miles to the northwest of St. Louis, if not for the fortuitous arrival of the Iroquois emissaries from the Salish Indians. This work was surely his destiny.

Details are few about why his superiors shifted position and decided to send De Smet to the Rockies. The official report stated that De Smet's eagerness, his zeal, and his remarkable energy made him the most suitable candidate for this new position.[6] This description is difficult to reconcile with the reality of his recent experience of a serious ailment and directive for complete bed rest. On the practical side, though, De Smet could tout more on-the-ground experience than the two new recruits who had first been selected. He had his missionary work among the Potawatomi, peacemaking experience, backcountry travel experience, and cartographic training as well. On the other hand, it is hard to imagine that his superiors would not have been concerned about his unreliability and erratic health issues. Just six years earlier he had quit his training and returned to Europe. Was he to be relied upon?

Perhaps his superiors changed their minds about De Smet because of the proposal he made to them just before returning to Council Bluffs. He offered to cover the costs if he were the one to go to the Rocky Mountains. Years later his fellow Jesuit Joseph Joset remembered that De Smet had proposed to use the annual pension provided for him by his family for this purpose. Apparently the Missouri Province was struggling at the time from "the want of means" and was unable to say no.[7] This was a time of terrible nationwide depression.

De Smet would embark for the Rocky Mountains as soon as travel conditions allowed. Just two weeks from his sick bed, he had only five weeks to prepare. That was when the spring caravan would depart for the rendezvous on the Green River, carrying trade goods from St. Louis to be exchanged for furs. De Smet's illness seems to have disappeared, and his overall state of exhaustion gave way to euphoria. All the eager Belgian could think about as he raised funds and organized supplies for this exciting journey was how the innocents of the mountains could be transformed from wild hunters to Christian villagers. Their lives would revolve around the cycle of the Catholic calendar as they learned to seek forgiveness for their original sin, from which only Jesus could save them. He would collect souls for Heaven.

The Missouri Province Jesuits launched De Smet toward the Rocky Mountains on March 27, 1840. He would be the only Black Robe heading west, due to a shortage of funds. He would have Ignace as an escort to the great gathering of the fur trade, where he would meet with tribal leaders about the potential for establishing a permanent mission among them. If circumstances were promising, he would return the following year with supplies and a crew. The words of the diarist at St. Louis University on that day marked the significance of De Smet's journey to the province: "The day eagerly desired of the Indians that dwell beyond the Rocky Mountains has dawned at last! For today Rev. Father De Smet departed alone to carry to them the light of faith and announce to them the way of salvation. . . . Fortunate Indians! Thrice fortunate Father to be chosen by God from all eternity as the instrument of his mighty work!"[8] Finally, at the age of forty, an impatient, impetuous Peter De Smet had a chance to prove himself in a worthy endeavor, one laudable enough for the history books.

Rocky Mountain Rendezvous (Summer 1840)

Pierre Gauché had survived a grueling journey back to the Rockies, but his young Nez Perce companion had not. The Salish people remembered that Lefthand had appeared alone in the springtime, when the people were camped on Eight Mile Creek in the Bitterroot Valley, digging roots and enjoying the sweet chew of Ponderosa cambium bark that comes with the season. The elders assembled to hear of his journey. Once they had passed the pipe, the Iroquois told of all that had happened on the trip to St. Louis and how Little Ignace had stayed behind so that he could accompany the Black Robe into their country. They should soon be arriving at Fort Hall. Chief Big Face immediately selected ten men to travel there to greet the long-awaited ones.[9]

The rendezvous was a small one because the fur business had changed so dramatically. In fact, this would be the last year for these legendary gatherings because silk hats had become the vogue style, and besides, hardly any beaver remained to be trapped. Buffalo hides had replaced them as the predominant trade item, creating an entirely new system of distribution. The inner mountain basins were no longer the hub of western commerce. The new center had shifted to the plains, and for the northwestern plains of what would become Montana, transport shifted to boats down the Missouri rather than overland pack trains.

In the spring of 1840 De Smet arranged for his party to travel with the American Fur Company's group of fifty men, thirty carts, and scores of mules, along with a party of emigrants. While De Smet addressed final details, he could not help but wonder about Pierre Gauché. The eager missionary knew that much depended on whether Pierre made it back home in time to alert the Salish of their arrival. Knowing the many perils of the journey, he understood the high chance that the Iroquois had not survived his travels across the lands of so many hostile tribes. If that was the situation, how would De Smet find the Flatheads, who could be anywhere in their vast territory? He and Petit Ignace would have to trust that the Almighty was overseeing all the moving parts. De Smet's state of mind was good. In those last few days before departure, he penned a letter to his brother in Belgium, telling him, "Never in my life have I been more tranquil or more happy."[10]

The eager Jesuit left Westport for this initial scouting trip on April 30, accompanied by Ignace and twenty-two-year-old Gabriel Prudhomme Jr. On the sixth day out Father De Smet developed a fever that plagued him throughout the overland journey and continued to a lesser degree throughout most of his time in the Rockies. He rode when he could but spent much of his time being jostled about with the provisions in one of the mule-drawn carts. During the long weeks spent crossing the Great Plains, the adventuring Belgian had ample time to consider the possibilities of his future. He did not need to limit his dream to a mission among the Salish. He pictured, instead, ten mission settlements among the Native peoples of the region, all under the umbrella of the Rocky Mountain Mission. The missions would be permanent agricultural refuges, like the reductions in Paraguay. His team of well-educated European Catholics would transform the lives of the pagan Natives, not only through conversion to Christianity but also through the benefits of civilization. The lives of these primitive people without wheels, agriculture, or an alphabet would be transformed by what he had to offer. The very determined Jesuit had no way of knowing that he was about to enter an ancient world with a brilliance all its own. The world he carried in his mind made little room for another reality. Complexity demonstrated superiority, and Catholicism was the road to personal salvation.

Bear Tracks, a renowned medicine man, had led an advance party to Green River to await the Black Robe's arrival. This contemporary of Charlo's father was one of the most reliable Salish headmen. He was strong in body and courage. His supernatural power allowed him to see into the future, change the weather, find enemies, locate missing animals and people, and attract bison by using his "magic buffalo-calling chant."[11] Perhaps his most remarkable ability was to project himself across space. Bear Tracks and the advance guard of the bravest warriors of the nation greeted De Smet at the rendezvous at the end of June. The Salish men, according to De Smet, greeted him with reverence and respect. It was not the meeting of strangers, he recalled later, "but of friends; it was like children running to meet their father after a long absence."[12]

Over the next several days the Salish delegation members told the Black Robe about their homeland and people and especially of how they had recently reigned supreme in a five-day battle with the Blackfeet, even though they were outnumbered by more than three to one. De Smet understood them to say that the Great Spirit had spared them so that they would be able to guide the long-awaited missionary to the hunting camp of their people.[13] They had been hunting with a group of Pend d'Oreille when their enemy attacked. Shining Shirt, the prophet, led them to victory. While the enemy suffered many losses and injuries, only two Salish men were seriously wounded, and none died.[14] The children back at camp would have spread the rumor that the two injured men had failed to bite the magic object.

On Saturday, Independence Day was acknowledged by the Americans, and on Sunday hundreds of native men, women, and children and a large contingent of Canadians joined De Smet in celebrating Mass under the open sky. From an altar decorated "with boughs and garlands of flowers" and overlooking the confluence of Horse Creek and the Green River, the priest reported that he "addressed the congregation in French and in English and spoke also by an interpreter to the Flatheads and Snake Indians."[15] The air filled with hymns of many voices. It was a moment that would stay with many as long as they lived.

The following day De Smet, with both Salish and Canadian escorts, all packed up once again for travel, headed northward across the divide that separates the Colorado River headwaters from those of the Columbia. They were aiming for the main camp of the Salish Nation west of the Tetons while traveling through "the Backbone of the Western Hemisphere" and some of the most magnificent mountain scenery in the world.[16] De Smet, who never in his life had seen such mountains, focused on the steep and narrow passages that they encountered. When the party reached Jackson Hole, he made note in his writings of the rare plants that covered the surrounding hillsides. Although his companions proceeded fearlessly across the rushing Snake River, the Belgian lowlander was stopped short with fear. Three Salish men made an impromptu raft for him, using his lodge cover as a floating device, and piled his belongings on top. They jumped in the water and instructed him to climb aboard. The simple yet ingenious system was safe, they assured him, while laughing as he was helped aboard. Ten minutes later he was deposited on the far shore; the short journey had been so smooth that it was as if he had been delivered there by a "majestic swan."[17] The following day they crossed Teton Pass and headed northward to the Flathead camp.

When they reached Pierre's Hole on the eighth day of travel, the priest's heart swelled at the sight of scores of lodges and perhaps two thousand people with thousands of horses in that spectacular setting. The Tetons swept up to the sky on the east, the Three Buttes dotted the northwestern skyline, and the wide-open landscape of the Snake River Plain seemed to go on forever. The delighted Black Robe found himself thronged by men, women, and children who wanted to greet him and shake his hand. Presumably Lodge Pole and his family were in the camp. This might have been the first meeting of the boy Charlo and the Jesuit missionary De Smet.

The long-awaited newcomer was escorted into the lodge of Tjolizhitzay, where the chief sat flanked by his councilors. De Smet felt himself welcomed "with the liveliest cordiality."[18] The missionary grasped the magnitude of the moment, thanked his god for the safe journey, and prayed that he would be successful. He had been planning this moment for a year, ever since learning of this chief and his people from Ignace and Pierre at Council Bluffs. His mind, so full of the world he would create among them, had little room for immersing in the moment or for grasping the depth of the man whose lodge he had entered. He could see why this large man, about sixty years old, with such a commanding presence, had been dubbed "Big Face" by French Canadian fur trappers, given the large size and elongated shape of his head, but he had no way of knowing that not long before this day the chief had experienced a life-changing moment, an enlightenment moment of epiphany. Some people might say he had been born again.

Tjolizhitzay was Crow by birth and had been adopted at some unknown point of his life into the Salish community.[19] From the time he was very young, this orphan boy had turned to spiritual sources for comfort and guidance. As an adult, he was admired for his spiritual depth as well as his natural leadership abilities. He thought deeply about the various religious ideas, both Native and Christian, that were spreading through the region during these years. Through this process he had developed or adopted a prayer that he recited with regularity, like a mantra. "Oh you, who know everything and are all-powerful and infinitely good," he would say, "have pity on me, come to my aid, grant my prayer."[20] On the winter day of the magical breakthrough, the old chief had been repeating his prayer in meditation when he was struck by "a most voracious light," and the experience brought a sense of "a new creation in the whole of his being."[21]

Big Face had prepared himself spiritually for this legendary meeting and received the Black Robe in a traditional manner. The still grieving father was keenly aware of all that had been sacrificed for this moment of possibility. With the interpretive help of young Charles Lamoose, he began by extending a warm welcome to the visitor. Next he recounted the historical record that pertained to their meeting. He spoke of the arrival of the Christian Iroquois and the many efforts on the part of the Salish to attract a missionary to their community, just as De Smet had learned from Little Ignace and Pierre. Now here they were, very grateful that a Black Robe sat among them and hopeful that what he would teach them would help them as they struggled through all their difficult challenges.

When it was his turn to speak, the stocky, clear-eyed Jesuit spoke to them about religion and then discussed the set of spiritual exercises he would schedule for them. They would meet for morning and evening prayers and for instruction during the day. That first evening, using the bell provided by one of the chiefs, he invited the people to gather around his lodge for evening prayers. The people expressed their desire for De Smet to show them "the road we have to follow, to come to the place where the Great Spirit resides."[22] After the long-awaited Black Robe recited the standard prayer, the people sang in unison songs of praise of their own composition. De Smet, with his ear attuned to the scale and tones of Europe, was astonished by the harmony of these unique creations.

Starting the next morning, with the help of an interpreter, De Smet assembled the council and preached to the members four times a day. In their language, through interpreters, they heard the Lord's Prayer, the Hail Mary, the Apostles' Creed, the Ten Commandments, and four Acts of Creation, Fall, Redemption, and Restoration. About two weeks into what would be a two-month visit in the traveling hunting camp, De Smet motivated their learning by promising a silver medal to the one who first memorized the prayers he had been teaching. Técousten, known to the fur traders as Little Faro, a quick-minded thirty-year-old, immediately demonstrated his accomplishment and claimed the prize. The intelligence of this young man so impressed De Smet that he appointed him to assist by helping others to learn.[23]

Every morning at the break of day, according to De Smet, Face-Raised-Up Grizzly waked the camp as he rode from lodge to lodge. He reminded his people to let the first thoughts of their hearts "be for the Great Spirit." Their prayers should express their love and beg the Great Spirit to be merciful. The sun is rising, he would tell them; they should get to the river to bathe and be ready for the sound of the bell and the teachings of the Black Robe.[24] After he had completed his round through camp, he would visit particular lodges that required some fatherly advice. Father De Smet was astonished to find such a "well-ordered and religious community . . . among Indians in the defiles and valleys of the Rocky Mountains."[25]

The missionary developed great respect for both Big Face and Face-Raised-Up Grizzly. Physically as different as they could be—Big Face was tall and powerfully built while Face-Raised-Up Grizzly was short and slight—they both commanded great respect. Regarding Big Face, De Smet believed that a more appropriate name would be "Nestor of the Desert," referring to Nestor, king of Pylos, from Greek mythology, for along with his age, "in stature and sagacity he has all the essentials of greatness." This chief, concluded De Smet, was to be "distinguished above all his fellows by intelligence, gentleness, and every good disposition."[26]

This mobile Salish village slowly made its way northward, heading toward the Three Forks of the Missouri. As the zealous missionary journeyed into the wilds of the Rockies, he carried with him a vision shaped in part by the Jesuit order and in part by the prevailing American understanding that tribal people had no choice but to make way for the white race. He would pave the way for the Salish transition. As they neared their home territory, near the border of what are now Wyoming, Idaho, and Montana, the priest climbed atop a high ridge between Henry's Lake and Red Rock Lakes along the Continental Divide and claimed this world for the Jesuits by inscribing upon a soft stone, in large letters, "Sanctus Ignatius Patronus Montium [St. Ignatius, Patron of the Mountains]. Die Julii 23, 1840."[27] Returning to the foot of the mountain, a tired yet enthused De Smet said a Mass of thanksgiving. Surrounded by Indians intoning chants to the praise of God, he installed himself in the land in the name of Ignatius, the Jesuits' founder.[28]

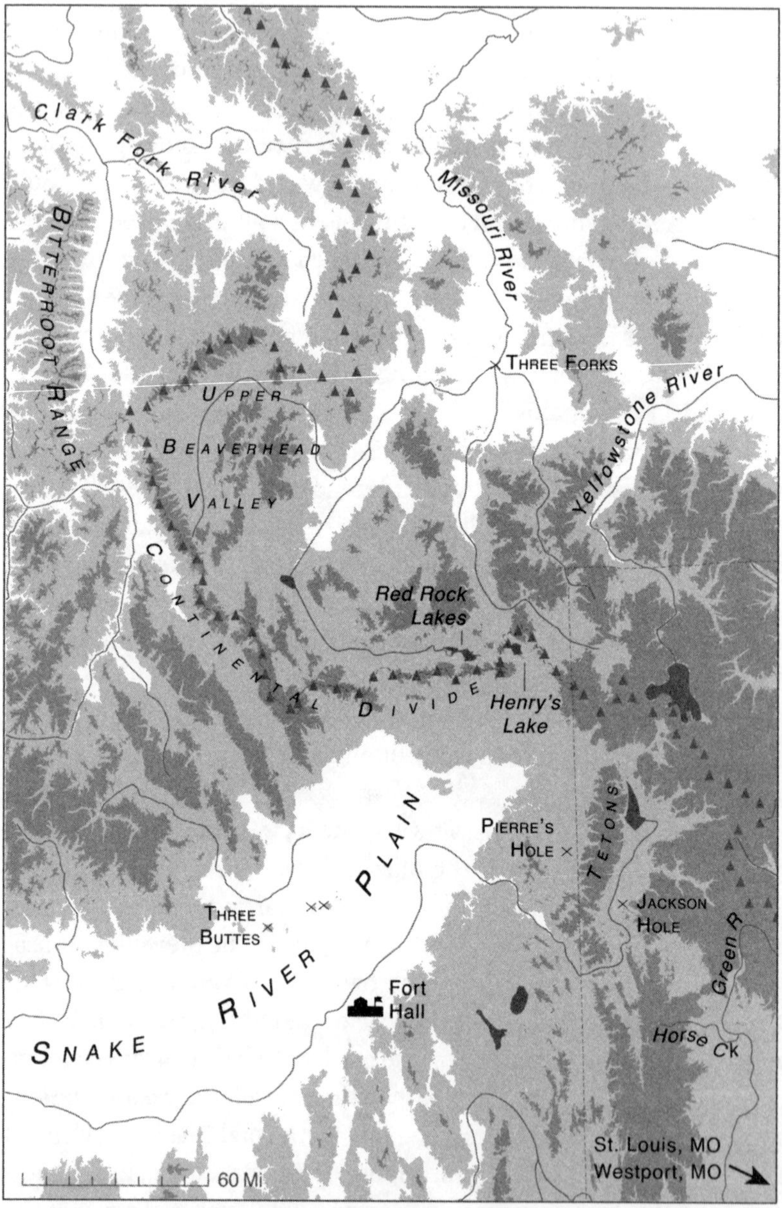

MAP 3. To the Rocky Mountains, 1840 and 1841. Hannah Shafer, cartographer.

De Smet had been in America for two decades and finally found himself among Native people he considered noble; they had not been compromised by negative influences of the Europeans. He observed these Indians to be honest, polite, and of good humor, as well as hospitable, well-mannered, and gay. He wrote in his account of this meeting that to help each other was their norm, and slander among women was unknown. "They share one another's sufferings, give help in time of need, and care for the orphans." He was grateful to see that these mountain Indians had not been subjected to the "insatiable greed" of white men on the frontier. He conveyed the absurdity that such dignified people as the Salish would be called barbarians by civilized men. "Their tent is open house; key and locks are unknown."[29] Despite their appeal, the Jesuit recognized that other than their gambling, these "elect of God" appeared ripe for full conversion of religion and culture.

The Salish responded positively to De Smet as well. He had a calming presence and seemed comfortable with their world, unlike some of the whites whose paths they had crossed. They were receptive to what he offered. Nearly six hundred of their children and elderly submitted to baptism during these weeks. The two chiefs were baptized that day. Face-Raised-Up Grizzly, once a poor orphan child, was christened Peter, the foundation, and Big Face was called Paul, in keeping with his patriarchal status.[30] The joy of the day was tempered by the requirement that all relinquish their guardian spirits. Big Face had received strong medicine from his life-long guardian, the crow. To formally renounce this special friend must have been done with mixed emotions.[31]

When the time came for De Smet to begin his journey back to St. Louis—through the country of the Crows (the Apsáalooke, Children of the Large Beaked Bird) to the American Fur Company fort along the Yellowstone River, then on to the Missouri—the Salish elders sent him out with an escort of some twenty warriors, with Insula, the Little Chief, in the lead. This chivalrous man, despite his small stature, was understood to be one of the most influential leaders among the Salish. He was brave in battle and could ride like no other. This war chief, just over fifty years of age, despite having only limited use of his right hand due to a war injury, still struck fear in the hearts of his enemies. From their first meeting De Smet and the Little Chief would remain close friends. As a sign of friendship and respect, Insula, although a decade older, adopted the missionary as his father.

When the Black Robe departed, he assured his hosts that he would return with others the following spring, ready to settle down with them. For the Salish their long-held dream was about to come true. With Black Robes among them, there was hope for a better world than the one in which they found themselves, one of incessant warfare and much sickness. The people hoped the new way to worship the Great Spirit brought by these black-robed men would give them extra power against their enemies and, perhaps, against smallpox and measles as well.

To the Oregon Country (1841)

In the spring of 1841, having had only six months to prepare, Father De Smet, Superior of the new Rocky Mountain Mission, set out from Westport on the Missouri by way of the new trail to Oregon. He was accompanied by two priests and three lay brothers, men who had taken the same vows of poverty, chastity, and obedience as the priests but who were not ordained. They traveled as part of a guided wagon train, with seventy emigrants eager to settle the rich lands of the Northwest. Gabriel Prudhomme Jr. traveled with them and served as De Smet's personal interpreter.

Of the three priests De Smet was the only one with experience among Indians. Gregory Mengarini, a young Italian aristocrat, was fresh off the boat from Italy and Nicholas Point, a poor Frenchman, had worked primarily among Europeans, most recently among the French Canadian community at Westport, where he had had some minimal contact with the Kickapoo Indians.

Non-Native travelers, in small numbers, had made their way westward along the South Pass route since the time of the Astorians, three decades earlier, but 1841 marked the beginning of the emigrant wagon trains. White settlers were already claiming what they perceived as their rights in the southwestern portion of the Oregon Country. Eventually they gained these perceived rights through renegade law and occupancy. Initial meetings were held in 1841 to discuss enacting Organic Laws of Oregon, intended to establish a temporary government until such time as the United States claimed jurisdiction, defined citizenship and rights.

FIG. 5. "Passage d'un ravin bourbeuse" (Trail through a muddy ravine). Nicolas Point Missionary Drawings Collection, JA-IX-C-9-031a, Jesuit Archives and Research Center.

The Organic Laws of Oregon mimicked a document crafted after the War of 1812 to open Indian lands for white settlement in the old Northwest. One difference in the new Northwest version was that wars against the Natives were to be commenced by "representatives of the people," commonly called vigilantes, instead of the Congress since Congress had no rights there. Under the temporary act, suffrage was extended to free white men and their male descendants. Consideration of the next generation made room for the fur traders, who had children with Indian women, to extend the right of voting to their sons. Technically Gabriel Prudhomme Jr. would have the right to vote, whereas the sons of Lodge Pole, Bear Tracks, and Insula would not. Of course none of the daughters or mothers could vote, Indian or white. Referring to anyone of color, the Organic Laws excluded Black people from occupancy. One result was that Hawaiians who had been brought over to work in the fur trade were forced to leave. Oregon was to be a haven for white Americans.

Native people were seen as an impediment to progress but not enough of one to stop white settlers from claiming land. Married couples could claim up to 640 acres—one full section—to "prove up" through certain improvements, and unmarried men could claim 320 acres.[32] These land claims were premature since the boundary with Britain had yet to be settled, but no higher authority stood in the way. The Organic Laws provided a semi-legal means for the lower Columbia River country to shift, slowly but surely, from Indian to white. The pioneers in Oregon were just continuing the long tradition of taking land from Native people based on a concocted construct of civil rights over natural rights, dating back to John Winthrop with the founding of the Massachusetts Bay Colony.[33]

Although the home of the Salish was in the Oregon Territory, its remote location between the Bitterroot Mountains and the main chain of the Rockies had protected it so far from emigrant incursion. The Black Robes would be free to sway the Indians toward the Jesuit vision, free from competition. They could not have found a better group to serve. The Salish were welcoming and generous people, eager to learn the ways of the Black Robes. They already prayed as a regular part of their lives. When they ate a meal, they would take a portion of their food, raise it toward the sun, and say, "Sun, be so kind as to allow these animals [or roots or fruits] to grow in abundance."[34] The morsel was then set aside in recognition of the spirit gift from which the food came. The priests just needed to help these innocents understand that the sun wasn't their savior.

Part 2. In the Salish World, 1841–60

Each place has a name and a story, each place has a name for something that happened in old time, and in the name and story is the people's greatness and proof of their favor in creation.

—Karen Fisher, *A Sudden Country*

5. Black Robes Enter Coyote's World

A Heartfelt Welcome

"They're coming! They're coming!" Upon hearing the scouts' announcement, everyone in camp looked expectantly toward the southeast, across the broad valley of the Upper Beaverhead River country, eager to catch a glimpse of the Black Robes. For two moons, since the time of Ripe Huckleberries, they had been waiting for this moment.

The missionaries and their escorts had made their way over the pass that divides the Snake River headwaters and the Beaverhead Valley, along the Continental Divide. They were arranged in several rows of riders on prancing horses, ten abreast. The three Black Robes were flanked by their Salish protectors, including the elderly sub-chief Oustilpo, "Walks Out into the Open," a modest and kind man who had been the one to officially welcome the Black Robes.[1] De Smet felt the comfort of knowing several of those present, including Little Ignace and the two sons of Grand Ignace, François Saxa and Charles Lamoose, in addition to Pelchimo, "Black-Edged Blanket."[2] Pelchimo, known for his courage, had demonstrated this trait soon after leaving Fort Hall on the party's journey northward, when he dove into the strong current of the Snake River to keep one of the supply wagons afloat after the mules had lost their footing.[3]

As it eagerly made its way toward the hunting camp of the main Salish village, the missionary party heard the sound of hoof beats just before hearing the exuberant greeting of Salish riders led by Titiche Loutso, "Crawling Mountain," a powerful war chief, draped in a scarlet sash. It was Crawling Mountain who had gifted De Smet with the magnificent white horse he was riding. The welcoming party had come to escort

FIG. 6. "Le petit Ignace. Iroquois, allié des Tetes plates." Nicolas Point, S.J., Fonds, Q-1.1602.909, Archive of the Jesuits in Canada/Archives des jésuites au Canada.

FIG. 7. "François Oulstilpo Chef T.[êtes] P.[lates]." Nicolas Point, S.J., Fonds, Q-1.1602.910, Archive of the Jesuits in Canada/Archives des jésuites au Canada.

FIG. 8. "Moise Titicheloutso, reputé le plus brave des Montagnes rocheuses." Nicolas Point, S.J., Fonds, Q-1.1602.359, Archive of the Jesuits in Canada/ Archives des jésuites au Canada.

FIG. 9. Pierre Jean (Little Faro) became a Flathead chief though very young. Nicolas Point, S.J., Fonds, Q-1.1601.931, Archive of the Jesuits in Canada/ Archives des jésuites au Canada.

FIG. 10. "Joseph Pepelchimo. Jeune encore, mais déjà reputé brave parmi les braves." Nicolas Point, S.J., Fonds, Q-1.1602.360, Archive of the Jesuits in Canada/Archives des jésuites au Canada.

FIG. 11. "Adolphe La plume rouge. Jeune chef Tête-plate," 184–[?]. Nicolas Point, S.J., Fonds, Q-1.1602.358, Archive of the Jesuits in Canada/Archives des jésuites au Canada.

FIG. 12. Michel Insila, called "Little Chief" (Insula). Nicolas Point, S.J., Fonds, Q-1.1602.911, Archive of the Jesuits in Canada/Archives des jésuites au Canada.

the priests the few miles remaining to the Salish hunting camp where everyone was eagerly waiting.

For a moment there might have been a hush. Perhaps even the trees held their branches perfectly still and the birds remained quiet as all beings acknowledged the significance of what was about to happen. People of a different belief system and a different way of life were coming among the Salish. Every being would feel the changes that would accompany these European men and others who would follow.

When De Smet first caught sight of Crawling Mountain, he couldn't help but be impressed. Still in his prime in his late fifties, this exceptionally skilled horseman was "the handsomest Indian warrior" De Smet had ever met.[4] The Jesuits would come to call him the "Bravest of the Brave." Others in camp who caught the eye of the head Black Robe were Five Ravens and "Little Chief" Insula. No mention is made of Lodge Pole, the father of Charlo, nor of Little Faro, a man who would befriend and later betray Father De Smet. Two of the most eager to greet the priests that day, especially De Smet, were the two old chiefs, Big Face and Face-Raised-Up Grizzly.

The exceptional and hopeful day was made more wondrous by the slanting golden light of late summer illuminating the late season grasses through which the riders passed as the sun approached the end of its daily descent. Beautifully dressed men and women surrounded the pale-skinned, black-robed men, eager to greet them as soon as they dismounted. They took their turns shaking hands, noticing how the firm hands of the priests, like other light-skinned people, made it difficult to get a feel for them. The usual giving and receiving that occurs among Native people through the gentle exchange of a hand clasp seemed blocked. But this did not dampen their enthusiasm. The priests had come to help them.

Ever since Grand Ignace had arrived among them and taught them about the white god, they had hoped to be strengthened by those who wore the black robes and carried crossed sticks. Now here they were, these men of high medicine, *skylax*, who had come to infuse the people with extra power against their enemies.[5] Without this extra help, the Salish people would surely disappear.

FIG. 13. Victor, the great chief of the Flatheads. Nicolas Point, S.J., Fonds, Q-1.1602.912, Archive of the Jesuits in Canada/Archives des jésuites au Canada.

Full of hope, the community welcomed these foreigners into their midst. The pipe was passed around the fire that evening while the greenhorn newcomers shared stories of their travels. Before the moon reached mid-sky, the tired priests and brothers made their way to the lodges. Father De Smet was pleased to find a fine buffalo robe upon his bed and gratefully snuggled in. Tired as he was, he might have found it difficult to calm his mind from all the excitement of this long-awaited meeting. Two years after Ignace and Pierre had landed their canoe at Council Bluffs, his dream was coming true. In the morning he would share his plan with the village.

When the ringing of a bell sounded through the circle of lodges, calling the camp to morning prayer, the people would have already greeted the sun's rise and bathed in the river. They were ready when the priests donned their robes and peaked caps and proceeded to the place of gathering at the edge of this magnificent valley at the very headwaters of the Missouri River, some 1,600 miles from St. Louis. Wafting incense and singing the entrance chant, they approached the large rock that would serve as an altar. Father De Smet stepped forward and looked around at the assembled crowd of nearly two hundred receptive people.

After a deep, grateful breath, he began to recite the first words of the traditional Mass in Latin.

> I will go in to the altar of God.
> To God, the joy of my youth.
> Give judgment for me, O God, and decide my cause against an unholy people: from unjust and deceitful men deliver me.
> For Thou, O God, art my strength; why hast Thou forsaken me? And why do I go about in sadness, while the enemy afflicts me?
> Send forth Thy light and Thy truth; for they have led me and brought me to Thy holy hill and Thy dwelling place.
> And I will go in unto the altar of God, to God, the joy of my youth.

The sentiment of this psalm would have instilled hope for those assembled on that day if the words had been translated for them. The people were already receptive. They believed in the holy water placed on their heads and wanted their children protected by its power. Mothers came forward to offer their little children for baptism, many of them probably for the second time. So delighted, the priests were able to overlook the nakedness of these wide-eyed innocents, at least for the time being. Lessons in modesty would come later.

Each person gathered there on that late summer day experienced the solemn yet joyous time with a sense of anticipation and expectation. The moment was ripe with potential and—as is so often the case—eventual disappointment, as each one believed the other understood his or her hopes and dreams.

Last Leg

With so much to accomplish before winter set in, the travelers began their journey to the place where the priests would settle among them, flanked in front and rear by guards. They made their way over a gentle pass back onto the Pacific Ocean side of the Continental Divide and into the massive basin of the Deer's Lodge, following the Great Salish River trail that had carried people to and from buffalo since before the days of the horse. With mules pulling two-wheeled carts loaded with their belongings and provisions—including an organ—the Jesuits traveled through a storied landscape. De Smet questioned his guides about sights along the way and waited for the interpreters to give him the answers. He had yet to learn that asking certain types of direct questions was not the way among these people. Stories were gifts to be received at the right time and place and from the right people. The chiefs were forgiving, though. The Black Robe did not know their ways. He would learn.

The entire journey was punctuated by place names that reflected the Salish world. Place names among Indigenous people characteristically tell of the plants and animals found there or of some rare sighting of some unexpected being. Or, like "Beavertail Hill" and "the Eyebrow," the land form might look like some animal part. Some places carried names that conveyed important materials or foods, like Silverbow Creek, where the reflection of spear-fishing bows shown as silver arcs on the water. (That stream was a good place to shoot huge bull trout during the fall spawning season.) Some names referred to orienting features on the landscape, like the tall mound that spewed steam from the ground in the big valley near the Divide. The Salish called it Momo, "Place Where the Smoke Comes Out." Their allies, a band of Shoshones from the upper Salmon River country, called it the Deer's Lodge because deer were often seen licking minerals around the cooled-down edges. De Smet may have been surprised to learn that none of the places were named after people, except maybe some mythological person. The European custom of honoring people in that way, like "Virginia" and "Maryland" for queens, was not the way among the people of these lands.

The people known as Flatheads called themselves Sqelio, a word spoken like a whispered wind, meaning "the People." The misnomer of "Flathead" may have been due to a misinterpretation of the sign commonly used for them, indicated by tapping the side of the head. Another possible explanation comes from an old story about strange people in strong canoes who came long ago "up the rivers from the great river which flows into the Great Salt Mystery."[6] The women were Coast Indians with flattened heads. Their children's heads were flattened too, pressed by boards when they were babies. The origin of the men was unknown; they were not *suyapi* (white people), nor were they Indians. They were smaller than the Indians of the mountains and the coast. "Their features were finer, but the color was the color of Indians."[7]

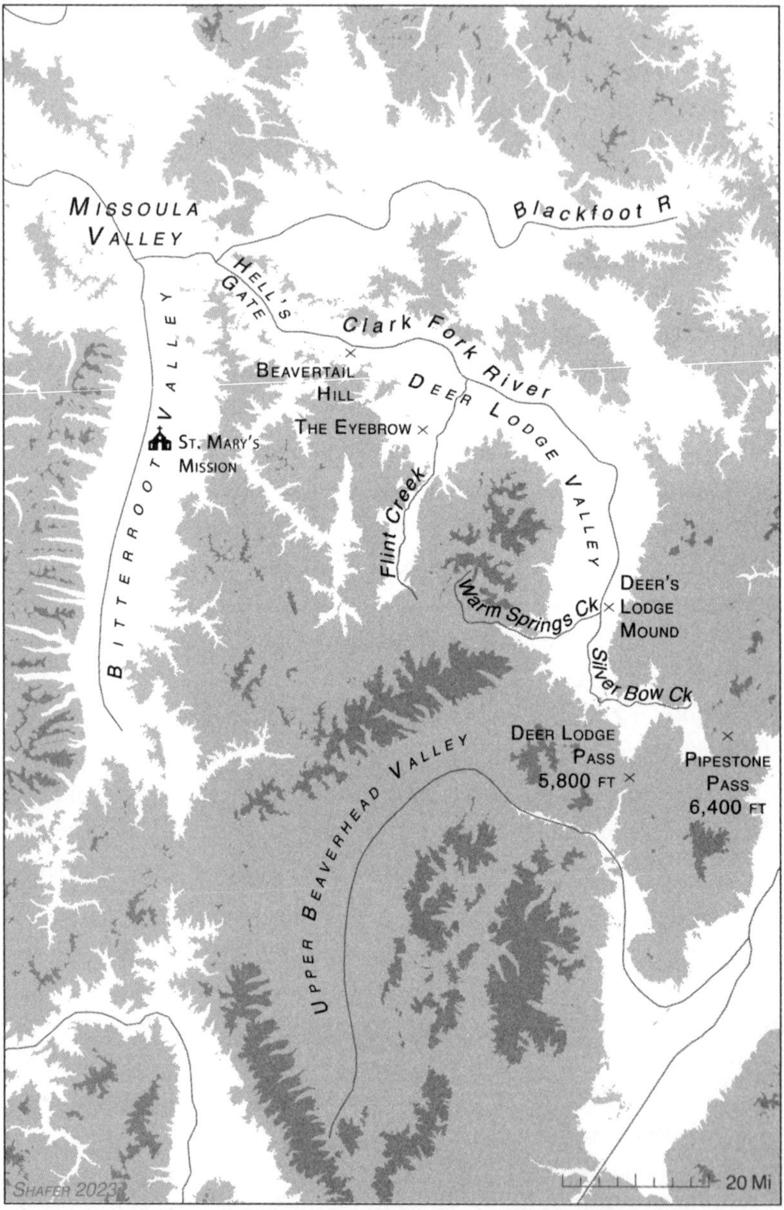

MAP 4. Between Beaverhead area and the Bitterroot Valley. Hannah Shafer, cartographer.

These people settled on the islands of Flathead Lake, where they lived on fish, small game, roots, and berries. They got along well with the locals. Sometimes they traveled to the west and would be gone all summer. They would return with dried red salmon, which they traded for buffalo pemmican, bitterroot, carrots, and camas. They were skilled healers and made good medicines. They taught the locals how to make a powerful salve of deer tallow and balsam pitch to be used on deep wounds. To treat eye ailments, which were common among river people, they applied clean bear oil. One of the most important skills they shared was how to strike two particular types of stone together over dry leaves, pitch wood, and moss to start fires. Before that the local people had rubbed sticks together to cause enough friction to make sparks, a very slow process. Sometimes they had the opportunity to collect embers from lightning trees. The strangers told the people that their fathers had come from a land beyond the sea. Winds had blown them off course and carried them to the mouth of the great river, where a storm broke apart their big canoe. Thinking they might find others of their kind to the east, they traveled up the river that led them to the big lake. When the first *suyapis* came, according to the story, before the time of Lewis and Clark, they saw the last of the old ones with flattened heads, and that is why they named the lake and the people "Flatheads."[8] Whatever the explanation, the Salish say that they never flattened their heads.[9]

The ancestors of the Bitterroot Salish once occupied a much larger homeland but had been forced to retreat to the Bitterroot Valley when their numbers had been diminished through disease and warfare and others had gained the upper hand.[10] The Blackfeet had gained access to European weapons long before the west-side tribes, who were left at a significant disadvantage. Because the confederacy of Blackfoot speakers had come to dominate the buffalo plains from the Yellowstone to the Saskatchewan, safety issues were critical. The Salish often traveled to the buffalo plains with Pend d'Oreille and Nez Perce allies.

Along the trail De Smet's traveling companions told him that distances were measured by a day's journey. A solitary traveler, or small group of men on horseback, could cover some fifty or sixty miles in a day, depending on conditions of the road. When a whole camp was changing location, as it was on this journey, the group made only a third that distance. Frequent river crossings slowed the progress. Arrowstone Creek (now known as Flint Creek) was the toughest crossing. A little way up that valley, De Smet was told, was a hill capped with a curve of trees, like an eyebrow, where the Salish used to get the stone to make their arrow tips. Since metal for arrowheads and knife blades had become accessible, they no longer needed to gather the stone for the hard work of flintknapping.

Past Flint Creek they traveled through rounded red-clay hills, skirting a canyon where red ocher deposits stained the steep walls. De Smet gave thanks for the clear skies and dry trail. The red clay would have made for a slick road. The last leg of the journey, the long valley of Hell Gate, on this September day was full of berries ripe for the picking. They were, after all, traveling during the Moon of Ripe Chokecherries. All the travelers felt grateful for their safe passage as they neared home.

Valley of the Red Willow

The Salish leaders had selected two of their winter village locations for the Black Robes to consider for their center, one in the Missoula Valley and the other in the Valley of the Red Willow or, more literally, Valley of the Red Osier Dogwood, after the River Nstetčcxʷétk, where now stands the town of Stevensville, Montana. Winter camps required a number of particular assets. They needed good water that would not freeze up; abundant wood for fuel; protection from cold winds; and resident food, preferably of the four-legged variety like deer, in addition to fish. These camps were located close to where the first roots would appear in the spring. Most of these same attributes were essential for the year-round residences envisioned by the priests, although they would have added good soil to the list.

Both sites held promise, but the priests preferred the latter—the Place of Wide Cottonwoods in the Valley of the Red Willow—because it was more protected.[11] This awesomely beautiful location was fed by two curving tributary streams, crossing a wide prairie, with gentle hills leading to spectacular mountains. The valley's rich grasses would provide feed for stock, and the ground should be good for growing grains. The creeks, gentle and clear, could be adapted for irrigation and a mill. The site was away from the main Blackfeet raiding trail, and the high

FIG. 14. Passing by the mouth of Lolo Fork, Bitterroot Valley. Gustav Sohon. Archives and Special Collections, Mansfield Library, University of Montana.

mountains on each side might serve as barriers from the influences of Europeans as well as marauding Indians. The priests looked at this pristine valley with great appreciation while imagining the European-style enclave they would build.

The eager priests soon began to realize the extent of the many and varied challenges to converting these people to Christianity and civilization. They were the same as those with which De Smet had struggled among the Potawatomi (with the blessed exception of alcohol), only more so, because the Salish were in their homeland, not in a refugee camp. De Smet's plan to replace the "varied life of a hunter" with "the innocent pleasures of the fireside" was going to be much more difficult than he had originally imagined.[12] Where the Potawatomi had been confined to several small villages within a relatively limited area, the missionaries were beginning to understand that the Salish were away from the village, often far away, as often as not. They crossed the mountains for buffalo twice a year and followed plant foods as they ripened in a perfect progression across the landscape of their vast homeland. Their travels weren't quick trips to a destination but rather a cyclical, rhythmic way of life from one camp to another, then back again, as earth completed each cycle around the sun. Home was wherever they were.

One of the most serious challenges for the Jesuits would be to replace the nature-dependent mobile life of the Salish with one where they would grow and raise their own foods in enough quantity to support a settled way of life. If this new self-sufficient settlement was to succeed, it would need barnyard animals and supplies right away. Father De Smet would go to the HBC trading fort of Colvile. Along the way he would have opportunities to visit with Pend d'Oreille and other tribes potentially interested in welcoming Jesuit fathers among them.

6. Reshaping Coyote's World

Place of Wide Cottonwoods

The Jesuit party and their Salish hosts arrived at the Place of Wide Cottonwoods on September 24, 1841, full of hope for what they would create together. Father De Smet put Nicholas Point in charge of planning the physical design of the first mission. The Frenchman had designed a college in Louisiana before heading west. They would build a great church, homes and fences, farms, storehouses, mills, schools, and an infirmary, and they would call it St. Mary's, based on a vision that had come to a little orphan boy. This child, christened Paul, had gone to the lodge of an old woman to learn the Catholic prayers. As soon as he had entered, according to what the boy told De Smet, he saw "some one who was very beautiful—her feet did not touch the earth, her garments were as white as snow; she had a star over her head; a serpent under her feet; and near the serpent was a fruit which I did not recognize." He could "see her heart, from which rays of light burst forth."[1] The Jesuits took it as a sign.

Fathers Point and Mengarini spent the first days considering the lay of the land and where best to erect residences, corrals, storage facilities, and, especially, the chapel and graveyard. In a world where even horses had never been fenced in, this new mission center would all be surrounded by what Father Mengarini called a palisade of three thousand "stout stakes." While the priests conducted their assessment of the location, the three lay brothers—William Claussens, Joseph Specht, and Charles Huet, trained in carpentry, blacksmithing, and tinning—got started with preparations.

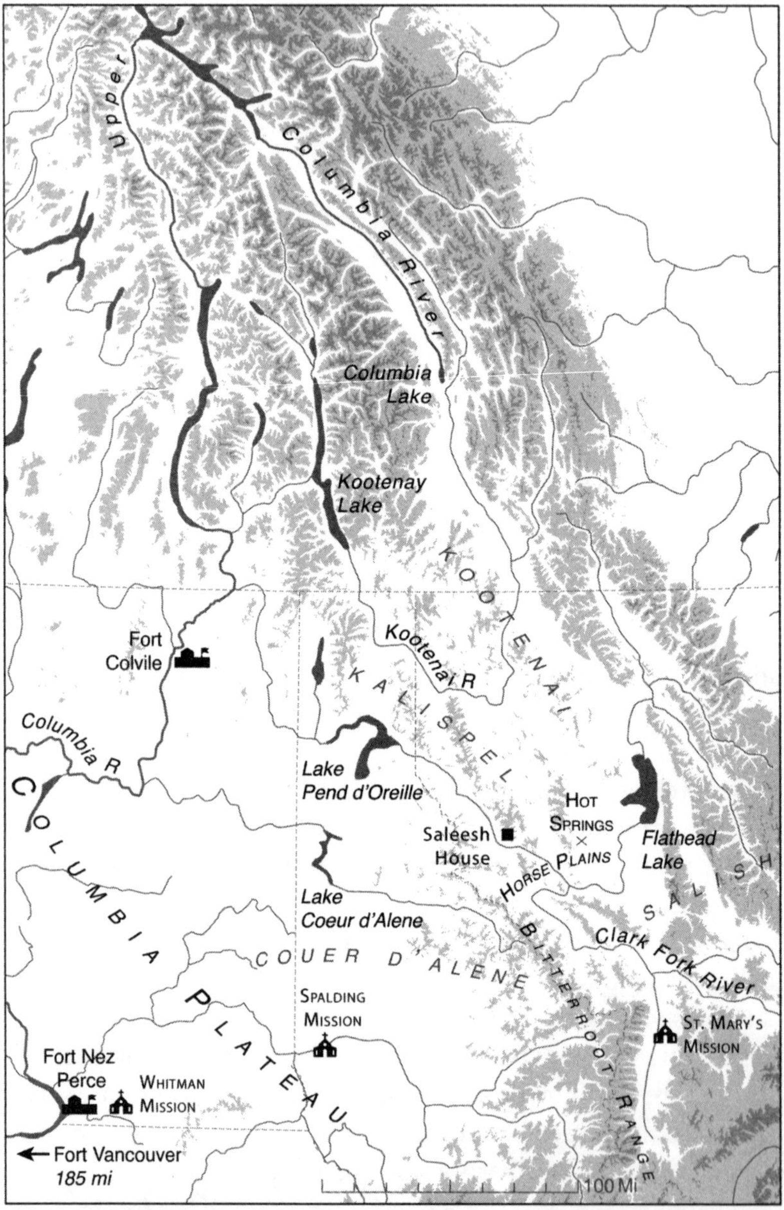

MAP 5. St. Mary's to Fort Colvile, 1841. Hannah Shafer, cartographer.

While the others constructed the physical center that would be their home base, Father De Smet went for supplies at Fort Colvile on the upper Columbia, the closest year-round European settlement, about three hundred miles to the west.[2] He set out with ten Flatheads, headed by Little Faro, known to be "imperturbable in the face of danger." Pierre Lefthand and Francis Lompry (Lumpré), a French trapper, served as interpreters.[3] The mission's meager funds restricted the quantities the missionary could purchase, but it would have to be enough to tide them over until crops were in ample supply and animals produced enough offspring to provide food for the community.

All these changes would take time. The people could not be swayed toward staying put until plentiful food was available at the mission. The Jesuits were so underfunded that they feared failure would come along before they filled their larder. In the meantime the Indians would need to go on their hunts in late spring and fall; fish and hunt in winter; dig roots, fish, and hunt in the spring; and follow the ripening berries and medicine plants into the mountains in summer and into the fall. Their lives would continue to flow with the seasons, defined by changing moons.

One of the missionaries' first tasks was to cut down a giant ponderosa pine from which to carve a cross. They would erect this focal point in the center of camp and thereby take possession of the land in the name of Ignatius Loyola. In this place where only tipis had stood, the workers hewed the cottonwood logs needed for the rectangular buildings under the direction of Claussen, the carpenter. Much of the labor for the log chapel came from the women and men of the community. It was the women who "hewed down the timber," with their husbands assisting.[4]

The Europeans thought what they built from logs was superior to the way the Natives lived, unaware of how their three poorly constructed cabins and chapel were not well suited to the environment. Heat would readily rise to the ceiling and escape through the thatching of the roof. The conical design of the Natives' lodges kept warmth closer to the space occupied, and the liner created a layer of insulation that wicked moisture away. Wind skirted the tipis while it pummeled and pierced the cabin walls.

To see the Jesuits cutting foundation trenches with axes from the already frozen ground shocked the Indians. The Salish men refused to participate. Among these mountain tribes men could not dig in the ground because they had spilled blood through hunting and warfare. To put their bloodied hands into Mother Earth was a desecration. Since women gave blood back to the earth with each monthly cycle, they had made their offering of reciprocity and had the right to dig roots.[5] The stalemate was broken by the influential Insula, who stepped forward, requested an axe, and joined Father Mengarini at the trench. He was choosing to override age-old traditions to support the priests. His lodge was the place they all gathered before the new chapel at St. Mary's was completed.

Father Mengarini, the well-educated newcomer from the Roman world of some two hundred thousand souls, had no frame of reference to understand the actions of the men who tried to stop them from cutting trees. The Salish found the slaughter of hundreds of trees difficult to witness. Father Point might have wondered if the Salish were like the Kickapoo in their attitude about nature. At Westport he had encountered a Kickapoo preacher named Kenekuk who stirred up his people against the whites. Kenekuk preached to large crowds, telling his people that ungrateful whites would not be saved because their actions made nature grieve. He waxed eloquent about how these interlopers injured the grass with their great scythes so that the grass wept; the trees wept too, from the injuries caused by axes; and the giant steamboats injured the rivers so that the rivers also wept. Father Point gave no credence to such a belief system about the feelings of nature and instead disparaged Kenekuk by noting that he practiced polygamy and worshipped an idol.[6] Maybe the Salish, like Kenekuk, believed that the trees and the ground felt pain.

The Jesuits misinterpreted the events of the day but learned from Paul, chief Big Face, and an aged Kalispel man who lived among the Salish that trees were a source of spiritual sustenance. When the Kalispel man was a child, he told the priests, he would go with his mother into the woods each morning where they would each find a tree "ravaged by time and nearly petrified," wrap their arms around it, and ask the tree for long life blessings.[7] This was their morning prayer. Paul told

Father Mengarini that as a poor orphan child, he had once sought the help of an old tree. Crying, with his arms encircling it, he asked the ancient being to take pity on him so that he might become a chief, have many horses and much tobacco. He could only conclude that the tree had come to his aid since he had become an important leader and had lived a good, long life.

The priests never came to fully understand cross-species spiritual assistance, which was core to the Salish worldview. Father Mengarini witnessed that the Salish prayed to "the first object appearing before him, even if it was a stone or a tree," for help with necessities or to ease their afflictions.[8] What he failed to grasp was that the rock or tree was not being prayed *to* but *through*, in the form of an intercessor.

The Jesuits had thought a great deal from their perspectives about what would be gained by the Salish through transforming their way of life from mobile to settled and by introducing the ingenious creations of civilized life, but they had given little or no thought to what might be lost to them through this conversion. Intimate knowledge had kept them alive in this homeland for thousands of years. They knew what the seasons would bring and what was needed to survive. They knew when and whence the food and medicines would come, and they trusted that in times of want, spirit helpers would intervene. The Jesuits' blindness would have consequences.

Becoming St. Mary's

By early December, Wide Cottonwoods had been transformed into St. Mary's. The chapel, twenty-five by thirty-three feet, could hold as many as four hundred to five hundred people, according to De Smet, and another priest explained such a large number was possible because "these people could be crowded into much less room than any other mortals."[9]

The Sabbath and the Gregorian calendar were shaping the rhythm of life in the village, taking attention away from the phases of the moon. The community spent hours each day learning the catechism. Father Point, a natural educator, spent his spare time creating visual teaching aids, and young Father Mengarini, the intellectual of the group, worked on learning the Salish language. They made good progress on all fronts.

FIG. 15. St. Mary's, Bitterroot Valley, ca. 1842. Nicolas Point Missionary Drawings Collection, JA-IX-C-9-033, Jesuit Archives and Research Center.

The missionaries kept the community on a regular schedule, initially working toward a goal to prepare people for baptism and, with further training, to prepare them for communion. To assist with the learning, the priests established two religious societies, one for men and one for women. The leaders of these societies were Lodge Pole and his wife, Slem-Hah-Kah, selected by their peers. Charlo and his siblings were active participants in the youth societies. The priests would come to depend on this family's influence to help transform the community.

The daily routine at St. Mary's began with the ringing of the Angelus, signaling time to rise for morning prayers and Mass. After breakfast men and women would separate into their instruction groups. Children would have their catechism lessons in the afternoon. Evening prayers followed at sunset, when the entire village gathered to kneel and recite the Angelical Salutation, the "Hail, Mary," the prayer recited with the rosary beads:

> Hail Mary, full of grace, The Lord is with thee.
> Blessed art thou among women, And blessed is the fruit of thy womb, Jesus.

Holy Mary, Mother of God, Pray for us sinners, now, And at the hour of our death.

Sundays and holy days had full schedules, with four sermons a day. The community learned about the acts of faith, hope, and charity and memorized the Lord's Prayer, Hail Mary, and Ten Commandments. All these were translated from French into the Salish language, and the teachings were put into practice.

The priests had hoped to have people prepared for baptism by the beginning of December but on December 2, the day before the sacrament was to be conducted, consummation of their plan appeared questionable. To start with, several key people were too ill to do the preparatory tasks assigned them. Included among them were the interpreter, Saxa; the prefect, Lodge Pole; and Father Mengarini. By evening, winds came up suddenly and hit the camp like a hurricane, tearing trees up by the roots and rendering each of the three cabins a "plaything of the winds."[10] The storm was so fierce that it blew out the scraped deer hide windows and disturbed the foundations of the church. On the same day some of the Indians accidentally broke the organ that had so carefully been transported from St. Louis. For people who look for signs from the natural world to guide their decisions, the litany of troubles of that day might have made them wonder about the power of the priests and the wisdom of moving ahead with baptism. Maybe some were afraid the storm had voiced the anger of Wind Maker, and they perhaps wished they hadn't burned their medicine pouches in preparation for baptism.

With the clear, calm dawn of December 3, the troubles of the preceding day were soon forgotten. Plans went forward, even though people had not recovered from their illnesses.[11] Father Point forged ahead and made final preparations for the big day. He wanted to inspire the community with great beauty to signify the importance of the occasion and to inspire devotion. In the literal calm after the storm, teams cleaned up the mess left by the wind. They hurriedly decorated the interior of the chapel with candles and framed pictures of the Stations of the Cross, transforming this house of worship from its humble appearance into a magical theater, ready for the rites to begin.

Twenty-four marriages were recorded that day. Some of the participants were already married in the Indian way, but the priests did not accept these unions as valid and enforced monogamy in the community. Many of the men had to choose which of their wives to marry and then to cast out the others. The priests gave no thought to why polygamy had recently become commonplace among the mountain tribes, nor to what might become of the discarded wives once the practice was eliminated. With so many men killed in battle, dozens of women had been left without a man to hunt for them. The solution was for married men to take on the responsibility of another woman, often a relative or the widow of the man's brother or cousin. Once they learned that the priests banned the practice, most of the men agreed to have only one wife, and polygamy became a practice of the past. Lodge Pole was one of these men. He chose Slem-Hah-Kah, the one who shared his strong faith and led the women's religious society. Her sister Kahkahpee, the mother of Charlo, would have to go.[12]

In planning for the baptisms, Father Point had paid attention to all the details. He knew how important ritual was to these people, just as it was to the Jesuits. As reported later by De Smet, who missed these important rites, Point had choreographed an impressive European-style procession with chiefs and married men first, followed by young men and boys, then married women, followed by widows and wives who had been cast off. Kahkahpee, baptized as Rosalie, would have been with the last group, no doubt struggling emotionally as they walked along. Young women and girls brought up the rear of the procession. On that day over two hundred Salish people were baptized into the Catholic Church in that simple, pew-less chapel.[13] Each participant was rewarded with a candle at the end of the ceremony, illuminating the chapel with the candles' combined light. Every single one of these baptisms, the priests believed, was the saving of a soul "who otherwise would perish unaided and forever."[14]

Delighted as the Jesuits felt about their success in conversion rates, the associated delays were keeping the Salish at the mission way past their usual time to leave for the fall buffalo hunt. They were feeling pressed to feed their bodies as well as their souls. The men needed to hunt, and the women needed to dry meat and gather and process late-season berries. Fall was the busiest time of year, when they traveled "camp to camp" as they stopped to gather the various foods and medicines and hides available for winter stores.[15] The intensive religious training was competing with other demands. Despite the conflicts, though, the people of the village embraced the Catholic teachings. They did so for various reasons, not the least of which was their hope to become invincible against the Blackfeet when they returned to the buffalo country. Until that time they would continue to practice their lessons, gather berries, hunt what they could find close by, and gather a winter's supply of firewood, all while completing their daily chores.

Messengers arrived in camp on December 8 to announce the return of Father De Smet and his escorts. Excitement flooded the camp, and people gathered near where the trail entered the village to welcome them back. Everyone tried to get close enough to see the farmyard animals the men had brought from Fort Colvile: cows, hogs, and chickens! What a challenge it had been to transport these creatures along wintry trails. That accomplished, the greater challenge would be to keep the animals alive until grass started growing again in the spring. An exhausted Father De Smet dismounted, and, after a rest, he related stories about his successful journey.

During his travels the peripatetic priest had met with people from the Pend d'Oreille, Kalispel, Kootenai, and Coeur d'Alene tribes, all of whom expressed interest in having Black Robes come among them. He was able to baptize hundreds of people over the course of his journey, mostly children but also ailing elders. Their eagerness gave him confidence that the Jesuits would be able to build the Rocky Mountain Mission beyond St. Mary's. He wrote to his superiors to encourage more investment in this monumental endeavor.

One reason for De Smet's eagerness to expand their operation was because there was a competition for souls with Protestants in the area. A Kalispel headman he met on the Colvile trip expressed his confusion about the two types of Christianity. The Kalispels knew about the Black Robes from the Iroquois and some of the traders, but they also had learned about those who didn't wear black robes and who were married and worked with their wives. What should the Kalispel headman believe, he wanted to know, and what should he encourage for his people? Europeans had been spilling each other's blood over this question for three centuries, since the time of John Calvin, and this war, now one of words, had persisted in the Oregon Country of North America. Father De Smet relished the opportunity to make clear that he represented "the only true church of Christ," and he advised the Kalispels to ignore the "calumnious attacks" the Protestants made against the Black Robes.[16] De Smet was a persuasive man, and in the morning the chief invited him to offer prayers and instruction to his people.

First Winter

In the winter world of the Bitterroot Valley, Father De Smet put his energy into instructing those who had yet to be baptized, while trying to ignore his growling belly. By Christmastime severe hunger affected everyone at Wide Cottonwoods. Not only did the Salish need to bring in meat and winter robes, but the priests too needed food. They could not eat the cows or hogs because they were needed as breeding stock, and their chickens were needed for eggs. The new seeds would not produce food until the next fall and then only if they were lucky.

On Christmas Day the Black Robes had the satisfaction of conducting marriages and baptizing more than one hundred Flatheads, with three chiefs at their head. The rites also included thirty Nez Perce, with their headman, and one man of the Small Robes band of Blackfeet, the Inuck'siks.[17] The easternmost Nez Perce band had suffered through two years of the small-hearted preaching of Presbyterian missionary Asa Smith and the disdain of his miserable wife Sarah.[18] Those Nez Perce who were baptized alongside their Salish allies on December 25 may have been seeking a more appealing way to encounter the power of the white man's sky god.

The chapel had been beautifully decorated by the women. They hung mats of woven grass on the roof and sides of the church and spread them over the floor and decorated the interior "with festoons formed of branches of cedar and pine."[19] That day the missionaries, assisted by those who had already accepted new Christian names, managed to baptize most of the Salish who had not participated in the early December rites. The Salish rejoiced as their important religious society leaders received this blessing. Lodge Pole became Victor—which the Salish pronounced as Mitt'to—and his wife, Slem-Hah-Kah, became Agnes.[20] Insula became Michael that day, after the archangel of war, for his brave and gentle spirit. Five Ravens became Ambrose. He was widely respected not only on account of his battlefield bravery but also for his integrity, unassuming generosity, and level-headed wisdom.[21] Pelchimo was baptized with the name Joseph, even though his mentor, Crawling Mountain, chose not to participate. Red Feather, known both for his courage and his harshness, became Adolph. Bear Tracks, the medicine man, became Alexander, although the baptismal name never seemed to stick.

De Smet took special pleasure in baptizing Little Faro. The Jesuit had been impressed by Faro since they had first met in 1840, and their relationship grew stronger on the Colvile journey. Faro had a remarkable mind and learned his catechism faster and more thoroughly than anyone else, and the missionary relied on him to help teach others. Father Point described him as having "an oval face, intellectual physiognomy, expression of kindness, smiling lips, thoughtful air, and easy manners."[22] Upon his baptism Faro was christened Pierre-Jean after De Smet.[23]

One great disappointment for these missionaries was Crawling Mountain's refusal to submit, although he had participated in the lessons throughout the fall. Perhaps his strong principles would not allow him to renounce his spirit helper.[24] Although his domineering personality stood in the way of his being well liked, his courage earned him great respect, and his opinions had influence. The priests did not want to alienate him.

The varied list of ethnic groups represented in the baptisms that day provides some sense of the complicated composition of the Bitterroot Salish people in that era. Nicholas, the father of a Small Robes family, was Blackfeet and married to a Salish woman. Big Face himself was Crow by birth, and Insula, the "Little Chief," was the son of a Salish father and Nez Perce mother. Crawling Mountain was also Nez Perce and Salish. Leaders were selected for their strengths more than their heritage. For the Salish, with their numbers so depleted, it made sense to welcome anyone of good heart with a commitment to join them and to help with providing food and defending their camp, as many Iroquois had done.

Once the ceremonies were completed, the missionaries could not stand in the way of the hunt, despite the fact that the mobile life was antithetical to the settlement they were attempting to create. Most of the able-bodied people in this village of forty lodges would be leaving soon for buffalo. They invited Father Point to join them, believing that a priest's presence would help them to be successful. Before Father Point had come America, the zoo in Paris was the closest he had come to wildness. With the invitation to the hunt, he had the opportunity to witness bison hunting and all that came along with it—even the Blackfeet. A challenge was something this Frenchman never avoided, and he carried a bit of the martyr in him. Let the excitement begin! Michael Insula was to be responsible for providing hospitality for the accompanying missionary. De Smet, Mengarini, and the lay brothers who supported them would stay behind. On December 29, as De Smet watched the women take down the lodges and load their horses for travel, he wondered if his team of missionaries would ever be able to convert these people to a settled lifeway, and he worried about his French companion as he ventured out on the adventure. Perhaps he felt a pang of jealousy.

A few hunters stayed back to assist the Black Robes and others who remained at the little outpost of St. Mary's. These were elders, some young children, and individuals too ill to travel, including the old chief Peter, Face-Raised-Up Grizzly, who sensed his end was near. Chief Big Face (Paul) also remained behind. Father De Smet faced his restricted winter reality with good humor. He and Father Mengarini instructed those who remained, and they took time to experiment with the best strategies for effective teaching. They drew on the wisdom of the old chief Peter to help them create this Christian refuge. Before they had time to establish a routine, though, he took ill and failed quickly. Peter was administered last rites, including the reception of his First Communion.[25] Mass was held following his death, and the priests led the procession to bury the mortal remains of this beloved leader at the foot of the cross in the consecrated ground near the chapel.

As he had requested, Peter was buried wrapped in the red flag that the missionaries raised on Sundays to mark the Sabbath. This burial marked a powerful transition from Salish tradition to the Catholic concept of consecrated ground. Among the people of these mountains, the tradition was to bury their dead near where they had died unless they needed to be removed from enemies' desecration. All these places were home; whether they were on the bison hunting grounds, in the high country, at fish camps, or in the root-digging basins, their relatives were laid to rest there. The landscape was made sacred with these burials, and they affirmed a sense of belonging for the Salish people. Now the priests wanted their remains to be gathered within the new graveyard, in ground made holy through a different sort of consecration, to ensure these people would rise again on judgment day. All these changes required some inner adjusting.

Winter in the Rockies can be fierce. The cold slows everything down, causing all living beings to draw into themselves. Anything moving is magnified by the white world of winter. Voices are quiet so as not to send the shock of sound through the crystalline air of a cold night. Even the sounds of flowing waters are turned to a gentle, high-tinkling song under the ice. Children too are quieter than usual, the growling of their hungry bellies sometimes the loudest noise in a lodge. When the air turns so cold it's hard to breathe, the quiet is pierced by the sharp cracking sounds that come when the sap freezes within the big trees.

Father De Smet was forced to move slowly in his own body and in implementing his designs for the planned community. The community could not plant the seeds from Fort Colvile until the ground thawed, and temperatures were too cold to continue with building projects. The priests and brothers suffered under the same conditions as everyone else and even more so because of the cabins' limitations. Extreme cold was beyond what the priests had previously known. Both Mengarini and De Smet grew up in wealthy families, where they were protected from weather in their well-constructed homes. The comforts of a nobleman's life in Rome might have filled Mengarini's thoughts each morning as he stuck his arms through the worn-out wool of his sleeves. His thin frame had become bony. De Smet's ample weight served him better through the lean times. Occasionally a hunter would bring in some meat, and fish were often available, but these gifts weren't enough to sustain them while their bodies fought the cold.

While the Belgian Black Robe focused his efforts on transforming this ancient tribal world, he must have thought about the creation story he had been told while traveling to Colvile. The Salish believed many stone features of this world had been created by Coyote, Sn̓k̓lip.

Sn̓k̓lip, "the little wolf," was the most powerful of the animal beings. At the beginning the world was not yet fit for humans because so many merciless beings called Natliskeliguten roamed the land. Creator, the Maker, sent Sn̓k̓lip and his brother Fox to make this great island habitable by ridding it of the evil beings.[26] The land finally became safe for Sqelio, the People, to arrive after all of the evil ones had been slain. Coyote stayed and taught the people skills and the knowledge needed to survive. Father De Smet had no intellectual framework or life experience to allow for him to fathom the deep history of the Salish with these places or the nature of their relationships with the world around them. They were living where they had been put at the beginning and where they intended to continue to live. They had been entrusted to care for this land and "to pass [it] on to succeeding generations."[27]

De Smet pondered the stories that taught the Salish everything they needed to know. Coyote stories taught them how to nourish their bodies, including "the traditional ways of hunting and fishing; the places used for gathering certain plants for foods and medicines." They also taught them how to take care of themselves and each other, including "the proper ways of child-raising, the relations between men and women, the relations between people of different tribes."[28] Other practical teachings included how to get and work the materials needed for clothing, tools, and weapons. Even "the spiritual dimensions of the world" were addressed with teachings about "human relations with animals; how things would be in the future"; music; and "even the sense of humor."[29] The Jesuit was a bit surprised to learn that Coyote was thought of almost like a god while, at the same time, he was guilty of all the worst of human nature. The people always laughed when they told Coyote stories, while the priest felt himself recoil. This belief system would have to be replaced by that of Christianity, believed the Jesuit, if these people were truly to be saved.

The quiet season gave De Smet an opportunity to work on the map he had begun during his Colvile journey. Always one to maximize opportunities, he used his new cartographic skills to create draft maps as he traveled along. His Salish companions told him about their methods of orienteering. If they needed to change their course to another destination, they composed a kind of map on bark or skin to clarify direction among themselves. De Smet found these maps to be astonishingly accurate, noting that "nothing but the degrees of longitude and latitude are wanting in some to make them exact." He marveled at this ability since, in his way of thinking, the people had "no knowledge of geography, nor of any science that relates to it."[30]

By early March 1842 the situation at St. Mary's was bleak. De Smet could wait no longer for the hunters to return and looked for the first opportunity to head west again for provisions and supplies. Spring travel required pre-planning, watching for the narrow window of time when snow conditions were such that horses could proceed over difficult trails but before the spring runoff, when river crossings became too dangerous. The restless priest left for Fort Vancouver in early April, accompanied by three Salish men and Charles La Moose, who would serve as interpreter. From that time forward Father De Smet would spend very little time at St. Mary's. Instead he would focus on expanding the Rocky Mountain Mission to other tribal nations.

De Smet was not, as many people believe, a resident missionary. Although he baptized hundreds, probably thousands, of Indians, he was not a pastor in the sense of tending a flock. Rather, he helped get the different missions started, traveling great distances in difficult circumstances, and he visited various tribes while exploring and mapping the region. In his administrative role for the mission, much of his time was spent out of the area, fundraising in the eastern United States and Europe. In fact, during his five-year tenure as superior of the ever-expanding Rocky Mountain Mission, he was resident at one center or another for a total time of only about twelve months.

The itinerant life suited him well, given his strong independent streak and driving desire to understand the world around him. He was an explorer by nature and a man of remarkable stamina. In a letter to a friend he described how on one of his ocean voyages he frequently played "shovel board," explaining that he "required motion to keep going."[31] While fundraising and recruiting in Europe in 1843, he edited his first manuscript, *Letters and Sketches*, 1841–42. Illustrated with sketches made by Nicholas Point and including De Smet's first Oregon Country map, the book would become a smashing success and the mechanism through which Peter-Jan became the famous Black Robe Pierre-Jean De Smet.

Surprises Await

Runners arrived in camp midway through the Moon of the Buttercup (April) to report the approach of the hunters and Father Point. What a great relief, after nearly four months, for those who had survived the long winter at St. Mary's to have their families return. Would they have meat? Each year it seemed to take longer to find bison, and some years the hunters returned home with nothing. As the bedraggled families straggled in on their pitifully thin and exhausted horses, they had smiles on their faces and parfleches packed with dry meat. The long famine was over for those in camp. Around the fires that night the hunters told their stories.

For over a month they had gone without. They had suffered greatly with extreme cold and destitute conditions on the buffalo plains. Desperate dogs chewed carelessly placed moccasins, horse gear, pant legs, and whatever else they could find, as Father Point learned the hard way.[32] Every day, though, despite all the challenges, the newly baptized Salish never failed to pray both at sunrise and sunset.

All winter the Blackfeet had threatened their camps, stealing horses and attacking when they dared. They had engaged in several small battles, including one where trapped Blackfeet were killed by the brave charge of Quilix (also Quilox or Quillox), "Red Dress" (also Red Robe or Red Gown), the famous woman warrior of the Pend d'Oreille. Then, during the second week of February, after many hungry weeks, they moved camp, desperate to find food. When hunger had grabbed so hard that they wondered if they would survive, the sun emerged, the wind dropped, and buffalo were found in abundance. Lacking any comparative frame for the basin where the Flatheads had successfully killed 153 buffalo, Father Point resorted to Parisian reference points. This basin he described as "an immense amphitheater of mountains, the least of which exceeds in height Montmartre, and in the midst of this majestic enclosure a plain more extensive than that of Paris, and on this magnificent plain a multitude of animals, the least of which surpasses in size the largest ox in Europe."[33]

Most of the Salish agreed that they had been saved from sure death by the Black Robes' medicine. Some Blackfeet were aware of the unusual luck of the Flatheads and sought for themselves the teachings of the white medicine men. Following proper protocols for visitors, especially those with a tenuous relationship to the Flatheads, they planted their pipe at the edge of the camp and sent a messenger to say that they wanted to learn from the Black Robe.[34] The camp leaders invited a small delegation to come, share the pipe, and speak of their intentions. The pipe ceremony established trust. Each person present drew on the sacred tobacco smoke and released its smoke to invoke the Great Spirit, the sun and moon, the earth, and the water as witnesses of their sincerity. Upon learning of their desire, Father Point shared with them the foundational prayers of the Black Robes.

The returning hunters learned that both of their old chiefs—Face-Raised-Up Grizzly and Big Face—had died right after they had left. A new head civil chief had to be appointed. The elders convened to begin deliberations. Various factors were considered in the selection process. The man needed to be wise, truthful, dignified, and brave and to have social influence, with the ability to command attention through oratory, according to Michel Revais, whose mother was Pend d'Oreille and whose father's mother was Salish. He also reported that a strong leader should be wealthy, be known for warlike exploits, and be of striking physical appearance. In contrast, he reported, "A loud talker, one boastful, or who could not control his temper, could not be chief. A chief should be considerate in dealings with others, modest in speech and behavior, quiet, cool, resourceful, and perfectly in control of himself. He should never talk in a loud voice, quarrel, show anger, fear, or jealousy."[35]

Three men, all in their fifties, would be considered for the position: Insula, Crawling Mountain, and Victor. These three had grown up together, and all of them, each in his own way, had shown strong leadership qualities since they were young. They were young adolescents when the first pale-faced strangers had arrived, when Victor's father, Three Eagles, had been chief. They all recalled that time before everything began to change, and they had their own particular memories of the occasion. Their age-mate Bear Tracks "recalled being mesmerized by the expedition's colorful flags snapping in the breeze, but his mother, wary of the strange supernatural power that lay behind the phenomenon, warned him not to let his eyes rest on the visitors' totems."[36] Since those first white men had arrived, the Salish had witnessed a significant shifting from one way of life to another, one where white men, weapons, and warfare had created a precarious future. Their fathers' generation had experienced lives changed by horses, smallpox, and the increased power of the Blackfeet, who came with rifles. The sons had grown to serve their downtrodden people as brave warriors and tribal leaders, while the white world encroached more and more.

Crawling Mountain was approached first, but he declined the offer; next approached was Michael Insula, who threw his support to Victor.[37] Victor accepted, as long as Insula would agree to serve as his second in command. These two very different men would be strong together for their people. Insula was small but mighty and full of vitality. Although the peak of his warrior days was behind him, he had other skills to offer. A natural leader and well liked, Insula had a gift for reconciliation. The priests were pleased because he too was a devout Christian. He agreed to Victor's proposal.

Chief Victor stepped naturally into his new position, his stovepipe hat with its two swaying feathers adding to his air of authority. A daring warrior, strong and agile, who had counted many coups, he was a solid choice: He had proven himself time and again in courage and kindness, two of the qualities most valued in leaders. His role as head of the Christian Men's Society was important, as the people were more and more depending on the Christian religion to secure a better future. The Jesuits were pleased. De Smet reported that Victor was appointed based on the same "noble qualities, both of heart and head" for which he had been elected prefect of the men's society.[38] The people trusted him.[39]

At the age of eleven, Charlo's future changed along with his father's. Not only the chiefs but also their wives and children were expected to have admirable qualities. Family members were to support the chief in his role.

Seed Planting

As soon as the ground thawed that spring, Father Mengarini organized workers to make the fields ready for planting. To find one hundred acres of tillable soil for the seeds Father De Smet had brought from

Fort Colvile required six different locations spread over a large area. Even then the rocky ground broke their plows. The Indians might have thought this damage was a warning from the spirit world to stop their activity. Watching the white men prepare the soil and plant the seeds made the Salish anxious. They could not understand why the priests tore up so much of the soil and grass that fed their ponies only to bury the little seeds in the ground. Having seen the chickens and hogs eat those seeds, they wondered, "Why bury something that can be eaten?"[40]

Caring for the life of this land had been their responsibility since the beginning of time, and disturbing the ground in this way was not included. Although the women dug for roots, they did so by creating the smallest opening possible, for the least impact, and they would leave an offering of thanks when they did so. Plowing up the ground was not just foolish but also disrespectful. Everything in nature—all elements and forces—has a spirit, and the Salish understood that other beings sacrificed themselves to keep the two-leggeds alive. The actions of the priests went against the traditional teachings of the Salish.

While the community focused on the beautiful time of year that came with the returning flocks, with longer days and warming temperatures, the priests tended their gardens and the morals of their charges. They banned gambling and so denied the Salish of their beloved stick game and horse racing. Individuals would bet almost anything on their team or favorite horse, with little concern for the risks of losing. Everything cycled around. A loser had family he could depend on and many chances to win back. Gambling carried none of the moral connotations it did for the Jesuits; the Salish felt no sense of sin, thus no guilt or shame over such practices—until the priests taught them otherwise. In fact, gambling was considered important practice in honing one's supernatural powers of intuition.

7. Covenant with Creation

Religion and the Source of Belief

In some ways the Catholic world, as it had been introduced to the Salish by the Iroquois a quarter of a century before, wasn't that far removed from their own. Like the Catholics, the Salish prayed to unseen forces for power and strength, chanted, burned incense, and shared a trust in visions from the mystical dimension of reality. They all gave thanks for their food. They carried amulets connected with spiritual experiences and valued the religious medals handed out by the priests. When needed, their healers drove out bad spirits. They did not have to abandon their beliefs to integrate those of Christianity.[1] They could claim a personal relationship with Jesus, much like the one they had with their guardian spirit. They weren't exclusive. Jesus Christ was a powerful spiritual force whom they gladly incorporated into their sphere of knowing. The spiritual lifeway of the Salish could continue alongside Catholicism.[2] These two roads to the Creator doubled their chances to live long lives with many horses and plenty of buffalo to eat. At least that's what they hoped.

The Jesuits, not accepting the limited space for their religion, struggled to replace the beliefs of the Salish with their own. But age-old teachings and experiences are not easily forgotten. Stories of Heaven and Hell did not fit with what they knew. In their beliefs this earth was like an island in the middle of a lake, only more enormous, and the sky was a hollow mountain that provided a lid over the land and water. Many other worlds existed beyond this one—located above, beneath, and around the one inhabited by people. When the people gathered around for winter storytelling season, they heard the stories of Coyote and all the gifts of Creation. Why would people deny their own origins and beliefs as told from the beginning of time? Father Mengarini was fascinated by their creation story and prepared a condensed version of the much longer, multilayered constellation of stories. He worked with a translator as he learned the language himself.[3] His documentation was limited by his biases and language limitations, but it stands as an important contrast to the belief system of the Catholics.

〉〉〉

According to Salish oral tradition, as told to others, Creation began when the Great Mother, Skomelten, "who had achieved existence independently, begot a son without the cooperation of man" (since none existed).[4] This son, Amotken, became the Creator of all there is. Like the Hebrew God in Genesis, Amotken eventually became disgusted by the behavior of his human creations and caused a great flood to remove them.

After the flood the next people to occupy the land were giants, but they were no better than their predecessors, so Amotken sent a "rain of fire" upon them. The third round of people was the worst yet, and they were destroyed by a series of plagues. The "fourth race of men" only managed to survive because Skomelten intervened on their behalf and gained Amotken's promise never again to destroy the human race.

This is where Coyote, Sn'k'lip, comes into the story, "when the Creator, the Maker, put the animal people on this earth." Back then, the animal people could reason and talk. At that time, according to tradition, "the world was in darkness, for there was no sun. Believing that the sole cause of their wickedness was the darkness, the people held a council [to find a volunteer to become the sun]." All of the animal people refused except Sn'k'lip, "the smartest and most powerful of the animal people." So Coyote became the sun. When he passed over the land and saw what everyone was doing, "he called out, so that all might hear, even the secret doings of people." Of course those who were behaving badly were very upset by having their deeds exposed, so they "angrily took Coyote by the tail, which at that time was very long, and brought him back to the ground," where he could be put to good use. Creator sent Coyote, along with his brother Fox, "to free this land of evils."[5]

When the land became safe for the Sqelio to come, Sn'k'lip stayed and taught them how to live in this world. He showed them to obtain food with tools of wood, sinew, and stone. He made them string for their bows, showed them which wood would make straight arrows, and showed them how to make arrow points from flint. It was Coyote who filled the streams with salmon and saved the land animals from the monsters so that the humans would have food. It was Coyote, at the behest of the Supreme Being Amotken, who brought buffalo to the land. Sn'k'lip taught the people how to use the meat and the tallow, the sinew and the bones, and how to make clothing, bedding, and tipi covers from the hides. He also brought healing herbs from the upper world and planted them for the benefit of the people. He taught the medicine people how to prepare their leaves, roots, and fruits for healing.[6]

Coyote also helped in times of trouble. When he heard that the salmon had been blocked from going up to the headwaters in the mountains by a landslide that had formed a great dam across the Columbia River, he went there and "struck it a mighty blow." The dam broke and freed the salmon, and this in turn relieved the mountain people of their hunger.[7] But Coyote could use his powers to take away food as well as to give it. He could keep salmon from certain streams if he felt the upriver people had done him wrong, like he did when he created the steep falls on the Spokane River. He could also fail at an important task, like the time he tried to put salmon in Lolo Creek, south of Missoula. To compensate the people for his botched job, he created a hot spring near the top of the Divide so they could refresh themselves on their journey across the mountain for salmon.[8] The people call Lolo Creek Tmsmłi, meaning "No Salmon."

⟩⟩⟩

From the stories about Sn'k'lip's travels, a road map of sorts was left for the people, showing them where to find roots, fruits, and places to hunt. Coyote stories are full of warnings about difficulties the people might encounter along the way, and they also teach the people about good qualities and bad so that they will know how to behave. With each telling, the

Salish people are reminded to honor the rules of reciprocity that keep the world intact and balanced. They are humbled by the gifts of food that keep them alive. Whenever they pass by the places where bitterroots grow, they are reminded of the tears shed by an old woman during a time of starvation and the gift of these roots that came with the spirit bird sent by Creator. They are surrounded by reminders of their dependence on other living beings. At the core of their culture is "a profound spiritual relationship with the land and the plants and animals, and a deeply engrained ethic against wasting any of this bounty."[9] The Jesuits at St. Mary's Mission knew that the traditional Salish belief system would have to be replaced with that of Christianity if they were to succeed in bringing salvation to these people. Jesus and God would have to replace Coyote and Amotken if they could figure a way around the wily trickster.

For the Salish, what they believed and how they lived were all intricately intertwined. The experience of hearing stories time and again in the place where the events had happened is vastly different from reading about a history that occurred someplace else. Salish history is embedded in a mythic reality, large enough to carry the story, with place names to serve as reminders—like Canaan must have been for Abraham's people. On their journeys the Salish see the places made safe for their first ancestors by Sn'k'lip. They are reminded, again and again, about their place in Creation, trusting in the wisdom held within the stories and believing that life will be good as long as they honor the covenant.

The deep roots of the people were invisible to Father De Smet—invisible because that's the nature of roots, to be buried, and because the eyes through which the missionary looked at the world had a pre-set cultural prescription shaped by another reality, a European worldview, from its roots to its full colonial expression. The head Black Robe, however, did come to understand how alive the stories were for the Salish people. His traveling companions would often point out to him some outcrop of standing columns of basalt, evidence of Coyote's efforts to make the land safe for the people, and say, "See there? That's a place where Sn'k'lip slayed Natliskeliguten."[10]

In recognizing their love of stories, De Smet set out to find a way to supplant Salish stories with those of the Bible. The Black Robe understood their appreciation for courage, so he picked tales of great valor to share. He started by telling of battles from the days of his youth in Belgium, during the days of Napoleon Bonaparte's wars. The Bible stories he chose also had a theme of courage and survival. He told them of Samson, of David and Goliath, and of Noah's ark and the flood.

As the people listened, they recognized similarities with their own stories, like the destructive flood, but they also saw the differences. Both belief systems had moral teachings. Moses was given the Ten Commandments—a list of things not to do—after being redirected by a burning bush. Coyote tales taught the people the same basic things, but the people liked them better because they were told as a narrative, animated with gestures by the light of the fire, not as a list, and they taught them how to behave in their own world, not a far-away land. Although they could imagine the parting of the Red Sea by picturing the waters of Flathead Lake, it wasn't their story, so it carried much less weight in the large scheme of things.

The people were especially interested in stories where dreams played a part because dreams were so important in their own lives. They wondered why the priests always spoke against dreams when they were so much a part of their own tradition. Why would De Smet judge the Indians' belief in dreams to be "remarkably superstitious"?[11] How were their dreams any less important than those in the Bible? What of Jacob's dream of the ladder connecting heaven and earth? And what of Joseph's dream of the angel's warning for the people to take Jesus away from Herod's wrath?

Before De Smet ever arrived in Salish Country, he had read in the journal of the seventeenth-century French Jesuit father Charlevoix about the power of superstition among the Indians with respect to dreams. De Smet found this strong connection to dreams to still be true, noting that different tribes interpret dreams in different ways. For some the rational part of the soul travels about during sleep. Others believe they receive important guidance for the future from their spirit helper or the Great Spirit. De Smet concluded that "all look upon dreams as sacred, and as the ordinary channels through which the Great Spirit and the Manitoos communicate their designs to man" and that "[the people] deem themselves bound to observe and obey them."[12]

The priests seemed more than willing to accept a vision if the apparition was of Mary, the mother of Jesus. De Smet loved to tell the story of young Paul, the orphan boy, who had a vision of the Blessed Virgin that led to the naming of St. Mary's.[13] Such visions were not unusual among the Salish and other Native Americans. Although the priests rejoiced at the appearance of this Christian saint, they attributed other types of visions to the dark realm. Perhaps the missionaries' inability to treat the dreams of the Indians with respect had to do with their preconceived ideas that would not allow them to accept the possibility that the dreams and visions of both traditions came from the same ultimate source.

The Salish showed interest in the Missionary Cross worn by the priests and the stories of the man who died for them. The Black Robes taught them of the miraculous birth and life of Jesus and of his mother Mary, Queen of Heaven. They told the Salish how Jesus taught forgiveness, even in his last acts on earth. (This teaching was difficult to accept, for the Salish would lose their honor if they did not take revenge on those who had harmed them or their families.) Of all the stories of Jesus, the people were particularly fascinated by the story of how he was put to death on a cross and how he returned as the savior. Maybe he could save them too.

Medicine and the Practice of Religion

One lingering problem surrounding baptism was created by the priests' insistence that individuals renounce their spirit helpers. The priests saw no choice but to insist on this severance. The people trusted the guidance of their guardian spirits and struggled with this unequivocal insistence to sever the relationship. To be a true Catholic, one could not serve two masters. To make this break official, each convert had to destroy his or her medicine pouch as an outward sign of ending the relationship with the guardian spirit.

Rarely, though, was the split so final as the priests supposed. The very premise of exclusionary access to the spirit realm was antithetical to the Indians. They knew what they knew, and their stories were their own. It would never have occurred to a Salish person to try to convince a Nez Perce or Kootenai to adopt Salish beliefs regarding origins and sacred ceremonies. They had their own relationships with creation, established through covenant with their Maker. It would have been inconceivable to try to make another person or group accept their history and beliefs as the one and only truth. Only Christians did that. This might have made sense to the Salish if they understood that cultural history and religious beliefs were not intertwined for Europeans, who had adopted these beliefs from a place of creation far removed from their physical surroundings.

Another difficult change that came with baptism was the imposition of a new name. The Salish recognized the importance of a name, and they still do. "[Names] anchor people to their culture and continue the beliefs, and also, [they] keep in our minds the ideas or concepts that are precious to us," explains Mary Jane Charlo.[14] At the time of the Jesuits' arrival, it was not unusual for the Salish to take a new name. What was notable about these baptismal names was their foreignness and their disconnection to anything about the life that sustained them. In the days before the Black Robes, birth names were generally changed at some point in a person's life. Individuals might be gifted with a name by a relative or gain one by accomplishing some notable deed. Traditionally when individuals acquired a guardian spirit and became medicine people, they received names in recognition of their spirit animal. Some people retained these names for the rest of their lives. In other cases significant events later in life gave cause for a new name, such as the one given to Bear Tracks, whose previous name would have reflected his spirit medicine. He became Bear Tracks after he hid evidence of his presence in a Blackfeet camp by "crawling with the four paws of a bear attached to his hands and feet."[15]

Charlo's father might have been known as Rabbit Protector until he acquired the name Lodge Pole following a death-defying encounter that involved a lodge pole being used as a horse picket. The brave young man had stolen into a Blackfeet camp, alone, to capture a particularly magnificent horse from its picket. Not wanting to make this capture too easy by sneaking quietly away, he leaped on the horse's back and rattled the lodge pole before galloping away under the dark night sky. The racket woke those sleeping in the lodge, and this daring horse thief was soon pursued by a mob of Blackfeet warriors.[16]

The brave young man suddenly found himself on the ground when the horse stumbled. In no time he was surrounded by angry Blackfeet. He

FIG. 16. Bear Tracks. Thomas Adams. Special Collections, Princeton University Library.

had no choice but to retreat to cover after he had overzealously drawn his bow, only to have it snap in two. He escaped into a thicket where he soon found himself bombarded by a fusillade of Blackfeet arrows, shot at point-blank range. According to eyewitnesses, the bushes were shredded and "not one branch . . . remained whole."[17] The Blackfeet assumed him dead and would return in the morning for his scalp. But when they returned, the young man wasn't there. He had slipped away under the cover of darkness, protected by his rabbit medicine. It was this audacious escapade, which began with the theft from a picket post, that earned him the name Lodge Pole.[18]

In the conversion process baptism was just the first step. Preparing the people for the next steps was far more challenging. De Smet underestimated the difficulty because of his limited understanding of the Salish world. He knew some of what they believed, but he was unable to fathom the depth and breadth of connection they experienced in their daily lives, nor did he realize how much more there was in their world than what met the eye.

The Jesuits were confronted on more than one occasion with events that tested their view of how the world worked. One of these times was soon after their arrival when the chief, Big Face, "Old Paul," a strong believer in the Catholic teachings, arrived at the priests' quarters full of anxiety about a disturbing incident. Through an interpreter he relayed the particulars of a visitation from his guardian spirit that very morning. This helper had come when Paul had gone out to check on his horses. Someone had repeatedly called him by name, but he could not see anyone, so he continued his walk. Again he heard someone calling his name. When he looked up, a crow was flying very close to him and said to him, "You are going to visit your horses, for you do not realize that at this very moment the Blackfeet are stealing your people's horses at Squtpkein." This was a place at the east end of the Missoula Valley known as Hell Gate on the Clark Fork River, a frequent site of ambush. Old Paul took the warning seriously and hurried to tell the missionaries. These well-educated Europeans did not believe in talking birds, so they persuaded Old Paul "not to give credence to the crow's ominous message."[19] The next morning, however, the priests must have wondered when they received a report that, indeed, twenty-three Salish horses had been stolen in the Missoula Valley by Hell Gate. Although Paul had renounced his spirit helper, the crow, at the time of his baptism, the crow apparently had not accepted the rejection.

The old chief told Father Mengarini about all the healing herbs and medicinal roots taught to him by this winged guardian spirit. The Italian, a trained physician, had to admit that these medicines were "useful in curing a variety of ailments." He acknowledged that some of the Indians' medicines against sickness were "real natural remedies" of a kind that a wise physician, in the European sense, would have prescribed. But Mengarini could not allow himself to honor these practices. Instead he concluded that the "apparent good served only as an excuse for the superstitious use of it against the evils and dangers of life."[20]

To deny one's medicine helper was to turn away from a trusted companion and protector from the spirit realm. The Jesuits understood that such a loss must in some way be compensated, so they handed out medals and picture cards of saints to encourage a new direction of focus. In the priests' world people prayed to a particular saint in times of need. By building on the perceived similarities between the saints and the animal helpers, the priests hoped to lessen the loss of the spirit helpers. The distant saints, though, were pitiful substitutes

FIG. 17. Devil's Gate. Nicolas Point Missionary Drawings Collection, JA-IX-C-9-039, Jesuit Archives and Research Center.

for the living relationships the people experienced with their helpers, and the active connections continued.

The Indians' medicine practices continued to be one of the greatest encumbrances to the work of the priests. Practitioners, *tlekiulsch*, who drew on the power given them by their spirit guides, continued to do their work.[21] Certain afflictions required attention beyond practical medicine for the body, and for these specialists were needed who had strong medicine for curing illnesses of the spirit. Others were seers, like Bear Tracks, who forewarned of dangers, predicted the location of herds, and found lost objects. Before the time of the white man's diseases, a cure existed for every ailment, thanks to Coyote and the spirit helpers. It is surprising that the Jesuits failed to mention the sweathouses that were placed near the Indians' lodges. To sweat was one of their most common health regimens.[22]

The priests believed the medicine practices of the Indians to be of the devil and referred to the men and women who demonstrated unusual powers as jugglers, conjurers, or sorcerers to convey their disrespect. "Let no one suppose that medicine among the Indians was, as among ourselves, a lawful product of human skill and science," declared Mengarini; "it was a means by which the evil one held possession of their souls."[23] The Jesuits had no place within their worldview to condone these spiritual connections. If the Jesuits were to succeed over the long term among the Salish, they would have to replace the Natives' spiritual belief system with their own. The priests might manage to control what went on under their noses, but some of the strongest practitioners lived beyond their reach and would not turn from what they understood of the spiritual world. While practitioners continued to exasperate the missionaries, at least the priests could stem the future tide by banning young people from going in search of a guardian spirit.

Whether Charlo went on a quest for a spirit helper is not known. Essentially nothing is written about Charlo until he stepped into the chieftainship at the age of forty. Given the important roles of his father and Agnes in the Church, it would seem unlikely that they would risk their relationship with the priests by enabling Charlo to seek what had been forbidden. His name, Słmx̣e Q'ʷox̣qeys, Claw of the Small Grizzly, might have been given to him in a dream, or it might have been given by elders after some brave ancestor.

Three years after the establishment of the mission, when Charlo would have been thirteen or fourteen, the influence of the spirit helpers continued. At that time one of the Salish men came to tell the priests that his sleep had been disturbed during the last three nights. This man, according to Father Mengarini, "who had always behaved as well as a savage can be expected to," needed help. Whenever he lay down to go to sleep "he would hear singing from above similar to that of the animals who serve as guardian spirits to the medicine men." He had spent these nights reciting rosaries, trying to drive the singing away. If he heard a message from the source of the singing, he did not share that with the priests. Their advice was for him "to protect himself by holding a crucifix, turning it in the direction from which the song came." Although it helped a little, he told the Black Robes that the singing did not go away.[24] Some might conclude that putting faith in the power of crossed sticks was "simple superstition," as the priests dubbed the man's experience, but the Jesuits could not step outside of their own belief system to impose an unbiased measure of spiritual truth.

For the Salish people, like Indigenous people all over the planet, direct experience of and with the spirit world was and is normal. Medicines were gifts of creation provided at the beginning of time and revealed through intermediaries. Back then individuals had learned about the common cures through their families, and special medicine gifts had come through their own guardian spirits. Why would they sever these connections?

The Basis for Learning

One of the most significant changes the priests brought to their mission communities was the way in which children—boys only—were educated. For the first time in their lives boys were expected to acquire an education by sitting indoors and reciting back what they were learning. Each student would learn a line, then go around in a circle, listening to and building on the ones before him. The boys struggled with this technique, prompting the Black Robes to employ some chicanery. The boys needed motivation to become competitive, like children in Europe. To accomplish their goal the priests encouraged pride or vanity, one of the deadly sins, "which, if properly directed, will always stimulate competition."[25] The child to first learn his prayers by heart was rewarded with a medal. The priests also used medals, painted pictures, and other tokens "to inspire industry" since the priests believed the Salish to be inclined toward idleness.[26]

On Sunday afternoons Mengarini employed a competitive children's game from Rome to teach Catholic doctrine to the Salish children. They were to memorize a predetermined set of questions and answers. Their parents and relatives would gather to watch the competition, "waiting anxiously to see who the victor would be." So uncomfortable were the boys with this game that they turned pale while sweat streamed down their faces, "even in the depth of winter." Charlo must have been among these boys, pressured to do well as the son of the heads of the religious societies. The winner of the final competition was rewarded by a present of arrows and was "made a kind of little chief among his playmates."[27]

Either the priests failed to understand how culturally inappropriate this game was for the boys or they disregarded the cultural norms entirely. Even today Native children from many cultures are uncomfortable sitting in rows with their backs to others while being encouraged to raise their hand to be recognized above their peers. They are more comfortable in a circle, where everyone's position is equal. "Getting ahead" is not a traditional concept. Whom would they be getting ahead of, and how would this cost the community? Cooperation, more than competition, was fundamental in their world. They competed in hunting skills and other ways important for their livelihood but not to be made "king for a day." Humility was an important virtue, and skills were to be used for the benefit of all.

De Smet remarked on the astonishing rate at which these Indians learned and marveled at their capacity to remember. "The Indian is endowed with extraordinary sagacity," he observed, "and easily learns whatever demands attention."[28] Whether it was the stories of their ancestors, the record of a peace council, or the stories of the Bible told by the priests, they could remember and repeat what they had heard. They were accustomed to listening to the stories of their people and their complex relationships with the world around them. Traditional stories would be repeated year after year in the winter lodges. Listeners would key into the imbedded teachings at different levels, depending on their age and perceptiveness. Through time they absorbed the guidance of the stories about how to live. They learned values, morals, and cautions. After a story concluded, no one would dream of quizzing listeners on the content in such a way as to extract isolated information toward a particular answer that would be either right or wrong. Life is way too complex for that and learning too intimate.

The natural world itself was the primary teacher. When traveling challenging mountain trails, De Smet marveled at his guides' ability to know the position of the sun, even when it was hidden behind the clouds. They could follow the path of a person or animal even when clues would be imperceptible to white men. These skills and knowledge, De Smet believed, came not from instinct but from "a constant application of the intellectual faculties."[29] They could determine direction along a forest trail by observing the way moss grows in greatest abundance on the north side of a tree and foliage is more abundant on the south side. Some of the men, whose intelligence he most respected, told him that this knowledge came to them "by long and close attention to the growth of plants and trees, and to the sun and stars." De Smet came to understand that these Natives were "conversant with things that are unknown to the civilized man."[30]

The ways of the Jesuits had evolved from a world where nature had been tamed and books carried the truth. Their schools were indoors because what they had to teach had little to do with nature or the gifts of creation. The subject matter was abstract and lacked local reference points. For the Indians the unknown terrain of classrooms was the new world. In their traditional methods of learning, all their relations of the natural world, along with traditional stories and games, served to teach children the skills needed to survive in their world. They taught children how to live, what to eat, how to find water and food, how to find their way, how to get along with each other, and how to take care of each other.

Images provided a common language and helped the priests break through some of their educational challenges. Father Point, a self-taught artist himself, noticed that the Indian was a visual learner, with "the eye of a lynx [who] never forgets what he has once seen." The priest went on to say that when an Indian "attaches any idea to a sensible sign, he can always recall it as soon as he sees the sign under his eyes." The Frenchman believed this was the basis for their gift of communicating through Indian sign language, as well as their "great inclination to render their thoughts by images."[31] When he implemented his visual teaching materials, the students' rate of success soared.

Father Point wasn't the only European to gravitate toward images over the written word as the best way to teach the Bible to Indians. Francis Blanchet, a French Canadian missionary who had been in the Willamette Valley since 1837, had a particularly difficult classroom challenge due to the presence of so many different languages spoken by his students. A natural educator, he followed their lead. He recognized that "totem poles" were a system of carved designs to record tribal history symbolically. He could employ the same strategy to teach Biblical history.[32] Rather than totem animals, though, he simply notched a pole with lines to represent the forty centuries from the creation of the world to the birth of Christ and dots to represent the years in the life of Jesus. Crosses at the top represented the death and resurrection of Christ. Natives on the lower Columbia called this portable mnemonic device the "stick from heaven."

Blanchet designed a portable form of this curriculum on a long narrow paper scroll pasted onto white cloth, about the width of a book, which he called the "history ladder." The ladder was composed of a series of colorful images, with one story leading to another and one important biblical figure to another in a systematic chronological progression. To the scroll Blanchet added the image of a withered branch to represent the Protestant heresy. Eliza Spalding, a Presbyterian missionary among the Nez Perce, appalled by this sacrilege, created a Protestant version to use with her charges. Her version showed two optional roads from Eden—the Protestant Road to Heaven and the Catholic Road to Hell. The final image at the top of her scroll showed the Pope falling into the fires of hell.

Father De Smet acquired one of the "Catholic ladders" for use at St. Mary's. When Father Point saw this ingenious device, he recognized immediately how appropriate the symbolic approach was to the Indians' way of learning and how easy it would be to teach Bible stories through time, from creation to the present day. His students would have the visual image to remind them of the associated story. From Adam, Eve, and the snake, subsequent images would take them through key stories of the Old Testament to the birth of Jesus and to the crucifixion, the resurrection, and the establishment of the Church. Loving to sketch and paint himself, Point created his own version of the ladder, with symbolic representations for instructing his pupils to facilitate better understanding of the catechisms. He included an image for each thing he expected them to learn, such as the faults and vices to be avoided and the virtues they should embrace. Whenever they saw a particular image, they could recall the accompanying lesson. The device was so user-friendly that some of the more advanced students among the Salish, both children and adults, began to teach others. They could focus on an image and easily remember the associated story. Their training in listening to stories served them well in adopting this system of learning.

Many of the Salish men created their own sticks of heaven to carry with them. They used an old technique of whittling symbols into a long stick to replicate the information contained in the ladder. Beyond the marks made on Blanchet's version, they added twelve other notches to represent the apostles, and finally they added eighteen marks for the centuries since Jesus had walked the earth.

With so much emphasis on memorization, music lessons provided a welcome break in the learning routine. Father Mengarini organized a

FIG. 18. Ambrose instructs a Blackfeet chief from the ladder. Nicolas Point Missionary Drawings Collection, JA-IX-C-9-067, Jesuit Archives and Research Center.

marching band with instruments of Europe. The Salish boys learned to march to tunes inspired by Turkish military marching bands that were in vogue in Europe at the time. Beethoven wrote his Turkish March in 1809, and Mengarini had grown up with such music. For the Native people of the Rocky Mountains all songs were created at the beginning of the world, even before humans incarnated, and they came to a person through the gift of nature. This "intimate magical" revelation of a song connects Native people to Creation—to the spirit side of the world.[33] Where the flute and the drum of the Salish world had been inspired by bird calls and the heartbeat that connects all living beings, European compositions were the work of an individual's creative process.

True Conversion of Belief and Lifeway

The larger, longer-term challenge for the Jesuits was to make true believers of the Natives. For lasting conversion, the Salish would need to accept the truth of the Jesuits' teachings over their own beliefs about the nature of the spiritual world. Where the Indians saw evidence of the creative acts of their sacred beings throughout their homeland and lived with the active spirits who gifted them with all they needed to survive—sustenance, shelter, clothing, and medicine—the Jesuits spoke of a god who lived in the sky, one who knew everything that people did and could condemn them to a burning world underground. This all-seeing and all-knowing god was somewhat like Sn'k'lip in the long-ago time when he had agreed to be the sun. Back then the animal people would not tolerate an all-seeing sky god, so they grabbed Coyote by the tail and brought him back down to earth.

As much as the people loved to hear the stories of Jesus, Coyote was more of a model for self-reflection. Sn'k'lip had all the faults of people, like greed, jealousy, envy, and anger, and his stories helped people see how not to be. The stories were funny, and the people never tired of hearing them. Even the children understood. In the Christian world these human attributes were mortal sins, treated with severe judgment. The Indians loved to hear the stories where good triumphed over evil, whether the stories came from their own world or that of the Christians, but some of the other teachings went against their ways. For true conversion the Jesuits would have to convince the Indians that they were part of the fallen race so that they too would desire salvation.

The priests had to face an inherent conflict in their plan. They assumed that the Natives would choose a settled, agricultural way of life once they had the opportunity and that they would come to accept the teachings of Jesus over those of Coyote. They failed to consider the underlying reality of the age-old Salish way of life. The people did not want to stop traveling along their beautiful road through the seasons. Everywhere they traveled they saw evidence of their own mythic history and understood that the mystery continued to reveal itself throughout one's lifetime. The core teachings of the Salish were antithetical to what the Jesuits understood about spirit and matter. After hundreds of generations had cycled through this homeland, Salish trails were strewn not only with memories and bones but also with relationships. Home was an unfolding sequence of spiritual gifts to be anticipated, relished, and cared for. Ultimately for the Salish it was impossible to both live and study inside square rooms within a village surrounded by a fence and still fully participate in Creation. How, in those confined spaces, would they be able to learn what yet was to be revealed?

8. Straddling the Divide

In the Name of Ignatius Loyola

Father De Smet returned to the Oregon Country in August 1844, accompanied by five Jesuit recruits, including Father Antonio Ravalli, a wealthy Italian with training in medicine and architecture; six Catholic sisters; and supplies they had brought from Europe for the new centers. After his long absence, De Smet had his sights on St. Mary's, but first he would need to deliver his charges to their posts. His plans changed, though, when he became ill with an extreme flu—known as the "bloody flux"—that had killed many Native people that fall. This terrible sickness forced him to spend the second half of September resting in Oregon City. He sent Father Ravalli on to St. Mary's without him. The new arrival carried with him the icons for the church, a grinding stone for the mill, and other supplies. De Smet was fortunate to recover from the debilitating illness. He had hoped to reach his "dear Indians of the mountains" before winter set in, but snow blocked his pathway across the Bitterroots and caused him to pause at St. Ignatius, the new Kalispel mission on the Pend d'Oreille River.[1] In February, once the ice broke up on the river, Kalispel boatmen escorted him upstream and on his way to St. Mary's and the Salish community.

The converts at St. Mary's—now including the prophet Shining Shirt—had not seen Father De Smet for nearly three years.[2] Doubts that had seeped in during his long absence were not quelled by his arrival. They had been disappointed by Father Ravalli's delivery of religious icons. These objects were not going to help them become more self-sufficient and less hungry, and they certainly weren't going to protect them from the Blackfeet. Their doubts increased when the head Black

Robe told them he would be leaving again after only one month. If he noticed their stirrings of dissatisfaction, he didn't try to soothe their concerns. He would count on Fathers Mengarini and Ravalli to settle ruffled feathers.

In early April, as soon as the road west was open for travel, De Smet headed back to the Columbia River country to try to assess the changing state of affairs. James Polk had been elected president in November on a platform that included the gaining of permanent control of the Oregon Country for the United States. This American dream was given justification that very summer of 1845 with the freshly minted phrase "Manifest Destiny," along with an energetic boost from President Polk's "Fifty-Four Forty or Fight" campaign. Father De Smet would have been eager to understand how this impetus was going to play out on the ground.

The geographically curious missionary visited fledgling and potential mission centers in and around the upper Columbia during that spring of 1845. Then, in a move reminiscent of the letter he had sent to St. Louis in February 1839, before his daring overland escapade from Council Bluffs, De Smet announced his decision to visit the Blackfeet, across the Continental Divide.[3] He would leave from Lake Pend d'Oreille and head north into and across the Canadian Rockies.[4]

This plan was nonsensical if his intentions were straightforward. He was choosing to follow the Kootenai River to its headwaters and then across the Rockies over a steep pass now in Banff National Park (at an elevation of roughly 7,200 feet), where snow comes early, when the much easier route to Blackfeet Country was directly up the Clark Fork and over the gradual trail over the much lower Lewis and Clark Pass (at an elevation of about 6,400 feet). His goal was not as outlandish as looking for a needle in a haystack, but it came close. Perhaps other factors drew him toward this convoluted and dangerous northerly route through Kootenai Country. He could use the opportunity to assess the possibility of drawing the Kootenais into the fold of the Rocky Mountain Mission. The potential border settlement no doubt had his interest as well. Given his strong desire to serve the goals of his adopted country, De Smet was likely to have been swept up in the energy of claiming the Oregon Country, especially when the role of

Catholic missionaries was so intimately intertwined. Despite having traveled non-stop, except for the bedridden weeks a year before, the forty-four-year-old De Smet embarked on what was probably the most challenging journey of his career.

After meeting with two bands of Kootenais along the way, De Smet got trapped by winter at Fort Edmonton on the east side of the Rockies, and the exhausted missionary had no choice but to accept the generosity of the chief factor, John Rowand, for his room and board until winter let go and conditions made travel possible. To give Rowand a break, he spent part of the long layover with a Catholic priest at St. Anne's Mission, to the northwest of the fort. Rowand was relieved by this respite because De Smet had such a hefty appetite. The Jesuit gained about twenty pounds that winter and worried about his ability to hike out by way of Athabasca Pass when spring came.

Although De Smet failed in his larger goal to meet with Blackfeet, except for a short visit with a small trading party, he used his time to prepare a record of his travels and to draft detailed maps of the Kootenai and Columbia headwaters and of the Canadian side of the western part of Blackfoot territory. Combining these new maps with ones he had already prepared on the U.S. side of the border allowed him to complete a map of tribal territories that would eventually be used by government negotiators at the 1851 Fort Laramie treaty council. He took great pride in this map. As he told Henry Warre, a British lieutenant he met as he had set out for this Canadian escapade, his map was more accurate than what was currently available, and with the new additions of the mountains and adjacent plains in the northern part of the Oregon Country, it was more complete than other maps as well.[5]

The utterly exhausted priest returned to his base of operations after his grueling winter up north, gradually finding his way back to St. Mary's. He stopped at Coeur d'Alene Mission on route, where he was joined in his travels by Nicholas Point. The two men were on their way to St. Louis, with a planned stop in Blackfeet Country.

De Smet Departs St. Mary's

While John C. Fremont and Kit Carson, two heroes of the day, were mapping a new route south of Mt. Hood, Fathers De Smet and Point arrived at St. Mary's Mission in August 1846, but most of the Salish were gone. Short on food, they had gone to buffalo. The Jesuits' efforts at agriculture still weren't enticing enough or productive enough to keep the hunters around the village. According to De Smet's spin on their efforts, the cattle herd had grown to forty head, the hog herd was "fast-increasing," and "a prolific progeny of domestic fowl" provided eggs and some meat.[6] However, the total sum available from stock and vegetables was far from adequate for the needs of the Salish and the resident Jesuits. No matter how hard the priests and brothers tried to create a self-contained community, the people continued their seasonal rounds. Not only did they require the food, but also the trade in bison hides (commonly called robes) had become ever more competitive. Forts on the Missouri and Yellowstone rivers served as collection points for the trade. Before 1830, when beaver skins were the primary trading commodity, the Salish traded an average of about two thousand robes per year. After 1845, by which time those numbers had quadrupled, the situation resulted in greater intertribal strife and an accelerated decline of the buffalo.[7]

The Jesuits' settlement at St. Mary's had grown to twelve cabins, and De Smet had not given up hope that the little log church they had built in 1842 would soon be replaced by one comparable to those found in what he termed civilized countries. He claimed that everything was ready for new construction except the stout rope needed to move the giant timbers onto the foundations, while the local missionaries, Mengarini and Ravalli, in contrast, complained to their superiors in St. Louis that they were challenged to function in an old and unimproved house and chapel.[8] The clay-chinked log house the disgruntled priests occupied had a roof made of saplings covered with straw and earth and small windows covered with scraped deerskin in place of glass. The log chapel still had no floor and no pews. Parish members sat on the ground, as they would in a tipi. The Indians felt at home there once they got used to the corners. An open fire provided warmth, and a hole in the roof allowed smoke to escape. The down side for the priests was that the opening also let rain and snow enter this sanctuary.

While De Smet dreamed of upcoming grandeur in an expanded Rocky Mountain Mission, he was unaware that seeds he was about to plant would lead to the demise of St. Mary's in just a few short years. He and Father Point were headed eastward across the Rockies to meet with the Pikunni—the Piegan Blackfeet—the southernmost tribe of the Blackfoot Confederacy. Father Point had long dreamed of working among the Blackfeet and hoped this outreach would open the door to his future. Both Black Robes hoped for better luck than De Smet had had in Canada.

Eager to catch up with the main Salish camp, the two priests headed east on August 16, escorted by hunters, scouts, and translators, who traveled with their Salish wives and children. Their French-speaking interpreters were Gabriel Prudhomme and a Pend d'Oreille man known to the priests as Charles (probably Charles Lamoose). Especially important on this particular journey was Nicholas of the Small Robes band of Blackfeet, whom the priests had baptized at Christmastime in 1841. He was accompanied by his grown son, Sata, and their families.[9]

This had been a very difficult year for the Blackfeet people. They had lost twenty-three warriors as the result of two clashes with the combined forces of Salish and Pend d'Oreille.[10] Nicholas was eager for his Blackfeet relations to benefit from the strong medicine of the Black Robes, as had the Salish, and hoped the tribes would come to more peaceful relations through shared beliefs under the banner of Christianity.[11] The priests recognized that these losses might make the Blackfeet more receptive to joining the Catholic flock.

Riding through Hell Gate Canyon, the Jesuits could not help but think of their first trip, when they had entered the country in 1841. Nothing significant had changed since then except that the white world had moved a bit closer. Fort Lewis had just been constructed near an important Missouri river crossing some thirty river-miles upstream from an earlier fort location.[12] The distance from St. Mary's Mission to Fort Lewis was two hundred and thirty miles, across the Continental Divide.

Father Point had already interacted with the Blackfeet—the "Arabs of this region"—during several hunts on the buffalo plains with the Salish.[13] He believed that if the Jesuits could awaken in them a desire for Christianity, they would be able to establish peaceful relations among the tribes. He and Father De Smet weren't concerned for their own safety, having learned that all would be well if they presented themselves as ministers of religion. Realistically, though, the Jesuits' intention to civilize and convert this tribe was premature.

Setting out, each of the two Jesuits held a dream that would never materialize. De Smet would not oversee the addition of more tribes to the Rocky Mountain Mission, and Point would never become missionary to the Blackfeet. Unbeknownst to De Smet, he had already been relieved of his responsibilities as superior of the mission. He had been fired for what some of his colleagues characterized as overzealous dreams of mission expansion. The mission centers were suffering from want, and their priests resented De Smet's overextending their resources and thereby depriving them of what they needed to function. The Indians, too, felt aggrieved that more was promised than had been delivered.

The superiors in St. Louis chose to shorten De Smet's leash. The letter with this news, sent from Rome on August 6, 1846, was waiting for him in St. Louis. He had already been replaced and was expected henceforth to serve in an administrative capacity at St. Louis University.[14] His vow of obedience must have been greatly challenged with this news. Point would later receive news of an assignment near Montreal. He had always been a bit unstable, easily agitated, and somewhat paranoid. As he aged, these qualities worsened, and his colleagues at Sacred Heart Mission complained about working with him. He was to be put out to pasture.

From Hell Gate Canyon the two Black Robes and their entourage traveled over a gentle pass across the Divide and headed toward the Three Forks.[15] While De Smet tended to focus on the geography, Father Point never seemed to know just where he was. His attention was drawn to plants and animals and interactions. In the general area of the Three Forks, he made note of the wide variety of flowers, large trees, and beaver activity since the decline of trapping. Areas of thick brush "offered ideal refuge for wolves, mountains lions and bears."[16]

With each passing day the priests grew more anxious that they had yet to locate the Salish village. Two days' journey past the Three Forks, they rejoiced when they came upon the remains of a camp and could identify who had been there. Along with the Salish, Nicholas and Sata "recognized the poles used as a means of transport by their tribe," the travois, and saw pickets such as only the Nez Perce employed.[17] The priests thanked God that they were finally on the trail of the Flatheads,

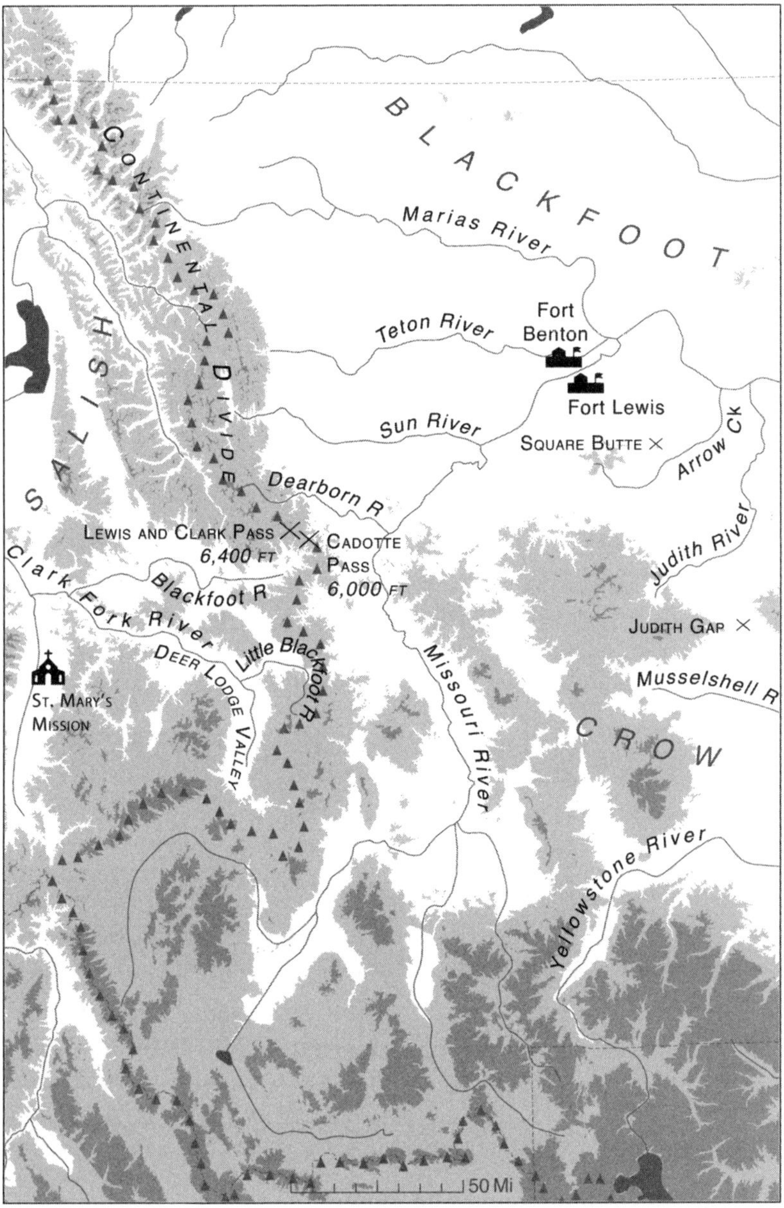

MAP 6. Route from St. Mary's to Fort Lewis. Hannah Shafer, cartographer.

FIG. 19. "Conjuncture critique et délivrance d'Adolphe par Abraham" (Critical circumstances when Adolphe was saved [from bears] by Abraham). Nicolas Point Missionary Drawings Collection, JA-IX-C-9-104, Jesuit Archives and Research Center.

and at the same time they felt concern about this particular alliance. Just a year before, the Crows had slaughtered a good portion of the men and boys of the Small Robes band of Blackfeet and captured scores of women and children. The united forces of Salish, Nez Perce, and Small Robes were likely moving toward trouble.

After several more days of stressful travel, having lost the track of the Salish camp, De Smet sent Gabriel and Charles ahead to determine the direction their people had gone and to learn what they could about "the dispositions of the Crows."[18] A few days later Gabriel returned with De Smet's Salish namesake, Peter John, "Little Faro," with news that the allied camp had repelled an attack by the Crows. The Salish expected retaliations, so the riders had hurried to tell the Black Robe of an impending battle one hard day's ride away.

Just about the time runners brought De Smet news of this conflict, Chief Victor was directing a successful counterattack, with the aid of Crawling Mountain and other renowned warriors, including Quilix.[19] Just the sight of this fierce woman scattered "a whole squadron of Crows" as she charged toward them with her hatchet raised in the air.[20] She

FIG. 20. "Quilox" at war. Adaptation by Thomas Adams of Nicolas Point sketch. Special Collections, Princeton University Library.

laughed and boasted, "I thought these great talkers were men, but I was wrong. They are not even worth pursuing."[21]

As De Smet and his escorts hurried toward the camp, still hoping to divert disaster, he must have wondered what had happened among these tribes since he had last seen them three years before when he was on route to St. Louis. He recalled their gathering at the mouth of Twenty-Five Mile Creek, near the big bend of the Yellowstone, when the Crows agreed to join them in a large camp of friendly nations—Salish, Pend d'Oreille, Nez Perce, Cayuse, and Shoshone. The Crows were eager to learn what the priest had to say, and they had many questions for him, including their wanting to know the number of white people. De Smet told them to count the blades of grass, and they would understand. They thought he was kidding until he described the eastern cities with their grand lodges of many stories, as high as mountains, and their roads full of travelers, as vast as herds of buffalo. Hearing his stories, they concluded the white race must be favored by the Master of Life. Some three thousand Crows participated in the teachings, aided by neophytes from the Bitterroot, including Eneas (Little Ignace) and Gabriel Prudhomme. De Smet taught them that only the Great Spirit could remove the sicknesses that plagued them. By fire God had destroyed the villages of sinners, he told them, and warned them to change their ways if they wanted to be freed of sickness, war, and famine. They had brought these woes upon themselves, he explained, adding that these were mild compared to what awaited them after death. Heaven would be the reward for those who repented of the evil ways and embraced the religion of the Great Spirit.[22]

They had seemed so convinced at the time. Now, roundly defeated in battle, they had fled south and into the mountains. De Smet would have no opportunity to further his work among them. Instead he and Father Point turned their attention northward, into the Blackfeet Country. The Salish and the Jesuits met with the largest band of Blackfeet somewhere in the Judith River country, between the Yellowstone and the Missouri. There the Black Robes introduced their intentions for the tribes to be at peace and for a mission to be established in Blackfeet territory. Victor led the discouraged Salish in search of buffalo before they returned to the Bitterroot, while the Black Robes and Blackfeet traveled to Fort Lewis, where the priests visited with various leaders, talking of peace with west-side tribes while planting seeds of conversion. While the Jesuits were patting each other on the back for their accomplishments in inter-tribal peace making, some Blackfeet stole over one hundred horses from the Salish camp on their return home, souring the Salish even more on what the Black Robes were doing.

Just a few days after a seemingly benign meeting with a fur trader named Charles Larpenteur, De Smet's opportunity to travel to St. Louis arose suddenly when the trader at Fort Lewis announced that he was heading downriver to Fort Union. Father Point would stay through the winter to visit the various camps and continue preaching the Gospel. On September 28, a day of torrential rain and thunder, the most famous Black Robe, Pierre-Jean De Smet, headed down the Missouri, armed with good news of the Black Robes' impressive success with the Blackfeet to share with his superiors in St. Louis. He had no idea that his meeting with Larpenteur would set into motion a series of interactions that would play into the demise of St. Mary's Mission.

As Father De Smet traveled down the river past the Mandan villages, he absorbed the dramatic changes that had occurred since his first trip in 1839, and he made a dire prediction. With buffalo numbers dwindling, competing bands of Indians would be forced into closer contact with each succeeding hunt. He forecast that the Blackfoot territory, from the Saskatchewan to the Yellowstone, would become "the last resort of the wild animals twelve years hence" and soon would be insufficient "to feed and clothe the hundred thousand inhabitants of these western wilds." His forecast was off by a decade but otherwise accurate. He further predicted that the tribes of the plains would continue "to fight their bloody battles" and would "become themselves extinct over the last buffalo-steak."[23] Chief Victor would live to see his people hungry for want of buffalo and the increasing competition for this most valued food, but Father De Smet underestimated the resilience of Native people. The outcome would not be as he predicted.

Indians in the New Territory of Oregon

The year Father De Smet left his position as superior of the Rocky Mountain Mission, 1846, was the beginning of the end of the ancient lifeways of the tribes of that region. With the Oregon Country boundary settled, nothing and no one was in the way of a legal U.S. takeover of lands within the new Oregon Territory except the Indians. They would need to be subdued and removed. The United States went to work on its new jurisdiction, preparing first for peace treaties and soon thereafter for land-cession treaties. U.S. Indian policy for the next century was in support of full assimilation; "the Indian needed to be killed" in order to save the man.[24] The priests, De Smet included, aided and abetted the process.

The hope that the Jesuits had brought to the tribes of the Rocky Mountains had all but disappeared by the time of De Smet's departure. It's not that he took it with him but rather that the people came to understand the inevitable: no matter what they believed, they weren't going to defeat their enemies, nor were they going to stop the onslaught of whites moving into their homelands. Nine years after the boundary settlement, tribes of the new Washington Territory would officially relinquish the vast majority of their lands and become dependent upon the government and its agents for assistance. At times the Indians found themselves engulfed in a living hell, and it mattered not if they believed Jesus rose from the dead to save them or whether or not they had confessed their sins.

The proximity of Salish territory to emerging routes of travel made these previously protected valleys vulnerable to white encroachment. Except for the Jesuits, no white settlers had yet claimed space in the interior mountains, but in the western part of the Oregon Country their numbers were growing exponentially. Propaganda of a promised land attracted many Euro-Americans. They were encouraged by former fur traders, government officials, and even missionaries to find a better life for themselves in the West.

One of these promoters was Presbyterian missionary Marcus Whitman, who, with his wife, Narcissa, had settled in the Cayuse homeland at Wailatpu, "Place of the Long Grass," near the trade center of Walla Walla, in 1837. Whitman traveled back east in the fall of 1842 to encourage people to join them in the rich Oregon Country. In the spring he returned with a wagon train of a thousand hopeful emigrants, many of whom settled around his mission. That same year, 1843, publication of De Smet's compilation of letters and sketches attracted attention to the area. Subsequent years saw significant increases in new settlers along with many thousands of cattle. The Indians started to feel the pressure of competition for their coveted grasslands. What had always seemed endless was now not enough. Anger accumulated in the lodges, while the *suyapis*, those bearded white people, invaded Indian lands.

White settlers spread eastward from the Willamette Valley, and from Fort Hall they took a branch trail northward, some right into the Bitterroot Valley. Some retired fur trappers and other multilingual men familiar with travel routes, like Gabriel Prudhomme, made their living guiding immigrants into the country.[25] Oregon Territory pioneers, or invaders, depending on one's point of view, were simply continuing the tradition of taking land from Native people, much as the pilgrims had done in New England. Even the label of "pioneers" imbeds the superior attitudes of discoverers, leaders, and innovators. These immigrants drew on the rationale articulated by John Winthrop two centuries before—that is, the civil right of those who could "improve" land over the natural right of those whose benefits came from land left in its natural state. It was Manifest Destiny for the superior race to claim and improve what was available. And claim they did, while the federal government focused on an expanded legal basis for land acquisition through treaties, reservations, and a military road designed with an eye to opening this previously remote region to Euro-American hordes. Like ants to a picnic, they swarmed.

Marcus Whitman's role in all this would lead to his murder in late November 1847. Whites were settling on Cayuse lands and grazing their cattle right along Walla Walla Creek. The Whitmans had taken more than two hundred acres themselves.[26] Even worse, measles was rampant in the Indian lodges, and the Indians did not understand why the white people did not die from it when they themselves did. They grew suspicious, and eventually violence erupted. A small group of Cayuse men set out to rid their community of an evil force. They took the lives of the Whitmans and other whites at the mission. The killings broke the trust that had long exemplified relations in the region. These Indians were by nature peaceful people.

St. Mary's Demise

Trouble was brewing at St. Mary's Mission in the Bitterroot Valley even before the Whitman killings. Grumblings began when De Smet returned to the Northwest virtually empty-handed after his long absence. The Salish had been expecting ample material goods to improve their diminishing quality of life, yet they received nothing they considered valuable. Father Ravalli identified this disappointment as the beginning of the troubles between the Salish and the missionaries.[27]

Gregory Mengarini, who had arrived with De Smet as an eager young man in 1841, had aged significantly under the duress of his assignment during the final few years. For his superiors in St. Louis he summarized his perceptions of the impediments and obstacles that blocked the mission's success and led to its closing in 1850. They included the character of the Indians, "lovers of freedom [who were] prone to the enticements of the flesh." From his point of view the chiefs were too "weak in spirit" to rule effectively, and parents were too lax in the religious education of their children. Furthermore, the priests believed that the Indians' continuing reliance on bison to provide the bulk of their food, keeping them away from the mission for long periods, impeded efforts at full conversion and success of the mission. Also the "infestation" of the Blackfeet was particularly destructive, especially in the final year, and the growing presence of whites and other Christians created many problems. In the eyes of this Italian Jesuit, how could the missionaries continue their work when many of the Indians backslid "into indolence?"[28]

The Jesuits were ridiculously underfunded, and their poverty influenced the attitudes of the Salish. Father Mengarini complained that twenty-two supports were needed to keep the chapel standing. Even the priests looked absurd. By 1847 their threadbare black robes had to be replaced, but they were unable to obtain their usual source of black wool from London. Instead, for the next two years, they dressed in the blue fabric sold to the Indians by HBC to make leggings.[29] The Salish understood that the priests were too poor to be relied upon for the help they truly needed.

Everywhere the Salish looked, their world was threatened. During the horrific winter of 1846–47, not only cattle, pigs, and horses died but also deer, antelope, elk, and bison. One report from the Columbia River country told of the death of five hundred horses, trapped in a little valley where they had sought shelter. So tightly huddled together, "a sheet of one mile square would have covered all of them, frozen fast where they tried to paw and stand, with little to be seen of them in the deep icy snow."[30] Closer to home, over a hundred bison died similarly when they were trapped by drifted snow just across the Sapphire Mountains from St. Mary's, between the hogbacks of upper Rock Creek.[31] The Salish had treated this small, west-side herd as their own larder for thousands of years.[32] Its loss was added to the litany of woes.

Many of those on the winter buffalo hunt that year took ill from tainted water, and measles descended upon the Bitterroot Valley.[33] The people survived all that only to face the worst smallpox epidemic in generations. Within the first few days of November, some forty people were infected, and a little girl died. The toll grew throughout the month. In total, eighty-seven people died from that sweep of smallpox.[34] No family was spared. Saxa, who as a young boy had lost his father, Grand Ignace, lost his young wife to the disease, and he himself suffered terribly for weeks, not knowing if he would live or die. He survived only to witness the death of his three little children. Then, on top of everything, he lost his entire horse herd, stolen by Blackfeet.

Tensions were rising. Many beleaguered Salish felt betrayed by the priests for teaching their medicine powers to the Blackfeet. For five years the Salish had allowed the priests into their lives and had done their best to strike a good balance between the two religions, their own and Christianity. Some recent defeats in battle convinced them that the special protection gained from the "white man's medicine" was no longer working.[35] Fur trader Thomas Fitzpatrick offered insight into why the tribes embraced the religion of the Black Robes and then often let it go. His understanding was that "the Indians would submit to the ceremonies of 'the medicine' with good grace until they found that those who had passed through all the ceremonies of religion had no better luck in hunting and war than they had had before. The only conclusion the Indian could accept was that the white man's 'medicine' is not so strong as his own."[36]

The Italian priests at St. Mary's were surprised by the cool reception they received from the returning hunters that fall of 1846, after De Smet's meeting with the Blackfeet. The situation worsened with the arrival of some Cayuse who had fled their country to avoid reprisals after the Whitman killings. They said the Salish should know that the whites had brought disease to kill the Indians and take their land. They should run the Black Robes out of the country. The Cayuse warned the Salish that the priests were not to be trusted, causing some to accuse Father Ravalli "of wanting to kill them in order to obtain their lands."[37] The Indians had cause to worry. Gustavus Hines, Methodist missionary in the Oregon Country, expressed his belief that "the hand of Providence is removing [the Indians] to give place to a people more worthy of this beautiful and fertile country."[38] Hines and others were continuing the attitudes brought by the Puritans to New England. His words echoed those of Puritan minister and president of Harvard College Increase Mather, who wrote that God had sent smallpox to the Massachusetts Nation as punishment for their lack of generosity toward the English regarding land ownership.[39] Just like the founding families of America, Oregon pioneers took no responsibility for the steady stream of Euro-American immigrants bringing new rounds of disease with them, diseases for which they themselves had some immunity while the Indians had none.

The uneasy alliance between the Jesuits and the Salish soon went from bad to worse, as did relationships within the community. One cause was an ignorant change in protocol instituted by the priests regarding the annual distribution of the potato harvest. They shifted the system from an egalitarian distribution to one based on merit, determined by the amount of time a particular Indian man had invested in planting the crop.[40]

One of the primary instigators of opposition to the Jesuits and their ways was the early Catholic convert Little Faro—Pierre-Jean—who had so impressed De Smet with his piety and zealousness in 1841. He accused the priests of failing to teach the Salish anything that would have use in their changing world. He encouraged them to reject the Jesuits in favor of Protestant missionaries, who would do a better job of teaching them to read, write, and farm. Theirs was a better road toward the future laid out by the Americans.

Of course these heretical ideas made the priests feel threatened. When Father Mengarini chastised Little Faro for his behavior, this malcontent led others in open hostility.[41] They joined a few white friends from the fur trade days in a camp across the river where they could avoid the reach of the Jesuits and enjoy old pleasures like gambling. For the first time in years, the sound of drums could be heard, and the rumors that flowed from that camp carried a more lasting effect than the drums.

Chief Victor seemed to lose his rudder during this time of challenge and, along with it, his effectiveness. He seemed unsure of how to proceed, and his hesitancy further undermined his authority. Insula, who had been his second chief, failed to step up. He is not mentioned at all by the record keepers during these years. The priests recognized a crisis in leadership. They had come to understand that a chief was "a friend who counsels, a father who exhorts, a guide who leads, a brave one who protects, sometimes a mediator who intercedes, and always a more or less perfect model who proposes nothing that he won't do or that he's not ready to do himself. If he were not all that, or at least if the strong side were not redeeming the weak side, soon those who had freely attached themselves to him . . . would abandon him to follow another."[42] Without strong leadership from within the community, individuals felt pressured to choose their path. Which leader had the strength to help them during these difficult times? Those who still believed prayed harder, and others sought solace wherever they could find it.

Father Mengarini took an overstep into tribal traditions by insisting that Victor appoint Crawling Mountain as his second in command. The

FIG. 21. Flathead Indians playing ring, a popular men's gambling game. Gustav Sohon. Smithsonian Institution. Reproduced in Ewers, *Gustavus Sohon's Portraits*, plate 7.

priests hoped the stature and strength of will of Crawling Mountain, whose chiseled features and "enormous, deep-set eyes . . . blazed with fiery intensity beneath a stern brow," would stabilize the community.[43] He had finally submitted to baptism in 1845, taking the name Moses, which the Salish pronounced as Moise. The priest believed this leader's more authoritative personality would bring strength and clarity to the challenges they now faced from within the community. Victor could only acquiesce and support the changes Moise implemented, so commanding was his personality. Even his fierceness, though, and the strong police force he implemented were not enough to quell the unrest and stem this tide.

At one point Moise became so incensed at Victor, apparently because of what he perceived as his weak leadership, that he struck him across the face. The priests were surprised that the head chief did nothing in response. To witness this scene would have been a terrible thing for Charlo, at the edge of manhood.

The Salish community gathered at the collapsing chapel in mid-November 1846 for prayers, led by Father Mengarini. Then in an unprecedented breach of etiquette, Little Faro interrupted the worship to vent his disgust at the priests and the chiefs that had become their pawns. Only Saxa, the son of Grand Ignace and Sinshe, tried to stop the harangue.[44] During Mass the following day, Little Faro again tried to interrupt the service. Instead of allowing for a repeat performance, the priests simply stopped the Mass and sent the worshipers home. They would close the church until they could be assured that the situation had been remedied.[45] Little Faro stopped his interference, but the priests' influence waned alongside Victor's, and they began to fear for their own safety. The people watched for signs and sensed a dark wind.

Escalating Blackfeet raids kept everyone on edge. George Simpson, who was helping to build the new Fort Connah, wrote a letter home in August 1847 in which he reported that the trading fort had lost twenty-nine horses to a "roving party of Blackfeet." Never before had they "been known to approach so near." Four of the horse thieves were shot, but no horses were recovered.[46]

Across the Continental Divide something was brewing that would bring even more trouble to the community. Charles Larpenteur was organizing to become the first trader to establish a trading post in the Bitterroot Valley among the Flatheads.[47] When he met with De Smet at Fort Lewis in September 1846 and learned of the peace council between the Flatheads and the various nations of Blackfeet, the trader sniffed the scent of a fresh-baked opportunity. Although his hopes to become a trader to the Flatheads never materialized, his efforts spawned a strong reaction that had consequences on both sides of the Divide.

Troubles between the Salish and their erstwhile allies, the Small Robes band of Blackfeet, presented the first stumbling block. In the fall of 1848, in a hunting camp south of the Missouri, a fight broke out between the two nations, leaving one dead on each side and many horses stolen. The Salish returned to their country as fast as they could. This left Larpenteur in a precarious situation. He still planned to take the trade to the Bitterroot Valley but needed horses to do so. To that end he visited the camp of the Small Robes. Things went well at first, and he was soon engaged in trading for horses. All was proceeding smoothly until “an old rascal commenced a harangue,” telling his people that they shouldn’t trade horses with this stranger, who planned to trade guns with their enemies. He encouraged them to “take what he has, and send him home,” along with “other bad talk.”[48] So the Small Robes took back their horses, repaid Larpenteur the goods he had traded, and sent the trader and his interpreter on their way on the two horses they managed to retain.

The trader at Fort Benton generously helped Larpenteur with enough stock to get across the mountains. It was late October, already past the season for good traveling. He and a crew made two attempts with different guides to get them across the Divide. The first guide disappeared in the night, leaving them stranded. The second one was Sata, who had accompanied De Smet and Point to Blackfeet Country. Despite the trader’s confidence in the small of stature but extremely capable Sata, they failed. Larpenteur concluded that he would spend the winter at Fort Benton and try again in the spring. But during that winter of 1848–49 the Blackfeet learned of Larpenteur’s plans to trade with the Flatheads and made clear their opposition. Those in authority advised him and his group not to go, saying that it would not turn out well; even if they managed to reach the Bitterroot, they would not find safety. Blackfeet war parties would stay close enough to carry on war with the Salish. The project was abandoned, but its ramifications lingered.

At St. Mary’s, although the heated confrontations of 1847 had ended, other challenges made these years difficult. The winter of 1847–48 found some eight or ten white men wintering among the Salish. These men were mostly former fur company employees, several of whom had taken Salish wives. They traveled with the seasons, spending summers on “the emigrant road,” where they traded good horses to travelers for hungry cattle and worn-out horses and then moved to a protected valley with reliable grass, where they all could recuperate during the winter. The Bitterroot and Missoula valleys were two of the best options due to luxuriant grasses. The Upper Bitterroot had the added advantage of its proximity to Fort Hall and the Oregon Trail. There these men could exchange their worn-out stock with the Salish for good horses. Each year the traders would repeat the cycle. Through this arrangement “many of the Flathead Indians became possessed of large herds of fine cattle" and also horses.[49] It might have been during these years that Victor became known as Xʷełx̣ƛ̓cin, Many Horses.

During these trying times the hopefulness the people had felt when the priests had first arrived was put into proper perspective. The spiritual medicine of the Black Robes wasn't going to save them. Horse raids and harassments from the outside had escalated, especially from the Blackfeet, and sickness had taken many lives. In addition to smallpox, most families lost at least one child to measles, while influenza took both young and old. The Indians were often hungry.

Even the traders at Fort Benton went hungry in the fall of 1849, so scarce were the buffalo. One American Fur Company trader at Fort Benton, Malcolm Clarke, wrote to his superior, Alexander Culbertson at Fort Union, to inform him of this serious problem. Nine traders had left Fort Benton for lack of food. Not only that, but also the company had lost two good traders in the war between Piegans and Flatheads.[50]

A violent storm set upon St. Mary's in the spring of 1850, not unlike the one that had ripped through their fledgling center in December 1841. For the priests this new tempest seemed to set into motion a dread that couldn't be stopped. It was like watching something fall inexorably: no matter what they wished, they could do nothing to stop it; the force had a life of its own. It had its own trajectory and momentum. At the same time, the priests witnessed the influence of those who lured more Salish away from the Church, and they witnessed many of them returning to their old ways.

One great irony in the drama of the Jesuit mission in the Rocky Mountains was the priests' inability to see how much the lives of the Native people conformed to the teachings of Jesus. Gregory Mengarini, in his frustrated attempts to learn Salish history, complained that they focused on "the present day, caring nothing for what is past, and leaving the future to take care of itself, provided that [they have] plenty to eat today."[51] Weren't they accepting their "daily bread," as Jesus had taught his followers? The priests called them profligate—wasteful—not of resources but of the opportunity to exploit them! Two worlds were operating in the same sphere, with two vastly different sets of values and understandings of life.

Charlo had been raised in these two worlds, the one of his ancestors and the one brought by the missionaries. He knew well the mythic tale of a lost paradise on earth. Although the image of a snake tempting Eve was etched in his memory, he had never accepted Eden as his place of origin. He had his own story, one of which he was reminded whenever he saw basalt columns that marked the places where Sn'k'lip had slayed Natliskeliguten, when the world was made safe for the Salish people. These and countless other reminders of his place in the world were embedded in the landscape. Charlo could not substitute this very real place of spiritual and material sustenance—the place where his ancestors lay buried—with a garden in some unknown land, nor would he want to.

Father Joset was sent from the mission among the Coeur d'Alenes to the Bitterroot to supervise and try to salvage the situation. Neither Fathers Ravalli nor Mengarini could hold the dismantled center together. Seeing that Father Ravalli was suffering from extreme anxiety, Joset sent him to another center to recuperate. Mengarini, too, was unstable. Three decades later Father Joset recollected that "some white people, repaying by ingratitude the many services which the Father [Mengarini] had lavished on them, began to spread calamonies [*sic*] against him among the Indians: some of those behaved in such a manner that the good Father was entirely disgusted: his courage having failed entirely he had to be removed, and there being nobody to take his place, the mission was disabled."[52]

No one knows for sure what all happened in that final year. The demise of St. Mary's wasn't due to Little Faro's rebellion. Three years had passed since that difficult time when he cursed the priests in their house of worship. Perhaps his challenge was like a dislodged boulder cascading down a steep slope, gaining energy with each roll. By the end of 1850 the Jesuits closed the doors of St. Mary's, afraid to stay. They leased the property for $250 to John and Frank Owen, brothers from Pennsylvania who were looking to establish trade with the Salish. The Jesuits retained the right to reclaim the property if they returned within two years; if not, the property reverted to the Owens. John Owen would manage to accomplish what Larpenteur had failed to do. This newcomer, with his steady companion, Nancy—a notably beautiful Shoshone woman—by his side, would soon establish a trading post on the property of the abandoned mission, right in the Salish heartland.[53]

Some of the Salish might have thought they had reclaimed their lives by ridding the valley of the priests, but they soon came to realize that the tribulations of their days would only increase. Their prophets had told them so. The time was coming when their lives would be whittled down to small reservations, just as De Smet had anticipated. Accepting the inevitable takeover by whites, the famous Black Robe continued to assist with their needs from his base in St. Louis during the transition.

Many of the Bitterroot Salish became good friends with the trader John Owen and watched with interest as what had been St. Mary's Mission became Fort Owen. Returning from buffalo hunts, the hunters would bring the jovial trader tongue, the choicest cut of meat, as a sign of respect and good will. He asked nothing of them, treated them fairly, and was generous to those in need. But his trading post attracted more outsiders into the valley, and it was not the gathering place that the mission had been. Both the stalwart Christians and the other Salish had lost some mooring at this time of rough seas.

For this small community, threatened on various fronts by enemies, strangers, and tension within, little was more important to them ultimately than social cohesion. From childhood on the Salish people were immersed in lessons of cooperation and conformity to the predominant viewpoint. This commitment to the good of the whole would protect them; it was essential to their survival as a people.

9. Atop a New Divide

Expansion and Contraction

With the creation of Washington Territory in 1853, the new governor, Isaac I. Stevens, accepted two extremely important responsibilities. One was to oversee surveys of a northern route for a transcontinental railroad, and the other was to negotiate land-cession treaties with tribes under his jurisdiction. To accomplish these tasks Stevens would depend on a large team of surveyors. The aspiring young governor, a recent graduate of West Point, had a plan to establish a base of operations for a survey crew in the Bitterroot Valley. His decision was influenced by the good reputation of the Salish. He had read the writings of Father De Smet in preparation for his duties and had tried, but failed, to convince the famous Jesuit to accompany the team.[1] De Smet's responsibilities for the Jesuits caused him to decline the invitation. Also, after all these years, he was preparing to take his final vows.[2]

The survey team, led by John Mullan, arrived at the Place of Wide Cottonwoods in the fall of 1853. One of the team members, Thomas Adams, upon arrival, noted that the "Flathead Village of St. Mary's . . . consists of a few scattered log huts," and the Owen trading fort he described as "strong."[3] No matter whom he asked, he was unable to determine if the abandonment of the mission had been caused by Blackfeet aggression or not. "The fort was the original Mission building," according to Adams, and John Owen turned it into a trading post.[4]

Most of the Salish were away on a buffalo hunt when the surveyors arrived. Pierre Lefthand was there to greet them, having remained in the valley to finish harvesting his ample fields. With the help of local information, Mullan decided on a base location fourteen miles south

FIG. 22. Fort Owen–Flathead Village, 1853. John Mix Stanley, Pacific Railroad Surveys. Archives and Special Collections, Mansfield Library, University of Montana.

FIG. 23. Cantonment Stevens, 1854. Gustav Sohon. Archives and Special Collections, Mansfield Library, University of Montana.

of Fort Owen and named it Cantonment Stevens. From that base the task of the surveyors would be to glean what information they could about the Salish, their allies and enemies, and their travel corridors.

One member of the survey team was the multi-talented Gustav Sohon, who served as an illustrator as well as cartographer and linguist. He got right to work on a Salish-English dictionary, and in the spring of 1854 he sketched portraits of Salish leaders. Having read De Smet's *Oregon Missions* in preparation for this work, he was thrilled to meet the men the priest described, many of whom were the same as those painted by Nicolas Point more than a decade before. Victor, the head chief, who still seemed young at an age close to sixty, gave his Indian name as Many Horses. Sohon caught up with him just as was preparing to leave with nine lodges to join the main camp for the buffalo hunt across the Divide.[5]

Sohon's notes about the various Salish leaders provide insights into their personalities, which would not necessarily be known through other means. Second Chief Moise is simply described as "a talented and worthy Indian." Alongside the sketch of Ambrose is a note of his bravery and generosity. Regarding Adolph, Sohon observed that he was "not much liked because he never fails to reprimand any of his tribe who may deserve it."[6] He helped to maintain public order. As a young man, he was known as a fearsome warrior, always recognizable by the red feather standing tall upon his head. He was also a devoted son. In 1842, when he was in his early thirties, his mother was thrown by her horse and knocked unconscious while on route to buffalo. Adolph carried her through many miles of snow until he caught up with the main camp. She survived.[7] Insula, "the Little Chief," nearly seventy winters, is noted for his piety. He officiated at Christian burials. Sohon recorded that "Bear Track" (Bear Tracks) was known as a "very brave and daring man, and is certainly one of the best looking men in the tribe." The artist also noted that "decision is written in every line of his countenance." Bear Tracks' integrity was conveyed in his clear-eyed gaze. Pelchimo, the youngest of these leaders, is noted for his "honesty and good sense." In a portrait done by Adams of Palchina "Parl-che-nar," thought to be the same person as Pelchimo, he notes the meaning of his name as "White Buffalo Calf."[8]

FIG. 24. Victor, head chief of the Flatheads. Gustav Sohon. Smithsonian Institution. Reproduced in Ewers, *Gustavus Sohon's Portraits*, plate 8.

FIG. 25. Moise, second chief of the Flatheads. Gustav Sohon. Smithsonian Institution. Reproduced in Ewers, *Gustavus Sohon's Portraits*, plate 9.

FIG. 26. Ambrose. Gustav Sohon. Smithsonian Institution. Reproduced in Ewers, *Gustavus Sohon's Portraits*, plate 10.

FIG. 27. Adolphe. Gustav Sohon. Smithsonian Institution. Reproduced in Ewers, *Gustavus Sohon's Portraits*, plate 11.

FIG. 28. Bear Tracks. Gustav Sohon. Smithsonian Institution. Reproduced in Ewers, *Gustavus Sohon's Portraits*, plate 13.

FIG. 29. Insula. Gustav Sohon. Smithsonian Institution. Reproduced in Ewers, *Gustavus Sohon's Portraits*, plate 12.

FIG. 30. Pelchimo. Gustav Sohon. Smithsonian Institution. Reproduced in Ewers, *Gustavus Sohon's Portraits*, plate 14.

FIG. 31. Mary "Quele-lox" or Red Gown. Thomas Adams. Special Collections, Princeton niversity Library.

FIG. 32. Alexander, head chief of the Upper Pend d'Oreille. Gustav Sohon, Pacific Railroad Surveys.

FIG. 33. Big Canoe, second chief of the Upper Pend d'Oreille. Gustav Sohon, Pacific Railroad Surveys.

FIG. 34. Michelle, successor to Alexander. Gustav Sohon, Pacific Railroad Surveys.

FIG. 35. Iroquois Peter (Iroquois Pierre). Gustav Sohon, Pacific Railroad Surveys.

FIG. 36. Iroquois Aeneas (Ignace). Gustav Sohon, Pacific Railroad Surveys.

FIG. 37. Charles Lamoose, mixed Iroquois–Pend d'Oreille. Gustav Sohon, Pacific Railroad Surveys.

FIG. 38. François or "Sarx-sar." Thomas Adams. Special Collections, Princeton University Library.

In addition to Salish leaders, Sohon sketched portraits of Pend d'Oreille leaders Alexander and Big Canoe. Forty-five-year-old Head Chief Alexander, he noted, was known "for his high-toned, sterling and noble traits of character. He is a brave man." Second Chief Big Canoe, older than Alexander by ten or fifteen years, was simply noted to be "dark-skinned" and "full-blooded." On the portrait of Alexander's son Michelle, Sohon noted that in addition to his "upright and manly conduct," he was known for his generosity.

Sohon also sketched portraits of the two men who greeted Father De Smet at Council Bluffs in 1839, Pierre Chalk (Pierre Lefthand) and Ignace Chapped Lips (Petit Ignace), fifteen years after that momentous meeting. The artist described Pierre Chalk, then in his fifties, his hair streaked with gray, as "the most industrious Indian in the valley, [who] cultivates a small farm raising wheat, oats, potatoes, etc. and owns a large band of cattle; he speaks the mountain French and English, besides several Indian languages." Sohon noted that Petit Ignace (Eneas) "came to this country with Pierre but had not the industry or forethought of his 'comrade.' . . . He is poor, but an honest and reliable man." Eneas, one of several men depicted wearing a Scottish tam, was able to advise Mullan on a trail westward over the Bitterroots.[9] A wanderer by nature, he had become geographically knowledgeable through his many travels. Unlike Pierre, he was not one to stay home to tend his garden.

Sohon's sketch of Charles, called Lamoose, the son of Sinshe and stepson of Grand Ignace, reveals the good looks and intelligence that Father Helias noted about the fourteen-year-old boy at his baptism in St. Louis. The caption with his portrait reads, "½ Iroquois ½ Pend d'Oreille, speaks English and French and lives with Flatheads." He is shown with his long black hair brushed back at the forehead with one hank held in a copper coil off to the side. Sohon notes that Lamoose had some eyebrow hair, "an exception amongst Indians" and indicative of mixed blood. Lamoose married a daughter of Bear Tracks. A portrait of Lamoose's half-brother, Francois Saxa, the son of Grand Ignace and Sinshe, was made by Thomas Adams. Saxa, also shown with a Scottish tam, had become a well-respected guide.

Stevens authorized Mullan to hire an interpreter who could also function as a guide, and he recommended Gabriel "as competent and reliable."[10] Gabriel Prudhomme would guide and interpret for the survey team as he had done for Father De Smet and so many other travelers during the previous decade. Like Eneas, this well-traveled man provided useful information to the survey team regarding the various passes across the mountains and laid down on paper the entire pathway from the Bitterroot to Fort Benton.[11] Despite all his years of service to the Jesuits and later surveyors, not a single identified image of Prudhomme remains.

The government agents claimed their purpose was to help establish a peace between "the Flatheads" and the Blackfeet and others who were stealing horses and attacking their camps. They did not speak of their plan for an intercontinental thoroughfare or about taking most of the Indian lands in the process. Stevens, back in Olympia, wrote letters and gave talks principally focused on the extinguishment of Indian title to lands between the Cascades and the Continental Divide. To the territorial legislature he conveyed his concern that the current situation made it impossible for non-Indian settlers to secure titles to land, "and thus the growth of towns and villages is obstructed." He wanted all impediments to "speedy settlement" by white immigrants to be removed, noting "much valuable land and an inexhaustible supply of timber east of the Cascades," where a population of about six thousand Indians in about twelve different tribes was blocking his goals.[12]

Significant land-altering changes were beginning even before road construction began. Two settlements—both established in 1854—bracketed Fort Owen and the Salish village at the former St. Mary's Mission. Cantonment Stevens consisted of a cluster of cabins located fourteen miles to the south, and the Kalispel Mission was relocated from below Lake Pend d'Oreille to a traditional gathering area some seventy miles to the north, in a beautiful valley south of Flathead Lake. The Indians had no way of knowing that the new mission would soon be located within the Flathead Indian Reservation. Fort Connah, the HBC post, had been established in that valley in 1847, six miles north of the new mission. The new St. Ignatius Mission provided the oppor-

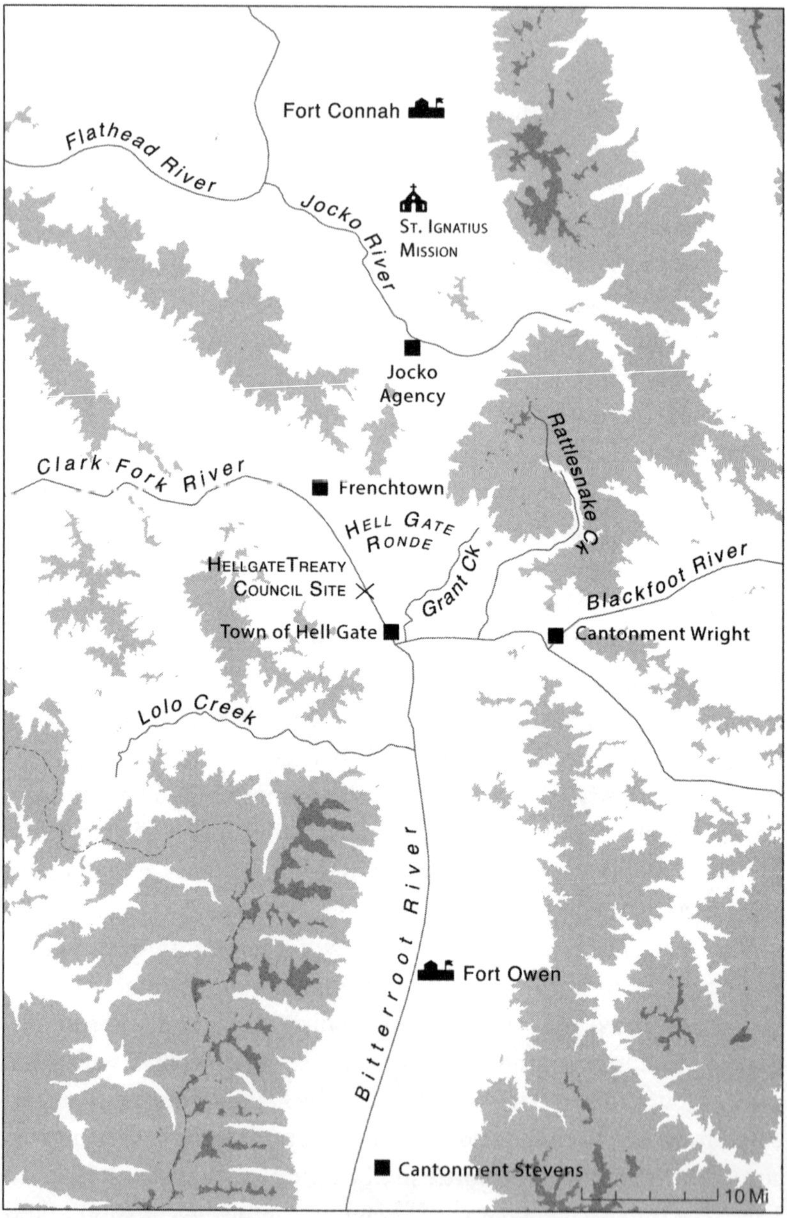

MAP 7. Five Valleys, 1850s. Hannah Shafer, cartographer.

tunity for the most fervent converts among the Salish, Pend d'Oreille, and Kootenais to participate in their Catholic religion.

While Governor Stevens laid the groundwork for land-cession treaties throughout the Washington Territory, using maps prepared by De Smet to shape the plan, De Smet wrote to the editor of *Précis Historiques*, the bulletin of Belgian Jesuit activities, that the "future prospect of the Indian tribes is very dark and melancholy." He noted that their geographic situation made certain their ruin, as they were "surrounded on every side by whites." Failing to address specific and often intentional causes, and seemingly unaware of his own role in promoting interest in the area, he lamented that "these savages disappear insensibly as the emigrations of the whites succeed each other and advance." He predicted that in a half century "there will be few traces of the Native races in the western portion of this hemisphere." The great tide of European emigration had to land somewhere, and that place was the West, he explained, adding that "the drama of population reaches its last scene at the east and west bases of the Rocky Mountains," the very home of the tribes incorporated within his Rocky Mountain Mission. With dramatic words appropriate to the very real tragedy playing out in the region, the famous Jesuit chronicler added his conclusion that soon "the curtain will fall over the Indian tribes and veil them forever. They will live only in history."[13] Again De Smet was wrong about the future of Native Americans, although there must have been times through the next half century that they themselves wondered if they would survive.

Beginning in December 1854, Governor Stevens moved systematically from west to east, negotiating treaties with the majority of tribes whose homelands were part of Washington Territory. At the Walla Walla Council his efforts to merge several tribes of the Columbia Plateau together on one reservation within the Yakama homeland met with strong resistance. The Nez Perce and Palouse refused, as did their neighbors, the Cayuse, Walla Walla, and Umatilla. One powerful Yakama-Palouse leader, Kamiakin, was so angry that he bit through his lower lip during the negotiations.[14] The treaty maker claimed victory with signed agreements and moved on, leaving a wake of dissent behind him as he headed eastward across the Bitterroot Mountains to negotiate with the Salish, Pend d'Oreille, and Kootenai.

Treaty Makers Bound the World

When the Indians gathered in early July for the council on the Clark Fork River, they were prepared for a peace treaty. Government representatives had talked to them about how the treaty would keep the Blackfeet in their own lands and allow for the mountain tribes to hunt buffalo more safely. Governor Stevens shocked them all when he started off the council by talking about "parting with their lands." The negotiators, assisted by interpreters with little command of the Salish language and essentially no facility with Kootenai, proposed that three tribes—the Salish, Pend d'Oreille, and Kootenais—be consolidated in the Flathead Valley, primarily in the home territory of the Pend d'Oreille. Neither the Kalispels nor the Coeur d'Alenes attended the council, although Stevens's plan was to lump them with other Salishan speakers. Stevens also assumed that the Kootenai-speaking Flatbows of the Bonners Ferry area would be settled with other Kootenais on the reservation. They didn't attend the council and did not relocate.[15]

Although it was least problematic for the Pend d'Oreille, the reservation plan was not to the liking of any of them. Unofficially they were told "that unless they sold their lands the whites would take them by force and give them nothing in return."[16] For the first days Victor, as head chief, waffled. They all felt caught in a web beyond their understanding. Charlo, married but not yet a father, must have struggled once again to witness his father's indecision. After several days of fruitless discussion Victor wisely suggested that the Bitterroot Valley be included in the reserved lands until such time that the federal government conducted a survey to determine which valley was best suited to their needs. This stipulation became Article XI of the treaty, specifying all lands in the Bitterroot Valley above the Lolo Fork would compose the conditional reservation (see Lolo Creek on map 7).[17]

No one suggested walking away. Despite many divisive and difficult issues, the head chiefs from the three tribes stepped up and placed an "X" by their names, and they were followed by their various headmen. Although the Iroquois had been welcomed into these communities as husbands and allies, none of their names appear on the treaty. Thus, it seems, they remained visitors, even after forty years. The most nota-

FIG. 39. The Flathead Treaty Council, July 1855. Gustav Sohon. Smithsonian Institution. Reproduced in Ewers, *Gustavus Sohon's Portraits*, plate 2.

ble exception to the signing was Crawling Mountain (Moise). He was infuriated by the entire process and the idea that they would give up their lands so easily. He was disgusted by Victor's acquiescence and told Governor Stevens that he never listened to the head chief. When the time came, he and his protégé, Pelchimo, refused to sign.[18]

Through the Hellgate Treaty, the combined Salish, Pend d'Oreille, and Kootenai tribes ceded approximately twenty-two million acres, lands roughly the size of Indiana, with the specification for their continued access to "open and unclaimed" lands for "usual and accustomed" purposes. "Usual and accustomed" purposes pertained to traditional cultural practices at those places within the aboriginal territories that provided for the tribes' livelihood. At that time every place within their homeland except for Fort Owen was "open and unclaimed," and it would have been a long stretch to imagine it otherwise; some particular places could be claimed, but such vastness could not.[19] Stevens's official account of the outcome reported "every man pleased and every man satisfied."[20]

Father De Smet kept abreast of the treaty negotiations through news that traveled with the traders up and down the Missouri. He understood that with the treaty "the mind of the poor Indian becomes uneasy, gloomy and apprehensive," and the recognition of their sad fate instilled a sense of hopelessness.[21] They would have to leave not only many of their hunting and fishing grounds but also the places where their fathers and mothers and all those they had loved were buried.

Treaty negotiators next called on all the bison-hunting tribes who hunted in the Upper Missouri and Yellowstone country to come together to make peace. Thousands of hungry Indians finally gathered at the mouth of the Judith River in mid-October 1855, having endured more than two months during a terrible drought, biding their time in lands essentially without bison, deer, or elk and only occasional scrawny pronghorn, while waiting for the delayed council to begin. Although they were committed to hear what the U.S. representatives had to say, their very survival had been threatened by staying for so long in these barren lands. It was for this reason that the council location was changed from Fort Benton to the mouth of the Judith River, sixty miles down the river. Chief Victor's horses were too far gone to make it the longer distance to the fort.[22]

The gathering was dominated by the tribes of the Blackfoot Confederacy and their allies, the Gros Ventres. The "western tribes" who attended this council included representatives of the Salish, Pend d'Oreille, Kootenais (in small numbers), and Nez Perce. After long negotiations, tribes from both sides of the Continental Divide agreed to some restrictions to hunting territories to keep the peace, although they argued for continuing access to traditional areas outside of the defined Common Hunting Ground in the Missouri River headwater basins. As they had just confirmed in their two-month hejira in search of food, the bison hadn't agreed to the proposed districts. Especially during a drought year, such as the one they were experiencing, hunters were required to spread out in many directions to find food. From the famine they had recently endured, the west-side tribes were adamant that they needed access to a hunting corridor that extended down the Yellowstone, as had always been their tradition.

The separation of hunters, it was hoped, would put an end to their ceaseless fighting and, more important, make it safe for whites to travel across the country unmolested. By treaty the common hunting area agreement would last ninety-nine years. Officials in Washington were thinking ahead to the time when a road and later a railroad would tran-

FIG. 40. Blackfoot Council, mouth of the Judith River, 1855. Gustav Sohon. Wikimedia Commons.

sect the land and Euro-Americans would come to claim it. They were not thinking of the gold rush that would take place just seven years in the future in the very lands set aside for the west-side tribes to hunt. They had no way of knowing that what was promised was not defensible, even in the short term. Eventually every tribal representative at what became known as the Lame Bull or Judith River Treaty council made his mark to the agreements—including Crawling Mountain.

On the days immediately following the treaty signing, according to Thomas Adams, "all hands were busy, early and late attending to the distribution of the large amount of presents (some 80 Tons,) brought up for the Indians." Feasting occurred on a grand scale, with the Indians enjoying the large quantity of flour, coffee, and sugar they received. "They are all extremely fond of sugar, of which they would make large kettles full of syrup, and drink with great gusto, and I expect that many a one was made sick thereby."[23] Silver medals made for the occasion were distributed on the following day to twenty headmen. They were each "very proud of the distinction as it was a guarantee of their authority among their people."[24] A military uniform was given to each head chief.

FIG. 41. Chief Victor, ca. 1860. Archives and Special Collections, Mansfield Library, University of Montana.

Treaty World Takes Hold

De Smet, from his removed perch on the grounds of St. Louis University, concluded that the Indians saw only a "dark and somber" future ahead.[25] The changes visible at that time were a mere fraction of what was to come. The treaties of 1855 opened vast tracts of land from the Olympic peninsula to the headwater rivers of the Columbia to be claimed by non-Indians. The U.S. military was ready and available to defend these takings except in the far reaches of the interior mountains in the homelands of the Salish, Pend d'Oreille, and Kootenai. Ceding vast areas of homeland through the Walla Walla and Hellgate treaties was akin to a family's losing almost everything of its home and property while being allowed to retain one small shed. The tribes did not truly understand what they had signed. They believed life would go on much as it had, except that now they would gain some agricultural and educational support from the U.S. government. Even if their interpreters had been capable, which they weren't, the Indian languages had no way to say "my land" because land was their source; they belonged to the land. The gifts of creation—the earth, trees, water, and all other beings—could not be owned.[26] Such a foreign concept was beyond their cognizance, and the mindset of the treaty negotiators was outside the capacity of most of the Indians to fathom. They had not yet fully realized that for Euro-Americans these gifts of creation were commodities, resources to be exploited. Resource, not Source: two concepts embodying oppositional views of the world. Although their leaders signed the treaties, that did not mean all was concluded in a "satisfactory manner," as reported in the official record.[27]

Many Salish stayed in the buffalo country after the conclusion of the Judith River Treaty council. They and their horses needed food and rest before they could make the long journey back across the mountains. After the long weeks spent with far too little food, in a landscape turned barren by drought and season, their leaders, responsible for the community's well-being, must have wondered if they would survive the winter. Some of their people did not.

After eight long months, capped off by a harshly cold winter, the various groups of hunters started arriving back in the Missoula and

Bitterroot valleys in late March 1856, returns that were timed to coincide with the beginning of the bitterroot harvest. As reported by Thomas Adams, at least one group, the one traveling under the leadership of Five Ravens (Chief Ambrose), returned with only a moderate meat supply. Adams was sorry to learn that the old man who had often fished for them the previous summer had died during the winter.

Returning families caught up on news. They learned that Gabriel Prudhomme, about forty years old, had died in January. As told by Thomas Adams, this "old Mountaineer" was well liked, and the entire community mourned his passing. He had lived among them since the arrival of the Jesuits in 1841. They also learned that "Pierre the Iroquois" had lost his house to a fire, just before the New Year. His "large two story log house" was located on Slocum Street in the growing little settlement of Stevensville. The building "was entirely consumed, as were also the furniture, which consisted chiefly of dressed Buffalo hides." Adams noted that Pierre had no insurance on the property. The estimated amount of his loss, according to the Indians' system of trade, was a "Pony, and a half."[28] As difficult as this must have been, the loss of his home would not be the worst thing soon to befall Pierre and his family.

Around the same time as the hunters' return, late April 1856, the Judith River Treaty passed through congress and was ratified by President Pierce. Soon thereafter the Blackfeet received their first annuities. The Salish, whose treaty had been made three months earlier than the Blackfeet treaty, wondered why the Blackfoot tribes were receiving benefits when the Salish weren't. To them it appeared that the U.S. government preferred rewarding enemies while neglecting old friends.[29]

The priests at St. Ignatius Mission wrote to their superiors in St. Louis to update them about life at the mission and on the new Flathead Reservation. Father De Smet was kept informed about people he knew well. Among other news, he would have heard that Pierre Lefthand, his old friend and interpreter, had died in a fall from his horse while he and his wife were hunting elk in the Big Hole in late May.[30] He survived their house fire only to die from an accident five months later.

In the latter part of July, Thomas Adams arrived at the traditional Salish camp known as Nłʔay, near Hell Gate, where the residents were fishing and gathering berries. Adams drove a wagon full of trade goods

FIG. 42. "Rattlesnake Creek—entrance to the Hell Gate Cañon." Thomas Adams. Special Collections, Princeton University Library.

he had acquired on a recent trip to Salt Lake City, which he hoped to trade for horses. He and his companions had traded their fresh horses to travelers on the "Emigrant Road" and then had used their profits to obtain goods desired by the Indians before returning home.

The Salish were moving from one traditional camp location in the Missoula Valley to another, every day or two, in a well-choreographed subsistence dance. From the east end they moved to the vicinity of where the Hellgate Council had been held. From the council ground they crossed the "Hellgate" and camped "at the foot of the mound on the St. Mary's," about five miles from their previous camp, at a place now known as McCauley Butte.[31] Fishing was good there, as it had been at the other locations.

Chief Moise and Bear Tracks, with some of the other Salish, visited John Owen at the fort on July 27, before they left for buffalo. Head Chief Victor visited Owen the next day. His camp was on the lower Bitterroot River, below Lolo's fork, where they were waiting for his wife, Agnes, to return from the Nez Perce Country. He told Owen that they would head up the Clark Fork for their summer bull hunt as soon as she arrived. A week later, on August 3, Thomas Adams arrived at this Salish camp at the Cold Spring, near where the Bitterroot emerges into the Missoula Valley.

The next day, upon the return of Agnes, the Salish prepared for their departure by hosting a great feast. Many of them would leave the next day to face a longer hunt than expected and a winter of great severity.

While in the camp, Adams visited with "Ignace the Iroquois" and noted in his journal that both Ignace and his wife, Julia, spoke English. Her "father was an old Spanish Mountaineer on Green river," and she "was raised by the whites at some of the trading posts."[32]

Trouble was brewing across the Bitterroots among the Nez Perce and other tribes of the mid-Columbia. John Owen's journal entry on August 21 reported, "Capt Chase arrived with his family from the Nez Perce Country."[33] Owen welcomed them to stay near the fort after learning that the Indians had burnt their house and drove them off. The Salish women must have been intrigued by the habits and manners of Mrs. Chase, the first white woman to live in their land.

While Victor and his people had headed up the Clark Fork for their fall buffalo hunt, on September 2 another group of Salish traveled up the Bitterroot, heading toward the Big Hole to hunt. Thomas Adams came to the camp of five lodges, joining up with his frequent associate, Charles Lamoose, the stepson of Big Ignace. Presumably he was welcomed to the lodge by Charles's wife, Eugenia, with their three young children. Eugenia was the daughter of Bear Tracks. These families generally moved camp each day during this season if circumstances dictated. At Ross' Hole, they took down a moose. On September 7, a Sunday, Adams noted that they moved camp, despite their preference not to move or hunt on the Sabbath, because the camp was low on meat. Two days later they managed to bring in only two small beaver, caught out of eight traps, but no other meat. Over the next few days, though, they managed to bring in five antelope. Another Salish camp of four lodges was camped a few miles down the creek. Joining forces, with everybody hunting, the only success of the two camps was one more antelope. Fat beaver meat was their main fare.

During these months the Salish crossed paths with the many itinerant stock traders who were settling in Salish territory. They were herding their poor "freight cattle" from the Emigrant Road to the valleys of the Salish homeland. Fred Burr, another of the Stevens railroad survey party, who had been assigned to Cantonment Stevens with Adams during the winter of 1854–55, planned "to establish a ranch for his cattle on the other side of the river," nearly opposite the cantonment. Some of these traders had settled into life around St. Mary's Village, near Fort Owen, and others established their winter quarters in the west end of the Missoula Valley, in the Hell Gate Ronde, which became known as "Grass Valley." Still others settled on the Jocko River on the new Indian reservation. Some of these men came into the area with Indian wives from elsewhere, and others joined up with women of the Salish and Pend d'Oreille tribes. They built corrals for their animals and lived well in Indian lodges while waiting for their stock to regain weight and strength. Whenever they could, they traded with Indians for horses. They paid little for the exhausted stock, then sold the rejuvenated animals at significant markup to needy travelers on their way to Oregon or California.

The new year commenced with such oddities at Fort Owen as a tea party given by Mrs. Chase for Nancy Owen and the other "ladies of the fort" (mostly Shoshone women).[34] John Owen made note of a wedding, during this long and dreadful winter, of "one of Mr Pattees' Men Named Silverthorn to one of the fair ones of the land[,] the ceremony performed in presence of witnesses by Mr Pattee." Owen added an interesting observation that "A man is not censured for so desperate an act during the Cold Season for the Nights are too Severe to Sleep alone and in fact the bible Says it is Not good for Man to be alone—So it goes." When the new Mrs. Silverthorn went missing a week later, Owen concluded, "She probably would rather lead the wild life of the tribe than be a White Mans fair bride."[35]

The Salish returned from buffalo in mid-January, and Chief Victor presented John Owen with a gift of buffalo tongues upon his return. They lost many horses due to the harsh winter conditions. John Owen reported that Chief Victor and his family spent much of April at St. Ignatius Mission, while Chief Moise remained mostly in the Place of Wide Cottonwoods.[36]

More than a decade after Father De Smet had brought seeds for crops and cattle, pigs, and chickens for meat and eggs, the Salish remained hunters and gatherers and continued to cross the mountains for buffalo at least twice a year. The hunters had to stay longer and longer in their quest for this staple food, so decimated were the herds. In the worst years they came home empty-handed. The women continued to gather roots each spring, relishing the earthy smell and tactile delight of removing the tough outer skins, as they visited together. As the months progressed, picking ripe berries always brought pleasure, regardless of the worries the women carried. Despite their best efforts to keep their precious children healthy, the white man's sicknesses continued to haunt them. The men worried about providing meat and hides for their families while they defended them all from increasing attacks by Blackfeet and from the ripple effects of new threats from formerly peaceful tribes to the west. Everyone sensed the rising waters.

John Owen decided it was time to reinforce the construction of the fort, and in April 1857 he set into motion a plan to transform the fort's wooden palisades and interior buildings into thick walls of adobe construction. By mid-May his crew had thousands of adobe bricks curing, and Owen figured the work would take the summer. But illnesses and injuries impacted the labor pool, and unusually wet and cool weather impeded production of adobe bricks in June and July. A shortage of laborers caused delays in August, and troubles with the sawmill kept the workers from producing the lumber needed for roof and floor construction. They could only work during the summer months, when freezing nighttime temperatures wouldn't restrict them from working the adobe. By the time they finished the job in 1860, they had dug out several large clay yards to meet their construction needs. No one mentioned what the Salish thought about digging so much clay from the earth. Perhaps, by now, with so many years of experience with white people, little surprised them.

The winter of 1856–57 was so severe that it completely ruined the bitterroot crop in the Bitterroot Valley, leaving the Salish in difficult straits. Their survival strategy was to try the root grounds in the Missoula Valley and for some of the men to leave immediately for bulls. HBC trader Michael Ogden—the son of De Smet's old friend Peter Skene Ogden and his Indian wife, Julia—went with them because Fort Connah as well was out of meat.[37] The hunters stayed out through June, then returned to the Hellgate Ronde long enough to dig and dry their camas before needing to return to the buffalo country to try again for

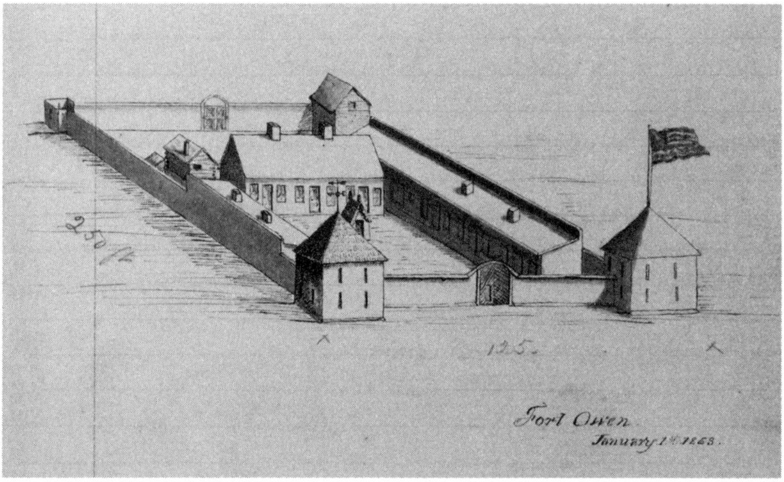

FIG. 43. Fort Owen. Thomas Adams. Special Collections, Princeton University Library.

meat. On July 10, 1857, John Owen, who had been appointed as Indian agent, noted that he believed a few of Flathead Indians were moving up the Bitterroot from the Missoula Valley "for the purpose of hunting up their cattle & mark[ing] the young calves."[38] Most of the Salish remained in the Missoula Valley during this time.

In these challenging years of transition some Salish families chose to move into the small village that had sprouted up around St. Ignatius Mission, where they found comfort in being near the priests. The family of Pierre Lefthand relocated at this time, as did Insula, the well-liked "Little Chief," who chose to live in a cabin by the mission, where he became a close friend of Father Hoecken. They adopted some of the ways of their white neighbors but not in a wholesale manner. They might have a cabin, but they also had a lodge pitched nearby. Many of them tried to integrate farming into their seasonal activities while continuing to follow their age-old rounds. They still crossed the mountains for buffalo.

In February 1858 De Smet wrote to a funder in New York about his concern for the "dear neophytes" of their missions. To help her understand, he invited her to "imagine two societies—one representing the manners and customs of barbarians, the other all the splendor of modern civilization—coming in contact" and to consider how long it would take for the two societies to fuse and "dwell together in complete harmony." Reflecting the thinking of European social scientists of the day, he continued with the conclusion that it would take longer than three generations for "the barbarous state" to "attain the height of the civilized," leaving open a dangerous period of transition. "The civilized society will have the advantage over the barbarous; it will have it entirely at its mercy, to make it subservient to its will and pleasure." Like children against "the malicious prudence of mature age," the Indians were not able to hold their own. He concluded that "the judgment of the savage is not sufficiently ripe to be able to compete with the wisdom of man born in the bosom of civilization."[39] He carried a worldview hard-pressed to imagine another way of measuring intelligence, aptitude, and success, regardless of all that he had witnessed.

De Smet, despite his concern about the vulnerability of the Natives, did not blame the difficulties on the American republic for their plight. The young country, in his view, had nobly succeeded at "extending her domination from the Atlantic to the Pacific, so as to embrace the commerce of the whole world." America, which had provided the Natives with "more means of civilization" than was the norm, was not to blame for "injustice and inhumanity" in the treaties with the Indians. Instead he blamed "private persons, new colonists, who act and place themselves in direct opposition with the good intentions of the government on behalf of the savages."[40] He did not question whether the government had any responsibility to protect vulnerable groups of people within its jurisdiction from exploitation. As a popular adage of the day affirmed, "To the victor go the spoils." What the tribal leaders thought about these matters was never put to paper. The next generation would become more outspoken as the number and magnitude of betrayals escalated.

The Salish continued trying to live the life that had long sustained them. Often during these years, according to John Owen, the Salish were "destitute of many things," and they continued to be hounded by the illnesses of white men.[41] Besides illness and extreme weather, there was rarely enough food, and conflicts with other tribes continued, regardless of peace treaties forged by U.S. authorities. In early May 1858 Bear Tracks was in a camp with Adams and other white traders when some Blackfeet arrived at night and, as reported by Adams, "drove

FIG. 44. Salish horses picketed at lodge. Thomas Adams. Special Collections, Princeton University Library.

off all the horses we had, but as the Hell gate River is swimming full, they could not, in the dark, drive them across so that they had to be satisfied with . . . riding . . . the best horses out of camp."[42] Two of those belonged to Bear Tracks.

During the summer of 1858 the situation was particularly bad. Because of troubles on the Columbia Plateau, the U.S. government banned the sale of ammunition to Indians. Fifty years after metal tools had been introduced, the old ways to make stone arrow points had been abandoned by everyone and forgotten by all but the most conservative old men, and they were too old to hunt. The young men were committed to hunting gear for which the government withheld the active ingredient. Salish hunters traded horses, hides, and dry meat, if they had any, on the black market for ammunition and iron arrow tips to see them through the buffalo hunt.

With adversity comes ingenuity. Nine Pipes (Ker-no-ta Sin-Man-hu) told Adams he wanted "to take two cows over the Mountain, & bring back some Buffalo calves." Presumably he would trade the cows and replace them with something he knew to be more valuable—buffalo. Adams agreed to let this respected entrepreneur borrow his navy pistol and "as much powder and lead" as he could spare.[43]

Agent Owen asked the chiefs what they needed to enable them to go on their summer hunt. They all recognized that their annuities would not provide what was needed. Their best chance at success, they told him, would be if he got them half of what they were due in ammunition and tobacco and for him to use the other half to "open us a field and get us a plow," explaining that through this two-pronged approach they "will sow wheat and have flour to eat as Buffalo are growing scarce."[44]

They left for buffalo in September 1858. In mid-October some scouts from Victor's camp on the upper Blackfoot River spotted two men traveling up the Clark Fork, near the mouth of Flint Creek. The men appeared to be traders, based on the abundance of goods they carried with them. These two were a white man named William Hamilton and Alex McKay, "a one-eyed half breed," posing as traders while actually conducting a little espionage for the U.S. Army.[45] Hamilton had been sent east from Fort Walla Walla to assess the state of affairs among the Blackfoot Confederacy tribes.[46] At that moment Hamilton and McKay were relieved to see it was Salish who were approaching rather than Blackfeet. They could get a status update to help them prepare for their time across the mountains.

Hamilton and McKay agreed to join the Salish on their eastward journey up the Blackfoot River to buffalo. Chief Victor welcomed them into his lodge as soon as they arrived. His son—presumably Charlo (then in his late twenties)—took care of their packs while they sat down to enjoy a meal and a smoke and to catch up on news. Afterward the headmen led the way to the large lodge of "old Moese," Crawling Mountain. Once the leaders and the visitors were seated, everyone else who could fit squeezed into the remaining space. The Indians were anxious to hear all about the end of the Spokane and Yakima war, and the government spies were eager to learn news of the Blackfeet. Their talking lasted through the night and ended only when they were called to breakfast by Bear Tracks, the old medicine man, just after sunup.

They traveled together up the river and across the Divide, and then a subset of them, led by Victor, rode toward the Piegan Agency on the Sun River, where they met with Agent Alfred J. Vaughn. No doubt Victor wanted to register a complaint about all the times Piegan horse thieves had attacked Salish camps since the signing of the treaty, just three years before.[47] Fifty armed Salish men approached the agency, around which were arranged some fifty lodges of Blackfeet and Bloods. The meeting between the Salish and Vaughn was productive, and afterward he distributed gifts. That night the Salish camp feasted on fresh buffalo meat. The young hunters presented the tongues to Chief Victor. The next morning, after six days with the Salish, Hamilton and McKay, the faux trading party, went their separate way. Before they left, though, they gifted Victor's people with much-needed ammunition. Buffalo were on the horizon.

De Smet Returns to the Rockies

William Hamilton was not the only government agent to be sent east from the Columbia Plateau in the fall of 1858; Pierre-Jean De Smet also received an assignment. The government understood that full implementation of American settlement of the Northwest could only begin with the end to Indian troubles, and the legendary Black Robe was just the man to help quell lingering unrest. De Smet's assignment came from General William S. Harney of the U.S. Army.[48]

The well-connected Black Robe was to go among the mountain tribes to rectify "false rumors" and to try to find war leaders who had escaped punishment, to assure them of amnesty if they agreed to peace.[49] Father De Smet delightedly found himself in a position to return to his beloved friends and mountains, and he trusted that his skills, experience, and relationships with several of the uneasy tribes would bring him success. Moreover, he might achieve a real coup if he managed to find Kamiakin and his brother Schloom, "two of the principal instigators" behind the war, and convince them to give themselves up. General Harney was aware that they had "fled to the Flat Head Country," and he felt confident that once these two were "given up . . . the Indians in this Department can easily be controlled."[50] What a story the adventuresome Jesuit might have to tell in his next book.

Father De Smet asked permission from his superiors in St. Louis to accept the assignment, explaining that "the tribes of the Columbia Plateau—the Yakima, Palouse, Spokane, Colville, Okinagans, and Coeur d'Alene—had joined together," and on May 17 they had attacked Lieutennent Colonel Edward Steptoe's battalion, killing two of his officers and several soldiers.[51] De Smet went on to say that the army was fearful "that a general uprising was imminent throughout the territory" in reaction to the increase in settlers, cattlemen, and miners. Even the peaceful Kalispels, Kootenais, and Salish, he reported, were uneasy about how the newcomers were claiming the most fertile locations as their own, in complete disregard for the treaty agreements of 1855, still not ratified. These mountain tribes "had resolved to drive back the whites, or at least to make resistance to their progressive encroachments."[52]

During the six weeks it took Father De Smet and General Harney to travel from New York down the Atlantic Coast, then across the Isthmus of Panama and up the Pacific Coast to Fort Vancouver, the fighting ended. Within a few months of the Steptoe debacle, when Steptoe's troops were humiliated by warriors of the plateau atop the butte now named Steptoe, the attempt by tribes to defend their sovereignty had been harshly met by the U.S. Army. Colonel George Wright's troops drove back the combined bands of Native warriors, then assured their defeat with the horrific slaughter of some nine hundred horses and the destruction of winter stores of grain and dried foods in the Coeur d'Alene Country. Then, to drive the defeat home, they rounded up and hung a dozen tribal leaders for their parts in the rebellion. These actions essentially put an end to the Plateau War; without horses and leaders the Indians were unable to mobilize an opposition to the military or to the whites overtaking their lands. They had come to the bleak realization that the "White race" was more than they could hold back. It was at that time that Colonel Wright conscripted William Hamilton to assess the status of the Blackfeet.

Although the tribes were subdued and quiet by the time De Smet and Harney arrived at Fort Vancouver, the general wanted the escapees accounted for and mollified. The multi-talented Jesuit could use his skills to convince them to attend a peace council in Vancouver. The aging priest was to go into the mountains to meet with tribal leaders and bring them to council with the general. De Smet later explained that the Indians "still retained their prejudices and an uneasiness and alarm which had to be dissipated, and there were false reports to be rectified. Otherwise, the war might soon break out afresh."[53] His was an unlikely scenario, but it justified the journey.

De Smet entered a somber world, echoing with sounds of grief, as he traveled through ancient homelands along the source rivers of the mighty Columbia. "The savages, formerly so numerous along the coast and the river, have almost entirely disappeared." In stark comparison to his first trip in 1842, white settlements dotted the riverfront, and a lighthouse guided ships into the Columbia bar. The Willamette Valley to the south of Vancouver had become home to a number of thriving towns and villages, alongside impressive farms with vast apple orchards; productive fields of barley, wheat and oats; and a wealth and variety of vegetables. Vancouver, having long served as the hub for the HBC, had become an American military fort and the center of a flourishing town of about one hundred houses. A military presence had been maintained since 1856, as was needed to keep the peace between the settlers and the Indians.[54] De Smet was pleased to find there a Catholic church and schools for both boys and girls, remembering how he had been the one to bring the first sisters to the region in 1844.

Upriver, at The Dalles, the once great gathering place for the Indians during the salmon runs had been replaced by a fort alongside a new town, as large as Vancouver, surrounded by outlying farms. De Smet predicted a fine future for The Dalles for white people by reason of its key position along this river corridor. As he continued to Walla Walla, the returning missionary saw a country "stripped of animals and game." Sounding like a land speculator, this well-traveled Jesuit reported that many new colonies would become established at inviting locations along this stretch of river. "Umatilla has fine forests," he observed, and the "abundant and nourishing grass" was well suited for "the raising of innumerable domestic animals."[55] Before the treaties, these had been the lands of the horse-rich tribes of the Yakama, Palouse, Cayuse, Umatilla, and Walla Walla. What De Smet did not see as he traveled up the river were any Native people. Diseases had nearly obliterated their presence from these ancient places. Survivors had retreated to their reservations.

Some settlers had moved into the area of old Fort Walla Walla at Walula on the Columbia, and a new town was getting started in the neighborhood of the new Fort Walla Walla, some fifty miles upriver. The town emerged to serve the needs of gold miners flocking to the region. In 1858 alone, over thirty thousand miners passed through, headed to the Thompson River in British Columbia, believing stories of rich finds there.[56] Though such stories were false, many of the seekers found the rich grasslands of the Palouse country appealing enough and chose to stay.

From Fort Walla Walla the De Smet party headed north. The party included Father Congiato, superior of the Oregon and California missions, who caught De Smet up on local affairs. The rapid approach of the "day of invasion by the whites," De Smet understood, was causing unease and apprehension for the Indians. They would have to leave "the place where repose the ashes of [their] fathers and of all those [they have] loved, and [their] hunting and fishing grounds."[57] The severe retaliation by Colonel Wright had convinced the Indians that they could not resist.

The returning Black Robe had hoped to cross the Bitterroot Range before winter set in. It was already November, and to his great frustration deep snow in the mountains kept him grounded at the Sacred Heart Mission. The Indian guides explained that travel would not be possible until the snow settled and hardened in February.[58] From November to February De Smet had no choice but to wait for the thaw. During these long weeks he wrote letters, tracked the weather, sketched, and visited. The church at the mission, designed by Father Ravalli and built just after De Smet had left this country, had replaced the little one made of cedar bark that De Smet had seen in 1846. The new one, so beautiful and well constructed, rivaled the cathedrals of Europe.

The priests had succeeded in making many changes since De Smet's departure, but some habits of the Coeur d'Alenes were difficult to curtail despite the best efforts of the priests. In his weather log for December 28, De Smet included a side note of "Departure of the Hunters." After nearly two decades agriculture merely supplemented the Indian diet—and not very well. Father Joset at that time had a request from boys who lived and studied at the mission to return to their parents for the deer hunt. Joset could not refuse the boys' request, for they were actually "suffering with hunger." This lack of food at the mission was especially bad this particular year. At the Indian villages, Joset reported, there was "no want of occupation or of companions; they have food in abundance, which is rarely the case at the Mission."[59] It is ironic that the Jesuits' stores of grain had been destroyed by Colonel Wright.

FIG. 45. Sacred Heart Mission, 1859. De Smet sketch.
Saint Louis University Archives.

By mid-February, as predicted, the snow had settled enough to allow for travel with a combination of canoe, horse, and snowshoes. Still weighing over two hundred pounds and twelve years older than he had been during his last difficult winter journey up the Clark Fork, De Smet drew on his extraordinary energy and his great desire to see his Salish friends and got himself moving. He was nearly thwarted on his first day out, when he badly wrenched his knee. With but a moment's pause to consider his options, he chose to tough it out, as was his tendency. After a grueling month on the trail, passing small winter villages along the way, he and his guides arrived in the Flathead Valley, where he got his first glimpse of St. Ignatius Mission, a thriving little village surrounding a simple chapel, nestled against a backdrop of some of the most beautiful mountains on the continent. He met there with Pend d'Oreille chief Alexander, "No Horses," one of his most devoted mountain friends.

After a brief rest followed by a visit with the Kootenais, near the north end of Flathead Lake, the still energetic priest headed south. In the Missoula Valley he met five Salish lodges on their return from buffalo. Their hunt had been successful, and they shared meat with him. Eager

FIG. 46. St. Ignatius Mission, 1859. De Smet sketch. Saint Louis University Archives.

to visit with the Salish, the long-absent Black Robe proceeded up the Bitterroot. Few of the Salish were in the valley at the time, having not yet returned from buffalo. De Smet had to have suffered to see Fort Owen thriving in the place of St. Mary's.

The returning priest must have learned of the tragic death of one of the Salish men, Ar-le-mah, the month before his arrival. Thomas Adams wrote in his journal on February 20, 1859, that this good man had not returned from elk hunting in the mountains. A search party went out and found him lying near the remains of a large fire. He had been badly burned, due to a large log that had evidently rolled onto him.[60]

Despite the absence of a mission among them, Father De Smet celebrated the fact that many Salish remained faithful. Their great chieftains—Victor (Many Horses), Michael (Insula), Adolph (Red Feather), Ambrose (Five Ravens), and Moses (Crawling Mountain)—had remained "true and zealous Christians," and in an interesting juxtaposition, he remarked that "real piety in religion and true valor at war are united in them."[61]

De Smet must have wondered what their future would hold now that ratification was working its way through Congress. The Pend d'Oreille and Kootenais would be expected to settle within the lands reserved in the Flathead Valley, and the Salish, for now, would be allowed to remain in the Bitterroot Valley, but once the survey was conducted, they might be forced to join the others. The final decision was in the hands of the U.S. government, which continued to think of the Indians merely as impediments to the government's extending its control over the territory through colonization by its citizens.

De Smet stayed just a day before heading back north to begin the return trip to the Columbia, only to find his departure delayed due to trail conditions. He was not the only one waiting to travel the road, nor was he the only one with a mission to accompany chiefs from the mountain tribes to visit U.S. authorities west of the Cascades. John Owen was waiting too. Finally, on April 18, the two groups set out for their respective destinations: De Smet to Fort Vancouver as special agent to the army for a meeting of the chiefs with General Harney, and Owen to Salem as Indian agent with tribal representatives to meet with the superintendent of Indian affairs. Coincidentally this was the same day that President Buchanan ratified the Hellgate Treaty, six weeks after Congress had approved it.

For reasons lost to history, De Smet and Owen did not travel together. The animosity between them seeps quietly through their journals, more by what wasn't recorded than what was. Afterward the two competitors wrote conflicting accounts of who had organized the chiefs and what had happened on route to Walla Walla. Each claimed their own initiative and blamed the other for interference.

Little detail is revealed in either of these journals, making it a challenge to understand the makeup of the two parties and their relationships. During a month-long trek Owen traveled with Francois Saxa and HBC trader Michael Ogden. The makeup of De Smet's party is unclear. Travels of both groups involved a number of unexplained or vaguely described events. In general the De Smet party stayed a day or two behind the Owen party. At the Spokane River crossing, after two weeks on the road, De Smet noted in his journal that he waited for the chiefs, who appear to have traveled with John Owen to Colville for supplies and possibly to pick up two more tribal representatives. Once the Owen party arrived, both groups headed south to Fort Walla Walla. Along the way

FIG. 47. Pierre-Jean De Smet, ca. 1859. Jesuit Archives and Research Center.

FIG. 48. Major John Owen, 1871. From Owen, *The Journals and Letters of Major John Owen*.

the famous "renegade chief" Kamiakin joined the travelers, although he followed at some distance rather than riding with them. Although he had apparently agreed to participate in the meeting with Harney, at Walla Walla he abandoned the plan and disappeared into the night. The next morning Father De Smet left the fort on his own and caught a steamboat for Vancouver, leaving Owen at the fort with the chiefs.

Four days later, on May 18, General Harney met with the chiefs in Vancouver. It is unclear whether De Smet met with them. Afterward some of the group traveled to Portland as documented in a famous photograph in which De Smet stands in the back row, flanked by the interpreter, Saxa, and a Coeur d'Alene delegate called Bonaventure, with Denis (Thunder Robe) of the Colville Tribe beside him. Seated in the front row are De Smet's dear friends, Salish sub-chief Red Feather (Adolph) and Pend d'Oreille chief Alexander, along with Kalispel chief Victor (Happy Man) and Coeur d'Alene sub-chief Andre (Andrew Seltice).

FIG. 49. Father De Smet and the chiefs, 1859. Jesuit Archives and Research Center.

These men had two things in common: a devout commitment to the Black Robes and to peace. Their people had not participated in the Plateau Wars. Spokane Garry, who also attended the meeting with General Harney, was not present with the group in Portland.

Father Congiato met with De Smet after his business with the chiefs was concluded, and the two decided they would travel back across the mountains "to negotiate business together at the Missions." After their visit Congiato wrote to his superior to express his dismay at how changed he found Father De Smet. Where he had been so "full of fervor" in the fall, as he headed into the mountains, nine months later he had lost that enthusiasm. De Smet, fifty-eight years old, told him his advanced age was causing him to suffer great fatigue.[62] The difficult months, both physically and mentally, had taken their toll.

John Owen had worries of his own. After returning home at the conclusion of the strange journey with the chiefs, he wrote to Superintendent of Indian Affairs Edward Geary in Portland that the "Flatheads" were leaving at the end of August for their fall buffalo hunt, and he expressed concern about potential trouble in the territory. "The Indian is becoming daily More & More unsettled, some of them alarmingly so," he warned. Where the Blackfeet had long been the Salish enemy, their threats had receded, while other tribes had stepped into the void. Not only tribal enemies concerned the Salish. They feared being "swallowed by the White tribe" and wondered what would become of them. New roads were being made all through their country, bringing more and more outsiders who hunted and fished in Salish haunts. When the Indians went hunting for deer, they had trouble finding anything to shoot.[63] As a long-time friend of the Salish, Owen felt responsible and feared the capriciousness of the U.S. government.

In a letter dated October 10, 1859, Owen wrote again to inform the superintendent of the misunderstanding among settlers that the Bitterroot Valley was open to them, a misunderstanding that was causing great distress among the Indians. Many men from Mullan's survey crew, as well as other non-Indians, intended to settle there. "The Indians have Serious objections. They have themselves large bands of Animals and Say there is Not More pasturage than they would like to have for themselves." Of course, he explained, the Indians believed that Article XI of the treaty of 1855 prevented "any whites Not in Service of the Ind Dept from Settling in the Bitter Root Valley South of the Lolo's fork."[64] He went on to describe the serious nature of the government's failure to make good on treaty agreements and noted that they, at the fort, were frequently unprotected because all the Indians went across the mountains to hunt. He called for a military presence to ensure the peace.

In another letter to Superintendent Geary on October 15, 1859, Owen communicated his preferences for the distribution of annuities. He prioritized blankets, cloth, ammunition, tobacco, and tinware. Although the Indians most wanted coffee and sugar, the agent suggested that the Indian Department prioritize rice instead since the Salish were "improvident" with the other staples. Owen recommended that funds should be made available for acquisition of "Stock & American Mares" so that the Indians could improve their herds. This would help them in the long run and would also be much pleasing to them. The agency would need tools and materials and workers for a carpenter shop, smithy, sawmill, and grist mill.[65]

Despite ratification of the treaty that spring, Superintendent Geary was unable to send the supplies and provisions guaranteed under the treaty. The Salish didn't understand why the annuities didn't come. Owen encouraged them to have faith in the government and explained to them the lengthy process. Letters between him and Superintendent Geary in Portland took three months to arrive. Once Geary had evaluated Owen's recommendations and passed them on to the Indian commissioner in Washington, they needed to go through a bureaucratic process just to get acquisitions approved before the goods could be shipped. If timing wasn't right, the annuities might sit in St. Louis for months, waiting for the next navigable season to Fort Benton. From there, freighters would haul the goods the 240 miles over the mountains to finally reach the Indians of the Bitterroot Valley.

Owen's letters revealed a growing despair over the situation. He feared Congress would fail to make good on its treaty promises. He was beginning to accept the unimaginable possibility that they could starve. Much would depend on the buffalo hunt.

Part 3. The People Surrounded, 1860–1910

Somewhere in the planetary history religious expression changed from participation in the sound, color and rhythm of nature to the abstractions of man outside this context pleading for temporary respite and hoping in the next life to return to the Garden.

—Vine Deloria Jr., *The World We Used to Live In*

10. Native World Turned Inside Out

Terrible Transition

The Salish left the Bitterroot Valley with hundreds of horses in late September 1859 and headed east toward the buffalo plains on a journey across a landscape they knew like their mothers' hands. They would eventually be joined by some of the Pend d'Oreille, Nez Perce, and other allies, but they would travel in separate groups because few campsites could provide for their combined needs and those of their horses. They traveled with dry berry cakes and roasted roots to get them through. All along the way the people stopped to acknowledge ancient trees and buried kin.

The landscape they passed through had changed very little during the fifty years since the first whites had arrived. Other than the tilled land around Fort Owen, the sod remained unbroken. The Clark Fork Valley looked much as it always had. On this trip, though, when Salish scouts went ahead to check for signs of enemy warriors around Snx̣ʷq’ʷpuʔsáqs the confluence of the Clark Fork and the Little Blackfoot rivers, what they saw instead was the cabin of a white settler, Johnny Grant.[1] There, where bison-skin tipis had been pitched since before the oldest among them could remember, now sat a rough shack of soft cottonwood logs, the bark still attached.

As the hunters proceeded over the mountains, they were weighed down by the knowledge that each year they traveled farther and found fewer bison. Their last good hunt had been three years before. Back when bison had been more plentiful, the camp stayed out for a few months at most, returning to the Bitterroot Valley loaded with dry meat just after the shortest day of the year. This year, as was common since the bison had become increasingly scarce, the Salish spent the entire fall and winter on the plains.

Returning hunters and horses were exhausted from having had to break trails through deep snow in the spring of 1860.[2] With each leg of the journey the Salish travelers saw signs of the whites' commitment to stay put. From Snx̣ʷq'ʷpuʔsáqs to the Bitterroot, their old trail was becoming the Mullan Road, widened and leveled yet still without bridges. The Stuart brothers, Granville and James, had settled down on lands not far below Snx̣ʷq'ʷpuʔsáqs, and Johnny Grant's father, Richard, had moved down the river with three hundred head of horses and cattle to settle in a nestled valley on the creek that would carry his name. Grant Creek flows into the Clark Fork close to its confluence with the Bitterroot River, near where the first white settlement in the Missoula Valley was forming.

In a letter to Superintendent of Indian Affairs Geary on March 25, 1860, Owen reiterated that "buffalo were becoming scarce and something had to be done to avert disaster. The People needed another means to subsist."[3] The Salish were hungry and needed support to expand their agricultural efforts for greater long-term security. They harvested bitterroots, then readied themselves to cross the mountains again, but the spring hunt was delayed by the highest runoff in memory. Hunt chiefs couldn't agree on a route with rivers overflowing their banks in too many places.

Tension mounted. At the end of June 1860, after receiving an account of goods making their way to the Flatheads, Owen sent a scathing letter to Geary about the absurdity of the character, quantity, and cost of the supplies selected. Bureaucrats had essentially ignored his on-the-ground perspective. Instead they had sent inadequate tools for Salish agricultural needs and had made no accommodation for the purchase of heifers and mares. They had sent "tons of Coffee, Rice and Hard-bread" and great quantities of sugar. Owen plead on the tribe's behalf for more sustaining provisions.[4] Then, when he thought things could get no worse, Owen learned that annuities had been held up at Fort Benton because of "the absence of a written order to release them." He detailed the situation for the superintendent in another letter on September 21. "The Indians remained thinking the Waggons nearly due would bring

FIG. 50. Victor's Camp, Hell Gate Ronde, 1853. John Mix Stanley. Archives and Special Collections, Mansfield Library, University of Montana.

them the much needed supplies for their fall and winter hunt. . . . Not a Blanket, round of Amunition, Kettles[,] Knives or Tobacco did I have for them[;] neither could I get them." He went on to ask what the poor Flatheads had done to merit such treatment. He was put in the terrible situation of sending them off on their hunt, poor and destitute, without essential supplies.[5]

The Salish, with some of the Pend d'Oreille, headed to the Musselshell that fall. Another group of Pend d'Oreille traveled to the Milk River country, where tragedy struck in November. Their camp near the Three Buttes—the Sweetgrass Hills—was attacked by a large party of Crees and Assiniboines.[6] Many died at that sacred place. The Pend d'Oreille had just reached buffalo and were in fine spirits when the attack occurred, according to Michael Ogden, who was with the party. "On the Evening of the Night of the attack the tired Camp on bended Knees offered their thanks to almighty God for the prospect then before them."[7] Then Chief Alexander, assuming no attackers were nearby since the buffalo hadn't been spooked, told his people that this was the place they would get their winter's meat. Instead that very night they lost twenty warriors, including Alexander's twenty-year-old son, and five others died later from their wounds. Nearly three hundred horses were taken, leaving them destitute. Alexander saw his son's terribly mutilated body. Michael Ogden told Owen that the only reason any of them had been left alive was because the attackers, who had arrived on foot, were so keen to escape with the horses and all the booty. Salish war chief Insula and his family had been in that camp on the Milk River, and he was one of the many who died.[8] The Little Chief, recalled Father De Smet, "was universally loved and admired as a brave and as a Christian."[9] The missionary kept a portrait of him close at hand, in remembrance of this cherished friend.[10]

Owen had been at the Jocko Agency when Alexander's people straggled in and was shocked by what he saw. In a letter to Geary at the end of December, he reported that he witnessed women, with children on their backs, arriving utterly exhausted. They had walked some four hundred miles from the point on the battle site on the Milk River. Because they had lost their horses to their attackers, they had been forced to abandon virtually everything on the battlefield. They returned with nothing but what essentials they could carry. Owen reported that he had immediately ordered the Indian Department pack train from the Jocko to proceed to Fort Owen for supplies and provisions and issued the Salish four head of oxen for transportation.

Imagine the distress of the returning Salish hunters in late February 1861, when they found even more white men with cattle herds consuming the spring grasses in the heart of Salish lands. While they were away, a general store had been built at the west end of the Missoula Valley, near where the treaty council had been held four years before. The Indians knew the area as Grass Valley—a favorite place to graze their horses when they were returning from the buffalo plains. White settlers had been congregating there for several years. The newcomers called the fledgling agricultural community Hellgate. Christopher Higgins and Frank Worden were the shopkeepers. Higgins had first come to the area in 1853 as wagon master for Mullan's team of the Stevens survey crew. With that work completed, he served in the army as a captain, fighting Indians during the Plateau War. Worden had clerked for Governor Stevens in 1855 and eventually opened a general store at Walla

Walla. In October 1860 the two men pooled their resources and, with goods carried by a pack train of seventy-five animals, established the trading post at what was a traditional camp location.[11] These newcomers had selected the spot because of its situation at the crossing of two important trails and between two other trading posts—Fort Owen and Fort Connah—knowing they would have a steady stream of customers along the nearly completed Mullan Road.

Many things had changed since treaty ratification, some connected to that action and others only tangentially. Bannock horse thieves, instead of Blackfeet, were disturbing the sleep of both Indians and whites. The newly established Missoula County held its first meeting. This easternmost county of Washington Territory had been created in response to a petition in 1860 from seventy-seven white men living in the extensive valleys between the Continental and Bitterroot divides. Forty-eight of them were from Mullan's road crew, and the others were cattlemen and opportunists who had been drawn to the area.[12] The basis for their request was the two-day ride required to get to the county seat in Spokane. They needed more ready access to a sheriff and judge, in addition to some resources.

The new county commissioners devised the rules by which they would govern this vast area where Indians still dominated the landscape by nearly twenty to one. The population of the Salish in the Bitterroot at that time was reported at 90 families, totaling 548 individuals. The Pend d'Oreille on the reservation totaled 895 souls, consisting of 184 families, including 604 adults and 291 children. The Flathead agency had yet to get a count for the fifteen or twenty lodges of Kootenais on and around the reservation. Many more of them were in Canada, having chosen to move among their relatives there rather than be relegated to the reservation.

At that time one of the few white settlers at the east end of the Missoula Valley was William Hamilton, the Indian fighter turned government agent who had traveled through the valley in the fall of 1858. He had returned at the end of his mission and built himself a rude little cabin just west of the mouth of Rattlesnake Creek. In his memoir he tells that he set up a trading post at that place, but local memory tells that he peddled whiskey, not food or supplies.[13] In 1861 a majority of the voters elected Hamilton as county sheriff, a title that, in those days, simply attested to the fact that he knew how to use a gun.

Agent Owen distributed annuities through the camp when the hunters returned in the spring of 1861. This was the first distribution to the Salish since the treaty ratification. The annuities were inadequate to keep most Salish in the valley beyond the time of the bitterroot harvest. While some members of the community stayed to plant and tend their farms, many others, led by a forty-year-old sub-chief, Nganta, or Nine Pipes, headed east for buffalo bulls in late May. Five weeks later they returned by way of the Clark Fork, laden with meat. This time the hunters had with them three buffalo calves that they had captured in the vicinity of the Three Forks of the Missouri, fulfilling the desire expressed by Nine Pipes three years before. When Granville Stuart saw the Flatheads passing by with such a treasure, he jumped at the chance to have the calves. They cost him "three plew of beaver skins and four buffalo tongues."[14] That night a huge comet streaked across the northwestern sky. The Indians must have wondered what this sky messenger was announcing. Experience had taught them that such visitors were omens.

Hungry and Haunted

Most of the Salish left again in September 1861 for buffalo under the leadership of Chief Victor. For the first time since settling on Gold Creek in 1859, Granville Stuart was bothered by drunken Indians. He blamed the whiskey traders, rather than the Indians, and wished they would move on "to the Blackfoot country or to Hades."[15] The source of the whiskey might have been Sheriff Hamilton.[16]

At the start of October, John Owen purchased three hundred cattle for the hungry people on the Flathead Reservation. In a letter to Superintendent of Indian Affairs B. F. Kendall, Owen, who had no funds with which to make the purchase, defended his decision to buy the cattle for the Flathead Nation as "an investment of the Flathead Annuity . . . calculated to promote the true interests & Substantial Welfare of the Indians." He further justified the expenditure as a response to the Indians' desire and great need for such animals.[17] It would have been a good thing to take this risk if they weren't about to experience the worst winter in fifteen years.

The weather that winter was noted by Granville Stuart to be "of unprecedented severity," and the Indians suffered terribly. "They lost most of their horses and were unable to kill many buffalo, consequently, they were without meat and were in a starving condition."[18] The Blackfeet remembered it as that time "When We Ate Dogs."[19] Mullan and his bridge-building crew also suffered in their camp that winter at the mouth of the Big Blackfoot, known to the Salish as Nʔaycčstm, "Place of the Big Bull Trout," a traditional fishery. By mid-January 1862 John Owen recorded temperatures at Fort Owen ranging from a low as 37 below zero to a high of 18 below zero. Snow at Hell Gate was three feet deep. By early February nearly every one of the Indians' cows in the Bitterroot had perished in the midst of the calving season.[20] Livestock were struck hard throughout the region. Freeze-thaw cycles made travel close to impossible. Fort Owen was nearly surrounded with the water overflowing from Mill Creek. The creek had almost frozen solid, "leaving No Channel for the Water to flow through."[21]

To make matters worse, Bannock Indians continued stealing horses, and some of the incidents resulted in bloodshed. Granville Stuart witnessed a party of Bannocks pass by on February 5, followed by "Flatheads." The next morning the Bannocks returned "with two Flathead scalps and a band of horses." With so many Indians "prowling about," according to Stuart, settlers in the Deer Lodge Valley left their ranches for the safety of Cottonwood Creek Village (eventually to be known as Deer Lodge).[22]

John Owen was concerned as well. The few Flatheads who had returned from the hunt were "talking of going off on a War party" to retaliate for the recent murders. He did his best to convince them of the futility of seeking out such formidable rivals, but "revenge & an insatiable thirst to Meet an Enemy" drove them.[23]

It turned out that one of the scalps with which the Bannocks returned belonged to Little Faro. An Indian known as William, whose sister had also been killed, was the one to bring the news to the fort on February 12. Owen was concerned these killings would lead to serious consequences and wondered how it would affect the destitute Shoshones who sought shelter in the Bitterroot Valley near the fort. Prior to these events, he noted in his journal, the "Snakes and Bannocks . . . have been friendly & in the habit of Visiting this Valley."[24] William told Owen that he had left the Flathead camp on the Yellowstone River some sixty days before. As of that time, they had seen no buffalo except a few roving bulls. Chief Victor planned to move his camp to the Musselshell, where he hoped to locate a herd.[25]

In the middle of February at the fort, Owen noted that "fat cattle & horses were dying in groups of from 3 to 10 Every day."[26] He had his own horses moved up valley, where a few bald buttes had some exposed grass. By February 19 he had not received word from the Flathead camp in the buffalo country, and he worried that the winter had been too severe for them to save their horses. He learned that two "Snake Indians" had been killed about ten miles up the valley from the fort. He advised some extremely poor Shoshones, who lived along the mountain streams without lodges or horses, to leave before the Salish took their revenge on them. They refused. Some of them had been subsisting on scant supplies of fish, roots, and berries during the wintertime in their little camps for so many years that they felt safe to stay. For the past few winters Owen had regularly issued them beef and flour.

Toward the end of the month Granville Stuart reported that "Eneas, and Narcisses, the Flathead, went up to Cottonwood last night and found a Snake Indian named Peed-ge-gee camped near there." They killed him and took his lodge and belongings, including eight horses and one of his wives. Stuart explained that the usual custom would be for the captive wife to be handed off to the women of their tribe to essentially become their slave, "imposing all of the drudgery of the camp on her and making her life anything but a bed of roses."[27] Both Granville and his brother James were married to Shoshone women, and James felt great sympathy for the captive. The following day, with the help of a friend, he paid ransom for her and returned her to her family.

Finally, at the time of the vernal equinox, the first of the Salish began to return from buffalo. They had suffered terribly. Granville Stuart reported that "they lost most of their horses and were unable to kill many buffalo, consequently, they were without meat and were in a starving condition."[28] As the Salish struggled their way along the Clark Fork, downtrodden, famished, and weather-beaten, they must have been alarmed by the heaped mounds of soil beside new sluice boxes and the murky condition of the water that colored the river below Snx̣ʷq’ʷpuʔsáqs. The Stuart brothers took pride in their "little settlement at American Fork," which Granville described as having "the lively bustling appearance of a new placer camp." They had used a thousand feet of lumber for sluice boxes.[29]

When Victor's camp passed through on April 7, 1862, the Stuart brothers had a long talk with the chief about Indian affairs. Victor was upset about the Snake and Bannock men who had visited Johnny Grant's wives and had then stolen Salish horses. He wanted them gone. Granville argued that the request was unreasonable because so many tribes used the important travel corridor. He wrote in his journal that the "old chief is too arbitrary in insisting that the Snakes and Bannocks should be forbidden to spend the winter and hunt there the same as all others, because of little squabbles common to all tribes."[30] Perhaps he had trouble admitting to his own role in the escalation in violence, which was blamed on Grant's arrival, since he too had a Shoshone wife and visiting in-laws.

John Owen received news at the end of the month—about the time the thaw finally came—that Victor was returning despite "not having sufficient Meat." He also heard word of some difficulty with the Crows, as did Granville Stuart.[31] Waves of returning hunters—Salish, Spokane, and Pend d'Oreille—continued to slowly make their way down the Clark Fork.

Crawling Mountain (Moise) reached the Bitterroot on April 22 and told Owen that Victor's camp was close. He arrived two days later with "his poor ½ famished Weather beaten Village . . . after an absence of Some Nine Months in quest of Buffaloes."[32] They had lost many horses and some men as well and had barely managed to get back with so little, only to learn that most of their cattle had succumbed to the harsh conditions in the Bitterroot. The Nez Perce camp arrived a few days after Victor. Once Five Ravens (Ambrose) with his camp arrived on April 27, Owen reported that "the Indians had a great Dance over the Scalps of their Enemies &c."[33]

On several occasions at the end of June the Salish chiefs visited with their trusted friend and Indian Agent Owen. In early July Crawling Mountain, with Saxa as interpreter, headed to the Jocko to claim the cattle Owen had arranged for them to get from the Jocko Agency. They all struggled to imagine how they would survive in this new world.

It is ironic that while the Salish suffered, Father De Smet found himself longing for the life he had come to know with them. In a letter to a friend from his Belgian homeland, he wrote of some poorly understood longing for what he had experienced among Native people in the Rocky Mountains. "I always miss something when I am not among my good Indians," he wrote. "I am conscious of a certain void wherever I go, until I come back to my dear Rocky Mountains. Then calm comes back to me; then only am I happy. *Haec requies mea,*" he quoted from Psalm 131. "This is my resting place for ever; here will I dwell, for I have chosen it." Pierre-Jean De Smet, who had entrée to powerful men on two continents—who had met with a pope, a president, and scores of Indian leaders—concluded by saying, "After having passed a good share of my life among the Indians, it is among them that I desire to spend a few years that are left me still; it is among them also, if it be the will of God, that I desire to die."[34] The famous Black Robe, who never again returned to live among the people of the Bitterroot Valley, longed for something he could not name in that fast-disappearing world.

The Gold Nugget Road

For people who had been horrified by the way the priests had dug into the ground to create the foundations for their buildings, the world unfolding in the early 1860s was beyond their imagining. Dynamite had blown out the rockiest sections of the Mullan Road, just in time for feverish Euro-Americans to flood the area in search of their yellow nugget fix. With steamboats now able to travel all the way upriver to Fort Benton, it was as if the road had been constructed, and the boats made ready, just in time to bring the miners who would permanently change the face of the land.

Fort Benton had been aptly named after Thomas Hart Benton, the Missouri senator who was such a strong proponent of opening the West to whites. Benton, a close friend of Father De Smet, focused his legislation on the accomplishment of Manifest Destiny. He had strongly supported the boundary settlement with Britain and then set his sights on the Pacific Railroad surveys and the first Homestead Act, while others

FIG. 51. Fort Benton, 1863. Gustav Sohon. Archives and Special Collections, Mansfield Library, University of Montana.

worked out the plans for land-cession treaties. The eastern half of the country was already filling up as new Americans spread into lands empty of Indians since implementation of the Indian Removal Act. Although England is approximately the size of the state of Alabama, and almost the entirety of western Europe fits into the eastern half of the United States, the European immigrants in America wanted more.

Broadened pathways and bridges irrevocably changed the land, while men like New York publisher and one-time congressman Horace Greeley paved a sanctimonious social path with affirmation of Manifest Destiny, as decreed by God himself. "God has given the earth to those who will subdue and cultivate it," he wrote in 1860, cautioning readers not "to struggle against His righteous decree."[35]

The completion of the Mullan Road finally fulfilled President Jefferson's dream to connect a trade corridor between the headwaters of the Missouri with those of the Columbia and paved the way for the homesteaders who would soon have a chance to own their own piece of the West. The new road carried newcomers between Fort Benton and the Missoula Valley and on to Fort Walla Walla, along the old trail that Gabriel Prudhomme and Eneas the Iroquois had sketched out for Mullan less than a decade before.

The Stuart brothers were at the vanguard of the new kind of men to arrive after the fur trade. Generally the earlier arrivals had accepted things as they were. In contrast, the cattlemen and gold seekers who followed new roads into the region were men who had a vision of what they could create in this new land. Some of them stayed and became pillars of their communities. In more than a few cases the substance of their pillars came from robbing Indians—not robbing in the sense of mugging but something much more insidious. Through the manipulation of a legal system that leaned in their direction, they would manage to take from Montana's Indians nearly everything that mattered. The rug these men would pull out from under the Native people was the land itself. The losses came in fits and starts but always worked toward the single end imagined by Horace Greeley, John Winthrop, and John C. Calhoun: productive land would be transferred into the hands of those who would subdue and cultivate it.

The Salish had a sense of what was coming. Some of them had been to St. Louis and knew how white people massed together like bees in a hive. When Adolph and Saxa had traveled to Portland with Father De Smet, they had seen the varieties of horse-drawn carts and wagons for which roads had been built.[36] These Native people, for whom cycles defined their existence, had seen how white people built square houses in rows, one after another and one on top of another, and they had smelled the city stench of slop buckets, butcher shops, saloons, and concentrated horse dung. Even with these experiences, their travels could not have prepared them for what this ancient travel corridor would become. They could not have imagined their precious fishing sites at the mouths of tributaries obliterated by industry, nor could they imagine hillsides completely denuded of trees to satisfy the accelerated demands for fuel and construction that came with the white settlers.

A tipping point was reached in the spring of 1862. Forty-five emigrants were working at the Stuarts' mine by early July, with a steady stream coming in behind them. By the end of the month a white woman appeared, the young wife of one of the emigrant miners.[37] The Indians might have been fascinated by her dress and hair, unaware, though, of the changes these Euro-American women would bring. In just a few years they would be dancing in the New Year at Fort Owen, carrying with them the superior airs of people who know which fork to use at a dinner party. The first white women to settle in the region distinguished themselves from the "primitive" ways of the local Indian women by wearing clothing of cloth, not hide; wearing shoes, not moccasins; eating with utensils of metal, not wood and horn; and they taught their daughters to embroider, not to bead. It was the women's job to "civilize" their men and their children. Fraternizing with Indians would not be accepted by the vast majority of these newcomers.[38]

While the tribes of the interior Rocky Mountains struggled against so many pressures, Father De Smet continued to work on their behalf from his base at St. Louis. The renowned Black Robe visited President Lincoln at the White House that spring, hoping to gain much needed support for the western tribes.[39] Lincoln conveyed to him his concern, but both realized that he had all he could handle with the Civil War and all of its ramifications, along with the Homestead Act, which was making its way through Congress as one strategy to add to the national coffers. The situation was like the story about the Illinois farmer who started planting before his field was completely cleared; one stump remained with a hornet's nest in it. The president would have to tend to what was ready for planting that spring of 1862 and deal with the rest when he could. The Indians' troubles would have to wait until a later time, and that would come soon enough.

Shifting Sands

For the first time in years the fall buffalo hunt of 1862 wasn't led by Victor. Owen, worried about his physical condition, convinced him to stay back. He told the old chief he would have "a good Comfortable house to live in & a field to Sow & plant for himself." Owen bemoaned the fact that he could not convince more of the Salish to plant gardens and raise stock instead of risking their lives on the bison plains, where the battles continued between east- and west-side tribes as if no peace treaty had ever been negotiated. He knew not to waste his words for "they are Indians & Indians they will Ever remain."[40] Owen worried for all of them. There seemed little hope for them to be able to support themselves, even if all the Salish put their energy into farming. There had been two decades of farming since the priests had first arrived, and the food provided was a supplement but not close to a replacement for the foods they gathered and hunted through the course of the year.

In early October, when the Salish camp was preparing to leave for buffalo, Owen issued them one thousand rounds of "powder & Ball," along with about fifty pounds of tobacco. He also presented three mules to Chief Ambrose, who would be the hunt chief in Victor's absence.[41] This trusted leader, still known to his people as Five Ravens, was "tall and solidly built, with pleasantly proportioned features, a well-groomed appearance, and a quiet dignity of bearing that bespoke sincerity of purpose rather than vanity."[42] He was known for his courage, especially during the Five Days' Battle back in 1840.

Ambrose was probably concerned about a potential run-in with some two hundred Paiute Indians, led by old chief Winnemucca, who were reported to be around the Beaverhead Mines at Bannack. Granville Stuart initially reported them to be an "insolent treacherous band," but it turned out they were just hungry people simply looking for food. They too had weathered a terrible winter, along with persecution from white settlers in their homeland.[43] They went over to the Yellowstone to hunt buffalo and caused no trouble.[44] With more tribes coming into the Yellowstone Country in search of bison, intertribal conflicts were bound to increase.

White settlers too felt the pressure. In the Missoula Valley newcomers to Hellgate and the nearby community of Frenchtown took precautions. In the upper part of the Bitterroot Valley, some Shoshones stole horses and killed an occasional cow as winter set in. Owen noted in his journal on December 8, 1862, that a party of Salish headed out in pursuit of them. He hoped they would be caught and severely punished.

Owen resigned his position as agent, so frustrated and outraged was he at the state of things. "The Dept. at Washington know No more about the Management of the Indian tribe than the Indians do about the cause of the Present [Civil] War," he wrote in his journal in December.[45] So ingrained were these ways between whites and Natives, he had come to understand, that nothing significant would occur to change the sad trajectory. More explaining would just waste his ink.

On the first day of March 1863 messengers arrived at Fort Owen from the Salish camp on the Yellowstone to report on the tribe's starving conditions. Entries from Owen's journal provide some details. The Salish had seen no buffalo, could find no other game for their subsistence, and suffered sickness. Some had died. On top of everything else, Blackfeet horse thieves preyed upon their weakened situation. A month later the first wave of returning hunters straggled in. They reported that Palchina (Pelchimo) had lost seventy horses to Bannock raiders while camped on Flint Creek, where he had waited for the trail through Hell Gate Canyon to be better beaten. Chief Victor sent horses to relieve those left afoot. Word then came that Palchina and one other Salish man had been killed when they had gone after the horse thieves. John Owen had come to rely on courageous Palchina, "one of our best Indians," and was deeply saddened by this loss.[46]

At the same time Owen bemoaned the troubles for the Indians, he took delight in the emergence of the new settlements of Frenchtown and Hellgate. Father De Smet was also of two minds about the paradoxical scene unfolding in the mountain world he had come to love. He was full of concern and sorrow for "his Indians," but at the same time he was full of hope for the progress emerging in little mining towns and commercial hubs. Manifest Destiny was a given. The Jesuits had paved the way and softened the blow, but the consequences were now upon the people native to these lands.

11. Disillusionment and Despair in Salish Country

Hornet's Nest

The new Montana Territory's gold helped to fund the deficit as the Union continued the long fight of the Civil War. Just a decade after the treaty with the Blackfeet, the west-side tribes were competing for meat not only with other Indians but also with the exploding population of miners and other newcomers arriving each spring on steamers to Fort Benton. From there they headed for riches in the mines of the Missouri headwaters, the same lands as the Common Hunting Ground, guaranteed for ninety-nine years in the Lame Bull Treaty as a place where the Indian people could hunt.[1] The peace agreed to in that treaty had been broken before it was ratified. Lame Bull himself, the first chief to sign the agreement, died in battle within a year of the signing. By 1865, just three years after the gold rush had begun, some fifteen thousand miners were working and exploring in this former hunting sphere, seriously disrupting the natural world.

New diseases for which the Native people had no resistance came west with the miners. Scarlet fever killed more than one thousand Blackfeet the same year that "Montana" was named. There was to be no slowing of the westward-flowing stream of *suyapis*, bringing with them very different values along with diseases. The Lakotas called them *wasichu*—"Fat Stealers"—because they always took the best.[2]

While Indians looked upon white people and saw greed and disconnection, white people looked at Indians and saw inferior beings. Europeans and white Americans were advancing theories of intelligence on an evolutionary scale primarily based on cranial measurements. In 1862, as the Civil War crystallized the emerging social philosophy of scientific racism, the army established a medical museum as a place to collect skulls. Dark people were baser, closer to animals than those with light skin, according to this theory, and dehumanizing language—such as "bucks" and "squaws"—reinforced it. After the war soldiers brought these attitudes with them. They came west as Indian killers. It was the work of the nation. Yet the nation was shocked to see these attitudes made manifest on Sand Creek in Colorado on August 29, 1864, when some 230 peaceful, white-flag-waving Northern Cheyenne and Arapaho women, children, and old men became victims of these racist beliefs and the politics of extermination.

By 1865 whiskey dealing in western Montana had become epidemic, and food shortages caused Chief Victor to encourage his people to plow up some ground and get it planted. They visited the agency in late March to get plows and other supplies. Not only the Indians were hungry, but John Owen was as well. He reported on April 5 that the fort was "entirely out of Meat . . . for the first time in 15 Years."[3] The cattle herds remained depleted from the terrible winter four years before.

After nearly ten months away, the mobile village of Salish buffalo hunters began their return to the Bitterroot in mid-April, carrying with them little meat on very poor horses. They always aimed to be back to the Bitterroot in time for the bitterroot harvest, a spirit food gifted them in the mists of time during a time of starvation. That spring of 1865 John Owen welcomed the hunters back and enjoyed a visit from "the old Chief Moese with a much-appreciated present of buffalo tongues and a small sack of pemmican."[4] He understood the great generosity behind this gift, knowing how little meat they had.

The Salish had more to worry about than food. Forty places in the Bitterroot Valley had become home to trespassers who were grazing their horses in all the best pastures. These settlers were planting apple trees, fencing property, building ditches, and applying to the county for licenses to run ferries across tributaries. Chief Victor sent a letter to the new territorial governor, Sidney Edgerton, in April. The letter was accompanied by a delivery of five horses—four to replace some stolen by young Flatheads and another, a horse belonging to Victor, as a gift to the governor, "the Great Chief of the Whites." Five branded oxen were also delivered to replace some stolen below the

FIG. 52. The Flathead Agency. Peter Tofft. In Meagher, "Rides through Montana."

Marias and found, not stolen, by the Salish. These gifts were a preface to the real purpose of Victor's letter. He wanted Edgerton to prevent white families from building houses on Salish lands. The Indians felt despondent at the daily sights of newcomers in the Bitterroot Valley. He also asked the governor to order the whites in the valley not to sell whiskey to their young people. Their drunken fighting kept him awake at night and in despair, "seeing the whites compelling by force our boys and girls."[5]

Chief Victor might not have bothered with the letter had he known of the new governor's view of Indians. At the first meeting of the territorial legislature, Edgerton expressed his hope that "the government will . . . take steps for the extinguishment of the Indian titles in this territory, in order that our lands may be brought into market."[6] As the United States expanded its artificial constructs into the remote Rocky Mountains of the northwest and superimposed lines across lands that had always been defined by the contours of ridges and slopes and rivers, a new "we" entered this world that excluded the Indian as surely as did voting rights. "Our lands" in the new territory were white lands.

In an ironic twist reflective of the transformed sense of ownership, the newcomers in the Bitterroot Valley resented the return of the Indians, whose hungry horses were now competing for grass with those of the newcomers. The white settlers began to plot and strategize ways to get the Natives out of their way. They petitioned President Andrew Johnson to have them removed, and that was just the beginning.

On May 19, 1865, just a month after the hunters had returned, a recovered Victor and Moise led another group eastward for buffalo.[7] Along the way Salish hunters would have seen emigrants and pack trains "over Stocked with good[s] & whiskey & many things Selling for less than they can be bought in St Louis."[8] Home was hardly recognizable. Salish leaders prayed they could get their people safely and soberly across the mountains without trouble.

Soon after the hunters left, Owen realized he was missing four horses, and he feared they had been stolen by some of the Flatheads. "The Indians of the Flathead Nation once proverbial for their honesty are growing tricky & worthless," he wrote, adding that only "rigid & great punishment" will get them to change their ways. The old chiefs, he concluded, seem to have lost all influence over the young men.[9]

Challenges came fast and furiously that year. If hunger and alcohol troubles weren't bad enough, by early July the Bitterroot Valley was "alive with Grass hoppers." John Owen reported that these voracious insects denuded the valley of grass so thoroughly "as though it had been burnt off." He worried that nothing would be left to harvest and the stock would suffer from lack of feed.[10] What a great disappointment to lose the wheat crop when he had finally got his mill functioning.

Owen went down valley for a visit in mid-October and found a large sawmill was up and running in the new town of Missoula, brought about "through the Energy & Enterprising Spirits of Mess Wordin & Co." Worden and Higgins had relocated their enterprise from Hell Gate, at the west end of the valley, to take advantage of the waters of Rattlesnake Creek. These men were thriving. In addition to the sawmill, they had acquired the necessities for a flour mill and were building a storeroom, "shops & dwelling houses."[11] Granville Stuart visited on Christmas Day. Even though the thermometer registered 34 degrees below zero, he stopped to make a quick sketch of the new town.[12]

FIG. 53. Missoula Mills, Christmas Day, 1865. Granville Stuart. From Stuart, *Forty Years on the Frontier*, 1:163.

Chief Victor received no response from Governor Edgerton, who was rarely in the territory, so Victor wrote to Thomas Meagher, the acting territorial governor, who had arrived in September. Again the chief complained of violations of the Indians' rights by settlers.[13] Meagher's response, ultimately, was to pick up the banner of the new settlers and call for a modification of the treaty to allow for at least two-thirds of this land to "be thrown open to the whites."[14] A barrage of efforts to dislodge the Bitterroot Salish from their homeland was set into motion that would not end until the people were removed. The six decades of Salish kindness and generosity—when no weapon was ever raised against Euro-American explorers, traders, priests, or trespassers—seemed to mean nothing in the Territory of Montana. Resentment simmered. Had President Lincoln still been alive, he might have concluded that the new territory had a hornet's nest of its own.

Two Worlds Colliding

Citizens of Missoula County elected John Owen to serve in the territorial House of Representatives in 1866, giving him the opportunity to serve as a bridge between cultures, informing each side about the other in a way that suited his sensibilities. He had no shortage of issues and worries to consider. Food had been scarce in the Salish villages both on and off the reservation that winter. People at Fort Owen welcomed fish to their table since they had run out of meat in February. Although January had brought respite from the frigid temperatures of Christmastime, cold and deep snow returned and lasted well into March. The Salish buffalo hunters struggled their way home during this time, gratefully laden with dry meat from a good hunt but mourning the loss of several men from conflicts with both Blackfeet and Crows. They had also lost a number of horses, making difficult the return journey to the Bitterroot.[15] A new agent, Colonel Augustus Chapman, arrived from the East, completely unprepared for the weather, the people, and the way of life. After Owen's resignation, Indian agents came and went as quickly as the tempestuous winter storms.

By late April "legions" of small grasshoppers lay in wait, clustered in the grasses throughout the Bitterroot Valley, ready for a feast. They did enough damage to the wheat crop to result in small harvests for both the Indians and the occupants of Fort Owen. In mid-September many of the Salish left for their fall hunt. Those who remained in the valley went to the Jocko Agency (as the Flathead agency came to be known) at the end of the month to receive their annuities just after the death of Pend d'Oreille chief Alexander.[16] The new chief would be his son-in-law, Many Grizzlies, known to the whites as Michel.

By early October scant food supplies at Fort Owen had once again reduced occupants to eating fish and an occasional mallard. They had no beef and little grain.[17] Many of the older Salish found solace in the resurrection of St. Mary's. A new chapel designed by Father Ravalli was being built near the fort, at the edge of the new settlement of Stevensville. Ravalli and a fellow Italian Jesuit, Father Joseph Giorda, would serve both the white Catholics of the valley and the Indians, whose septuagenarian chiefs—Victor, Moise, Adolph, and Ambrose—remained devout.

Colonel Chapman didn't last the year. Although the agent had sold some agency goods for personal gain, the reason for his dismissal was more political than righteous. A number of the previous agents had done worse. In mid-December Acting Governor Meagher, who was also

FIG. 54. St. Mary's chapel and Victor's cabin, Stevensville. Rollin McKay, photographer. Archives and Special Collections, Mansfield Library, University of Montana.

superintendent of Indian affairs in Montana, replaced him with John Wells, a personal friend of President Johnson.[18]

New Year's Day, 1867, dawned bright and frigid. John Owen was delighted that the Indians who had remained in the valley, including Chief Victor, "made their usual time-honored Calls" to Fort Owen, offering a hearty handshake to all who were gathered there. The jovial trader marveled at the return of the old chief's good health and his astonishing agility. Owen described this elder, whose hair remained "Black as a coal," as one who could "jump upon the Back of his horse with as Much Sprightlyness as the youngest of his people."[19] Victor regaled guests from Philadelphia with stories of Lewis & Clark.

Once again for those who remained in the valley, fish got them through the winter. In early March Owen received sad news of a terrible skirmish between the Flatheads and the Blackfeet. The Flatheads lost several men, and the old chief, Crawling Mountain, had been shot clear through his body. Then terrible weather arrived as if it were December, and the deep cold lingered for two full weeks. Cattle died by the hundreds before the herds had had a chance to recover from the last disastrous winter.[20] The Indians still prayed, but it seemed like no one was listening.

In April Owen learned that "[Governor] Meagher was authorized by the War Department to raise & Equip 1000 Men."[21] Red Cloud's War made citizens around Bozeman concerned about Indian troubles spreading their way.[22] The Salish managed to avoid becoming embroiled and finally returned to the Bitterroot Valley in early May on skinny, run-down horses carrying little meat after an absence of eight months. The rumors of war had been true. Crawling Mountain had been shot but had survived. Owen found him "very feeble" and looking "as though he has had his last hunt on this Earth. Poor Man."[23] The brave and powerful Crawling Mountain had been brought to the edge of death's door in the escalating Indian wars on the buffalo plains.

On June 6, 1867, Agent Wells held council near Fort Owen with seven Salish leaders in a lodge bearing a U.S. flag. The Salish were represented by the two leading chiefs, Many Horses (Victor) and Five Ravens (Ambrose), and three war chiefs—Red Feather (Adolph); Red Night, whose baptismal name was Henry (pronounced "Arlee" by the Salish); and Red Coyote, known to the whites as Isaac. Also present for this important council was Bear Tracks.

Non-Indian attendees who joined Agent Wells included Napoleon Fitzstubbs ("Stubbs"), postmaster at Fort Connah; Judge Thomas M. Pomeroy; and Judge Jasper Rand, who was serving as a member of the fourth territorial council that year. The other three non-Indians to attend this gathering were close friends of the Salish: John Owen, Father Giorda, and HBC trader Angus McDonald. McDonald, long based at Fort Colville, had been visiting old friends among the Salish during the previous week. "Mac," whom the Salish called "Oops-chin," was a tall, good-looking man, "straight and slim."[24] "He had a dark complexion, with long jet black hair, reaching to the shoulders, and a thick, long and very black beard and moustache." His shirt and pants were of deer skin, and around his neck he wore a black silk handkerchief. He was known to prefer "Indian ways to those of civilization," and he often joined the Salish for their hunts.[25] According to Owen, the old Indians revered him, perhaps in part because he was such a gifted storyteller and he loved to sing and play his bagpipe. Imagine "the echoes from the mountains of the land of the Flathead-Salish of western Montana reiterated the rhythm of Salish chants, augmented by the melody from the 'bag that whistles,' as the Indians called the fascinating Scottish pipes."[26] He was always a good friend to them and could be counted on to provide reliable counsel.[27]

Agent Wells invited all present to exchange views. Over the course of two days Victor and Adolph spoke about the Stevens treaty, annuities, and Indian land titles while lamenting the intimidation they had experienced from white invaders in the Bitterroot and all along their trails to buffalo. The agent finally broached the subject of removal, the most contentious issue looming over them. The chiefs told him that "they would die rather than leave their homes" unless that directive came from the "Tyee at Washington."[28] They shouldn't have to move since they had never ceded these lands.

Wells was sympathetic. Based on what he heard from chiefs Victor and Adolph, he believed they would move with their people to the Jocko Reservation if the president requested them to do so. They understood that the president had this right, following an official survey and examination, if he determined the Jocko to be better suited for their needs. At least one other attendee at the council held different views.

The agent's sympathy for the Salish had stirred up the opposition, leading to a hatchet job of an article being printed in Helena and Virginia City's *Tri-Weekly Post* on June 15, under the penname "Union." The author reported that Agent Wells had not been clear about the most pressing issue of removal and had failed to address damages claimed against the Indians by white settlers for butchered cattle. Even more troubling, the agent had responded inappropriately to the Indians' concerns. Not only had he failed in the council, but the writer also alleged that Wells was incapable of performing his duties at the agency, adding that perhaps the reasons were that Wells was a heavy drinker who experienced occasional episodes of irrational behavior and didn't get along with the employees of the agency. The article concluded by announcing the council a farce and the agent "entirely unfit" for the job.[29]

Wells determined that Judge Pomeroy, the agency clerk, was the author "Union." Wells understood the clerk to be resentful because he had hoped to land the job of agent for himself. Wells blamed Pomeroy of stirring up trouble between Indians and whites in the Bitterroot, after years of peaceful coexistence, and using "overzealous newspaper correspondents" to further his aims. The agent challenged the judge to a duel for besmirching his reputation.[30] The duel never happened. Agent Wells turned his focus back on his duties and wrote to the commissioner of Indian affairs for permission to escort a delegation of Salish chiefs to Washington to clear up the matter of removal. The proposal was not accepted.

During these years after the Civil War larger forces than inadequate governmental support were affecting the Salish and all the other bison-hunting tribes. The first transcontinental railroad, the Union Pacific, was forcing its way through Lakota and Cheyenne Country, and along with it came the mass slaughter of bison. Declining numbers of this primary food source forced tribes to compete in ways that made the old days look like child's play. Life and death now hung in the balance of this diminishing equation.

On July 20, 1867, Congress authorized an Indian Peace Commission "to establish peace with certain hostile Indian tribes of the buffalo hunting nations." Four civilians and four military leaders were appointed to serve on the commission. The title "Peace Commission" was misleading, given that half of the commissioners were military men, warriors of the Civil War. Civil War general William Tecumseh Sherman, one of the members, advocated for the Plains tribes to be forced onto reservations, adding that those not in compliance be declared hostile and treated as enemies. "We must act with vindictive earnestness against the Sioux, even to their extermination, men, women and children," he wrote to President Grant.[31] Resistance was especially strong from the Lakotas and Cheyennes because of their proximity to the path of the railroad. The Salish and their neighbors were far enough removed not to feel the scorched-earth strategy of General Sherman, but they felt the domino effect of greater competition for the buffalo and increased military presence.

In mid-June, while grasshoppers again covered the ground, some of the Flatheads left for the camas grounds and others for buffalo. Owen could see that these age-old practices were what kept them going. With buffalo growing scarce and requiring such great effort to find, the Indians needed something that kept them "on the Move to Keep Soul & body up."[32] The drought continued. It was the driest season Owen had seen since coming into the country sixteen years before.

Some people had to stay back because they didn't have buffalo horses. Some had been lost to theft and others to exhaustion.[33] What horses they had were like magnets to newcomer Shoshones who were lurking around the valley that summer, waiting for their chance to ride off on fresh mounts. On the Fourth of July Owen's herder was shot at during one of the Shoshone raids. Even then the horse thieves didn't let up but continued raiding well into summer. Although the grasshopper infestation ended, crops suffered from lack of rain. Owen's journal entry on July 14 summed up his feelings with "Things look gloomy."

The personal attacks on Agent Wells escalated in August with interference by the newly elected Republican senator from California, Cornelius Cole. He charged that Wells was unfit to hold office not only because Wells didn't understand the Indians' nature but also because of his excessive drinking. The senator demanded the agent's immediate removal from office. One might wonder about the political shenanigans behind getting a California senator involved in this Flathead Indian agency situation. Whatever the backstory, Agent Wells, after only four months in the Indian service, had his reputation ruined by underhanded political manipulations. "Union" wrote another libelous article, this time to the *Montana Post,* in which he claimed that employees were bailing from the "perfect Babel" that the agency had become. He described collapsing buildings and the loss of crops from inattention.

Short-term territorial governor Green Clay Smith, from his base in Washington DC, suspended Wells and assigned W. J. McCormick, a Missoula land developer, to serve as a temporary special agent, while advocates stepped forward to help with Wells's defense. Fourteen agency employees signed a statement that Wells was a good agent and a capable farmer. Wells traveled to Virginia City to meet with Acting Governor Meagher and then set out for Washington DC to clear his name and the charges against him.

The summer hunt of 1867 was surprisingly successful after so many difficult years. The Salish hunters journeyed back to the Bitterroot feeling hopeful that they would survive another season. Along the way they might have passed Camp Baker, west of White Sulphur Springs, and wondered at the presence of mourning drapes. Thomas Meagher had fallen overboard and into the Missouri River under suspicious circumstances. The acting governor was dead.

By the time the Flatheads returned from their bull hunt, Special Agent McCormick had found the accusations against Wells to be false. He appeared to have been a good agent, well liked, "honest, thrifty, and industrious."[34] The agency buildings and crops were in good order. Rumors regarding liquor sales by Wells proved to have been falsely generated by men with their own eyes on agency positions.[35] Wells, on route to the nation's capital, was unaware of these findings.

Considering Options

Within days of the hunters return, the Flathead leaders held a council on the Lolo Fork, according to John Owen, who heard rumors of the gathering on August 20. Their purpose was "to take into Consideration the propriety of ordering the Whites to leave the Country &c." Owen dismissed the talk as "all Bosh." The Flatheads were apparently upset about the hanging of one of their young men for stealing horses the previous spring on the Gallatin.[36] Settlers in the Bitterroot Valley got wind of the Indian council and started amassing guns. Things really heated up when an unarmed Judge Rand, traveling to Fort Owen from Missoula on August 25, was shot at by a group of inebriated Indians somewhere near the mouth of Lolo Fork.[37]

Sometime that fall the Salish headed back on the long journey to the buffalo plains. Lodges were packed up, gear stowed in parfleche bags, and travois organized and hooked up to the horses, and once again, in a rhythm they knew like a lullaby, they headed out. This year, though, they carried an uncomfortable tension about what they would find when they returned to their beloved Bitterroot Valley. Relationships with white neighbors had devolved to such an extent that recovery might not be possible. Chief Victor, who had always made the effort to sustain good relations, was at a loss to know what to do.

Word reached Wells in Washington DC just before Christmas that the Flatheads were reported to be on the warpath. This was just one of many rumors about Indian confederacies aiming to drive white people out of their lands. Wells cautioned patience and requested support to return to the Flathead agency. The government failed to act on the request. John Wells, who had done his best as a public servant, was left adrift and penniless in the capital city of the nation he served.

Fort Owen celebrated New Year's Day, 1868, in traditional fashion with a visit from the Indians. Owen marveled at the mild weather during those first days of the year. An old-timer in the valley told him that "the three first days in January govern the remainder of the Winter." It seemed winter had decided not to come until January 4, when dense snow drifted in every direction, followed by a north wind and extreme cold that didn't let up for weeks. It was cold enough to cause grown chickens to "tumble over[,] frozen stiff in day time." Owen sat by his fire, keeping the ink and his fingers from freezing, to write about an issue he couldn't get off his mind. He sent a letter to the Hon. James M. Cavanaugh, the territory's lone delegate to Congress, concerning the troublesome issue of the removal of the Flathead Indians to the Jocko Reservation.[38]

During the third week of the difficult month, McCormick arrived with a sled-load of some very coarse flour, along with tobacco and flannel shirts and blankets he had purchased in Missoula for "the destitute ½ starved Inds."[39] Chief Victor, assisted by his interpreter Francis Saxa, was informed and would notify the Indians to gather on January 24 to receive the distribution. The people were very appreciative that the agent had gone to great trouble and expense to get these "Much Needed Stores" in the middle of winter. For two frigid days "hungry & half clothed Indians" crowded into the fort yard to receive these essentials.[40] Before McCormick returned to Missoula, he distributed flour and goods to some suffering Shoshone camped near the fort, as had Owen before him. The remainder of the flour was stored for future distributions. Owen, relieved for the Indians, couldn't help but worry about the growing competition from Missoula firms. His business was falling off, and his debts were mounting as he suffered through one year of drought after another.

FIG. 55. "Mission of St. Ignatius." Peter Tofft. In Meagher, "Rides through Montana."

When winter finally loosened its grip on February 10, 1868, Owen traveled to the Jocko Agency to get a sense of improvements there. This had been the longest cold spell he had seen during the eighteen years he had been in Montana. The whole year had been unusual. The past summer had been the driest he had known and the fall—"Yes Even up to Christmas"—had been the wettest. The predictable January thaw never came. Little snow had fallen during the deep cold, so the ground remained bare, making for easy travel to the agency.[41] At St. Ignatius Mission Owen caught up with the "Revd Fathers" and visited the new convent of the Sisters of Providence. He found their efforts to be very successful. Their fledgling school had "quite a Number of Scholars. Half Breed & Ind. Girls," who, to him, seemed cheerful.[42]

By the time Owen returned to the fort, the Indians were ready for another issue of flour. Chief Victor oversaw the distribution. Owen was intrigued to learn that Lompry was recovering from the near blindness he had been suffering for nearly two years. Both Dr. Baker from the agency and Father Ravalli from St. Mary's had treated him to no avail. More recently Lompry had been under the treatment of an Indian doctor and was improving. "Strange though true," Owen wrote in his journal.[43]

It was at this same time, in early March, that Chief Moise, Crawling Mountain, died after suffering through a year since he had been shot.[44]

On the day following the old chief's burial, Bitterroot Valley settlers in Stevensville met to discuss their rights. They prepared a petition that thirty lodges of non-farming Indians be removed to the Flathead Reservation. Twenty lodges of farming families should be allowed to remain. Removing the Indians, the petition argued, would be less expensive than moving the whites. The 170 residents who signed the petition claimed a population of 700 whites in the area, significantly more than the Salish. Although Owen signed the petition, he sent a letter to Indian Agent Wells in Washington DC the next day, "inquiring the Necessity of having the Valley throw[n] open" for settlement given that "the Flatheads will never leave of their own volition for the Jocko."[45]

The likelihood that Agent Wells ever received Owen's letter is slim. Word came to the Bitterroot Valley on April 16 that Wells had committed suicide. The distraught man had failed in his struggle to right himself after being thrown off kilter by dishonest, conniving opponents, while his wards continued their own struggle for survival under increasingly difficult circumstances.

The first wave of returning hunters appeared in the Bitterroot on March 19, 1868. Owen noted they had some meat, but their horses were in very poor condition. Although they had found bison closer than usual, they had suffered through several skirmishes with the Blackfeet. Everyone at the fort had hoped for the hunters' success, given their own shortage of meat. While they were gone, Nancy Owen kept her husband of a decade fed with "fine fresh trout." Owen updated Chief Ambrose on the meat shortage at Fort Owen and was assured that word would be carried to the village for people to bring some meat and tongues for trade. Owen gave him a bag of flour "in the Name of his Great Father." Ambrose returned two days later with twenty-five pounds of pemmican. Owen gratefully gave him some sugar in return.[46]

A Wide Divide

The New Moon of April—the Bitterroot Moon—was soon followed by swarming grasshoppers. Charlo and other perceptive Indians must have recognized similarities between these devouring creatures and some of the greedy newcomers clamoring for the removal of the Indians. In late May Territorial Representative Cavanaugh took advantage of the growing fear among white people caused by the Sioux-Cheyenne alliance (sometimes referred to as the Sioux War) and used his influence in the U.S. House of Representatives to shape attitudes with ugly racist words. "I like an Indian better dead than living," he told the assembly. "I have never in my life seen a good Indian—and I have seen thousands—except when I have seen a dead Indian."[47] It didn't matter to him—the only delegate from Montana Territory—that the tribes of western Montana were paragons of diplomacy and nonviolence.

Just before the summer solstice of 1868, the Black Robe most famous for peacemaking, Father De Smet, was called in by the Peace Commission to save the day. The federal government was desperate to get the Plains tribes to sign a new treaty at a second Fort Laramie council, but the powerful Hunkpapa Lakota leader Sitting Bull was refusing to attend. The government needed a miracle worker, and the sixty-seven-year-old Jesuit was the best bet. Despite his poor health, De Smet journeyed several days to reach Sitting Bull's camp on the Powder River in Montana, and there he was allowed to meet with the legendary war chief. The Belgian had walked into many an Indian village through the course of his years in the West, but this occasion must have caused the most trepidation. Maybe something in his steady gaze convinced people to trust him, or maybe Sitting Bull saw his ancestors' spirits there, assuring him that the old missionary could be trusted. Whatever the reason, Father De Smet somehow convinced Sitting Bull to send delegates on his behalf to the Fort Laramie treaty council, giving a nod to the possibility of peace.

Good news finally came in August. The harvest of barley and peas was the best the people had ever seen at Fort Owen. Things were looking up. Owen barely had time to keep up with correspondence now that the fort was receiving tri-weekly mail. Things took a terrible turn, however, when Nancy Owen suffered what must have been a stroke that left her partially paralyzed and unable to speak. Her doting husband tended to her like a nursemaid. Then cold weather surprised them at the end of the month and dashed all hope for preserving food for winter. Heavy frost killed the tomatoes, although they had been covered, and it even destroyed the more weather-resistant crops like cabbage. Even the wheat crop was damaged. Owen concluded that the Bitterroot Valley was no place for farming.

During the dog days of September, Salish leaders knew they must be more proactive in protecting their rights to the Bitterroot Valley. The Indians held a council to discuss how best to respond to threats to their lifeway.[48] Chief Victor delivered a message for Owen to carry to William J. Cullen, the new superintendent of Indian affairs. For the first time this position was made separate from the governorship. Victor's visit was prompted by the removal petition and by Salish concern about a road through the Bitterroot recently approved by the Missoula County commissioners.[49] The chief's message voiced strong opposition to leaving the Bitterroot Valley. These homelands had been set aside for the Flathead tribes by the Stevens treaty, and the white men who had settled in the valley and made improvements there had done so in defiance of that treaty.[50]

Chief Victor must have been aware of an impending meeting with Cullen and various other governmental representatives when he gave Owen the message. He wanted them to know his stance before they gathered. Four days later Owen returned from Missoula with Cullen and the new acting governor, James Tufts, along with two employees of the Jocko Agency, Francis Blake and Judge Pomeroy (the infamous journalist "Union"), and unnamed others to whom Owen referred as friends. The group met with the Indians and discussed the difficult situation in the valley. Although Victor attended, sub-chief Ambrose (Five Ravens) served as their spokesman. He began by voicing concern about the planned road improvements. He then offered a surprising proposal. Perhaps they should all consider the possibility that the more isolated part of the upper Bitterroot Valley might be better suited for their reservation.[51]

Nancy Owen had seemed better, but her condition worsened in mid-September. In the early afternoon of September 24, 1868, she lost consciousness. A few hours later, surrounded by her Shoshone friends, she "quietly & peaceably relinquished all that was Mortal. . . . Poor Woman She is No More."[52] After two decades together, John Owen lost his beloved wife. He hardly had time to be lonely, though, with visitors passing through almost daily. The traditional homeland of the Salish, once so quiet and so Indian, had exploded with white people. The Indians began leaving for buffalo on September 22, led by Five Ravens. Many Horses, feeling his advanced age, stayed in the Bitterroot in the cabin Owen had built for him and his family, close to the fort.

M. M. McCauley, a personal friend of Territorial Representative Cavanaugh, arrived in October to replace Agent Wells, after a seven-month vacancy in the office. This was the same month that war broke out on the buffalo plains despite the efforts of Father De Smet and the Indian Peace Commission. Chief Victor and company traveled to the agency to monitor the distribution of annuities. They might have traveled along the new wagon road being constructed along the right bank of the Bitterroot River, now known as the Eastside Highway. Owen, a lifelong Democrat, was distressed to learn of the election of Ulysses S. Grant as president. Adjusting to life on his own, he left the fort for Missoula on Christmas Day and didn't return until the spring equinox. Duncan McDonald (the son of Angus), who had become clerk at Fort Connah, accompanied him back to the Bitterroot to trade for furs with the Indians.

Five Ravens and the Salish hunters returned to the Bitterroot around the same time as Owen, at the end of March 1869. Once again they carried little meat and returned with exhausted, broken-down horses. In the decade following treaty ratification, hunger had become a steady companion. They had lived through grasshopper plagues, drought, harsh winters, and poor hunts, and the government wasn't holding up its end of the bargain. The Salish were not receiving the help promised by treaty to transition to a more reliable economy. The chiefs felt a great burden as they watched their people suffer. Doing their best to help those in need, they ended up with the least.

In April Owen received a response from a letter he had written in late November to his "old friend" Lieutennent General Phil Sheridan, who would become one of the most hated men known to the bison hunting tribes.[53] Owen must have met Sheridan when they were both involved in the Yakama War on the Columbia Plateau in 1857. Sheridan seems an odd choice of friend for Owen, given his reputation in Indian Country. The Civil War veteran was allied with Major General Sherman and agreed with his policies of extermination. In 1869, when Sherman moved to the top of the ranks, Sheridan took over command of the Great Plains and continued to implement Sherman's strategy to eradicate the food source of the Plains tribes. Phil Sheridan has been attributed with coining the saying "The only good Indian is a dead Indian."

Father Ravalli visited Owen on April 27, 1869, to discuss the growing tension in the valley. This Jesuit, who had first arrived in 1844, was one of the few white men with whom the Indians had a long-term relationship. The Salish trusted these two men, Owen and Ravalli, as confidantes during these times of tumultuous change. In contrast, no government official stayed long enough or cared sufficiently for the Salish to be relied upon. They had watched a steady flow of changing Indian agents, governors, acting governors, and superintendents, the newest of which arrived that month.

General Alfred Sully, the son of a portrait painter from Philadelphia, was a West Point graduate who had fought Indians in Florida, California, and then the Great Plains before he arrived in western Montana. He was appointed superintendent under a new policy of the Grant administration. Drawing on the tide-shifting recommendations of the recently concluded Peace Commission, Grant replaced civilians in the Indian service with military appointees.

Regarding official relations with the Indians, the Peace Commission recommended that the United States no longer recognize tribes as sovereign nations and that all Indians be relegated to reservations. Instead of making treaties with them, the federal government should dictate the particulars and send in the military against those who refused to relocate. Of course these changes wouldn't make their way into the lives of Indian tribes immediately or in one swoop. They would come like a freezing river, where the ice slowly expands to the point where it drives the flooding waters through the villages, like Burnt Fork had done a few years before. For the Bitterroot Salish this time would come in a few short years with the arrival of James Garfield in 1872 but wouldn't climax for more than twenty years.

Victor understood that although their problems were taking place in what the white people considered the Territory of Montana, the solutions would have to come from the Great Father in Washington. He had tried to go there to meet him, without success. He would try again.

In early May the old chief conscripted John Owen to prepare a letter to Ely S. Parker, an Iroquois of the Seneca Nation who was Grant's commissioner of Indian affairs. He wanted Parker to understand the serious problems faced by the Salish. Owen started the letter by noting, "Scarcely a day passes without some of them [the Flathead Nation] visiting me to know what their great American Father has done regarding the lands of this valley." Victor had Owen tell Parker of the rapid turnover of Indian agents since 1862, when Owen had resigned. In the seven intervening years six agents had passed through. Owen explained that the Salish were challenged beyond their capacity and needed the government to come to their aid. Liquor had become a terrible problem that the chief wanted stopped. "The country [is] being filled up with white men [who] have driven the buffalo off," he explained. "They are not close or plenty as they were before the white man came among us to hunt for gold which they seem to love so much. We must farm or starve." He closed his letter with a plea: "May my words reach your heart. . . . Please hear us and help us."[54]

Many Horses joined his people on the spring buffalo hunt. They left on the last day of May, after the women had finished the bitterroot harvest and packed the dried roots away. It was a good thing that most of the community had gone on the hunt, for farming conditions in the Bitterroot Valley were as bad as Owen had ever seen them. Even areas usually moist were completely dry by the end of June after a killing frost had already ruined the corn and potatoes. Food was scarce. All residents, Indian and white, scoured the hills and small valleys for whatever four-legged food they could find. Both John Owen and Granville Stuart often reported on the impressive numbers of fish, ducks, deer, and occasionally antelope that their neighbors had bagged. Whether the hunts were driven by hunger or sport mattered not to the critters. Their numbers were plummeting. The Montana territorial legislature enacted the first game bird hunting laws in 1869 by establishing a restricted season. Otherwise hunters could shoot as many deer, sheep, antelope, goats, or moose as they liked whenever they liked.

Serious troubles were brewing at the Jocko Agency, just in time for the new agent to step into the mess. A. S. Galbreath, a brevet major for the U.S. Army, was appointed to replace McCauley. He arrived about the time of a nearly total solar eclipse along with a fire that destroyed the agency mills, barn, and stables. The new agent wrote to General Sully to explain the circumstances of the fire—actually two fires. Galbreath had been told that the first one originated when an Indian boy who was fishing in the Jocko made a fire to cook his meal and the flames got away into the tall grass. The second fire, however, had to have been started, intentionally or carelessly, by someone smoking in one of the buildings. Many rumors were flying about, including one in which some Indians were blamed for intentionally setting the fire as an expression of their dissatisfaction with a recent governmental decision to assign army officers rather than civilians to serve in the Indian Department.[55]

General Sully assessed the Indian situation and, in a report to Commissioner Parker written on August 3, 1869, recommended an increase of military force to prevent serious difficulties. His concern came from escalating incursions of war parties from all directions—Powder River country to the southeast, "British possessions" to the north, and Washington Territory to the west. These Indians often "commit depredations on the whites." He made an exaggerated estimate of as many as sixty thousand Indians—men, women, and children—in Montana Territory, at least on occasion, while he had fewer than four hundred troops available. In the report Sully included a description of a certain white element that, "from its rowdy and lawless character, cannot be excelled in any section, and the traffic in whisky with Indians in this Territory is carried on to an alarming extent." He told of one recent cowardly murder of two Piegans—a "harmless old man" and a boy barely in his teens—that had occurred in broad daylight on the streets of Fort Benton. He intended to arrest those responsible but doubted they would be convicted in any court. So common were these hostilities that General Sully was surprised that "open war with the Indians" had not yet erupted.[56] The civil authorities openly acknowledged their inability to act. Only with the power of military force, the general concluded, could the situation be reversed and lawful order be restored.

With the ink of Sully's report not yet as dry as the parched earth of that summer, tension erupted on the east side of the mountains. On August 13 the front-page headline of the *New North-West* was "Indians on the War Path." News had reached the Deer Lodge weekly newspaper from Fort Benton that on August 8 about 150 Blackfeet had attacked an ox train on Eagle Creek, near the mouth of the Judith River. Two Indians had been killed. The location was only twenty miles from Camp Cooke, an army post established three years before.[57] General Sully quickly responded that the Blackfeet should be considered to be in a state of war. In addition to the wagon train attack, horse thieving had exploded. Then on the morning of August 18, twenty-five miles from Helena, a ranch was attacked, and two men were shot, one of whom was Malcolm Clarke, an influential and politically powerful pioneer. Miners, cattlemen, and sutlers—all—were ill at ease in this unpredictable world, and they demanded that something be done. General Sherman would investigate, and the debt would be paid, not by the perpetrators but by hundreds of innocent Indians.

12. The Shrinking World

A New Voice with a Bullhorn

Life in Montana Territory during the first half of the 1860s is known only through glimpses that found their way into the historical record. The journals, letters, and reports of John Owen and Granville Stuart, along with reports of Indian agents, compose the bulk of information for lands west of the Continental Divide that became known as Missoula County. Beginning in 1864, the first newspapers in the state served the mining towns of Virginia City and Helena. Only on rare occasion did these papers address events occurring in the valleys west of the Divide. The weekly *New North-West* published its first issue in Deer Lodge in the summer of 1869, and it soon became a force that both shaped and reflected the world around it. Like a village crier with a bullhorn, it initiated "group think" for literate people throughout western Montana.

The introduction of newspapers marks the time when Montana history shifted from stories of white men in Indian Country, like Lewis and Clark, Father De Smet, and John Mullan, with all the fascination that came through encounters of white men and Indians, to the stories of men founding towns and the suppression of hostile Indians. Reconciling these two kinds of stories and incorporating Native histories from the points of view of the Natives is not a simple task, but finding a bridge between the stories is essential if our history is to serve truth. It was at this juncture in Montana history that the honorable and generous Salish were colored with a different brush. For those who wanted their lands, they became the enemy.

Headlines in the August 20, 1869, issue of the *New North-West* summarized the themes of the day from the perspective of white settlers:

"The Destruction of Timber" addressed impacts of massive fires; "Indian Troubles" alerted readers to travesties committed by Indians east of the mountains; "Another Indian Outrage" told of the murder of Malcolm Clarke; "Trouting" told of a fishing and hunting excursion to Lost Creek (now a state park near Anaconda) when six men brought in 526 trout in one day; and, perhaps, the most important headline, "RAIN, at Last!" From the paper locals could learn the news carried by buffalo-hunting tribes as they traveled along the Clark Fork. When a party of Nez Perce passed through Deer Lodge on return from a productive buffalo hunt, local citizens were told "Heap Sioux on Yellowstone."[1]

That fall the paper ran its first of many articles on the trouble brewing in the Bitterroot Valley. The September 24 edition posted a copy of a letter report to General Sully from a group of Bitterroot Valley citizens under the caption "The Bitterroot Troubles." These white settlers had met twice to consider recent issues concerning "the proposed expulsion of the whites from the valley, and to protest against it to the authorities." They claimed that when "whites first came into the valley, the Indian Agents advised them to settle and the Indian chiefs made no objection, so that they felt fully warranted in supposing their rights and titles would never be disputed." Bitterroot Valley citizens behind the letter reported that they had fenced 4,900 acres, with 2,900 of them cultivated. They had 1,500 horses and cattle and had raised 21,900 bushels of grain that year. In good faith they had "improved their farms, placing good and substantial fences and costly buildings upon them, at considerable outlay of money and years of labor." They had built schoolhouses, flouring mills, and sawmills and had improved highways. Their town of Stevensville, at the former Salish village site of Place of Wide Cottonwoods, touted stores, saloons, a hotel, and a post office, and it served as a center where folks could find a butcher, blacksmith, and a carpenter. They paid "taxes regularly and cheerfully" and had collected ample funds to support a school and the poor.[2]

Such impressive facts led to the main point of the letter: these 175 white settlers in twenty-five families should be allowed to stay put, especially because such a "small number" of Indians would "be given" the valley, and they already had an "ample reservation elsewhere." The authors of the letter asked General Sully to use his "influence with the proper authorities" on their behalf, to the end that they "may retain undisputed possession of . . . homes and property."[3]

On the same page as the Bitterroot Valley letter, the *New North-West* presented its own editorialized view of the situation, beginning with its slant on the 1855 treaty. In the editor's view, instead of recognizing the cession of millions of acres by the Indians, the Hellgate Treaty with the Salish, Kootenai, and Pend d'Oreille granted them a reservation of five thousand square miles—"a little State in itself." In fact the reservation was less than two thousand square miles, totaling about 1.25 million acres of the more than 20 million acres of their original homeland. The paper continued with a twisted version of the facts, claiming that the Indians had been content with these arrangements while they were in the council, but before signing the treaty, the Flatheads had insisted on "a monstrous folly" in the form of "an additional special reservation in the Bitter Root Valley." Now, "for some reason or other," the Indians wanted to dispossess whites and "drive them out homeless and in want" from the lands "they have wrested from the wild." Expelling these farmers, they claimed, "would cap the climax of outrageous follies and crimes perpetrated by the government upon its pioneers under the mistaken idea of philanthropy and the advice of ignorant or designing parties." Beyond their own protection, the editor proposed, all occupants of the valley—red and white—should gain clear titles to their improved lands. The paper ignored the fact that the Salish, by treaty, had rights to all the Bitterroot Valley and therefore had no need for clear title. "If these Indians are peaceable and industrious," the editor continued, "protect them in their home. No one will be injured or complain." However, for the government to evict the families of industrious pioneers in favor of "rovers," "is the perpetration of a diabolism a fiend would grin at." In his hyperbolic conclusion, the forward-thinking businessman/editor reminds the governor and general not to recommend the removal of whites from the Bitterroot Valley and thereby avoid "establishing as a valley of barbarism one of the finest garden spots on the line of the Northern Pacific Railroad."[4]

Who could honestly use the term "barbarism" in connection with the Salish? One can almost see the Deer Lodge boosters rubbing their hands together and licking their lips as they thought about the riches that would come with the railroad—as long as the Indians didn't ruin everything for them. In a more just world, someone would have written a companion piece about the good fortune of the white settlers of western Montana to be sharing land among such peace-loving and generous Indians.

Efforts by whites to justify their claims on Bitterroot Valley lands were based in arguments that the chiefs and the agents had let them stay, thereby overriding the treaty. In the early days Chief Victor had in fact allowed some white men to stay to help protect his people from Blackfeet raids, just as he had always welcomed new men into their shrinking tribe. Owen, in 1859, had allowed a Mormon trader and his non-Salish Indian wife to graze their stock in the valley, then corrected his error the following winter by denying them permission to continue the practice because they were trespassing on Indian lands.[5] The treaty had been ratified, and the Indians resented other animals consuming the feed needed by their hungry horses and cattle. The arrival of white families in the 1860s brought entirely new considerations for the Indians. These people were not there to become friends and neighbors with the Salish, as had been earlier arrivals, and their view of what the valley should become was not one shared by the people who had been cared for by these lands since Coyote had slayed the monsters.

The next issue of *New North-West*, in October 1869, continued the harangue. It focused on attempting to discredit Article XI of the Hellgate Treaty, which kept the Bitterroot homeland out of the land-cession agreement until such time that the president made a decision regarding the better option for the Salish—the Bitterroot or the Jocko. Governor Stevens had not intended "to give them the entire country," readers were told, but rather he was only compelled to do so "by the perversity of the dissatisfied chiefs to make this eleventh article."[6] The "few Flatheads," who balked at removal from their homeland, the article claimed, were responsible for the current difficulties. Of course Chief Victor was the leader of the Salish at that time, when they believed they were going to a council focused on peaceful relations with the Blackfeet. Instead they found themselves blindsided by Governor Stevens with a land-cession treaty.

The news article presented the current situation as a choice between a return to barbarism or the opportunity for the land to be officially opened to settlement and civilization. Essentially these representatives of the white farmers, most of whom had arrived within the last five years, were outraged that such industrious members of society might be evicted from lands they occupied—despite ownership limbo—while feeling great disdain for the Salish people who stood in their way. The same edition noted above extols the probable coming of the Northern Pacific Railroad (NPRR) and reports on mine expansion between Gold Creek and Racetrack Creek in the Deer Lodge Valley. The white people had arrived in a land of phenomenal potential, if only the Indians would get out of the way.

General Sully, as superintendent of Indian affairs for Montana, arrived in the Bitterroot Valley in early October 1869 to see for himself what was at issue. He held a council with the Indians, represented by Victor, Arlee, and sub-chief Nine Pipes (known as Joseph Nganta to the whites). Arlee had stepped into this leadership position a year earlier, after the death of Ambrose (Five Ravens), who had been second chief since the death of Crawling Mountain in 1868.[7]

Sully submitted a proposition for them to consider.[8] Based on his assessment of the situation on the Flathead Reservation, Sully understood that troubles would continue to escalate if the Indians continued to experience hunger and the agency continued to malfunction. The government needed to make good on the treaty. In a letter to Commissioner Parker, echoing recommendations made by former agent Wells, he urged the establishment of a military post close to Missoula from which whiskey peddling could be brought under control and trouble-making Indians of Washington Territory could be kept out of Montana.[9]

During his negotiations General Sully offered generous terms for the Salish to relocate to the Jocko, but they refused. He then proposed a smaller reservation for them in the upper Bitterroot Valley, as Ambrose had suggested, but this they also refused. The agreement signed on October 7, 1869, between the Flathead representatives and Sully permitted both Indians and whites to remain in the valley. The Salish leaders must have had some eye-rolling moments when they heard essentially the same promises that had been made in 1855 but never honored.

Article I of this agreement detailed lands to be ceded by the Flatheads above Willow Creek—essentially all lands in the upper valley beyond where Corvallis sits today. This agreement reduced the size of their reserved lands by approximately two-thirds. Article II prevented further white settlement within the revised reservation boundaries unless permitted by chiefs and their agent. Existing settlers could remain but could not acquire more land without permission. Problems between Indians and whites would be mediated by the superintendent of Indian affairs of Montana and the agent. Article III guaranteed white settlers a right-of-way through the reservation. Indians retained their inherent rights, as protected in the Stevens treaty, to hunt, fish, and gather anywhere on the reservation that was not fenced. Unfenced land was to be used as common grazing land. Article IV addressed monetary restitution methods.

The next three articles addressed what the Indians would receive and what they would relinquish. Under Article V each Indian family would receive a wooden house valued at no more than $400, along with a fenced farm area of two acres, a good plow, and a yoke of oxen; every two families would receive a farm wagon. Article VI promised the erection of a grist mill plus necessary repairs for a period of twelve years. During these years employees at the reservation would include a miller, physician, engineer, blacksmith, and suitable agent. Article VII required the Flatheads to relinquish rights under the Stevens treaty except for the annuities.

Article VIII, requested by the Flathead chiefs, protected John and Nancy Owen's land sections, which had been obtained under the Oregon Territory Donation Act of 1850, and the priests at St. Mary's Mission would be provided 640 acres to support the church.

General Sully returned to his office in Helena, where, on October 24, he wrote to Commissioner Parker recommending the building of a new saw and grist mill and barn on the Flathead Reservation, to replace the ones destroyed by fire in early August. Instead of rebuilding them in the Jocko Valley, though, he suggested that they be built in the Mission Valley, which would become the new location for the agency because that was where all the Pend d'Oreille and many Kootenais lived and farmed. General Sully understood the importance of getting the agency back in "good working order" so as to convince at least some of the Salish to move to the reservation.

Sully remained apprehensive about fallout from this agreement, knowing of the degenerating attitudes of whites toward Indians. The Sioux War was in full swing, and Blackfeet, Bannock, and Shoshone horse thieves threatened even the recesses of the Bitterroot Valley. Many white settlers wanted the Indians entirely removed to the Flathead Reservation as a necessary precursor to Bitterroot Valley lands being declared open for homesteading. They didn't intend to continue living on an Indian reservation with all its limitations. Sully's fears were well founded. White settlers kicked into gear shortly after the treaty terms were made public.

Little Food to Dig or Snare

General Sully's attempt to respect both sides of the Bitterroot dilemma—by honoring the treaty while at the same time acknowledging the investments made by white settlers—initiated a force like a cannonball wafting through the air, too mobilized to fall short of its goal. The idea that white settlers in the Bitterroot Valley would have to continue to live on Indian lands was completely unacceptable. Sully's proposal unleashed the same forces that had driven Manifest Destiny—the pent-up desire for more and the rationale for making it happen.

The *New North-West* expressed outrage over the newly proposed Bitter Root Reserve, which, it observed, was to remain in the possession of the undeserving Salish, whom it accused of having acted "with the usual Indian treachery" in their refusal to sign the Stevens treaty back in 1855. The paper overestimated the number of white farmers and underestimated by a third the Indian population in the valley. It described the Salish people as "a band of mongrels . . . bucks, squaws, papooses and dogs." Given Sully's "evil deed," it concluded, good citizens needed to exercise their "imperative duty" to denounce the treaty and to bring whatever influence they may have to prevent ratification by the Senate.[10]

Other papers echoed the same sentiments. The *Helena Daily Herald* described the Bitterroot Salish as "vagabond relics of various tribes of Montana known as Flatheads."[11] If Missoula had been publishing a paper in 1869, its voice against the Sully agreement likely would have been the loudest. Missoula entrepreneurs were already eyeing opportunities on the remaining home turf of the Salish.

In October 1869 white settlers in the Bitterroot met to discuss their options, then sent a letter to President Ulysses S. Grant requesting that the Flatheads—at least the non-farming ones—be removed from the valley. A commentary in *New North-West* addressed the "baleful treaty" made with "the miserable squad of squalid savages styled the Flat Head tribe of Indians."[12] A few weeks later the paper ran a letter from "Old Stone" of Missoula, in which the author noted that those settlers "working like beavers to defeat the Sully Treaty" expected help from Deer Lodge neighbors who received "half of their produce from Bitter Root farms."[13]

Meanwhile, the Jocko Reservation had troubles of its own. Agent Galbreath deplored the state of conditions at the agency and throughout the reservation. He wrote to General Sully in late November to report the destitute condition of the Kootenais and Pend d'Oreille, who had little meat and no ammunition to acquire it. The agent had denied them (and the Salish) ammunition because of all the trouble in the region. Whites were reporting depredations, primarily in the form of horse stealing. Galbreath concluded that the reservation Indians would be less hungry and therefore less apt to be causing trouble if they received necessary support. In response to the agent's letter, Sully ordered twenty thousand pounds of flour for the Indians, some of which Galbreath issued to the Bitterroot Salish, along with blankets on a day in mid-December that was cold enough for the Fort Owen mill to freeze up.[14]

The year 1869 had been terrible for everyone in western Montana but particularly for the Indians, who truly faced famine. A killing frost had been followed by drought, and the Salish found few buffalo on their hunts, leaving them hungry going into winter. Sickness stalked them. Grief was no stranger, and death came through many doors. Charlo and his wife, Margarite, like so many of their people, lost a child that winter, a four-year-old daughter. For parents, the terrible grief for these lost children was compounded by the fear of a future without their people in it. They were forsaken by the buffalo and by the greed that surrounded them like the waters of an epochal flood.

With construction of the transcontinental railroad reaching completion, the plains were being emptied of buffalo. Bison-focused Indians in the northwestern plains, converging from all directions, found themselves competing for the diminishing herds. The end of the ancient ways was visible on the near horizon. Soon there would not be enough buffalo to feed the people.

The railroad hadn't killed the shaggy beasts. The intended annihilation of the American bison can, instead, be laid at the feet of President Grant's general-in-chief of the U.S. Army, William Tecumseh Sherman, who focused his attention on exterminating buffalo so that the Indians would have no choice but to become dependent on the government for help. He told Lieutennent General Philip Sheridan, who had become military commander for all lands from the Mississippi to the Rocky Mountains, that "it would be wise to invite all the sportsmen of England and America . . . for a Grand Buffalo Hunt, and make one grand sweep of them all."[15] Sherman and Sheridan conscripted Buffalo Bill Cody to assist in such a spectacle, and their efforts were wildly successful. In a period of one and a half years in 1867 and 1868, Cody, on his own, is reported to have killed more than four thousand buffalo.

The slaughter was keenly felt by all Native people throughout buffalo country, regardless of whether they were friends or foes of the U.S. government. By January 1870 decreases in all quadruped populations were significant enough to prompt Granville Stuart to address these changes from the perspective of one decade in the Deer Lodge Valley in an article carried by the *New North-West*. "Game, once so abundant," he wrote, "is now almost exterminated, there being few deer, mountain sheep or antelope remaining." He added that "a few white Rocky Mountain Goats" could still be found on the most inaccessible peaks and that elk managed to survive "in considerable numbers in the densely timbered mountains, where are also a few bison, but all have learned to avoid the hunter."[16]

End of an Era

Bone-chilling cold continued into the new year, with temperatures reaching 38 degrees below zero. *New North-West* advertised for twenty-five thousand miners to come to the diggings in the upper Clark Fork basin. Late in January, at a time when smallpox was killing Blackfeet and Bloods on the Marias at a rate of about seven per day, the paper reported on a military attack on one Blackfeet camp—in a case of random retaliation for Malcolm Clark's murder—later to be known as the Baker Massacre (named after the colonel in charge).[17] In its next issue *New North-West* printed a related letter in which R. D. Leggatt and J. Anderson from Red Mountain City, a mining camp southwest of Helena, congratulated Colonel Baker on a job well done.

For those in western Montana the Baker Massacre was of less interest than the news they had received a week before that the Flathead Removal Bill had passed through Congress. The Flatheads became aware of this impending disaster when they returned from their winter buffalo hunt. Instead of a ratified treaty to protect rights to their ancient homeland, their lands would be declared open to settlement.[18] The chiefs pondered this threat while they worried about feeding their people. Those who had stayed home, both in the Bitterroot and on the Jocko Reservation, were suffering from a desperate lack of food, and the hunters had failed to find adequate buffalo.

The 1870 U.S. census for Montana counted 18,306 whites, 1,949 Chinese, and 183 African Americans. The estimated Native American population was 19,300.[19] More than eleven thousand of the white people in the territory had found their way to the traditional Salish homeland. Those with power—called "pioneers" and "founding fathers" by those who inherited the results of their efforts—used their collective influence on politicians to have the Salish people removed from their homeland. By summertime a fledgling Missoula newspaper in a booming little town would help strengthen their cause.

John Owen conducted a census of the Flathead Nation in April. He counted 446 Indians in the Bitterroot Valley, noting that only 217 of them were "full-blooded Indians." These numbers showed a decrease of nearly 20 percent since the last census in 1861, when the total population was reported as 548.

Deaths outpaced births among the Salish that year, including the death of Chief Victor. He had left with his people for the bull hunt in early June. A reporter for the *New North-West* had witnessed their passage and reported "250 or 300 Flatheads with some 600 horses . . . bound for

FIG. 56. Two-wagon freighter in Missoula, Montana Territory, 1870. Amos Buck is driving, and Will Cave is riding next to him. Archives and Special Collections, Mansfield Library, University of Montana.

the Muscleshell."[20] Victor, at least eighty years old, died somewhere on the buffalo plains on July 14, 1870. Little is known about the particulars of his death except that he was killed by Indians and died by a "wound in the leg," held in the arms of Charlo.[21] Charlo, approximately forty years old, stepped into the role of chief soon after his father's passing.

When word of Victor's death reached John Mullan in San Francisco, he drafted a tribute, then arranged with the *New North-West* for publication. Mullan had known Victor since the Pacific Railroad Survey began in 1853 and considered the chief a good friend. His words were addressed to the Indians of the Flathead Nation, but they were also meant to be read by white people living in traditional Salish lands. As the Flatheads' friend, he began, he felt "great sadness" and expressed sorrow for their loss of "the great and good Chief Victor."[22] He wrote with patronizing yet unequivocal praise that Victor, "mild and gentle as a woman, and innocent of wrong as a child," was a leader who "had no superior among the red man of America." During the years of road surveys and construction Mullan had experienced "many and constant acts of kindness" from Victor and never had a man injured or a horse stolen. He had joined the chief "at his camp fires, traveled with him to the hunt, had seen him help the widow[s] and orphan[s] of his tribe." He had witnessed the chief "go in person on missions of peace to the Blackfeet, to the Crows, to the Sioux and to the Bannacks, endeavoring to maintain with them friendly relations." Victor, "brave in battle and generous in peace," was so exceptional that he "set an example worthy of imitation, to all Indian tribes." Mullan hoped the Indian Department would erect a monument to commemorate Victor's "worth and his acts, and at the same time to teach all Indians that their good deeds shall never die." The white man, Mullan affirmed, "has lost a friend."

Unaware that Charlo had been made chief, Mullan prompted the Flatheads to choose a successor who would carry on Victor's ways, one, "if possible, with all his virtues." He hoped that "the mantle of his wide-spread greatness [would] fall on his [successor's] shoulders." In conclusion Mullan told Victor's people that "Father De Smet, Sohon and all your friends among the whites, have many reasons for feeling exceedingly sad to hear of the death of the great and good Victor."

Politics of Removal

A new governor, Benjamin F. Potts, arrived in July 1870, after a great deal of turnover and inconsistency in that office during the previous year. General Sully was replaced by Jasper Viall in September, and Charles S. Jones replaced Flathead Indian agent George Ford after only a short stint. These replacements were due to a federal policy reversal that excluded military officers from civil positions. Viall, another political appointee from Vermont, had no background or interest in Indians prior to taking this lucrative position. He and the new governor were allies.

When Agent Jones arrived in the Jocko Valley in October, he found that the only annuities ordered for the 1,900 destitute reservation occupants were eight hundred blankets. He got to work repairing fences around the agency and putting up a new building to serve as the kitchen and mess hall. He continued the practice of distributing "two pecks of potatoes/week to each head of family" to stave off starvation.[23]

Returning hunters shifted the tide from famine to feast. The November 10, 1870, issue of the weekly *Missoula and Cedar Creek Pioneer*—one of two new local newspapers—reported the return of the "Calaespelles" (Pend d'Oreille) from their fall hunt, heavily laden with buffalo meat and robes. Such good fortune had not been theirs for many years. They also returned with dozens of horses they didn't have when they left. Led by Chief Many Grizzlies (Michel), they had captured more than seventy horses from their Blackfeet enemies in retaliation for their own losses the year before.

Another hunting group, composed of Pend d'Oreille, Salish, and Spokanes, led by Pend d'Oreille sub-chief Big Canoe—the man the future agent Peter Ronan would called "one of the greatest war chiefs the tribe of the Pend d'Oreilles ever had"—had no such luck.[24] They had left for buffalo in September and, according to the article in the *Pioneer*, the combined forces had lost everything in the Yellowstone Country to Crow and Sioux warriors. "Stripped of all they possessed," they returned home on foot in a "destitute and dilapidated plight . . . without an ounce of meat." Instead of compassion for their imminent suffering, the journalist suggested readers "would hope that this severe lesson might prove beneficial to them," while reflecting on how the bison "predominates too much in the 'noble son of the forest,' to permit him to profit by past experience."[25]

Agent Jones held his first council with the Bitterroot Salish in December. He was surprised that War Chief Arlee stepped forward to do most of the talking while Head Chief Charlo said little. The subject of removal stirred up strong emotions, which were quelled somewhat when the agent proposed the alternative option of homesteading for the Salish and their becoming U.S. citizens. Arlee and Nine Pipes followed up with a visit to the agency to further discuss matters in the Bitterroot.[26] Why Charlo was not present for this three-day discussion is unclear. Perhaps the head chief was not there because Arlee and Nine Pipes were considering a move to the agency if conditions were right, and they chose not to include Charlo in the negotiations.

One can imagine that Chief Charlo, Claw of Little Grizzly, like his father before him, kept abreast of the news and must have suffered from each heartless blow from his white neighbors and government officials. But he, perhaps better than anyone, understood differences in worldview and moral compass between Europeans and Native Americans. He and his people had suffered through an astounding series of manipulations and lies by the whites, nearly since first contact, and they continued to do so. Charlo had watched his father, Victor, struggle to lead their people through these mystifying, soul-sucking years, and now he had to carry the burden forward himself.

By the start of 1871, newspapers and politicians clamored for the removal of the Salish from their Bitterroot homeland, while encouraging white Americans and Europeans to discover the riches of Montana. In late January Governor Potts, the seventh territorial governor, was encouraging Swedish immigration, causing the *Missoula and Cedar Creek Pioneer* to remark that it hoped he would "direct the attention of new-comers to our part of the world."[27] The newsmen didn't need to waste their ink to encourage people to settle in the valleys of western Montana. That inviting world was a magnet to people dislocated by choice or circumstance after the Civil War. Even more people might have come if they had known that prime movers in the federal government were set on removing the Salish from the Bitterroot Valley. Father De Smet learned of this reality during a visit to Washington and shared the news with Father Giorda at St. Mary's Mission.

That spring the Salish faced serious hunger, and their struggles continued with their white neighbors. In May, Charlo, accompanied by elders who had been advisors to his father, met with Father Jerome D'Aste. The group included Arlee, Adolph, Joseph Nganta, and two others.[28] They asked the priest to dictate a letter petition to President Grant regarding the failure of the government to accomplish an official survey of the Bitterroot Valley. Now, eleven years after treaty ratification, they needed his clear direction. They were "encompassed on all sides by white settlers" with very negative consequences. White settlers had created "whole towns." The Salish continued to worry about their young people being led astray by freely dispensed liquor. Echoing Victor's letter of May 1868, they wanted to meet with the president so that their land status could finally be settled. They noted that other, less friendly, tribes had been allowed to visit the president, and they hoped he would agree to hearing their vital business.[29] They never received a reply. Agent McCormick's report to the commissioner spoke of the exacerbation of "conflicting interests of the opposite races"; conveying his doubts, McCormick added, "That the two races should live together in amity and good accord is not to be expected." Like history has shown, he concluded, "the weaker must sooner or later yield to, or be destroyed by, the more powerful."[30]

After the long and hard winter the hungry Salish people were thankful for the drought-resistant bitterroot crop when spring emerged. Following prayers of gratitude, the women picked up their elk-handled digging sticks and returned to this joyful annual gathering of the "first foods." From then on they could anticipate the unfolding cycle of gifts that would follow. In early June, just after the camas harvest, Salish and Pend d'Oreille families left for buffalo, with Chief Charlo in the lead. On June 9, 1871, the *New North-West* reported that Deer Lodge—a town of over 4,300—"was fairly swarming with aborigines yesterday from the lower country, en route to buffalo grounds." It offered an estimate of "300 braves, with the usual number of squaws, papooses, cayuses, and dogs." Formerly the summer hunt was a smaller affair, conducted at a leisurely pace. Back then the traveling village took its time and relished the multitude of foods available as the people went up the valley and into the mountains as part of the journey. Women dug high-elevation root crops and picked berries while men hunted and fished. Plant medicines were collected as well, in a perfect matchup of a healing plant for each illness, except in the case of white man's diseases. Now, as they moved eastward, hunger drove them more quickly toward buffalo, with less and less assurance that buffalo would be found.

A reporter for the *Missoula and Cedar Creek Pioneer* suggested to readers that the "Soreheads" in the Bitterroot Valley had an excellent opportunity "to jump, squat, or pre empt the Indian Reservation in that portion of Uncle Sam's ranch. Its occupants have all vamoosed the premises in search of 'chemuck' [a Chinook jargon term referring to food] and revenge."[31] The seventy lodges of the combined Salish and Pend d'Oreille, led by Charlo and "the bellicose Michel" respectively, had passed through Missoula on their way to the Big Horn and Yellowstone Country for buffalo and to take revenge on the Crows who had sacked them the previous year. They were expecting to be joined in the Deer Lodge valley "by some 150 friendly Snakes," who were "also the life long enemies of the Crows."[32] While on the Yellowstone, instead of finding Crows, they were attacked by Sioux. Meanwhile, in a revolving drama of allies and enemies, another hunting camp of Pend d'Oreille and Kootenais forged a peace pact with two hundred lodges of Blackfeet.[33]

The summer hunt was a three-pronged disaster for the Salish and Pend d'Oreille. Crickets and continuing drought impacted the grasses, and therefore the buffalo and the Sioux attack left eighteen of their men dead. As Charlo led his long-suffering people toward home at the height of summer, he carried more than the mantle of goodness from his father that John Mullan had envisioned. The new chief felt the weight of the world on his shoulders.

Three days after their mid-August return from buffalo the Salish set aside time to come together to mourn their dead. A feast was held near St. Mary's Mission and reported on by the *Missoula and Cedar Creek Pioneer*. Two fine buffalo cows and two buffalo calves were the main dish, along with some cattle. "Flour, sugar, coffee, etc., were also furnished in great abundance for the feast," which was attended by several hundred mourners and friends. A second feast, even larger than the first, was held the next day on the Burnt Fork, some two miles above Stevensville. It appeared to the reporter that the entire tribe and many distinguished members of the neighboring tribes were there.[34]

The families of the murdered braves had pooled together the "considerable property" of the deceased to provide for their guests, and "their entertainments were conducted on the grandest scale." They served barbecued meats and other refreshments in "picnic style." During the feasting various people stood and expressed their "condolence and . . . sad feelings." Then "the Chief, or some head man, having collected together all the remaining effects of the deceased, publicly invites all creditors to present their claims against the estate, and pays up till the effects are exhausted." After the feast "the bitter wailing of the multitude for the dead [was] indulged in for about half an hour, then prayer, the interchange of social feelings, etc., and the final dismissal."[35]

Unfortunately John Owen wasn't around to provide more details of the state of affairs during this time of crickets and drought and heat. He had stopped writing in his journal. His business had continued to drop since the Mullan Road was completed and the Missoula Mercantile got established. His debts mounted alongside the tension and increasing ugliness that had come to characterize the valley he had chosen for his home. He missed his wife. After receiving a blow to the head from a windmill blade, he never seemed quite the same. While others had gathered to mourn their dead, Owen was confined to a hospital in Helena. He would never return to his beloved Bitterroot Valley.[36]

13. Shadows Abound

Garfield's Betrayal

The chorus for Salish removal strengthened in October 1871, when Superintendent Viall announced his support. Despite the estimate by Agent Jones of forty-four good Salish farms in the Bitterroot, Viall justified his position by claiming there were only three such farms of value, and his statement was backed by the surveyor-general for the territory, a Potts appointee.[1]

Viall had visited the Jocko Valley that summer with Governor Potts and William H. Clagett, the man they had just helped get elected as the lone delegate to Congress. All three Republicans aligned to conclude that removal was the most "humane course" of action. To influence public sentiment, this political posse, like the newspapers, distorted reality and used dismissive language about the Salish, calling them "remnants" and "almost extinct."[2] Surely the administration couldn't ignore the legitimate pleas of the good people of the Bitterroot Valley, the territorial advocates conveyed, when only a few Indians stood in the way of developing this most desired of all valleys of the territory.

Governor Potts requested the president to order the survey that would pave the way for removing the Bitterroot Salish from their homeland. On November 14, 1871, President Grant ordered the removal. Appraisals of Indian property were to begin immediately. This administration, which had withheld support for distribution of annuities and other treaty obligations and ignored Charlo's request for a meeting, kicked right into gear to make removal happen. The bill introduced by Clagett made its way through Congress, and the act was approved seven months later. Enacting the law was easy; getting the Indians to move was not.

In December, when the hungry Salish left again for buffalo, joined by a large party of Pend d'Oreille, Kootenai, and Nez Perce, white citizens of the Bitterroot Valley worried about trouble. The Salish might fight, they thought, rather than leave this beloved homeland. Other Indians might come to their defense, and the only military in the territory was across the mountains, focused on the Sioux. The white settlers of western Montana needed protection and again called for a military post. They had much to defend.[3]

The winter was made difficult by steady snow and cold. In February 1872 the *Missoula and Cedar Creek Pioneer* reported that some Kootenai Indians had camped on Rattlesnake Creek in the vicinity of town.[4] In early March, snow accumulations were so great that bighorn sheep could be seen on the slopes across the river from town, "gently nipping the luxuriant bunch grass on the mountain side."[5] The Salish hunters returned home with meat in March, but the bitter cold winter was so hard on them and their horses that they barely managed to drag their exhausted, depleted selves back through deep snow. They had no idea of the disaster awaiting them, like a slow-moving wrecking ball, but they could sense it.

The little town of Missoula, with a population approaching five hundred white men, women, and children, was becoming less and less tolerant of the Natives. On April 20, 1872, the *Missoula and Cedar Creek Pioneer* called for restriction of Indians to the Flathead Reservation. "Of course, we have no objection to their passing through the country on their way to and fro their hunting grounds," the editors offered, "but we do protest against their being allowed to go into, camp in and about our town and remain there for weeks, as some of those here at present have done." That summer saw Salish, Nez Perce, and Pend d'Oreille Indians camping in Missoula on their trek to buffalo and again on their return. It made no difference to the citizens that these people were camping in places used by countless generations of their ancestors. These places were no longer "open and unclaimed," so the Indians no longer had rights to be there.

The long-dreaded official notice of their removal was delivered to the Salish by Viall on June 28, 1872, giving them only one month to prepare. It is surprising that little is known about the response of the

Salish to this ultimatum. A gleeful Viall might have joined the governor and other cronies to enjoy a well-earned round of drinks at the Pioneer Bar, a favorite hangout in Virginia City.

Once the act had passed on June 5, the bureaucracy moved quickly to mobilize a special agent, in the form of Representative James A. Garfield, to implement the plan. Garfield, a Republican from Ohio and a major general in the Civil War, was a man of great energy, known for his eloquence and charm. At the time of his special assignment, he was under scrutiny for his role in the Credit Mobilier railroad-funding scandal. Removing himself from the nation's capital for a while might not have been a bad thing.

Congressman Garfield spent time preparing in Ohio, then traveled west and on August 16 arrived in Virginia City, where he soon met with Potts and Viall for details. He learned that a committee of Bitterroot Valley citizens had visited the governor about feared hostilities from "the Flatheads and from their allies the Nez Perces, a thousand of whom were encamped near Hell Gate."[6] Since no action had been forthcoming from the government, the citizens had organized militias of approximately one hundred men throughout the valley in the towns of Missoula, Aetna, and Corvallis. As reported by Garfield, they made a formal request of the governor "to issue arms and ammunition" and to urge the president to establish a cavalry post somewhere in the valley.

The governor, accepting the point of view of the white settlers, seemed to carry little hope of avoiding an armed conflict. After all, the Modocs were showing the U.S. government what they thought about being forced onto a reservation in the Klamath country of Oregon, and skirmishes had characterized relations between white settlers and Modocs all summer. In north-central Texas, Kiowas had attacked a military supply wagon in May, killing half of the teamsters along a lonely road. Closer to home, the Bannocks had been raiding white settlements and Indian villages for the last few years, and across the mountains to the east, Sioux and Cheyenne warriors were constant threats to the territory.

In Garfield's report of findings, he included his own observations of the background causes relevant to the situation. The governor, fearful of violence, "had ordered three hundred muskets and thirty thousand rounds of ammunition sent to Missoula." Garfield sensed "that much of the apprehension was groundless," given the long friendship that characterized relationships between white men and both the Salish and Nez Perce. He had reservations about arming the citizens and the negative impact that might have on his ability to reach a peaceable agreement with the Flatheads regarding their removal. He requested Governor Potts to accompany him to the Bitterroot Valley, where he could better assess the situation. They were joined by Viall, Clagett, and Wilbur Sanders, a member of the territorial House of Representatives and a fellow Republican. The four Montanans, who had the ear of Congressman Garfield, carried a vision for the future very different from that of the Salish. The four men must have felt stirred up by the potential this trip to the Bitterroot Valley held for manifesting their dreams.

According to Garfield's accounts of proceedings, the government officials traveled through Helena, then Deer Lodge, then on to Missoula, where they visited with citizens who expressed to him that their primary anxiety "was to secure the establishment of a military post, and that the market which would thus be afforded for their home products was really a matter of greater consideration than protection against hostile Indians."

On Wednesday morning, August 22, 1872, they proceeded to the Salish village near Fort Owen.[7] Consultations began the next day. Three lodges had been put together to create a space large enough for the council and to provide shade from the intense summer sun.[8] Garfield reported that the Salish were represented by Charlo, first chief, the second chief Arlee, and Adolph, the third chief, in addition to "a large number of the principal men of the tribe."

Garfield started off by reminding them of the provisions of the 1855 treaty, particularly the specification that gave the president power "to determine whether the Bitter Root Valley should be set apart as a special reservation for the Flatheads, or whether they should remove to the Jocko reservation." Next he explained the Presidential Order of November 14, 1871, and the supporting congressional act of June 5, calling for Flathead removal. The president's order claimed that the valley had been carefully surveyed and examined in accordance with the eleventh article of the treaty, and the president had judged the Bitterroot *not* to be better adapted for the wants of the Flathead tribe than the Jocko Reservation. Accordingly Indians residing in the Bitterroot should be removed to the Jocko Reservation or declare themselves willing to accept the conditions of the homestead and preemption laws. The Salish would be compensated for improvements to their lands made after the 1855 treaty and the lands would be made open for settlement by others. Garfield told Charlo and the others that $50,000 had been set aside to compensate them for their lands.

Chief Charlo shook Garfield's hand, then this "commanding presence, tall and of strong frame," spoke for his people.[9] He began with the Stevens treaty, pointing to the copy he had brought with him, the one left to him by his father. That document, he attested, guaranteed their rights to the Bitterroot Valley. The most important stipulation of Article XI—the survey and subsequent examination by the president—had never been completed, despite what was claimed. Given that seventeen years had elapsed without any action, the Indians took the inaction and silence to be tacit recognition of their rights.

Over the course of several hours the Salish leaders told the senator they opposed the removal plan. Arlee, the short, thickset second chief, explained that many treaty stipulations had never been met—they had never gotten the promised teachers, blacksmiths, carpenters, or farmers. They had been promised that they "should be taught for twenty years how to read and write, and then they would be like the white men, and know how to do everything—but nothing had been done." Every speaker claimed the Bitterroot Valley as his home and declared he was "wholly unwilling to leave it." This intention was not delivered as a threat. The speakers "affirmed their steady friendship for the whites and disclaimed any hostile intentions, declaring themselves willing to suffer, peaceably, whatever the Government should put upon them, but that they would not go to the reservation."[10]

Representative Garfield understood their perspective and perhaps sympathized with the way they felt blindsided by Governor Stevens. He was feeling blindsided himself by their staunch opposition to removal. This was not what he had expected. The letter of instructions he had received from Francis Walker, commissioner of Indian affairs, had indicated that the Flatheads had expressed willingness to leave the Bitterroot Valley, "and it was supposed their removal could be accomplished without opposition." Garfield assured the Salish that the government recognized that they "[had] been badly treated; your money and goods have not come as they should; but the Great Father does not intend this shall happen anymore."[11]

The Salish told the officials about how white settlers, whose numbers had grown to more than their own, had "crowded into the valley without their consent." Garfield attributed this situation in part to the friendly disposition of Victor, "who permitted many white men to settle in the valley, and in several instances invited them there." These men tended to be known by Victor through the fur trade or railroad surveys, and many of them had Indian wives. They were different from the white settlers that Salish leaders had never welcomed, and they had not consented to their presence on Salish lands. The congressman acknowledged that within the past five years white settlements had significantly increased "without the invitation or consent of the tribe."[12]

Before he closed the meeting, Garfield asked the chiefs if they would intentionally disobey the president and Congress. He told them he would expect their answer in the morning, after they had consulted with their people. He also invited them to accompany him to the Jocko Reservation to look at the possibility of relocating. That evening the Indians went to the head priest at St. Mary's, presumably their dear friend Father Ravalli, to hear his thoughts on the matter.[13]

The Salish chiefs met again with the commissioners on Friday morning and conveyed their good will to the president. They would travel to the Jocko Reservation, but this agreement "should not imply any promise to leave Bitterroot Valley."[14] They adjourned early to prepare for their travels northward.

Two Nez Perce leaders, Looking Glass and Eagle Against the Light, were camped near Fort Owen. General Garfield wanted to understand their intentions toward the whites and whether they had made any kind of commitment to the Salish to help them protect their rights to the Bitterroot Valley. They had no such agreement. On the whole their relationship had long been one of banding together to hunt buffalo to better their odds against the Blackfeet and other enemy tribes.

The Salish delegation met up with the Garfield party at the Jocko Reservation on Saturday and spent time through the weekend looking

FIG. 57. "When Garfield Visited Montana," 1872. *Anaconda Standard*, May 24, 1908, pt. 2:7.

over agency buildings, fields, and the Jocko Valley, with an eye toward settlement. They reconvened on Monday for another long meeting. Garfield reported that he began to realize through the course of their discussion "that the chiefs had at last become divided in opinion among themselves about removal." He understood them all to carry "a deep-seated distrust of the promises of the Government" and that they feared they would lose both the Bitterroot Valley and the compensation promised by the government.[15] To assure them, the commissioner promised them comfortable cabins if they relocated, along with tilled land and grain for one year.

Garfield drew up a contract for removal and had it translated paragraph by paragraph to ensure that the Salish understood all the provisions, and he urged the chiefs to sign. Then the Salish leaders were asked "to answer by signing or refusing to sign."[16] Charlo held fast and refused to sign the contract. He would not leave his cherished homeland. In a stunning reversal from the pledges made on the first

FIG. 58. Chief Arlee and family. From P. Ronan, *Historical Sketch of the Flathead Indian Nation*.

day of meetings to never leave the Bitterroot, both Arlee and Adolph signed. But why? What caused the two chiefs to change their minds? According to James V. Sanders, who at the age of thirteen attended the proceedings with his father, Wilbur Fisk Sanders, the "very affable and approachable" Arlee had held his own meetings with various members of the delegation outside of the official sessions.[17]

In a move reminiscent of Father Mengarini's appointment of Crawling Mountain when Victor was chief, the government officials appointed Arlee as chief of the Salish, at least for those going to the reservation. A former war chief, more than a decade older than Charlo, Arlee was a powerful warrior of Nez Perce and Shoshone heritage who had been adopted into the Salish nation. It seems this appointment was a coup orchestrated by outsiders, and it did not sit well with Charlo. A few years later, when leadership troubles were emerging on the Flathead Reservation, the agent at that time reported that Arlee did not have the support of the Salish people. He had come to his position through a bribe offered him by the agent to get him to agree to move to the reservation when Chief Charlo would not.[18]

Garfield left the conference having failed to accomplish what he was sent to do. In the stage to Deer Lodge, traveling along the once pristine Clark Fork River corridor, which he described as "permanently ruined by miners," the congressman reviewed conversations with Arlee, Adolph, and Viall.[19] The sub-chiefs had confidence that Charlo would come around if treaty stipulations were finally met. Somewhere between the Bitterroot Valley and the nation's capital, James Garfield decided how he would turn his loss into a win. He concluded that he would "proceed with the work in the same manner as though Charlot, the first chief, had signed the contract," as he explained in a letter to Viall.[20] He also wrote to his wife about his decision, claiming that he felt bound to do what he could "to save these noble Indians from the mistake they will make it they refuse. Moreover I greatly dislike to fail in anything I undertake."[21] The copy of the document included in the commissioner's annual report appeared with a forged "X" marked beside Charlo's name.[22] The government proceeded as if Chief Charlo had signed the agreement. When Charlo denounced this forgery, he was vilified in Montana's press as a liar and a treaty violator.

Father De Smet was seventy-one years old and ailing at the time of Garfield's betrayal. What must the priest have thought then about the American republic, which he had earlier held blameless for the troubles of the Indians? The blame could no longer be left with the private citizens who took advantage of the Indians, for Garfield and the Montana cabal that aided and abetted his work were all government officials.

Chief Charlo held Garfield as the one responsible for this manipulation of the Hellgate Treaty that would abrogate Salish rights to the Bitterroot Valley. For the time being, nothing changed. Charlo and Arlee coexisted in the Bitterroot Valley in an uneasy truce.

Fewer Options

Pend d'Oreille and Salish hunters returned from their winter hunt in late February 1873 with little meat. A week later the *Missoulian* reported that Indians had taken some cattle belonging to white settlers in the Bitterroot. "These are the same Indians that Gen. Garfield came all the way from Ohio to move, but didn't."[23] These same Indians were hungry. The foods on which they had always relied were no longer available to them, at least not in adequate yields; there was too much competition. Even their horses were hungry.

In late April, the day after a tornado-like storm blew through Missoula, "unroofing a barn and uprooting hundreds of large pine trees," the *Missoulian* printed a lengthy article about efforts to persuade the Bitterroot Salish to move to the Jocko Reservation. Agent Daniel Shanahan would meet with them to understand why Arlee and Adolph and their people had not yet moved. To sweeten the pot he invited them all to first share food, then talk. More than four hundred Indians joined the agent that day, all of them needing some food in their bellies. Arlee explained the delay on the fact that fifty-two families had planted crops and didn't want to leave until fall, after the harvest.[24] Chief Charlo remained firm in his refusal of all offers to relocate to the Jocko Reservation.

A week after the meeting a new Indian superintendent, C. C. Wright, joined Shanahan for further discussion with the Indians who were refusing to move.[25] The Flatheads put little faith in these officials, who came and went like the wind and rarely made good on promises. Even the promises of Representative Garfield had not materialized. Why should the people move when no houses had been built for them?[26] They had nowhere to go. They respectfully but firmly refused, and they repeated the request, made many times since the time of Chief Victor, that their chiefs go to Washington to meet with the president, the one person who could bring final resolution to this treaty issue.[27] They knew that the Bitterroot Valley was best suited to their needs and trusted that the president, with full examination of the facts, would agree.

In synch with the seasons, on June 6, after the bitterroot harvest had been completed and early camas had been gathered, the Indians were beginning their journey across the mountains for buffalo. "Our town for the last week has been full of Indians, and some fifty lodges more are in the canyon on their way down," reported the *Weekly Missoulian*. "Our valley is literally alive with Indian horses."[28] A week later fifty lodges of the Nez Perce and fifty Pend d'Oreille and Flatheads were camped across the river from the town of Missoula at the traditional village site on the flat at the base of Mt. Sentinel. The *Weekly Missoulian* reported rumors of "medicine talks" held by these Indians, but the only specifics it learned were that "the Flatheads" intended to meet with Agent Shanahan to demand guns for their hunt.[29]

The first group of hunters to return came through Missoula in late July, in time for the huckleberry harvest, around the same time that white sportsmen were slaughtering "chickens by the hundreds."[30] Duck hunting was reported to be "all the rage" for Missoulians, and "fine fat, wild geese" were sold in the market on Wednesday for one dollar each, in the small but growing town.

In August, as the heat of summer intensified, western Montanans learned of armed conflict near Big Horn between Sitting Bull's band and the U.S. Army. The Peace Commission's work had failed. In early October the Flathead agent reported the appearance of a troublesome bunch of Modoc, Piute, Yakima, Spokane, and other Indians from the Columbia River country as a matter of concern to the Pend d'Oreille's chief, Michel. The agent was concerned because of the determination of the travelers to acquire whiskey on their way to buffalo country. To avoid trouble, Michel led his people away from the alcohol dealers. The Pend d'Oreille were aware of the Modoc hangings near Tule Lake in northern California and wanted to stay out of trouble.[31] The Pend d'Oreille hunters would leave the next day with their second chief, Andre, for the hunting grounds. He would carry with him an American flag in addition to papers from Shanahan to remind authorities across the mountains to enforce whiskey trade regulations.[32]

During the same month as the Modoc scare, October 1873, a year after the Garfield agreement had been reached, Arlee and ten families, after they had harvested their crops, finally made the move to the Jocko Reservation. Agent Shanahan sent a letter to *New North-West* announcing the success, while downplaying the lack of provisions available at their arrival. He made clear the job had been made more difficult due to "the determined efforts of some white settlers in the Bitter Root Valley, to retard the removal of the Flathead Indians to this Reservation and provoke a war between them and the government."[33] Apparently the Salish still had friends in the valley.

Arlee almost immediately regretted the move. In mid-October he met with Shanahan to voice an official complaint about all the promises that had not been kept. He was looking for reassurance that the situation would be remedied because his people had nothing to eat. He spoke of the many white friends in the Bitterroot Valley who had warned him not to relocate to the reservation because the Salish "would be poor there and starve." Now they faced winter in a worse situation than before. Arlee asked that the president hear this plea and help them.[34]

Missing John Owen

From April 1851 through February 1871 John Owen's jottings had provided a local perspective about the lives of the Bitterroot Salish, as had those of the Jesuits before him. Without the old trader, a void was created. News came from the outside and not from the Indians' point of view. The 1874 new year came and went, with only snippets known of the Salish. Some of them on the reservation engaged in a birthday ball in late February in honor of George Washington's birthday. In March crowds of "Indians" passed through Missoula from their annual buffalo hunt, surprisingly well supplied with buffalo meat and robes. They managed to bring home the gains even after losing a large number of horses, some to the winter and others to the Crows. "The horses which they still have are almost in a famishing condition from their long march and the scarcity of feed," according to the *Weekly Missoulian*.[35]

Three weeks later Indians still remained around Missoula, a situation not to the liking of the citizens. The *Weekly Missoulian* ran a story on April 2 that began with, "Whose are they? We mean the gang of insolent, pilfering Indians encamped on the flat just above town, who spend their time lounging about the streets, intruding themselves upon private grounds and residences, gawking in at windows, rummaging out-buildings, begging, stealing, etc." The same issue of the paper advertised "Bitter Root for Sale."

With barely six weeks since the last of the Indians had left Missoula, the town found itself "swarming" again at the end of May. An editorial in the *Weekly Missoulian* reported "somewhere in the neighborhood of one hundred lodges of Indians within one mile of town—Pen d'Oreilles, below, Flatheads above and Nez Perces at the South end of the bridge, flanking us on every side except the hills to the north."[36] One hundred lodges in those days equated to some five hundred people or more. Their numbers surpassed those of the nervous Missoula residents. Citizens felt vulnerable with no quick way to get help if it was needed. Without a direct mail route to the nearest military help in Washington Territory, it was quicker to send messengers than to wait for the mail to travel to San Francisco on route to Olympia.

The *Weekly Missoulian* writer questioned why all these Indians had come and why they were camped so close to town. Since "the feed is not so good here as elsewhere and there is no game to attract them hither," he pondered, perhaps they had come simply to dispose of "a few peltries" and to purchase supplies. The journalist must have been new in town and was unaware of the constancy of this pattern since long before white people had settled in the valley. History happens in particular places, and newcomers don't always know what has occurred. They bring their ignorance with them and impose it on the place, distorting its reality. The journalist lacked knowledge of the age-old practices that brought people to the Missoula Valley at this season, when the hills had greened up and the waters ran high. No doubt at least some of the Indians had come to dig camas from moist meadows before they headed eastward, over the mountains, to hunt buffalo bulls. Perhaps the spring runoff was forcing them to pause in Missoula before heading up the river.

A week later the Indians were still there. The *Weekly Missoulian* reported a recent incident west of town involving a Mr. Geo. A. Baker, who "was riding along the road through the Pend d'Oreille encampment just below town," causing Indian dogs to rush out, "yelping and barking." Mr. Baker "drew his pistol and commenced unloading it among them, when an Indian from one of the lodges let his gun go off. The Indian was arrested on a warrant from Judge Pomeroy and lodged in jail." The correspondent expressed the belief that "the Indians have no business to camp so near to town," while recognizing the dilemma that existed because nobody seemed to have the authority to exclude them and "neither their agent or the Fathers have influence to prevail on them to choose another location." In fairness the writer concluded that Mr. Baker, under the circumstances, "ought to have put up with the annoyance rather than adopt a course calculated to precipitate matters."[37] The article ends with a call for troops to be established in the area.

In mid-September a new agent, Peter Whaley, reported the reservation to be almost completely deserted. The Indians had left for their hunt in August, when their situation, according to Whaley, was so dire that they had no choice—they had to get buffalo meat or starve during the upcoming winter "as the government has made no provision for their subsistence, and they raised nothing this summer."[38]

Growing disdain for the Indians simmered on the pages of the *Weekly Missoulian*. On September 28, 1874, it featured an article about Pend d'Oreille horse stealing. It was especially concerned about the ones taken from Bannocks on the Lemhi reservation, the ones that would bring reprisal. Missoulians feared they would be subject to a visit from Chief Tendoy and his band, who would come for horses, no matter whose. Since the Indian agent didn't have legal authority to deal with these horse thieves, the paper offered an alternative. It suggested that "a few of Uncle Samuel's blue-coated missionaries would do the business and educate these simple-minded children of the forest in the ways of godliness." The citizens could "call on all those who desire the thorough conversion of the Indians to aid us in this direction." In other words, bring in the military and vigilantes to help take care of the problem.

The hunters again were successful. Maybe their luck was changing. According to an unnamed source of a letter sent from St. Ignatius Mission on December 21, 1874, the 183 lodges, with about six hundred hunters of the Pend d'Oreille, Coeur d'Alene, Kootenai, Spokane, Colville, and other nations who had left in August and September, had had the most successful hunt in a long time.[39] Having weathered so many difficult years, this treasure trove of buffalo must have seemed miraculous. In addition to the impact of five years of Sherman's policy of buffalo slaughter, an economic depression had sent thousands of white men flocking to the plains to kill bison and sell their products. For those men buffalo were "slow-grazing, four-legged bank rolls," to quote writer J. Weston Phippen. "They sliced their humps, skinned off the hides, tore out their tongues, and left the rest on the prairies to rot."[40]

During the successful hunt of the allied west-side tribes in the late fall of 1874, the Indians did essentially the same thing. The total number of bison killed was so great that the hunters couldn't take all the meat. The women could never have processed that much food and still have been able to get home in time for the bitterroot harvest. So they "secured only the hides, tongues, borses, sinews, and dupuis, or back part of the animals."[41] At least some of them must have felt remorse, and perhaps a sense of dread, to behave in ways antithetical to their moral teachings.

The winter of 1874–75 was exceedingly cold in western Montana, with temperatures plummeting between 20 and 40 below zero during most of January. By April many animals on the Flathead Reservation were "dying by droves from starvation."[42] The Indians suffered significant losses and weren't allowed to leave the reservation without a military escort, according to orders received from the Indian Department in December. This order went against Article III of their treaty, guaranteeing them the right to hunt, fish, and gather in open and unclaimed land. Like the buffalo, fewer and fewer of them were increasingly surrounded by threatening forces and constraints.

In May, when large flocks of mallards, teal, and whistlers congregated around ponds in the Bitterroot Valley, the reservation Flatheads, under a military escort, traveled south along well-known trails and "pitched their tents on their old stamping ground" around Fort Owen to engage in some lively trading. The spectacle was witnessed by a *Missoulian* writer who noted that "Buffalo robes and pemmican were in active demand, and business was consequently brisk."[43]

Major T. C. Medary arrived in mid-July 1875 to replace agent Whaley, who had lasted less than a year. Medary's father had been governor of Minnesota and a family friend of Martin Maginnis, a two-term Montana Territory delegate to Congress as a Democrat. Barely a month into the job, Agent Medary found himself accused of being ineffectual by Governor Potts, who wanted to know why reservation Indians were hunting near Deep Creek, in the Musselshell Valley, without an escort. White settlers wanted them back where they belonged. The agent felt his hands tied by conflicting laws, orders, and treaties: "An act of Congress requires the Indians to remain on their reservation, their treaty permits them to hunt and fish anywhere, and an order from the Interior Department instructs that where a party of Indians are permitted to leave the reservation an escort of soldiers shall accompany them." Lacking troops to force them to stay on the reservation and unable to find military escorts since the closest post was hundreds of miles away, Medary had been unable to enforce the Indian Department's order for escorts. For these reasons and because he was responsible for the oversight of some 1,800 Indians (and even more during the semi-annual treks to and from the buffalo country)—thankfully peaceful—he heartily concurred with the white populace that a small post should be established near Missoula.[44]

Medary must have wondered how long his wards would remain peaceful, given the federal government's continuing failure to honor its treaty provisions. In a letter that fall to the commissioner of Indian affairs, the agent complained about the government's failure to provide an expected purchase of six hundred bushels of wheat along with appropriate equipment and seeds for the Indians to be successful on their farms. The promises made to the Salish to coax them to the reservation had never been fulfilled.

Like a Wolverine

The few hundred Salish people who remained in the Bitterroot Valley faced growing resentment from white residents of the county for not paying taxes. Charlo, as the son of Many Horses, still believed the Hellgate Treaty protected the traditional lands of his people and their right to be there and that they shouldn't be taxed on lands they had never relinquished. Many of the Salish had improved their allotments, while others declined to accept the allotments assigned to them by the government and proceeded to live as they had before, adjusting as well as they could to the increasing number of transplants in the valley.

That fall Charlo's people rebuffed Agent Medary. He reported to the commissioner that the Indians appeared to "have abandoned all relations with the Government, believing that the Garfield treaty will never be fully carried out." Three years had passed with no follow-up. He expressed his belief that the majority of them would "probably remove to the Jocko within another year" as long as the U.S. government made good on its promises in the Garfield agreement.[45] The agent was doing his best to stem the tide of this impending disaster, but he clearly failed to understand Chief Charlo and the many who agreed with his commitment to their homeland. They had never been allowed to meet with the president, the only avenue they believed was appropriate for bringing clear resolution to this impasse.

Salish food sources had changed dramatically since the days of Chief Victor. Even the once plentiful "Deer Cache Hills" near Flint Creek had been decimated. Bison were becoming so scarce on the plains that Congress passed a bill to protect buffalo. It didn't become law because President Grant refused to sign it. The goals of his military commanders to exterminate the bison had not yet been reached.

In mid-February 1876, in the midst of a bitterly cold winter, Agent Medary wrote a special report to his superiors about the failures of the federal government to meet its treaty obligations and the many ways this was having negative impacts on the people. Not only was this situation affecting those on the reservation, but it was also fueling the argument of the Bitterroot Indians that the promises made would never be kept. If the government wanted to succeed with the removal of Charlo's people from their homeland, the agent recommended that the treaty promises be fulfilled. He expressed confidence in his capacity to bring the matter to satisfactory conclusion as long as the government did its part. His confidence was based on a recent meeting with Charlo and a delegation of his men.[46]

Charlo had visited the agent to discuss proposed taxation on the Salish properties in the Bitterroot Valley. Since the Garfield agreement had moved forward with Charlo's forged signature, those Indians who had stayed in the Bitterroot were no longer provided annuities promised by the treaty. That was unjust enough since the treaty stipulation regarding their lands had never been met, but now the county wanted to tax them for land that was their own. Medary explained that he himself had no jurisdiction over the county and so could not protect them from *nolen volens*—the condition of citizenship the Indians accepted when they refused to relocate to the reservation, including being subject to taxation. The agent told Charlo that he had already spoken to the commissioners and encouraged them not to be hasty in regard to taxing the Indians. If they chose to go forward with their plan, they should implement the amount incrementally so as not to overwhelm anyone. At that meeting the agent coaxed Charlo toward relocating with promises of assistance and financial support and assured him that he, like his father before him, would be head chief.

The meeting with Charlo made a strong impression on Medary. He was moved by the chief's profound sadness. The agent could feel the deep love Charlo had for his Bitterroot Valley home and how he honored the words of his father, who told him never to relinquish those lands. In his letter Medary expressed sympathy for Charlo and his people, given their challenges and poverty, and presented his best case for the federal government to do its part to make matters right.

No record exists of how Charlo responded in the meeting with Medary. From the agent's written record we can assume that Charlo might have felt hopeful. He had every assurance that the agent would do his best for him, and he could surely feel the man's sympathy. But as Medary had explained, he himself had no jurisdiction over the county commission. Despite the agent's efforts, the commissioners chose to move forward with taxation, as they struggled through the impacts of a third year of a nationwide depression. That decision set in motion the occasion for Chief Charlo's bitter but eloquent speech to his people on February 26, 1876.

No Mincing of Words

The people gathered on that frigid day at the St. Mary's commons to hear their chief and to share their thoughts about this latest threat to their treaty-guaranteed lands. Charlo began, and his disgust and anguish at the white people who "filled graves with our bones" seeped through every word.[47] His people listened intently, as did some of their white neighbors. Although his words were translated into English, they don't begin to communicate the differences between what his Salish words carried and what the English words conveyed. When Charlo complained that they were being asked to pay the white man, to "pay him for our own—for the things we have from our God and our forefathers; for things he never owned and never gave us"—his words carried his deep knowing of the gifts of life residing there, given to the Salish at the time of creation.

No doubt the reporter for the *Weekly Missoulian* did his best to record the words of Charlo as translated into English by his unnamed interpreter. Some of Charlo's allusions could not be confused. When he scowled and said, "To take and to lie should be burnt on his forehead, as he burns the sides of my stolen horses with his own name," the chief imagined a situation where the Creator had branded the white man to warn the Salish about him. Perhaps, he wondered, "had Heaven's Chief burnt him with some mark"—like the mark of Cain—might they have known to refuse him? Lacking such a warning, Charlo recalled to his people how they had aided the Lewis and Clark party, how they "did not refuse him in his weakness; in his poverty we fed, we cherished him—yes, befriended him"—yet now the Salish found themselves being treated with no such generosity and no compassion.

The chief asked his people to consider the time when the treaty makers met them at Clme, "Tree Limb Cut Off," a traditional camp area rich in chokecherries in the Missoula Valley, along the river named after William Clark. What became known as the Hellgate Treaty was the beginning of the problems they now faced. Charlo could not help but think of the irony that they were gathered at a place always known as Łq éł mlš, "Place of Wide Cottonwoods" but called Stevensville since 1864, named by the unsympathetic former governor Thomas Meagher in honor of the treaty maker Isaac Stevens.

Charlo asked his people to recall Governor Stevens. Did he not "feast us with our own cattle, on our own land, yes, on our own plain by the cold spring?" Many of those assembled remembered that time just after the summer solstice, when over a thousand people gathered to meet the negotiators. Charlo himself had been a young man then and was proud of the way his father, Many Horses, had stood up to Stevens and successfully negotiated for his people to retain the Bitterroot Valley. Remembering that time, Charlo continued with what he had come to say. "Did he not invite our hands to his papers; did he not promise before the sun, and before the eye that put fire in it, and in the name of both, and in the name of his own Chief, promise us what he promised—to give us what he has not given, to do what he knew he would never do?"

Murmurs of resentment must have flowed through the downtrodden Salish people gathered there that day, knowing full well that treaty promises had not been met. Their chief continued. "Now, because he lied, and because he yet lies, without friendship, manhood, justice, or charity, he wants us to give him money—pay him more." Looking out over the crowd, he asked the question he knew could not be answered: "When shall he [the white man]"—referring to the avaricious intruders who were demanding that taxes be paid—"be satisfied?"

During this speech the *Weekly Missoulian* reporter's ears must have perked up when the chief's oration turned from historical references to comments about the nature of white people and how they differed from the Salish. "His horses, his cattle, his sheep, his men, his women have a rot," the chief declared. "[Do] not his breath, his gums, stink?" The bitter leader went on to describe how the jaws of the white men lose their teeth, a condition he could not fathom. The low-carbohydrate diets of the Indians, like those of nonagricultural people everywhere, kept their gums healthy and their teeth intact. He remarked how astonishing it was that even though they had to replace their own teeth with false ones, the white men were not ashamed.

Charlo's sadness was palpable as he looked out over these long-suffering, hungry people, and his stinging words pierced the air. "He spoils what the spirit who gave us this country made beautiful and clean. But that is not enough; he wants us to pay him besides his enslaving our country." Not only the country, the chief continued, but the Salish people as well, with the "degradation of a tribe who never were his enemies."

Charlo had known good men of European heritage, but, so overwhelmed by tragic losses and sick to death of unkept promises, he had completely lost trust in these displaced people. The white man, in his view, was a "roving skulk, first; a natural liar, next." Through time and experience he had come to understand the hairy-faced man as "a long-tailed, skulking thing, fond of flat lands, and soft grass and woods [who] often smiled like a rabbit in his own beard." Charlo went so far as to imagine that the Salish people "would be all safe now," and their country their own, if the white people who had been raised with the stories of Genesis had died alongside "the virgin's son" when he was "nailed to death on two cross sticks to save him."

Having missed their chance to turn these covetous and insatiable orphans away, the bitter and careworn Salish tribal leader had come to accept that his people would never be free. White men, whether they be neighbors or government officials, could not be trusted. "No, no," the chief bemoaned, "his meanness ropes his charity, his avarice wives his envy, his race breeds to extort."

Charlo reminded his people of the deep cold they had recently suffered through "in a destroying night when the mountains and the firmaments put their faces together to freeze us." He asked them to recall their white neighbors' response. Did they help? "No. Four times in one shivering night," he reminded his people of an old one-eyed Indian, "that gray man of full seven tens of winters was refused shelter in four of the white man's houses on his way in that bad night." These neighbors, he concluded, are "cold and merciless, haughty and overbearing." So ingrained are these qualities, the chief declared, that "stealth and envy" fit the white man, "as do his hands and feet." The whites have come "like the wolverine that steals your cache," he reminded his people, "and comes as long as he lives, and takes more and more, and dirties what he leaves. The rascal is also an unsatisfied beggar," he concluded, "and his hangman and swine follow his walk." And this walk had led them all to this moment. "Pay him money! Did he inquire, how?"

The chief then expressed his views about the causes that had led the white man to the current situation. "His avarice put him in debt, and he wants us to pay him for it and be his fools." Charlo had come to realize that the sacred agreements made between nations would never be honored. His people were hungry. Salish children were dying of diseases that came with the invaders. His daughter Agnes had died the year before, joining over fifty Salish children over the previous five years. Given such a small population overall, these losses were devastating. No wonder he was led to the sad conclusion that "night enters our future with him." He could see only darkness ahead.

He looked around at the faces of his people and posed a rhetorical question. "Did he ask how many a helpless widow, how many a fatherless child, how many a blind and naked thing fare?" All of those gathered there thought of the suffering they had endured during these years, with rare aid offered from their encroaching neighbors.[48]

The priests at St. Mary's were an exception. They had always offered support to the best of their ability. Charlo must have taken comfort there because he and his wife had both chosen to be confirmed just the year before. From the world Creator had made for them, where all their needs were met, the Salish world had become a place of bare survival.

Nez Perce Scare

The Salish people continued their seasonal rounds, even though their world was becoming less and less recognizable. In early May they were in the Missoula area before they started up the Clark Fork and across the mountains for buffalo. A *Weekly Missoulian* editorial on May 10, 1876, complained of "The Indian Problem." The Natives, who "toil not . . . are now sharpening their scraps of old iron that they have purloined during a season of vagabondage into pruning hooks to pry up from the ground the esculent cammas." For the citizens of Missoula—like those of Philadelphia in 1821—these Indians were not the worthy poor but the profligate, who "toil not." But the Salish were attempting to make their living the way they always had; it was just harder now. Roots were essential to their livelihood, yet fewer and fewer traditional locations remained "open and unclaimed." White farmers plowed the moist camas meadows for other crops. The Indians needed dried roots to sustain them as they crossed the mountains, praying for buffalo.

One very positive change happened in their lives in the spring of 1877 in the form of the new Flathead agent, Peter Ronan. This kindly Irishman would turn out to be the most stable, competent, and dedicated of all the agents that had passed through the Jocko Agency since John Owen. Ronan and his wife Mary and their six children would become a steady presence in the region until Peter's death in 1893.

Soon after the Ronans' arrival, white settlers of Missoula County received a long-desired improvement to their lives. In June 1877 a military post was finally established at the outskirts of Missoula, just in time for some high drama. Citizens were alarmed about the Nez Perce War in Idaho and fearful that it would spread to their doorsteps. They didn't know what to expect from the Salish and the Indians on the reservation, given their long alliance with the Nez Perce. The presence of both the military and Agent Ronan made possible the management of a potentially explosive situation, one that could ruin the already fragile relationships between Indians and whites in Missoula County.

Charlo and his people were following camas roots and fish runs at that time. When the twenty lodges of Salish arrived back in the Missoula Valley on July 8, 1877, Agent Ronan sought Charlo out for a meeting about the potential for trouble. What could the white citizens expect from the Salish if there were to be a confrontation with the Nez Perce? As reported by the new agent in a letter to the Indian commissioner, Charlo's response was thoughtful and thorough. At the outset he assured Ronan that he didn't need to worry about their position. He told him that his father, Victor, who had made the treaty with Governor Stevens, took pride in the fact that his people had never spilled the blood of a white man. Charlo was committed to the same path. Not only would they not turn on the whites, but if needed, his people would also help defend them.

Chief Charlo was good to his word, as he had always been. That summer, before the Nez Perce arrived, he escorted white settlers from their isolated ranches to Fort Owen and other comparatively safe places. He then traveled up the Lolo Fork, where he met with Chief Joseph and warned him not to cause trouble, not to even "steal a calf, or a little chicken from Charlot's friends" or they would suffer.[49] The Nez Perce bypassed Missoula and traveled through the Bitterroot Valley without serious incident.

In mid-August, when the danger had passed, Father Palladino, who at the time was an assistant itinerant priest in an enormous parish, traveled a loop from Missoula through the Bitterroot to the Big Hole and into the Deer Lodge Valley to get a read on the mood of the citizens. On his return he met with Ronan to share his concern over what he had seen and heard. The Nez Perce had stirred up the hornet's nest, and the result was that the white men no longer distinguished between the warriors of the plains and the trustworthy tribes from west of the mountains.

The priest counseled Ronan to keep the Indians on the reservation because of danger from white men east of the mountains. The agent should provide food to both those on and off the reservation so that they wouldn't go on the fall hunt. Within a few days, though, a terrible hailstorm ruined their crops, leaving the Indians with no choice but to go for buffalo or starve.[50] Ronan reported the Bitterroot Salish as being in "a most deplorable and unsatisfactory condition."[51]

Chief Charlo left in October 1877 with forty lodges on route to the Musselshell Valley for buffalo. The travelers followed the Mullan Road along the Little Blackfoot River and camped near the Ten-Mile Hot Springs on their way into Helena.[52] A second group of Bitterroot Salish hunters headed for buffalo under the leadership of old chief Adolph. In the Upper Musselshell country, with ever more cattlemen appearing, they had to pull down fences to continue along their well-worn paths. On that journey they encountered sheep, not cattle, instead of buffalo, and they couldn't stop their dogs from attacking and killing seven. The sheepmen reported their losses to the military, and the citizens of Meagher County began strategizing. Something had to be done with these Indians.[53]

Meanwhile, General Sherman made a visit to the Flathead Reservation to meet with Agent Ronan and a priest at the Mission about the recent scare from the Nez Perce, the hunting habits of the Indians, the approach of the Northern Pacific Railroad, and other issues affecting their administration of the Indians. In a letter to *New North-West* about his visit, he acknowledged the dilemma of an agent without "a dollar and no authority to promise them meat." He blamed the Indians for not working and not stocking up on food for the winter, while he failed to address the diminishing food sources and the plight of farmers in a land where crops were so easily wiped out by freeze, drought, grasshoppers, or freak hailstorms. Although the Indians from the reservation promised to stay north of settlements, Sherman opined that "once out and hungry they will steal tame cattle, and the next thing will be shooting and war." The Indians were most concerned by the fact that the traders were forbidden to sell them ammunition, as per an order issued by the Indian commissioner. Sherman, more aware than anyone of the near demise of the bison herds, having orchestrated that symphony, understood that these friendly Flatheads "must go for buffalo or starve." He warned that in the buffalo country "they may come in contact with white settlers, who do not know the difference between the Nez Perces and Flatheads and trouble may result."[54]

The reservation Indians who had gone for buffalo despite limited supplies of ammunition had been unsuccessful. In December a group of over one thousand hungry Indians camped by the Jocko Agency, trusting that Agent Ronan would find a way to help them. He put young men to work around the agency and paid them in supplies he obtained from a Missoula merchant with his own money. He was able to obtain wheat during the week of Christmas and had it ground into flour as a stopgap to starvation.[55]

In early April 1878 Charlo's people somehow managed to return from their winter trek with meat, although they had lost 140 head of horses to Sioux raiders a month before.[56] Their hunt the next winter was also successful, so much so that when Charlo's people returned in the spring of 1879, they needed help to bring in the food, and Arlee sent fresh horses.[57]

Their lucky streak of two good hunts was about to end. Pressure from cattlemen in the eastern part of the territory had influenced the legislative assembly to write to President Hayes about confining Indians to reservations. The cattlemen claimed that Flatheads engaged in depredations, including burning fences and killing livestock, and they also served as shields for war parties. They lumped together all the Indians of Montana as nomadic troublemakers who "roam at will through our agricultural and pastoral regions, frequently entailing losses upon our settlers." Casting a line that rarely failed to hook their objective, the legislators noted that if Indians were confined to their reservations, immigration and industry would flourish.[58]

Agent Ronan was incensed by the accusations and had proof that the reservation Indians had not been involved. The only hunters that left the Jocko Reservation during the winter of 1878–79 had gone under military escort. No evidence materialized to stain the unblemished track record of the tribes of the Flathead Reservation, but these facts were overridden by the demands of white settlers. Despite troubles, hunger drove the Pend d'Oreille to leave again for buffalo after hearing that herds had been seen across the Divide. Big Canoe, seventy-years-old and essentially blind, joined the hunt that would be his last.

The winter of 1879–80 was frigid. The Indians on the reservation needed meat, and so did the Salish who remained in the Bitterroot Valley that winter. Toward the end of the season the *Weekly Missoulian* reported on a group of Indians around town who were "bringing in the hides of frozen cattle," and "an enterprising squaw was observed dragging home a piece of veal which had succumbed to the rigors of

FIG. 59. Charlo's people in front of tipi by St. Mary's Mission church, 1880s. Archives and Special Collections, Mansfield Library, University of Montana.

winter."[59] The situation was pitiful, and the return of Salish hunters during the first week of April brought no relief. Their scrawny animals carried riders but not provisions. The Pend d'Oreille hunters fared better. They managed to get meat, but the scene on the bison plains left everyone uneasy.

14. Charlo's Lament

The Ghost of Garfield

The speed of news had changed exponentially since the 1850s, when it might take a year for a letter from New York to reach someone in the Oregon Country. It still took weeks, with the mail route long and convoluted and before telegraph lines started connecting the dots of towns alongside the rail lines. In November 1880 it took just two days for Montana papers to report that James Garfield had won the presidency. No record exists to tell what Chief Charlo thought when he learned that his nemesis had become "the Great Father" of the land or of the assassin's bullet that slowly resulted in the president's death on September 9, 1881.

In January 1882 Granville Stuart was at Fort Maginnis, northeast of the fledgling town of Lewistown. He had moved to Helena in 1879 and soon acquired four hundred head of cattle to run on the eight hundred acres he owned on the southern slopes of the Judith Mountains, acres recently removed from Indian treaty lands. As the cold wind blew across this winter white world, his mood was dark. He was not pleased by the constellation of Indian tribes hunting in this country and was mulling over the impending wreck when Indians would collide with cattlemen like himself.

So full of thoughts about Indian buffalo hunters in the Musselshell, this old friend of the Salish composed a letter and sent it to a Helena paper. Part of the problem, in his opinion, was that the tribes who were meant to be hunting in the common hunting ground established by the Lame Bull Treaty of 1855 were not hunting there, except in rare instances. That area, instead, was regularly used by "the Snakes and

Bannacks," who, he pointed out, "were not parties to this foolish treaty." Stuart failed to mention that the herds had abandoned that area when the miners took it over. He elaborated on the many changes that had occurred in the intervening years, highlighting the fact that Indian lands had become "the most heavily populated parts of Lewis and Clarke, Meagher and Gallatin counties, and *all* of Jefferson, Madison and Beaverhead counties." The government had surveyed and sold land "to actual settlers" in those places. In his mind those actions were tantamount to abrogation of the common hunting ground part of the treaty. Accordingly, he ranted, it was time for elected officials "to formally and actually abrogate it." This, he proposed, was a better option than the government's "making a spectacle of itself by seeking about to find a means to convoy a lot of able-bodied pauper savages across counties having a little game, into the central ones, where there is none at all." Ultimately everyone understood that "as Indians cannot live on air, they must inevitably subsist almost entirely upon the cattle of the citizens, while hundreds of starving Indian dogs chase the cattle for miles and kill many calves."[1]

Stuart had read that the Interior Department hoped stockmen would be "prudent and conciliatory" when it came to incidents with Indians. He wanted the U.S. government to understand that "the stockmen of this vicinity propose to be about as prudent as wolves, and conciliatory as rattlesnakes, and the predatory savages can count on our welcoming them with bloody hands to hospitable graves."[2] While it may be that Stuart was thinking only about the east-side tribes and not the Salish, his rhetoric made no such distinction.

By December 1882 General Sherman's prediction and Granville Stuart's worry had come true. With no buffalo to eat, some of the Bitterroot Salish hunters were killing cattle on Careless Creek and Swimming Woman Creek, on the south side of the Snowy Mountains.[3] The Salish needed blankets almost as much as meat. The people were not part of the cash economy, and blankets at the time cost around three dollars a piece.[4] Fortunately none of the needy west-side Indians ended up dead and buried, as Stuart had warned, or if they did, their killings were never reported.

When they returned to search for buffalo the next summer, some unidentified Indians stole all of Charlo's horses. The *Weekly Missoulian* reported that "he was compelled to remain at White Sulphur Springs until ponies were sent to him from the Bitter Root." He received "five or six ponies" from fellow tribesmen, and the reporter emphasized that those ponies represented "about all the wealth of Victor's son, the hereditary chieftain of the Flathead Nation," along with his Bitterroot farm.[5] Charlo's farm consisted of a two-story log house of four rooms; it sat at the back of a "pretty little park" consisting of some "seven or eight acres," all fenced, where he grew wheat.[6]

While the Salish focused on surviving, men in Washington were conceptualizing a new strategy of land allotments for moving Indians toward self-sufficiency, on the one hand, and freeing up the land for eager settlers, on the other. The gist of their thinking was that when Indians no longer held lands in common but instead held them separately—in severalty—through an allotment process, they would come to know the pride of individual ownership. The concept was an easy sell. By 1882 advocates promoted the notion that the allotment system "has the effect of creating individuality, responsibility, and a desire to accumulate property." By owning their own land, the Indians would learn "habits of industry and frugality" and would achieve the highly valued accomplishment of self-reliance.[7]

A group of Protestant reformers began meeting in the Catskill Mountains to consider ways in which they could help the Indians become more self-sufficient. Among this group was U.S. senator Henry L. Dawes of Massachusetts, a name that would become synonymous with allotments. Many in the nation's capital were beginning to agree that pride in ownership could be the culminating shift on the long road to move Indians from barbaric to civilized and a whole lot more.

As the Northern Pacific Railroad was nearing completion, the NPRR company petitioned for a right-of-way through the Jocko Reservation and sent assistant attorney general Joseph McCammon to negotiate an agreement. Indians on the Jocko Reservation were not pleased. "This reservation is a small country and yet you want five depots upon it," Kootenai chief Big Knife complained. "My country was like a flower and

I gave you its best part." Unlike the white men, the Indians preferred their country to money. Big Knife explained to the negotiators that the land "is like our parents."[8] Ultimately they had no choice. The land would be taken. Allowing the creation of roads through the reservation had been agreed to by treaty. McCammon concluded an agreement that ceded a fifty-three-mile swath across the southern portion of the reservation, where Arlee and Adolph had settled.[9] The railroad divided more than the land.

In the Bitterroot Valley the railroad had devastating results for Chief Charlo's people, in part due to efforts on the part of Washington Territory land claims attorney John Mullan, the man for whom the first road through Salish territory had been named and the old friend who had extolled Victor's virtues in a widely publicized obituary. The NPRR had claimed its due in odd sections within the affected townships under its land grant of 1864. Nearly two decades later, Mullan, representing non-Indian settlers in the Bitterroot in their fight against the railroad, argued that those sections should be declared open for homesteading based on legal history in the valley since 1864. The judge's decision in January 1883 went against the railroad and opened its previously held sections for settlement under the Homestead Act. The Salish who had taken out patents on their lands after Garfield's visit were protected. All other places could be claimed. Thankfully, fifty-one patents had been prepared for Salish men, including Charlo, and had been kept safe for them at the agency. Without these they would have had no legal claims to their homes and lands.

Congress sent Missouri senator George G. Vest and Montana delegate Martin Maginnis to western Montana in September 1883 to report on the condition of the Indians. They took the train to the new Arlee depot to meet with the reservation Flatheads. Pend d'Oreille chief Michel expressed the Indians' strong desire to maintain their system of holding lands in common and not to be severed from each other.

The members of the delegation concluded their business on the reservation and headed south to the Bitterroot Valley to meet with Charlo and his advisors. First, though, at St. Mary's, they met with an ailing Father Ravalli, who assured them that Charlo had never changed his mind about his commitment to stay in the Bitterroot and had not made his mark on the Garfield agreement.[10] When the delegations met, Senator Vest, a skilled orator, explained the purpose of their visit. Charlo listened to the removal proposal, then expressed his complete lack of confidence in their promises and made clear to them he would never leave. "Your Great Father Garfield put my name to a paper which I never signed," he told them, saying that Ronan had their own unsigned copy in safe keeping at the agency. Based on all his experiences, he continued, he would never trust them or any white man.[11] The meeting's frostiness might have also been due to Charlo's awareness of Maginnis's negative track record concerning Indian lands.[12] It had been one of the hallmarks of his political career.

A reporter for the *Helena Independent* described the council as dramatic. Senator Vest, looking across the room at Charlo, explained, through the interpreter, the purpose of their visit. Charlo paused for a moment while keeping a steady gaze directed at Vest, then responded in his usual manner, by bringing context to the situation. Speaking "with all the confidence and dignity of a chief backed by five thousand warriors," he told them that "from their former strength," now they were "only a few . . . poor and weak."[13] The chief reminded them that Salish hands were "free from the white man's blood," and since their last meeting about removal in 1872, his people had protected their white neighbors from the Nez Perce. Considering this history, he wanted to know why the white man, would "take his heart from us now?" The Salish had not changed their minds. They did not wish to leave their homeland. In graphic language, he described how this situation felt to his people: "You place your foot upon our necks and press our faces into the dust." Even so, he made clear, he would never give up this place for the reservation. The option he proposed instead was to go to the plains.[14]

Senator Vest—who would later coin the phrase "history is written by the victors"—reminded Charlo of what happened to Joseph and the Nez Perce when they attempted to go to the plains. "Look where he is now! There are no more plains. The white men are as thick as leaves from ocean to ocean." The senator told Charlo to forget his dream. "Either get a patent to your lands here or go upon the reservation."[15]

The Indians reiterated their refusal to leave the Bitterroot. For dramatic effect Charlo removed his hat, threw it to the floor, and shouted,

"You may take Charlos to the reservation, but there will be no breath in his nostrils! Charlos will be dead! He will never go there alive!"[16] The senator stood up and answered, in language as emphatic as the chief's, that the Salish must obey the white man's laws. They must go where the government chooses to send them.

The council reached a stalemate. The commissioners met afterward with Agent Ronan, who offered a lifeline. He reminded them that the Salish, since the time of Victor, had frequently asked to meet with the president to resolve this issue. Before the council broke up, a decision was made that Charlo would go to Washington to talk the matter over with the Great Father, President Arthur, the fifth president to serve since Chief Victor had sent his first request to President Lincoln.

When Senator Vest returned to Washington, he ordered a clerk to dig up the original of the Garfield agreement that had been sent to the commissioner and determined that it had no "x" mark next to Chief Charlo's name. The honesty of the brave and beleaguered Salish leader was affirmed, but he never forgot and never forgave the whites for this and countless other abuses he and his people had suffered. The revelation of the forgery ultimately changed nothing. The federal government continued to put pressure on the Bitterroot Salish to move.

Charlo Goes to Washington

Deep snow and cold marked Christmas of 1884 in the Bitterroot Valley. Salish families set up their lodges around St. Mary's and went to confession. Father D'Aste wrote of the "pitiful sight to see the poor women . . . trying to keep up their supply of firewood. Their cotton lodge covers did little to shield them from the cold." Seeing them, he went on to say, "you would think they had plenty of everything, for they looked content and happy." He pondered what would become of them and feared much suffering ahead. "They are now very poor, and if the government fails to come to their help . . . I am afraid that starvation will get the lot of them."[17]

Just three months after Senator Vest returned to Washington, the Salish delegation prepared to leave for the nation's capital. In addition to Agent Ronan, Chief Charlo was accompanied by Sandhill Crane's Necklace (Antoine Moise, the son of Crawling Mountain); Far-Away

Grizzly (Louis Vanderburg, the son-in-law of Bear Tracks); Hand Shot Off (John Hill); and Thomas Abel Adams. The group included their trusted interpreter, One Man Walking (Michel Revais).[18] Gathered on the platform on a crisp morning in January 1884, they were observed by a traveler who, as "Babbler," wrote a newspaper article about this unusual scene. "Babbler" did his best to bring the scene to life. He described Chief Charlo, who was in his early fifties, as an "old Indian, with a massive, stern face, on which Father Time had chiseled deep wrinkles, who walked with dignified step and upright form, was of heavy square build, clothed in a handsome mantle of fur, wore a white felt hat, with two eagle feathers sticking up at the back of the hat from the band, handsome beaded moccasins on his feet." Charlo was followed by a man who "was being led by two Indians." Behind them were another trio, described as "two Indians and a half-breed in regimentals—that is, he wore a blue coat, with brass buttons."[19] The man being led by others that "Babbler" described was the blind interpreter, Michel Revais.

Their journey by train took six days. The route took them up the Clark Fork, a corridor they had been avoiding since railroad construction began. The starkness of the barren hillsides made this ancient landscape seem unfamiliar. Across the Divide they dropped into the Three Forks, past the boom town of Bozeman, with nearly one thousand people, and on to the Yellowstone Valley across what used to be buffalo country. That very winter, in that buffalo ghost land, Indians were starving to death. The Blackfeet remember that time as Starvation Winter, when hundreds of their people died.

Hurtling through the bleak white landscape in a loud capsule, removed from the frosty air and the creaking of winter trees, was disconcerting. It must have been particularly hard on One Man Walking, who could feel the speed but not see it. Charlo's eyesight was also compromised but not to the extent of Michel's.

In Washington the members of the Salish delegation were treated as dignitaries. Their list of activities included attending a party given by President Arthur. The official business regarding Salish removal from the Bitterroot began after a few days of sightseeing and visiting. Secretary of the Interior Henry Teller was the point person for negotiations. In addition to Chief Charlo's entourage and Agent Ronan, Senator Vest and Delegate Maginnis also attended. The first day, the officials focused on all the reasons that Charlo should accept the government's offers and agree to removal. The offers included a house, fenced and plowed land sufficient for a farm, cattle, horses, seed, and agricultural implements. These same benefits would be given to each head of family among his people. In addition, Charlo would receive $500 a year and, once again, would be head chief of the Salish and all the Indians of the reservation.

The officials didn't understand that Charlo had never been motivated by money. Perhaps he remembered the Bible lesson of St. Paul's warning that the love of money was the root of all evil. He might have learned that lesson from Fathers Mengarini or Point when he was young; but his understanding went deeper than that. In his 1876 speech, when the Salish were being asked by the county commissioners to pay taxes, Charlo had reminded his people that this was a request for them to pay the white man "for the things we have from our God and our forefathers; for things he never owned and never gave us."[20] The essential things were what mattered to him, and white men could not provide them. Charlo refused all offers, telling the representatives he just wanted to die in peace in his homeland.

Over the course of their meetings, according to a story that ran on the front page of the *Helena Weekly Herald* on February 21, 1884, Secretary Teller concluded that "he did not feel that the Indians ought to be compelled to go. The chief . . . hasn't much confidence in the promises of white men, and he is sharp enough to know that the Secretary cannot carry out his promises unless Congress is willing."

The delegation arrived home on March 7, after an absence of nearly six weeks. Charlo returned with his vision restored, but Michel was not so lucky. Both men had surgery on their eyes at the conclusion of their official business. Charlo's operation was a full success. Michel had been blind for over three decades, and his condition was not responsive to the surgery.

Charlo's return to the Place of Wide Cottonwoods might have seemed shocking after his exposure to the opulence of Capitol Hill. His people were suffering, and they had to face a world totally bereft of buffalo. The year before they had had good luck hunting elk and moose in the Big Hole and around Skalkaho and other places in the upper Bitter-

FIG. 60. Chief Charlo and delegation in Washington DC, 1884. From P. Ronan, *Historical Sketch of the Flathead Indian Nation*.

root Valley, but white citizens resented the competition. New game laws restricted hunting seasons that pertained to white citizens but were ignored by the Indians due to their 1855 treaty rights. The *Weekly Missoulian* ran a short opinion piece on March 14 from a county correspondent based in the upper Bitterroot Valley at Como, reflective of the growing tension. "A party of Indians passed up a few days since, on a big hunt. By the way, is not our game law a regular Bonanza for poor Lo, as it withdraws competition by the whites and leaves him [the Indian] a clear field? If the Indian is so much better than the white man that he can violate the law with impunity, why not let him run the machine for a while himself?"[21]

That summer, when the Salish were hounded by hunger, Stevensville citizens called for speedy agreements for the railroad spur up the Bitterroot, and a monument was erected in Cleveland in honor of James Garfield. The *Weekly Missoulian* reported the Indian presence around the booming town to be "quite an annoyance to many of our settlers. They [the Indians] seem to feel that their time worn trails are public roads which the white man has no rights to fence in and they very inconsiderately tear down (and leave down) the obstructing fence wherever they wish to cross the old track." The article continues with a note about the presence of thirty Blackfeet lodges on a fishing and hunting incursion right in the neighborhood. Although Missoulians did not fear for their personal safety, "there is a feeling that a strange Indian in a strange land will not hesitate to break into a cabin or drive off a good horse if he finds the opportunity."[22] Like the Salish, the Blackfeet survivors were hungry and couldn't face another winter like the one before.

After the meetings in Washington, Charlo might have hoped that he and his people were going to be left in whatever peace they could find. But hornets remained active, buzzing with steady reminders that other people wanted them removed, and they wouldn't rest until that happened. Another government official would eventually find his way to the Bitterroot Valley to consummate the deal.

Meanwhile, a new collision course was being laid out that would pit the traditional collective values of the Salish against the values of individualism, self-reliance, and material wealth. The *Weekly Missoulian* ran an article from a Diamond City newspaper in March 1886 that alluded to a scheme for acquiring Indian lands. The report built on the same reasoning that had been used to sell the concept of allotting lands to promote good stewardship. The new version for "the planned break-up of the tribal relations of the Indians" would not only allot "to each a certain portion of land," but also the balance of the reservation lands would be sold "for their benefit." In other words, instead of simply breaking up the reservation into individual properties, the Indians would receive individual parcels of predetermined size, mimicking the Homestead Act, and all remaining lands would be taken from them. It was a brilliant scheme for undermining the treaties. "Excess" land would be made available to non-Indians. It was justified as the solution for long-term support as promised in the treaties. The author concluded with the rationalization that this "is the only plan that has been hit upon which promises a permanent and positive solution of the question for their support."[23] This idea was working its way through the halls of Congress. The act would go down in infamy in Indian Country and would be keenly felt on the Jocko Reservation more than two decades later.

Paradise Lost

By 1886 the traditional Salish camp locations along Silver Bow and Warm Springs Creeks, at the head of the Clark Fork, were spoiled by industry, as were the foods they had traditionally acquired there. A half century before, fur trader Warren Ferris had described the Deer Lodge Valley as a virtual paradise, "decorated with groves and thickets of aspen, birch, and willow, and occasional clusters of currant and gooseberry bushes," with rich bottomlands, "resorted to by great numbers of deer and elk."[24] This valley was becoming a wasteland.

Traditional fisheries had become unfishable all along the channelized Clark Fork due to mills and the industry of the towns now dotting the valley along the railroad. Timber was so scarce as to almost cause a local war on Cramer Creek, an upper Clark Fork tributary. Because the lower Blackfoot and Clark Fork valleys had been stripped of timber, the owner of a mill on the lower river set his eye on Cramer Creek. When his crew arrived, they found another team from a headwaters mill. The men were going to fight for this last stand of timber until some cool head suggested they split the take. They competed to see who could haul out the most timber, each working one side of the drainage, leaving the slopes denuded.[25]

Cramer Creek is located about forty-five miles below Snx̣ʷq̓ʷpuʔsáqs. When the railroad came through, that place became known as Garrison Junction, a name imposed on the landscape like an American flag on the moon—"Garrison" for the famous abolitionist from Massachusetts and "Junction" because the railroad surveyors too recognized the place as where the trail split for Helena or Bozeman. The name comes from a world of heroes and individualism, born from a culture that usually names mountains and rivers and towns after outstanding men, while Snx̣ʷq̓ʷpuʔsáqs tells of the place itself, from a people finely tuned to the foods and waters and pathways of their homeland. The changing names along old pathways were telling the history of the takeover that Charlo was trying to survive.

Charlo's own life felt as denuded as the hillsides. His wife, Margarite, had died the previous summer at the age of forty-six, not long after the death of their nine-year-old son Peter. The buffalo were gone. The off-reservation fishing, hunting, and gathering rights offered the Salish little in these industrial wastelands, stripped of life. Women asked farmers if they could follow behind their plows to gather camas roots, and, as a pitiful replacement for the bison hunt, the Salish camped near the slaughterhouses to trade for meat and scraps. What had for many years seemed bleak had now shifted into the realm of hopeless.

During these dark months the concept of allotment had evolved into law through a bill carried by Senator Dawes. It passed on February 8, 1887, and provided for patents to be given to individual Indians for their reservation lands. It went so far as to confer citizenship on Indians who would foreswear their tribal affiliations. In October 1889, after Chief Arlee's death in early August and when the details were finally worked out for the Salish to sell their patented lands in the Bitterroot, the government appointed a special commissioner, Henry Carrington, an aging lawyer and retired general from the Sioux wars, to take care of the details.

The well-versed special commissioner headed to the Jocko Reservation in Montana after preparing for his assignment by reading pertinent background material. There the sixty-five-year-old Carrington met Chief

Charlo and other Salish representatives as well as Agent Ronan. They began their time together with a mass at St. Ignatius led by Father D'Aste, assisted by Michel Revais. They moved on to the home of Agent Ronan to get acquainted.[26] Carrington and Charlo were strikingly different in their physical presence, both in size and manner. The solid gravitas of Charlo, the younger by about six years, set off Carrington's thin frame and officious manner. The general knew what it took to make things happen, though, and he created a relaxed social atmosphere for establishing relationships. Work could wait until later, when they would get down to business in the Bitterroot Valley.[27]

In the bumpy ride by coach to Stevensville, Carrington took in the beauty of his surroundings, accented by the turning cottonwood leaves reflected in the river. The white caps on the mountains completed the idyllic scene. He mulled over the reason for his journey. His primary responsibility over the course of the next weeks was to address the particulars necessary for removal of the Indians who remained in the valley, and it included the appraisal of more than two hundred quarter sections.[28]

The commissioner visited Charlo's farm, a couple of miles west and a little south of Stevensville, and found the chief out in front of his cabin fixing a plow. In the corner of the yard, munching dry corn fodder caught around the fence, were a few skinny horses, chickens, hogs, dogs, and a cow. A half-covered tipi that served as a summer dwelling stood out among a small smokehouse and a scattering of broken farm equipment. The chief's small fields of corn and wheat had been harvested. The only furnishings inside the cabin were piles of blankets and robes that served as bedding. Charlo spoke to the general of his hunger and that of his people. Carrington had come prepared and provided food in abundance for the chief and for many others who came forward that day.[29]

The general then got to work on the detailed work before him. He carefully documented all the patented lands and then, with the help of Michel Revais, Father D'Aste, and old Eneas—"Petit Ignace"—he certified land rights through documentation of family lineages. As a member of the U.S. Supreme Court bar, he was able to handle the legal work.[30] He prepared necessary documents for the Indians to relinquish their patents and to agree to removal.

The astute negotiator invited the Salish to meet with him, one by one, to discuss particulars of moving and to sign their consent. He rented a room in a Stevensville hotel for the meetings. His strategy was to meet with the men separately and thereby avoid the influence of Charlo. Carrington did not understand the limitations of Charlo's authority and the process required among the Salish to come to consensus. Immersed in the military hierarchy, the general had no understanding of "the Salish tradition of collective leadership."[31] He deemed Charlo to be obstinate. Charlo observed the proceedings from a distance. He held fast to his rights to remain in the Salish homeland until the moment he witnessed his trusted companion Distant Grizzly (known to the whites as Louis Vanderburg) step to the table and sign. His dear friend had broken with the chief and was prepared to move. Other headmen also agreed to take the deal offered. Charlo wavered.[32]

On the day after an exhausted Carrington completed the negotiations with all those who had stepped forward to sign, he met for six hours with Chief Charlo, and they still didn't reach an agreement. Charlo held steady, saying he would sign no more papers and he would not move. Carrington reported Charlo's concern that if he changed his mind, he might be perceived as "a coward and a liar." He preferred suicide. The next day, though, Charlo (Claw of Little Grizzly) arrived at the general's door with his young son Victor. He sat there a while before knocking, then made his presence known. Carrington welcomed him to enter, and he was followed by others who had waited for their chief to decide before they made their own decisions.

Charlo sat on the floor smoking his pipe while his friends and relatives signed their contracts. Finally the worn-out chief reached a decision. He would move to the reservation for the sake of his hungry people. Before signing the removal agreement, the chief asked that the graves of their ancestors in the St. Mary's cemetery be protected, to which Carrington agreed. He also wanted assurance that his people would be provided good cabins at unoccupied sites in the Jocko Valley and that the government would provide food for them during the winter, after this stressful time of drought, while they waited for Congress to approve the agreement. Charlo asked for Arlee's house as a way to reassert his chieftainship, and he asked that a covered, two-seated spring-wagon be provided for him. Once he was satisfied that his requests had been agreed to, he stood up and said, "I will go with Big Heart to the Jocko. I will sign." He told Carrington that the Great Spirit had spoken to him in the night, telling him to "trust the white Chief."[33] The general responded by placing "the chief's hand over his own heart as a pledge."[34] What Carrington wrote that day to satisfy Charlo didn't completely match up with his official report.

Claw of Little Grizzly and Many Horses before him had always vowed to stay where their ancestors were buried. In a poignant twist to this story, in May 1889, more than two years before they had to leave the Bitterroot and several months before General Carrington came to negotiate the removal, the Salish were observed "digging up the remains of their comrades in the old Fort Owen burying ground and removing them to the reservation."[35] The timing of this removal of ancestors' bones followed just a few months after the former special agent to the Flatheads, W. J. McCormick, had been blown off the roof of the fort during one of those occasional ferocious Bitterroot windstorms and had died of head injuries as a result. McCormick had purchased the fort at a sheriff's auction in 1872. It is ironic that John Owen, the founder of Fort Owen, also died that year, in July. Perhaps the McCormick family had asked the Salish to remove the burials, or maybe the Indians were concerned that the land would be sold and they might lose access. Whatever the reason, the remains of those ancestors who had been buried since the time of the Jesuits' arrival would be waiting for them at the St. Ignatius Mission cemetery.

Carrington promised Charlo that he would return the next spring to arrange for the land sales and for the move. Charlo and his people, counting on Carrington's promised 1890 return, did not plant crops that spring. According to historian Robert Bigart, "The drought of 1889 had left them so impoverished that they could not afford seed, and in spite of the promise of assistance, the government failed to provide more than starvation rations." The Salish dug roots and sought meat in their usual haunts, where little remained. Congress failed to provide funds for costs associated with the move. All was in order except that Carrington failed to return at the expected time. By December 1890 conditions were so dire the Salish "were forced to barter away their horses, harnesses, plows, and even stoves in order to feed themselves."[36] Ronan provided them with bare necessities to get them through until spring. According to Charlo, if their horses and cattle hadn't died in great numbers that winter, his people would have starved. By March provisions were gone, and the bitterroot crop was not ready. Desperate, they risked violations of state game laws and visited nearby slaughterhouses to eke out a living.

On July 1, 1891, Congress finally approved, and the president ratified, the necessary funding to relocate the Salish. When General Carrington returned to the Bitterroot Valley to assist with the effort in late July, more than a year later than expected, Chief Charlo refused to talk business until his people were fed.[37] He truly feared his people would die before food could be obtained. Carrington acted swiftly and convinced the Buck brothers, Stevensville merchants, to provide the needed food and supplies while they waited for land sales to manifest. The hungry families gathered around to partake of the offerings laid out on the boardwalks of town. Chief Charlo stood out in his red vest and the felt hat with its upright eagle feather while he looked over his flock to make sure all were fed.

Hunger continued its tight grip. The people hadn't the strength or the horsepower to travel far. They sought food in the upper valley and up Burnt Fork. A letter from an Upper Rock Creek rancher to the *Philipsburg Mail* on October 1, 1891, complained that "the Indians who are tramping across the east side down to the Bitter Root are killing any and all kinds of game they happen to see." His only particular example was the killing of an elk and a moose in the upper canyon by "a small band of the Redskins." He had been motivated to write after reading a recent article entitled "Trapping Elk by the Hundred," about a white man in Idaho abusing game laws by killing large numbers of elk and shipping them back east for profit.

Only four land parcels had been processed by early October 1891. Carrington and others feared the Salish wouldn't make it through another winter in the Bitterroot without intervention. He and Ronan wanted them to go ahead and move to the reservation, where food security had greatly improved, rather than waiting for their payments, but some of their own people on the reservation cautioned them to stay put until they were paid.

The Salish chiefs met General Carrington on October 11 at the office of the justice of the peace, Joseph McLaren. According to M. L. Rickman, pastor of the First Baptist Church in Bozeman and friend of Carrington, "Main street was filled with Indians on their ponies in constant motion like bees when the queen is lost." The first to enter were some "two dozen braves," who seated themselves in the space where trials were held. Their chief, Charlo, then entered, escorted by Antoine Moise, the son of Crawling Mountain, and two others. They passed through a door marked "private" and entered a room that doubled as a lawyer's office and a pastor's study. Charlo took a seat across the room from General Carrington, who, according to Rickman, rose and addressed the chief, using metaphors to convey that it was time for the Salish to agree to move. He likened the United States to a "big train coming down the track" and the Salish to "a little calf" in the way of the train. The general was "the whistle," there to warn them it was time to relinquish their Bitterroot lands and move to the Jocko.[38]

Rickman described the suspenseful scene while everyone waited for Charlo to respond. The chief "sat with arms folded," without speaking, "his superb head erect, his dreaming eyes looking out of the window, silently smoking his pipe, preserving an attitude of dignity blended with disdain." Although the silence was deafening, all remained quiet. "No one moved." Charlo then "gave a little start like one checking a sleepy sensation in company" or confirming some inner resolve. Then he stood and removed two handkerchiefs from his chest, "one as white as the driven snow, the other red as blood." He leaned over and spread them side by side on the carpet. "Pointing toward the white one, he said, 'Flathead is like that. He never killed white man. He never shed white man's blood.' Pointing toward the red one, he said, 'The Crows, Snakes, Sioux, Nez Perces are like that. They want to kill white man. Flatheads fight for him. Chief like that. He never killed white man.'"

Then Charlo revealed something about his father's death, otherwise lost to history: "When Charlot fight for white man [was when] he see Indians kill Chief Victor." They were somewhere in the Musselshell country in the summer of 1870, and Charlo was doing something to protect a white man when his father was killed. As Victor fell, Charlo caught him in his arms. "Charlot chief then." He went on to tell about how the Flatheads drove the Nez Perce away from the Bitterroot and saved the white man, referring to 1877. He brought his remarks to a close by saying, "No white man hates Flathead. White man drives Flathead away. Charlot wants white man to live. White man wants Charlot and his children to die. Charlot has spoken."

Charlo sat back down with "sadness in his majestic bearing." Rickman saw that his friend, "the old soldier, was overcome with feelings and shed tears as if Charlot had saved his own life." When he could speak, the general said, "Chief Charlot, I am your friend. I love your children. I will do all I can for you, but I must do what the Big Chief tells me to do. You must leave your homes, Charlot, but the Big Chief will pay you for your lands."

Charlo stood to deliver harsh words, ones he had spoken on many an occasion. "Flathead always tell truth to white man. White man always lie to Flathead. Many times white man has lied to Charlot. Charlot still fights for him." He gazed out of the window toward St. Mary's, then turned back and addressed Carrington: "Charlot and his children will go, not for money; but Charlot want peace with his white brother." Those words brought the meeting to an end.

The next day the chief had changed his mind. He told Carrington that he hadn't been able to fall to sleep until he sent word to his people "to come together in the morning as soon as the sun was up to say prayers to the Great Spirit." That eased his distress, and he was able to sleep, and while he did, he told the general, "The Great Spirit gave me these thoughts. 'Charlot, go with your people. They will starve, or freeze here. Nobody will buy your land if you stay. Go and pick out good land and build houses before winter. Shut your ears to lies which bad people tell you.'"[39]

The Salish people gathered together for prayer at daybreak on October 12. After thirty-six years of peaceful resistance, their fight was over. They would all go together to the reservation. Charlo told the general that he didn't want any soldiers along, and the only white men he wanted to travel with them were Carrington and Joe McLaren, a U.S. circuit court commissioner. The thirty-seven-year-old Irishman had moved to Stevensville with his family in 1883 and had become a trusted friend of the chief.[40]

FIG. 61. Charlo and Salish men, with General Carrington and others, in front of St. Mary's chapel, 1891. Archives and Special Collections, Mansfield Library, University of Montana.

The chief received word that troops would be arriving on October 15 to escort them to the reservation. The Salish should pack up their belongings and assemble at St. Mary's the day before. They would hold a feast that night and recount their stories. The scene was one worth remembering. As described by Rickman, rows of tipis had been erected at the commons next to the church. Nearby the Salish had arranged criss-crossed lodgepole pines on the ground, with kindling placed beneath the logs. "The entire length was lighted by the Indian torches, making a huge, fiery cross." Within a grand circle created by seated women, the men circled around. As each angle of the cross was reached, they moved "as if they would dash into the flames" then out again and back into the circling dance. One group would follow another while the women sang.[41] The entire night was spent feasting, dancing, and recounting their age-old history.

The scene the next morning was all confusion until Chief Charlo, Claw of Little Grizzly, rode through the crowd, "steady as a beaver moves on his lake, holding aloft the white wing of a crane." The Salish people later remembered that their chief led them in Catholic prayer, then gave instructions to prepare for departure. He had worked out a plan for them to travel in three groups of about fifty each, one to be led by Charlo, one by Saxa (Francis Xavier Lamoose, the son of Sinshe and Grand Ignace) and the other by Louis Vanderburg (Distant Grizzly), a relative and close companion of Charlo. (Louis's wife, Mary, was the daughter of Bear Tracks, who had died in his nineties about a decade earlier.)[42] Horses and wagons were loaded up with children and belongings and organized into the three groups, while the People waited for their chief to give them the signal that it was time to go. When he did, "in perfect order the Indians rode away." One Bitterroot settler contrasted the older Salish men, who sat astride their horses straight and tall and silent, with the women, who "were bent over crying."[43] The white residents, according to Rickman, seemed to have "mingled feelings" of both relief and grief as they watched them go, accompanied by a military guard despite Charlo's wishes.[44]

The proud Salish people, caretakers of these lands since they had been given to them by the Creator, proceeded in silence down the Bitterroot Valley. The three groups followed along wagon roads, often in sight of the Bitterroot spur line of the Northern Pacific Railroad. They passed by the town of Florence at the place they knew as One Horse and made it several miles more before rain forced them to stop earlier than expected. Descendants remember that their families joined together for the night on the property of a friendly settler named David Maclay, south of Lolo, or "No Salmon," where the railroad had built a switchyard. Carrington, who traveled with Charlo's group, remembered that after the livestock was secured and the meal consumed, visiting went on until the chief called for quiet.

People awoke early to the sound of a ringing bell as the chief called them to prayer, a familiar sound ever since the arrival of the first Catholics. The plan was to pass through Missoula before dark. They passed near Fort Missoula and the camas grounds and then gathered together before they reached the Clark Fork. As was their way, they removed their finest apparel from their parfleches in order to present themselves proudly. An honor guard of painted defenders led them toward the river. Details of the crossing have been lost. Salish historians believe

FIG. 62. "Removal of Flatheads" from the Bitterroot Valley, Montana, 1891. Penn Museum, image #P175348.

one group may have crossed the rickety Higgins Avenue bridge while the others forded the river, one close to the bridge and another a short distance downstream.

Missoulians gathered along Higgins and gawked at Distant Grizzly's heartbroken group as they crossed over the Clark Fork. Carrington found this town of some 3,500 non-Indians surprisingly quiet as the Indians moved through streets lined with curious onlookers. The displaced Salish travelers kept their eyes averted and "gave no hint that many were weeping and longing to get away from the gaze and criticism of the white observers."[45] Charlo, ever the dignified chief, looked straight ahead, willing his people to get through this gauntlet without trouble.

Their passage must have seemed interminable. This multi-day journey from the Bitterroot took them along a trail that their ancestors had known since the beginning of time. Many familiar places were now built upon by the square buildings of the white world. Once across the Clark Fork, they headed west on the Mullan Road. The elders felt relieved that none of their young people got coaxed into trouble as they passed the enticements of town. They passed by the site of their treaty council and camped near a train station named for De Smet, in the west valley, near Frenchtown.

From there the trail branched northward to the crest of what is known as De Smet Hill and through what was called Coriacan's Defile—named in memory of a Hawaiian who had been ambushed there by Blackfeet in the 1830s; it was later known as Evaro.[46] The canyon's entry was narrow and steep. Over their heads a train ran along the elevated Northern Pacific track across the gap. Its ear-splitting clacking and the sound of the whistle blasting through the morning air caused the livestock to stampede. The wife of Joseph Lomprey flew off her bolting horse and broke her hip on the landing.[47]

They stopped again near the racetrack atop the canyon, just miles before they reached the agency and again donned their fine clothes and painted their faces. Many people had gathered at the agency to welcome them, including a proud and relieved Agent Ronan. His wife, Mary, described their arrival in her journal: "Within a mile of the agency church, the advancing Indians spread out in a broad column. The young men kept constantly discharging their firearms, while a few of the number, mounted on fleet ponies, arrayed in fantastic Indian paraphernalia, with long blankets partially draping the forms of the warriors and steeds, rode back and forth in front of the advancing caravan, shouting and firing their guns until they neared the church."[48]

This last hoorah of the young men came to a halt as they approached the church where the priest stood with open arms to welcome the weary travelers. Although Agent Ronan felt proud to have helped bring this long chapter of Flathead history to a close, Mary found it one of the saddest and most pathetic scenes she had ever witnessed.

Chief Charlo dismounted to stand and shake hands with all those who had come to welcome him as they made their way into the little Jocko church, warmly greeted by Father Canestrelli. As noted by the *Spokesman Review* on December 3, 1891, in its reporting of this historic dislocation, the Latin verses they chanted that day in their unique hybrid expression—"O Salutaris" and "Tantum Ergo," scribed by Thomas Aquinas in the twelfth century—must have touched their hearts. Within the verses were words that meant "Our foes press on from every side; Thine aid supply, thy strength bestow." The Christian god and saints had long provided strength and hope for these long-suffering people. The Jesuits had arrived among them fifty years before and planted seeds of Christian faith that had sprouted and remained strong for many Salish families, including Charlo's. After the benediction of the mass, Peter Ronan welcomed everyone with a feast.

The *Missoula Weekly Gazette* observed that "the travelers are apparently pleased with the change, if one is to judge by the may grunts of satisfaction expressed along the line and they feel that they are going to meet friends and will be well cared for."[49] But the Salish survivors experienced it differently. Mary Ann Combs recalled it like "a three-day funeral march."[50] Some remembered that "the soldiers did not allow people to go to the brush to relieve themselves, warning them they would be shot if they ran away." Children wondered why their elders were crying. This forced march from the Place of Wide Cottonwoods to the Jocko Valley became known as "the Séliš Trail of Tears."[51]

After this painful exodus, the bitter chief, with his second wife and the youngest of his four children, eleven-year-old Victor, settled into a home provided by the government. There he lived quietly among his people for his remaining years.

Reservation Blues

Homelands of the Confederated Salish, Pend d'Oreille, and Kootenai Tribes originally comprised all of western Montana and adjacent parts of Idaho and British Columbia. The terms of the 1855 Hellgate Treaty reduced their holdings to 1.25 million acres of the Jocko Reservation and 1.7 million acres of the provisional Bitterroot Reservation. Once the Bitterroot lands were taken from the Salish, they joined others on what became known as the Flathead Reservation. By the time Charlo and the Bitterroot Salish got settled in the Jocko Valley in 1891, their holdings had already been reduced by the railroad, and more were soon to follow. Their stalwart protector, Agent Ronan, died in 1893, leaving them even more vulnerable to political manipulation. Even the reserved land was not considered inviable by those who imagined how much more they could do with it. Since the time of John Winthrop, Euro-Americans had never stopped thinking of Indians as those who wasted the land, and the lands of the Flathead Valley were no exception.

FIG. 63. Flathead Indians at Jocko Agency, 1894. Charlo is in the back row wearing a hat. Archives and Special Collections, Mansfield Library, University of Montana.

The first agent to replace Ronan was unscrupulous, and the next, the first non-Catholic agent, W. H. Smead, had no respect for Salish traditions. This former state senator from Missoula was appointed in 1897, just two years after introducing a bill to open the Flathead Reservation for general settlement. This bill and its author were despised by the Indians but extremely well liked by the white community, as made clear by a *Weekly Missoulian* op-ed on February 3, 1895. Daniel Bandmann, a Shakespearean actor from New York who had bought a ranch in 1887 near the mouth of Hell Gate Canyon, asked the question, "Why should this fine tract of land be reserved for a few dozen half casts who reap the benefit of it, to the detriment of thousands of willing and anxious home seekers?" He added that more white settlers on the reservation would help influence the process toward civilization for these Indians, who live "in a half barbarious [*sic*] state." He questioned the fairness of these people having all these "millions of acres" when they pay no taxes, while "the white man struggles and labors" in the building of civilization. From his point of view, "A few half cast Indians live in clover and keep the white man in a sort of bondage." Bandmann came to Montana after the buffalo were gone and had no idea about the treaty history of the Native people of western Montana, nor of all they had ceded already for white settlement. Readers are left to wonder if it would have made any difference if he had known that the Flathead Reservation represented such a small fraction of their original lands.

One source of tension at this time involved dwindling herds of deer and elk. White citizens complained that the Indians seemed to get away with hunting wherever and whenever they wanted. Members of the local chapter of the League of American Sportsmen made their voices heard. In 1899 the superintendent of the Lewis and Clark Forest Reserve reported that the Flatheads slaughtered game and often used fire to drive the animals where they wanted them to go. The land commissioner passed the complaint on to the secretary of the interior, and soon a mandate came down from the commissioner of Indian affairs that "Indians refrain altogether from entering forest reserves for the purposes of hunting at any season of the year."[52]

For Indians on the Flathead Reservation, this news was devastating. The vast majority of their traditional hunting places had been integrated into the Flathead, Bitterroot, and Helena National Forests, created in 1897. Agent Smead posted the new restrictions and informed the local forester that he would implement a system of passes for Indian families to access the forests on a controlled basis.[53] The Native hunters recoiled at being treated like leashed animals.

The nineteenth century drew to a close with little for the Salish to celebrate. Reservation life bore little resemblance to what had been told them by Governor Stevens all those years before. They lost not only their lands but many of their human rights as well. Agent Smead was enforcing government schooling for their children, regardless of what the parents desired. An Ursuline Nun who worked at the Jocko Agency school reported that although the chief "had always been on good terms with the whites, he detested their ways." He was concerned that the Salish children would speak English, not their own tongue. "When they know English, they will go to the white towns and buy whiskey." He did want their hair to be cut like the white men's. "God made the Indian with long hair" was his belief. He feared that schooling would initiate a process that would ultimately take their children away from them. "Our children will become like whites in other ways in school, and when they grow up they will fly away like birds and leave their parents." Although Charlo protested the opening of the Jocko school, "he sent his own son, Victor." Echoes of his lament still waft across the land as many of his fears materialized.[54]

As the white world surrounded them, more and more people participated in the mid-winter Blue Jay Ceremony, adopted from the Columbia River people. The multi-night healing dances connected them to the old ways of Coyote's world and, for those precious days, allowed them to leave the white world behind.

On the reservation in the early years of the twentieth century, the Salish were making necessary adjustments to life without buffalo. Many of them raised cattle and horses and some families excelled at raising crops of grain, hay, and vegetables. Covetous non-Indian cattlemen and merchants dreamed of ways to get Indian grazing lands for themselves. In 1903 Agent Smead imposed a grazing tax on owners of more than one hundred animals. Each horse or cow beyond that number would cost the owner one dollar. Horses had long signified wealth to the Salish, and those who could spent their days tending their herds. This tax was devastating for horse-raising Indians who were still living outside the cash economy.

As if this tax weren't enough, a larger and more devastating effort was put into motion that same year. Montana congressman Joseph Dixon, a Quaker from North Carolina who had lived in Montana for only twelve years, introduced a bill to Congress to impose the Allotment Act on the Flathead Indian Reservation. Based on the same rationalization conjured up by John C. Calhoun in the 1820s, this law allowed for the breaking up of collective landholdings and the switching of ownership to fee simple title, and "excess lands" could be sold off or made available to white homesteaders.

The bill passed easily and became law in 1904. Tribal members would be allocated either 80 acres of farmland or 160 acres of grazing lands for heads of household, and half that would be allocated for single adults.[55] As census workers manipulated the system, tribal members received allotments totaling 245,000 acres, about one-fifth of the reservation.

FIG. 64. St. Ignatius Mission and Flathead Agency. From P. Ronan, *Historical Sketch of the Flathead Indian Nation*.

FIG. 65. Father and son at their home near St. Ignatius Mission, Flathead Reservation. Archives and Special Collections, Mansfield Library, University of Montana.

Government agents assigned allotments, often on rocky ground, so that the richest grazing and agricultural lands would be declared "surplus" and thereby be opened to homesteading.[56]

Of course Charlo was vehemently opposed to allotments. He and other elders understood the consequences to their way of life once they were moved apart through this checkerboarding of their lands. Since time immemorial they had lived in close community, tending to each other as needed and celebrating successes as children grew into adulthood. Fearing how this splintering of lands would affect them, the elders needed to ensure some safeguards. They wanted some lands to be held in common, and they wanted their people to be cared for into the future. In March 1905, feeling railroaded by the white people making the new rules, Charlo, at seventy-five, set out again for Washington. He would ask President Roosevelt to support three requests as his people faced this excruciating transition. First, the Salish elders wanted the president to create a forest preserve out of their lands so that they would have a source of firewood and lumber for cabins. Second, they wanted guaranteed water rights for irrigation. Third, they wanted assurance that their poor, crippled, blind, and infirm community members would receive care.[57] The elders understood that these stipulations had been incorporated within the articles of the 1855 treaty and wanted to assure their continuation. Arriving during the week of inauguration festivities, Charlo was allowed only a brief audience with the president and received no assurance that his requests would be honored.

White men eager for their chance to grab the best of the Flathead lands found the old chief to be more than an annoyance. The *Weekly Missoulian* ran an article about Charlo's efforts to gain a timber reserve and long-term support for the reservation. It began with a sympathetic picture of the "irreconcilable" chief, "a grand and pathetic figure . . . a crownless monarch on a seatless throne"; then it shifted gears, "putting all sentiment to one side" to get to its point.[58] "The Indian is no more entitled to a special timber reserve than the white man nor should the government provide for him in any way after tribal relations are severed." The article went on to say that "Charlot is too old to adapt himself to conditions" and noted that "though we may feel sorry for the old man, a grand old man, we also feel that he must bow to the inevitable."[59]

Despite the *Missoulian*'s opinion, Senator Dixon amended the Flathead allotment act to provide for a five-thousand-acre timber reserve.

Over the course of his lifetime Charlo had witnessed the many political shenanigans and outright lies that had cost his people their beloved Bitterroot Valley. In exchange they had been promised the Jocko Valley within the protection of the Flathead Reservation. A federal inspector of reservation lands reported Charlo's "bad influence," claiming that he was "opposed to everything which tends to civilization or advancement of the Indians."[60] Of course his opinion about Charlo makes perfect sense from the vantage point of a nation coveting the lands promised by treaty to the Indians. But Charlo didn't live in that world. What the *suyapis* considered advanced had no appeal to the dignified old chief. He was holding dearly to the world he knew, not the one these interlopers embraced. They were the ones who should open their eyes and bear witness to the degradation of life that followed them wherever they ventured. He had chosen to remain in the world of his ancestors to the extent that was still possible.

During the summer of 1907, in the midst of the drawn-out land appraisal and eligibility determination process for allotments, Secretary of Interior James R. Garfield arrived at the Arlee station, where he was greeted by "nearly five hundred mounted Flathead."[61] Missoulians had invited the secretary to visit for the Fourth of July, as part of his multi-city Montana tour. He had accepted their invitation and one from the Flathead Reservation leader as well. Both Chief Charlo and Secretary Garfield must have noted the irony of their meeting, thirty-five years after the first Garfield had come to their lands. With his son Martin, Charlo welcomed Secretary Garfield and his son to the place where they had been forced to move. When the chief had the chance, he told the secretary of the Indians' opposition to opening their reservation. He hoped he could count on his support back in Washington.

Garfield's entourage didn't stay long. The Salish were just beginning to celebrate the first large summer gathering since coming to the reservation. Indians had come from far and wide; tipis were pitched everywhere, like in the old days. This joyous gathering boosted Charlo's spirit. In an unusual move he invited white friends and neighbors to join with them in this multi-day celebration.

FIG. 66. Chief Charlo and Secretary Garfield with their sons, 1907. Edward Boos, photographer. Archives and Special Collections, Mansfield Library, University of Montana.

FIG. 67. Three Indians receiving camp meat ration. Lo-me Joseph is on the wagon. Archives and Special Collections, Mansfield Library, University of Montana.

Joy was short-lived. The wrecking ball might have paused momentarily, but its momentum was building, and devastation was just ahead. During the difficult years between the passage of the Allotment Act and its implementation, Charlo continued to lovingly serve his people. Louise Vanderburg, great-granddaughter of Louis Vanderburg and descendant of Bear Tracks, remembered him as a true chief, like his father, Victor, who put the needs of his people first. She remembered when he stopped at the cabin of an old woman at Evaro one fall and learned that she had no meat. He went out and shot and butchered a deer for her. When he came back, he saw that her axe was broken. He repaired the axe and cut firewood for her so that she could make dry meat to see her through the winter. This was how those old chiefs were, she remembered. If someone was sick, they would find an appropriate medicine person. Whatever they could do to help, they would.[62]

The old chief was called to testify in a water suit in the Bitterroot Valley in May 1908. According to a newspaper article about the case, it was the first time the seventy-nine-year-old chief had returned there since the Salish had been marched to the reservation seventeen years before. Nearly blind, he was accompanied by "Indian Policeman Lum-

FIG. 68. Flathead women cutting up and carrying away one of the buffalos that was choked to death while being loaded on a train, ca. 1908. Archives and Special Collections, Mansfield Library, University of Montana.

phrey" to serve as interpreter. The reporter noted that Charlo had a good memory, ironically referring to him as the "old warrior."[63] The only way that moniker fit was in the context of legal battles that he had bravely fought and never won.

Chief Charlo's health took a serious downturn soon after the first tribal allotments were made during the summer of 1909. Liver trouble took his energy and kept him close to home. By Christmas the valiant protector of the people and their traditions was bedridden. The priest from the Jocko church came each day with soup and tenderness.[64] Through all of Charlo's life since the arrival of the first three Jesuits in 1841, despite his attitude about their rejection from Creation, he found solace among them. He died in the Jocko Valley on January 10, 1910, just before the land grab was implemented. His descendants and many of the Salish people continue to participate in both the Catholic Church and the midwinter dances of Coyote's world.

Epilogue

The Worlds We Carry

> Until the lions have their own historians, the hunt will always glorify the hunter.
>
> —Chinua Achebe, "The Art of Fiction"

The lives and times of Salish chiefs Victor and Charlo were intertwined in space and time with Father Pierre-Jean De Smet but remained worlds apart in core beliefs and perspectives. Chief Charlo cursed the day that white men first stepped foot onto his treasured homeland. Raised in the church, he knew well the mythic tale of a lost paradise on earth. Although the image of a snake tempting Eve was etched in his memory, he had never accepted Eden as his place of origin. He had his own story. The spiritual wellspring for the Salish was embedded in their homeland. Charlo could not substitute this real land for a mythic garden in an unknown place. The chief understood the consequences that came from being "rejected and cast off" from the place of creation. As he had told his people when they faced taxation in 1876, this rejection from Creation shaped the very essence of a European and made him "take more and more, and to dirty what he leaves."[1]

Twenty years after founding St. Mary's Mission, Father De Smet found himself with an ineffable longing for something of the Salish life. The irony of the situation is in De Smet's desire for his chosen resting place to be the same place where generations upon generations of Salish people had found their ultimate rest. Victor and then Charlo refused to leave the Bitterroot Valley because that was where their ancestors were buried. To live where ancestors' flesh and bones fed the trees and grasses was to be part of the great circle of life. Perhaps the aging missionary had absorbed some deep feeling for this interconnected way of life, despite his contrasting worldview.

Over the past several hundred years, the dominant worldview carried to the Oregon Country by De Smet has marched relentlessly across much of the planet. While the white world has approached land and nature from a material viewpoint of usefulness and value, the Salish understand the subject as one of spiritual connectedness. The contrast can be seen in the story of the bitterroot from its mystical beginnings to its struggle to survive in today's world. The valley that sits at the heart of this story carries the common name of this gift of food: Bitterroot. Now the state flower of Montana, this exquisite burst of flowing pink petals carries the scientific name *Lewisia rediviva*. "*Lewisia*" is for Meriwether Lewis, who made the first record of the species near the confluence of Lolo Creek and the Bitterroot River in 1806. "*Rediviva*" is for the plant's capacity to revive after long periods without water or soil.[2] *Séliš redivivia* would be a more appropriate name. These plants are incredibly resilient; they manage to find their way back to life, even through cracks that eventually form in pavement. Bitterroots, cared for and sustainably harvested since time immemorial by the Salish people, are like the people themselves. They have the capacity to be resuscitated when life appears lost, as their way of life must have felt to Charlo at the time of his death. The bleak future of allotted lands that loomed on the Salish horizon in 1910 was metaphorically akin to pavement poured over bitterroot grounds.

What is astonishing about the story told here is that against overwhelming odds—given the epic efforts on the part of the U.S. government in partnership with the Jesuits to change them—the Bitterroot Salish people are still here, still grounded in their worldview. They have never forgotten who they are and where they came from, and they continue to uphold their values, so distinctive from those of Euro-Americans. People of the white world assumed the Confederated Tribes of the Flathead Reservation, along with Native people all over America, would want to become like them. But for people who define wealth by family and believe their success as human beings is defined by "what you give, not what you have," the acquisitive tendencies of Europeans were not something to emulate.[3]

The differences in expression of these two distinctive worldviews were monumental when Father De Smet arrived in the Bitterroot Valley and remain so today. We don't have to wonder long or travel far to know the costs of the dominant American lifeway. Without rooted ethics, we forget our actual place in creation; we fail to remember that we are dependent on everything else. This forgetting is how forests become clear cuts, fish become toxic, drinking water ends up in plastic bottles and toilet bowls, and domestic animals are raised under conditions that should break our hearts. We see the consequences of our neglect in extinctions, soil depletion, shrinking aquifers, tainted waters, and rising seas. At the center of these discouraging and unsustainable losses is a view that regards life solely as a material resource rather than a sacred Covenant with Source. The Salish, by contrast, with resilience grounded in their worldview, continue to embrace the values of pan-species kinship that have defined them since Creator placed them on this earth. They are holding true until such time that others join them.

This is the time to remember that we *are* all related. *Lemlmts*!

Notes

Introduction

1. *Weekly Missoulian*, April 26, 1876. All of Charlo's quotes in this chapter come from this source. The content of Charlo's speech was later confirmed by Salish people who had been there that day, as related in Salish–Pend d'Oreille Culture Committee, *The Salish People*, 135.

1. Separate Worlds

1. Ewers, "Gustavus Sohon's Portraits," 28; Point, "Notes Biographiques," in "Souvenirs des Montagnes Rocheuses," 25–26, Nicolas Point, S.J., Fonds, Archive of the Jesuits in Canada; Capps, "Leadership in Eastern Salish Communities," IN 9.
2. Ewers, "Gustavus Sohon's Portraits," 28; Capps, "Leadership in Eastern Salish Communities," IN 9.
3. Turney-High, *The Flathead Indians of Montana*, 70.
4. Karamanski, "The Iroquois of the Fur Trade of the Far West," 4–13.
5. Binnema, *Common and Contested Ground.*
6. Face-Raised-Up Grizzly, band chief of the Mission Valley and Horse Plains divisions, was head civil chief of the eastern Salish bands. Myers, "The Flatheads"; Capps, "Leadership in Eastern Salish Communities," IN 7.
7. Turney-High, *The Flathead Indians of Montana*, 41–43; Salish Kootenai College, *Challenge to Survive*, 2:44; Salish–Pend d'Oreille Culture Committee, *The Salish People*, 127.
8. Ferris, *Life in the Rocky Mountains*, 162.
9. Stuart, *The Montana Frontier*, 168.
10. Ferris, *Life in the Rocky Mountains*, 182–83, 185, 191, with further descriptive details on 403–5.
11. Ferris, *Life in the Rocky Mountains*, 410–12.
12. Capps, "Leadership in Eastern Salish Communities," IN 6.2.1, citing Ball et al., *Autobiography of John Ball*, 75–76.
13. Ferris, *Life in the Rocky Mountains*, 413–14.
14. Capps, "Leadership in Eastern Salish Communities," IN 6.2.1. Based on two primary sources, Capps concludes that Insula's feat "almost certainly occurred at the 1834 Ham's Fork Rendezvous," located north of Kemmerer, Wyoming.
15. Turney-High, *The Flathead Indians of Montana*, 76.
16. Anderson, *The Rocky Mountain Journals of William Marshall Anderson*, 164–65.

17. Victor, *The River of the West*, 199–200.
18. Jerome D'Aste, untitled manuscript, quoted in Capps, "Leadership in Eastern Salish Communities," IN 9.
19. Peterson, *Sacred Encounters*, 14; Salish Kootenai College, *Challenge to Survive*, 2:44.
20. Holterman, *Shining Shirt*, 4.
21. Charlo referred to Face-Raised-Up Grizzly as his uncle in an interview with William E. Myers, a colleague of photographer Edward Curtis. GC 1143, box 7, 7.6.10, Edward S. Curtis Papers, Seaver Center for Western History Research.
22. George Capps, fur trade scholar, personal communication, August 3, 2023.
23. Research by Dale Morgan for his book *Jedediah Smith and the Opening of the West*. Morgan sorted through disparate primary sources to pull this story together. He shows that "Pierre Cha-cha-wea-te" was, in fact, alive.
24. Morgan, *Jedediah Smith and the Opening of the West*, 396n14. The original group had been a "whole party of hunters [originally] from Montreal and Canada, mostly Iroquois and half-bloods."
25. Mengarini, *Recollections of the Flathead Mission*, 181.
26. Ignace told Gustav Sohon in 1854 that he had come into the country with his companion Pierre Chalk, or Gauché, and Sohon left the note about it on a sketched portrait of Ignace. Ewers, "Gustavus Sohon's Portraits."
27. Ignace's Indian name meant "Layered His Creeks." Capps, "Grand Ignace," 51–54.
28. Capps, "Grand Ignace," 56.
29. Capps, "Grand Ignace," 59.
30. For further reference to prophecies about Circling Raven (Coeur d'Alene) and Shining Shirt (Flathead), see Mellis, "Coyote People and the Black Robes," 53–64.
31. Laveille, *The Life of Father De Smet*, 168.
32. Garraghan, *The Jesuits of the Middle United States*, 3:95.
33. Garraghan, *The Jesuits of the Middle United States*, 3:95. Garraghan points out that the instinct for "holy wanderlust" was in keeping with some who had reached sainthood.
34. Charlevoix, *History and General Description of New France*, 3.
35. Davis, "Peter John De Smet: The Years of Preparation," 169.
36. Adams quoted in Crosby, "Jesuits Go Home."
37. Joset, manuscript held in Davis Papers, Jesuit Archives and Research Center (cited hereafter as JARC).

2. *Westward Ho*

1. The 1800 census shows a little over five million people in the United States, but the numbers do not include Native Americans or anyone west of the Mis-

sissippi. Categories include free men and women, "all other free persons," and slaves. American Indians living among the general population were included for the first time in the 1860 census.

2. Cappon, *Adams-Jefferson Letters*, 573.
3. Clement, "The Philadelphia Welfare Crisis of the 1820s."
4. Devitt, "History of the Maryland–New York Province."
5. James Monroe, "First Annual Message," online by Gerhard Peters and John T. Woolley, "The American Presidency Project," https://www.presidency.ucsb.edu/node/205560.
6. Stephens, *To the Indian Removal Act*.
7. The Office of Indian Affairs was renamed the Bureau of Indian Affairs in the mid-twentieth century.
8. J. H. Buckley, *William Clark*.
9. Jones, "Iron Will."
10. Clark adopted the two children of Sacagawea, Jean Baptiste "Pomp" and baby Lizette Charbonneau, in 1813. For several years prior to the adoption, Jean Baptiste was being educated in St. Louis under the sponsorship of Clark. Lizette's life appears to remain undocumented.
11. Wunder, *Native American Sovereignty*, 175.
12. Genovese and Landry, *US Presidents and the Destruction of the Native American Nations*. Also see "James Monroe: Pushed Tribes off Land, but Boosted Indian Education," an interview by Alyssa Landry with Dan Preston (editor of "The Papers of James Monroe," an editorial project at the University of Mary Washington), in *Indian Country Today*, February 2, 2012.
13. Quoted in Akers, "Native Nations in an Age of Western Expansion," 69.
14. Garraghan, *The Jesuits of the Middle United States*, 1:45–55.
15. Judge John Marshall's decision on *Johnson v. M'Intosh* in 1823 applied the Doctrine of Discovery, a colonial tool that allowed European governments to claim territories "discovered" and occupied by their subjects—for example, Columbus in North America—as if Indigenous people had no claim to their own lands. See Miller, *Discovering Indigenous Lands*, and Charles and Rah, *Unsettling Truths*. In March 2023 Pope Francis repudiated the decree, five centuries after its implementation. See Bill Chappell, "The Vatican Repudiates 'Doctrine of Discovery,' Which Was Used to Justify Colonialism," NPR, March 30, 2023.
16. Although none of the published writings of the Jesuits included the names of the enslaved people who cared for their needs while they were traveling or in their new settlement in Missouri, recent scholarship has uncovered records and descendants. See "What We Have Learned," Jesuits: Slavery, History, Memory, and Reconciliation Project, https://www.jesuits.org/our-work/shmr/what-we-have-learned/missouri/.
17. Jefferson, *Notes on the State of Virginia*.

18. Bright, *Native American Placenames*, 344.
19. Sleeper-Smith, *Indigenous Prosperity and American Conquest*, 228.
20. McNutt and Parish, *Cahokia in Context.*
21. A significant difference between these early schools and those implemented a half century later was that these were voluntary, not mandatory.
22. Laveille, *The Life of Father De Smet*, 54–55.
23. Garraghan, *The Jesuits of the Middle United States*, 1:350–59.
24. Garraghan, *The Jesuits of the Middle United States*, 1:351.
25. Garraghan, *The Jesuits of the Middle United States*, 1:352.
26. Garraghan, *The Jesuits of the Middle United States*, 1:359.

3. *Like Braided Streams*

1. Josephy, *The Nez Perce Indians and the Opening of the Northwest*, 94.
2. See De Smet, *Letters and Sketches*; Garraghan, *The Jesuits of the Middle United States*, 2:249; Capps, "Grand Ignace"; Mellis, "Ignace Partui"; Salish–Pend d'Oreille Culture Committee, *The Salish People*, 136; Sperlin, "The Story of Grand Eneas (Big Ignace)."
3. Capps, "Grand Ignace," n144; Garraghan, *The Jesuits of the Middle United States*, 2:237–48; Mengarini, *Recollections of the Flathead Mission*, 173–74.
4. Josephy, *The Nez Perce Indians and the Opening of the Northwest*, 96–98; Palladino, *Indian and White in the Northwest*, 10, reports that the two men who died there had been baptized as Narcisse, a Nez Perce pipe carrier who was buried on October 31, and Paul, of the nation of "Tetes Plattes," who was buried on November 17.
5. George Catlin sketched two survivors of this delegation to St. Louis in 1831, identified as Hee-oh'ks-te-kin' (Rabbit-skin-leggins) and H'co-a-h'cotes-min' (No-horns-on-his-head) (see Palladino, *Indian and White in the Northwest*, 8–19).
6. Cox, "Gabriel Prudhomme Estate."
7. Capps, "Leadership in Eastern Salish Communities," IN 19.
8. Garraghan, *The Jesuits of the Middle United States*, 2:246–47.
9. The seven tribes were the Salish, Nez Perce, "Panthéres" (Pend d'Oreille?), Kootenai, Spokane, Cayuse, and Ochazères (Colville?). Garraghan, *The Jesuits of the Middle United States*, 2:247.
10. Garraghan, *The Jesuits of the Middle United States*, 2:247.
11. Evans, *St. Mary's in the Rocky Mountains*, 17.
12. Quoted in Cebula, *Plateau Indians*, 186.
13. Sperlin, "The Story of Grand Eneas (Big Ignace)."
14. Salish–Pend d'Oreille Culture Committee, *The Salish People*, 136; compare Bigart and McDonald, *"You Seem to Like Your Money,"* 111.
15. Julie Cajune, personal communication, 2004.

16. Salish–Pend d'Oreille Culture Committee, *The Salish People*, 136; Evans, *St. Mary's in the Rocky Mountains*, 17.
17. Mengarini, *Recollections of the Flathead Mission*, 181.
18. Garraghan, *The Jesuits of the Middle United States*, 1:432n23.
19. Jaenike, *Black Robes in Paraguay*.
20. Nicole Winfield and Pedro Servin, "Pope Praises Jesuit Missions in Paraguay after Apology," *San Diego Union-Tribune*, July 11, 2015, https://www.sandiegouniontribune.com/sdut-pope-praises-jesuit-missions-in-paraguay-after-2015jul11-story.html.
21. Carriker, *Father Peter John De Smet, S.J.*, 50.
22. Point, *Wilderness Kingdom*, 43.
23. Through my years of working with Native elders, I have inevitably heard their deep regret that they are not able to tell me their history or a story in their own language because there is no way to do justice to their verb-based, and therefore visual, languages with English.
24. See Whitaker, "Pierre-Jean De Smet's Remarkable Map."
25. Variously spelled Padekoshek, Pedagoshok, Patogoshuck, or Pah-eh-go-shuck, the name meant "Pile of Lead," as reported by Clifton, "Billy Caldwell's Exile in Early Chicago." Caldwell was a highly respected leader in Kansas during the removal era and pre-removal. Personal communication from Blake Norton, curator, Citizen Potawatomi Nation Cultural Heritage Center, 2019.
26. Pierre-Jean De Smet to Jan Roothaan, December 1, 1838, in Chittenden and Richardson, *Life, Letters and Travels of Father Pierre-Jean De Smet, S.J.*, 1:163–64.
27. Pierre-Jean De Smet to Mother Superior, Carmelite orphanage at Termonde, July 1838, in Chittenden and Richardson, *Life, Letters and Travels of Father Pierre-Jean De Smet, S.J.*, 1:185.
28. Chittenden and Richardson, *Life, Letters and Travels of Father Pierre-Jean De Smet, S.J.*, 1:437.
29. Garraghan, *The Jesuits of the Middle United States*, 1:438.
30. Garraghan, *The Jesuits of the Middle United States*, 1:441.
31. Garraghan, *The Jesuits of the Middle United States*, 1:442.
32. Garraghan, *The Jesuits of the Middle United States*, 1:431.
33. Whitaker, "Pierre-Jean De Smet's Remarkable Map." Also see Garraghan, *The Jesuits of the Middle United States*, 1:442n33.
34. Quoted in Garraghan, *The Jesuits of the Middle United States*, 1:439.
35. Garraghan, *The Jesuits of the Middle United States*, 1:439.
36. Mengarini, *Recollections of the Flathead Mission*, 181.
37. Letter from Bishop Rosati to Jesuit general Roothaan, in Garraghan, *The Jesuits of the Middle United States*, 2:249; Mellis, "Ignace Partui," 212–15.
38. Capps, personal communication, 2023.

4. Prayer and Possibility

1. Garraghan, *The Jesuits of the Middle United States*, 2:250.
2. In November of the following year, 1840, De Smet, on arriving at Fort Vermilion from his first Rocky Mountain journey, found that his diplomatic success with the Yanktons the preceding year had been undone. See Thwaites, *The Jesuit Relations and Allied Documents*, 30:67.
3. Laveille, *The Life of Father De Smet*, 93–94.
4. Davis, "Peter John De Smet: The Journey of 1840," 168.
5. Laveille, *The Life of Father De Smet*, 94.
6. Garraghan, *The Jesuits of the Middle United States*, 2:252.
7. Joset manuscript, held in Davis Papers, JARC.
8. Quoted in Garraghan, *The Jesuits of the Middle United States*, 2:252.
9. P. Ronan, *Historical Sketch of the Flathead Indian Nation*, 26.
10. Pierre-Jean De Smet to his brother, Francis, March 16, 1840, in Davis, "Peter John De Smet: The Journey of 1840," 35; Laveille, *The Life of Father De Smet*, 137.
11. R. T. Malouf, "Family Histories," 242, citing Claude E. Schaeffer Fonds, series 2, M-1100-118.
12. Chittenden and Richardson, *Life, Letters and Travels of Father Pierre-Jean De Smet, S.J.*, 1:220.
13. Chittenden and Richardson, *Life, Letters and Travels of Father Pierre-Jean De Smet, S.J.*, 1:261–62.
14. Turney-High, *The Flathead Indians of Montana*, 42–43; De Smet, *De Smet's Oregon Missions and Travels*, 93–94.
15. De Smet, *Letters and Sketches*, 137. The site of this Mass is about ten miles west of Pinedale, Wyoming, where it is marked with a monument.
16. De Smet, *Letters and Sketches*, 212. Geographers of the day used the phrase "Backbone of the World," now commonly associated with the Blackfeet phrase for the Rocky Mountains.
17. Chittenden and Richardson, *Life, Letters and Travels of Father Pierre-Jean De Smet, S.J.*, 1:222.
18. Chittenden and Richardson, *Life, Letters and Travels of Father Pierre-Jean De Smet, S.J.*, 1:223.
19. Capps, "Leadership in Eastern Salish Communities," IN 7; De Smet, untitled manuscript, October 10, 1841, C3 35-30, Missouri Province Collection, JARC.
20. Quoted in Capps, "Leadership in Eastern Salish Communities," IN 7.
21. Capps, "Leadership in Eastern Salish Communities," IN 7, quoting from a translation of Nicholas Point's unpublished "Notes Biographiques," in "Souvenirs des Montagnes Rocheuses," Nicolas Point, S.J., Fonds, Archive of the Jesuits in Canada.
22. De Smet, *Letters and Sketches*, 142.

23. De Smet, *Letters and Sketches*, 142–43; compare Chittenden and Richardson, *Life, Letters and Travels of Father Pierre-Jean De Smet, S.J.*, 1:226.
24. Laveille, *The Life of Father De Smet*, 109.
25. Chittenden and Richardson, *Life, Letters and Travels of Father Pierre-Jean De Smet, S.J.*, 1:264.
26. Chittenden and Richardson, *Life, Letters and Travels of Father Pierre-Jean De Smet, S.J.*, 1:325.
27. Garraghan, *The Jesuits of the Middle United States*, 2:254–55; Davis, "Peter John De Smet: The Journey of 1840," 121–42.
28. Garraghan, *The Jesuits of the Middle United States*, 2:254–55.
29. Quoted in Laveille, *The Life of Father De Smet*, 110.
30. Chittenden and Richardson, *Life, Letters and Travels of Father Pierre-Jean De Smet, S.J.*, 1:325–26.
31. Mengarini, *Recollections of the Flathead Mission*, 163.
32. The delineation of sections was based on a rectangular survey system that began at the end of the American Revolution, establishing a formal method to divide up the land conceptually into one-mile squares, four of which composed a section.
33. Winthrop, "Generall Considerations for the Plantation in New England," 118.
34. Mengarini, *Recollections of the Flathead Mission*, 157.

5. *Black Robes Enter Coyote's World*

1. Capps, "Leadership in Eastern Salish Communities," IN 32, citing Point, "Notes Biographiques," in "Souvenirs des Montagnes Rocheuses," 31, Nicolas Point, S.J., Fonds, Archive of the Jesuits in Canada.
2. Pelchimo's name is spelled various ways, including Pelchino and Palchino/a. (According to George Capps, the evidence suggests that the two might be different people; Capps, "Leadership in Eastern Salish Communities," IN 36.1 and 36.2.)
3. Capps, "Leadership in Eastern Salish Communities," IN 36; Point, *Wilderness Kingdom*, 38; Point, "Notes Biographiques," 36.
4. De Smet, *Letters and Sketches*, 251; Chittenden and Richardson, *Life, Letters and Travels of Father Pierre-Jean De Smet, S.J.*, 1:305; Point, *Wilderness Kingdom*, 39.
5. De Smet, *Letters and Sketches*, 342.
6. Story told by four elderly Kalispel-Salish men through an interpreter in 1923. Published in Clark, *Indian Legends from the Northern Rockies*, 92–95.
7. Clark, *Indian Legends from the Northern Rockies*, 94.
8. In his 2005 book *1491: New Revelations of the Americas before Columbus*, Charles Mann argues a case for an early Chinese presence along the Pacific Coast of North America, including the Columbia Basin.

9. Human remains recovered from the region that date to a time before contact with Europeans show no signs of head flattening.
10. Salish–Pend d'Oreille Culture Committee, *The Salish People.*
11. Point, *Wilderness Kingdom*, 39; map by Michael Louis Durglo Sr., in Salish–Pend d'Oreille Culture Committee, *The Salish People*, 40.
12. Point, *Wilderness Kingdom*, 43.

6. Reshaping Coyote's World

1. Chittenden and Richardson, *Life, Letters and Travels of Father Pierre-Jean De Smet, S.J.*, 359.
2. The center was spelled "Colvile" when it was the HBC post and "Colville" when it became a U.S. Army post in the 1850s. Close to the town of Colville, Washington, it was constructed close to the major fishing site of Kettle Falls, now flooded by Lake Roosevelt.
3. Capps, "Leadership in Eastern Salish Communities," IN 46. "Lompry" is variously spelled as Lomprey, Lumpry, Lampere, and Lompré.
4. Palladino, *Indian and White in the Northwest*, 43, quoting De Smet.
5. Rob Collier (Nez Perce), interview by Sally Thompson, 2005.
6. Point, *Wilderness Kingdom*, 24.
7. Mengarini, *Recollections of the Flathead Mission*, 158.
8. Mengarini, *Recollections of the Flathead Mission*, 158.
9. Chittenden and Richardson, *Life, Letters and Travels of Father Pierre-Jean De Smet, S.J.*, 1:331; De Smet, *Origin, Progress, and Prospects*, 5–6. Palladino, *Indian and White in the Northwest*, 42–43. According to Palladino, that first chapel was replaced a year later with one somewhat larger.
10. Point, *Wilderness Kingdom*, 42.
11. Chittenden and Richardson, *Life, Letters and Travels of Father Pierre-Jean De Smet, S.J.*, 1:340.
12. Palladino, *Indian and White in the Northwest*, 85. I have not been able to find good documentation of the ages and genders of Charlo's siblings. Charlo family records on Ancestry.com list "Kahkapee" as Iroquois. Her baptismal name is shown as Rosalie. She had four children with Victor. Charlo was the second, and the other three were girls.
13. Chittenden and Richardson, *Life, Letters and Travels of Father Pierre-Jean De Smet, S.J.*, 1:354.
14. De Smet, *Letters and Sketches*, 344.
15. Salish–Pend d'Oreille Culture Committee, *The Salish People*, 26.
16. Chittenden and Richardson, *Life, Letters and Travels of Father Pierre-Jean De Smet, S.J.*, 1:357.
17. Chittenden and Richardson, *Life, Letters and Travels of Father Pierre-Jean De Smet, S.J.*, 1:359; Juneau, "Small Robe Band of Blackfeet."

18. See Harden, *Murder at the Mission*, for more details about the Protestant missionaries among the Nez Perce.
19. De Smet, *Origin, Progress, and Prospects*, 5–6.
20. Johnson, *Flathead and Kootenay*, 337.
21. Capps, "Leadership in Eastern Salish Communities," IN 35; Point, "Notes Biographiques," in "Souvenirs des Montagnes Rocheuses," 33–34, Nicolas Point, S.J., Fonds, Archive of the Jesuits in Canada.
22. Capps, "Leadership in Eastern Salish Communities," citing Point, "Notes Biographiques," 38.
23. C. M. Buckley, *Nicolas Point, S.J.*, 281; Capps, "Leadership in Eastern Salish Communities," IN 46.
24. Capps, "Leadership in Eastern Salish Communities," IN 34.
25. Mengarini, *Mengarini's Narrative of the Rockies*, 26–27; Point, *Wilderness Kingdom*, 53 (illustration).
26. The understanding that North America is an island is widespread through Native America. Many tribes refer to this land as Turtle Island.
27. Salish–Pend d'Oreille Culture Committee, *The Salish People*, 7.
28. Salish–Pend d'Oreille Culture Committee, *The Salish People*, 7.
29. Salish–Pend d'Oreille Culture Committee, *The Salish People*, 7.
30. De Smet, *Letters and Sketches*, 303–5.
31. Letter from De Smet to the monseigneur, sent from Liverpool in May 1847, in Davis Papers, JARC.
32. Chittenden and Richardson, *Life, Letters and Travels of Father Pierre-Jean De Smet, S.J.*, 1:361. This content is part of a letter from Nicholas Point about his first buffalo hunt with the Flatheads (1:361–66).
33. Chittenden and Richardson, *Life, Letters and Travels of Father Pierre-Jean De Smet, S.J.*, 1:362.
34. Chittenden and Richardson, *Life, Letters and Travels of Father Pierre-Jean De Smet, S.J.*, 1:363–64.
35. Revais quoted in Teit, *The Salishan Tribes*, 376.
36. Capps, "Leadership in Eastern Salish Communities," based on Calcium, "Up the Bitter Root: With Notes on the Side," *New North-West* (Deer Lodge MT), November 16, 1872, p. 2, c. 4–5.
37. Nicolas Point to Pierre-Jean De Smet, January 13, 1863, BO 0043-5, Nicolas Point, S.J., Fonds, Archive of the Jesuits in Canada.
38. De Smet, *Letters and Sketches*, 356.
39. Not only the chiefs but also their wives and children were expected to have admirable qualities. A chief's wife was expected to be dignified, unassuming, quiet, and hospitable. Teit, *The Salishan Tribes*, 376.
40. Mengarini, *Recollections of the Flathead Mission*, 97.

7. Covenant with Creation

1. Peterson, *Sacred Encounters*, 23–24.
2. Cebula, *Plateau Indians*.
3. Mengarini, *Recollections of the Flathead Mission*, 149–52.
4. Here and in the next several paragraphs the quotes are from Mengarini, *Recollections of the Flathead Mission*, 149–50. This telling is based on the writings of Mengarini, the SPCC, and Ella Clark.
5. Statements by Salish-Pend d'Oreille Culture Committee and Elders Cultural Advisory Council, Confederated Salish and Kootenai Tribes (CSKT), 2020.
6. Clark, *Indian Legends from the Northern Rockies*, 68–70. This account is based on interviews with Lassaw Redhorn, Queauesah, and Domicie Michell, who shared stories from Seliš and Ql'ispe oral tradition.
7. Clark, *Indian Legends from the Northern Rockies*, 82.
8. This became Lolo Hot Springs.
9. Statement by Salish-Pend d'Oreille Culture Committee and Elders Cultural Advisory Council, CSKT, 2020.
10. Mengarini, *Recollections of the Flathead Mission*, 156–57.
11. De Smet, *Letters and Sketches*, 305.
12. De Smet, *Letters and Sketches*, 305. Manitoo (also Manitou) is an Algonquian word for spirit beings or those with supernatural powers.
13. De Smet, *Letters and Sketches*, 347; Point, *Wilderness Kingdom*, 42; De Smet, *Origin, Progress, and Prospects*, 8.
14. Quoted in "Flathead Indian Reservation History," Facebook group posting, December 1, 2022, https://www.facebook.com/groups/264160831141937.
15. Mengarini, *Recollections of the Flathead Mission*, 167–68. A bridge in Missoula was renamed in 2021 for descendants of Bear Tracks.
16. Point, "Notes Biographiques," in "Souvenirs des Montagnes Rocheuses," 25, Nicolas Point, S.J., Fonds, Archive of the Jesuits in Canada. Later oral tradition makes the enemy faced in this episode Crows, not Blackfeet.
17. Point, "Notes Biographiques," 25–26.
18. Point, "Notes Biographiques," 26.
19. Mengarini, *Recollections of the Flathead Mission*, 162–63.
20. Mengarini, *Mengarini's Narrative of the Rockies*, 27.
21. Mengarini, *Recollections of the Flathead Mission*, 161.
22. Johnny Arlee, personal communication, 2021.
23. Mengarini, *Mengarini's Narrative of the Rockies*, 10.
24. Mengarini, *Recollections of the Flathead Mission*, 164.
25. Point, *Wilderness Kingdom*, 20.
26. Chittenden and Richardson, *Life, Letters and Travels of Father Pierre-Jean De Smet, S.J.*, 1:337.

27. Mengarini, *Mengarini's Narrative of the Rockies*, 34; see also Mengarini, *Recollections of the Flathead Mission*, 142–52.
28. De Smet, *Letters and Sketches*, 303.
29. De Smet, *Letters and Sketches*, 303–5.
30. De Smet, *Letters and Sketches*, 303–5.
31. Letter no. XXIII of the Rev. Father Point, S.J., in De Smet, *De Smet's Oregon Missions and Travels*, 314.
32. White and St. Laurent, "Mysterious Journey," 70–90; Hanley, *History of the Catholic Ladder*.
33. Thompson and Egesdal, *Salish Myths and Legends*, xxxi.

8. Straddling the Divide

1. Chittenden and Richardson, *Life, Letters and Travels of Father Pierre-Jean De Smet, S.J.*, 2:451, 452.
2. Shining Shirt was baptized on Easter Day, 1845, and christened Peter. In an unusual move, he asked permission from De Smet to continue to use the name Shining Shirt because this was the way his guardian spirit addressed him, and he didn't want to lose this important relationship. Surprisingly, De Smet agreed. Capps, "Leadership in Eastern Salish Communities," IN 30.
3. See Garraghan, *The Jesuits of the Middle United States*, 2:324–28.
4. See map 5, chapter 6.
5. Sir Henry James Warre Fond, Public Archives of Canada, MG24, F71, vol. 27:2211–12, H-1701. The map in question is most likely one in the collection of De Smetiana held by the JARC in St. Louis. One rendition of this map was published in an 1847 account of this journey. David Thompson had prepared a map of the entire Kootenai region for the Northwest Company that De Smet had never seen, for it was no doubt kept under lock and key. Competition in the region was intense, and accurate maps were priceless. De Smet's 1851 map can be seen on the Library of Congress website.
6. De Smet, *De Smet's Oregon Missions and Travels*, 321.
7. Fahey, *The Flathead Indians*, 68.
8. De Smet, *De Smet's Oregon Missions and Travels*, 321–22.
9. Through extensive research, George Capps uncovered impressive evidence that Nicholas was Rides Behind of the Small Robes band, as documented in Capps, "Blackfeet Peacemaker."
10. De Smet, *De Smet's Oregon Missions and Travels*, 327–28.
11. Capps, "Blackfeet Peacemaker."
12. The earlier fort was Fort McKenzie, located near the mouth of the Marias River. Fort Lewis was on the south side of the river, a short distance upstream and across from what would become Fort Benton.
13. Garraghan, *The Jesuits of the Middle United States*, 2:295, quoting Joset.

14. See Carriker, *Father Peter John De Smet, S.J.*, 107–10, and Garraghan, *The Jesuits of the Middle United States*, 2:421–25, for a discussion of the reasons for De Smet's dismissal.
15. De Smet, *De Smet's Oregon Missions and Travels*, 365. De Smet's description is too vague for readers to know which pass they traveled. The most likely is Cottonwood Pass from the Deer Lodge Valley into the Boulder River Valley.
16. Point, *Wilderness Kingdom*, 118.
17. C. M. Buckley, *Nicolas Point, S.J.*, 279.
18. De Smet, *De Smet's Oregon Missions and Travels*, 341.
19. C. M. Buckley, *Nicolas Point, S.J.*, 283–84; Point, *Wilderness Kingdom*, 192; De Smet, *De Smet's Oregon Missions and Travels*, 298–99.
20. C. M. Buckley, *Nicolas Point, S.J.*, 284; compare Peterson, *Sacred Encounters*, 72 (illustration); De Smet, *De Smet's Oregon Missions and Travels*, 302.
21. Quoted in Point, *Wilderness Kingdom*, 192.
22. Chittenden and Richardson, *Life, Letters and Travels of Father Pierre-Jean De Smet, S.J.*, 1:391–93.
23. De Smet, *De Smet's Oregon Missions and Travels*, 365.
24. "Kill the Indian, and Save the Man," Capt. Richard H. Pratt on the Education of Native Americans, in *Proceedings of the Nineteenth Annual Conference of Charities and Correction*, Denver, Colorado, June 23–29, 1892, 46–59, reprinted in Prucha, *Americanizing the American Indians*, 260–71.
25. In 1843 Gabriel Prudhomme married Mary Trise Boisvert, "I-Yos-Cha-A-Ni" Enos. According to her family history, her Iroquois father was Ignace Moses Enos (Anayos), born in 1780 at Kanawaga, and he died in 1850 on Flathead tribal lands. Her mother may have been Mary Marie Washakie, the daughter of a Salish mother and a Shoshone father who was killed by Blackfeet in 1805.
26. See Harden, *Murder at the Mission*, for a detailed description of the mission at Wailatpu.
27. Ravalli to Roothaan, June 29, 1847, quoted in Garraghan, *The Jesuits of the Middle United States*, 2:376–77.
28. Mengarini, "Rocky Mountains (Concluded)," 150–52; Garraghan, *The Jesuits of the Middle United States*, 2:375–83.
29. Mengarini, *Recollections of the Flathead Mission*, 75–76.
30. *Weekly Missoulian*, July 22, 1875.
31. Hilmo, "The Rocky Fork of the Clark Fork"; Oakley, *The Philipsburg Story*; Siria, "Rock Creek, Past and Present."
32. The presence of skulls and other heavy bones in Flint Creek Valley archaeological sites attests to local bison hunting over several millennia, as does the stippling on George Catlin's 1832 map of North America documenting the presence of bison.
33. Mengarini, *Recollections of the Flathead Mission*, 233–36.

34. Mengarini, *Recollections of the Flathead Mission*, 193.
35. Letter report from Lt. John Mullan to Governor Stevens, November 18, 1853, in Fuller, "The Confederated Salish and Kutenai Tribes," 40.
36. Thomas Fitzpatrick letter, 1847, quoted in Mengarini, *Recollections of the Flathead Mission*, 120.
37. Gloria Ricci Lothrop, introduction, in Mengarini, *Recollections of the Flathead Mission*, 120.
38. Quoted in Robbins, *Landscapes of Promise*, 4–5.
39. Mather, *A Brief History of the War with the Indians in New-England*.
40. Mengarini to Roothaan, September 26, 1844, in Capps, "Leadership in Eastern Salish Communities," IN 9.
41. Mengarini, *Recollections of the Flathead Mission*, 233–36.
42. Point, "Notes Biographiques," in "Souvenirs des Montagnes Rocheuses," Nicolas Point, S.J., Fonds, Archive of the Jesuits in Canada.
43. Capps, "Leadership in Eastern Salish Communities," IN 34; see also Ewers, "Gustavus Sohon's Portraits," plate 9. Compare Point's portrait, misidentified as "Adolphe, or Red Feather," in Point, *Wilderness Kingdom*, 49.
44. Mengarini, *Recollections of the Flathead Mission*, 234; Ravalli to Roothaan, April 5, 1849, quoted in Garraghan, *The Jesuits of the Middle United States*, 2:378; Mengarini, "The Rocky Mountains (Concluded)," 150.
45. Mengarini, *Recollections of the Flathead Mission*, 234–35.
46. Chalk Courchane, "Fort Connah, MT and Its Managers," Oregon Pioneers, http://www.oregonpioneers.com/bios/FortConnah.pdf.
47. Larpenteur, *Forty Years a Fur Trader*.
48. Larpenteur, *Forty Years a Fur Trader*, 260–61.
49. F. H. Woody, "Historical Sketch of Missoula County," *Weekly Missoulian*, July 19, 1876.
50. Letter from Malcolm Clarke to Alexander Culbertson, Ft. Benton, November 5, 1849, Missouri Historical Society, Chouteau Collection.
51. Gloria Ricci Lothrop, introduction, in Mengarini, *Recollections of the Flathead Mission*, 79.
52. Joset manuscript, in Davis Papers, JARC.
53. Owen, *The Journals and Letters of Major John Owen*, 1:129; Sangiovanni, "Overland Trips across the American Deseret"; Chalk Courchane, "Owen, Nancy," Oregon Pioneers, http://www.oregonpioneers.com/bios/NancyOwen_1824.pdf.

9. *Atop a New Divide*

1. The Jesuit Archives and Research Center (St. Louis) holds the telegram sent by Stevens. I have not encountered any record regarding De Smet's response.
2. Garraghan, *The Jesuits of the Middle United States*, 3:99.

3. Thomas Adams, September 29, 1853, Thomas Adams Papers, Princeton University Library.
4. Thomas Adams, October 26, 1856, Thomas Adams Papers, Princeton University Library. This document contradicts a belief that the original mission was burned, as instructed by the departing priests.
5. Stevens, "Report of Explorations for a Route for the Pacific Railroad," 1:416.
6. Quotes and captions from Sohon in this and the next several paragraphs are in Ewers, "Gustavus Sohon's Portraits," plate 11.
7. Mengarini to Jan Roothaan, September 26, 1844, Missio Montium Saxos, vol. 1, folio 7, item 1, Archivum Romanum Societatis Iesu, Rome (cited hereafter as ARSI).
8. Thomas Adams, Journal II, p. 104, Thomas Adams Papers, Princeton University Library.
9. Ewers, "Gustavus Sohon's Portraits," plate 20.
10. Weisel, *Men and Trade*, 6.
11. Weisel, *Men and Trade*, 6.
12. Stevens letter to Comm. Indian Affairs Mannypenny, December 29, 1853, U.S. Congressional Serial Set, vol. 741, H. Misc. Doc. 38:9.
13. "Indian Question," December 30, 1854 (Letter XIV), in De Smet, *Western Missions and Missionaries*, 210.
14. Pambrun, "The Story of His Life as He Tells It."
15. "Kootenai Tribe of Idaho" became established as an official entity in 1974, when the remaining sixty-seven individuals declared a war of words and awareness on the United States that resulted in an award of 12.5 acres of land to the tribe. The Coeur d'Alene tribe secured land in 1873 by executive order. The Kalispel tribe secured its reservation in northeastern Washington by executive order in 1914.
16. De Smet letter report to Captain Alfred Pleasonton, from Coeur d'Alene Mission, December 4, 1858, 393(1)-E 3573, Letters Received, 1858–1860, National Archives and Records Administration (cited hereafter as NARA).
17. For a map of the conditional reservation, see Montana Tribes Digital Archives, https://montanatribes.org/wp-content/uploads/2018/04/1857Stevens11x17MT.pdf.
18. See Bigart and Woodcock, *In the Name of the Salish and Kootenai Nation*, 79.
19. Bigart and Woodcock, *In the Name of the Salish and Kootenai Nation*, 61.
20. Stevens, "Report of Explorations for a Route for the Pacific Railroad," 12:209.
21. Chittenden and Richardson, *Life, Letters and Travels of Father Pierre-Jean De Smet, S.J.*, 2:758.
22. Report of Special Agent Thomas Adams to Gov. I. I. Stevens at camp near Fort Benton, October 4, 1855, NARA. Also see S. Thompson, "A Summer Like No Other," in S. Thompson, *Disturbing the Sleeping Buffalo*.

23. Thomas Adams, Journal III, October 18 and 19, 1855, Thomas Adams Papers, Princeton University Library.
24. Thomas Adams, Journal III, October 20, 1855, Thomas Adams Papers, Princeton University Library.
25. Chittenden and Richardson, *Life, Letters and Travels of Father Pierre-Jean De Smet, S.J.*, 2:758.
26. April Charlo, TEDx Talk, March 27, 2015, University of Montana.
27. Doty, *Journal of Operations*.
28. Thomas Adams, Journal III (1855 July 30–1859 November 10), notes made December 26, 1855, Thomas Adams Papers, Princeton University Library. "Pierre the Iroquois" is assumed to be Pierre Lefthand (Gauché).
29. Owen, *The Journals and Letters of Major John Owen*, 1:129.
30. Owen, *The Journals and Letters of Major John Owen*, 1:129.
31. Thomas Adams, Journal III, notes made July 21–25, 1856, Thomas Adams Papers, Princeton University Library.
32. Thomas Adams, Journal III, notes made August 3, 1856, Thomas Adams Papers, Princeton University Library. Ignace was a common name among the Iroquois. (See Bigart, *Life and Death at St. Mary's Mission, Montana*, 124.)
33. Owen, *The Journals and Letters of Major John Owen*, 1:139.
34. Owen, *The Journals and Letters of Major John Owen*, 1:152.
35. Owen, *The Journals and Letters of Major John Owen*, 1:154.
36. Owen, *The Journals and Letters of Major John Owen*, 1:160.
37. The tribal affiliation of Julia Ogden is unclear. In various instances she is referred to as Flathead, Nez Perce, or perhaps Spokane. Prevailing evidence suggests she is Salish and possibly also Nez Perce.
38. Owen, *The Journals and Letters of Major John Owen*, 1:171.
39. De Smet letter to Sophie Parmentier, in Chittenden and Richardson, *Life, Letters and Travels of Father Pierre-Jean De Smet, S.J.*, 4:1197–98.
40. De Smet letter to Sophie Parmentier, in Chittenden and Richardson, *Life, Letters and Travels of Father Pierre-Jean De Smet, S.J.*, 4:1197–98.
41. Owen to Col. James Nesmith, in Owen, *The Journals and Letters of Major John Owen*, 2:185.
42. Thomas Adams, Journal III, May 8, 1858, Thomas Adams Papers, Princeton University Library.
43. Thomas Adams, Journal III, May 25, 1858, Thomas Adams Papers, Princeton University Library.
44. Owen, *The Journals and Letters of Major John Owen*, 2:185.
45. Alex McKay is likely the son of Thomas McKay, a Metis fur trader, and the Chinook daughter of Chief Concomly.
46. Hamilton, "A Trading Expedition amongst the Indians in 1858." Also see "Clark Fork Journey," in S. Thompson, *Disturbing the Sleeping Buffalo*.

47. Bigart and Woodcock, *In the Name of the Salish and Kootenai Nation*.
48. S. Thompson, "Clark Fork Winter," in S. Thompson, *Disturbing the Sleeping Buffalo*.
49. Chittenden and Richardson, *Life, Letters and Travels of Father Pierre-Jean De Smet, S.J.*, 2:743.
50. De Smet letter report to Captain Alfred Pleasonton, from Coeur d'Alene Mission, December 4, 1858, 393(1)-E 3573, Letters Received, 1858–1860, NARA.
51. Chittenden and Richardson, *Life, Letters and Travels of Father Pierre-Jean De Smet, S.J.*, 2:730–31.
52. Chittenden and Richardson, *Life, Letters and Travels of Father Pierre-Jean De Smet, S.J.*, 2:730–31.
53. Chittenden and Richardson, *Life, Letters and Travels of Father Pierre-Jean De Smet, S.J.*, 2:743.
54. Chittenden and Richardson, *Life, Letters and Travels of Father Pierre-Jean De Smet, S.J.*, 2:743–744.
55. Chittenden and Richardson, *Life, Letters and Travels of Father Pierre-Jean De Smet, S.J.*, 2:740–42.
56. Bancroft, *The Works of Hubert Howe Bancroft*, 349.
57. Chittenden and Richardson, *Life, Letters and Travels of Father Pierre-Jean De Smet, S.J.*, 2:758.
58. De Smet letter report to Captain Alfred Pleasonton, from Coeur d'Alene Mission, December 4, 1858, 393(1)-E 3573, Letters Received, 1858–1860, NARA.
59. Joseph Joset to Pierre-Jean De Smet, S.J., in De Smet, *New Indian Sketches*, 66–67.
60. Thomas Adams, Journal III, Thomas Adams Papers, Princeton University Library.
61. Chittenden and Richardson, *Life, Letters and Travels of Father Pierre-Jean De Smet, S.J.*, 2:766.
62. Congiato to Beckx, Vancouver, May 20, 1859, Mont. Sax Collection 2-iii, ARSI. Translation by Laura Wagster.
63. Owen to Geary, August 16, 1859, in Owen, *The Journals and Letters of Major John Owen*, 2:193. In this letter Owen states, "The Flathead tribe will leave about the last of this Month for their Summer & fall hunt."
64. Owen, *The Journals and Letters of Major John Owen*, 2:195–96.
65. Owen, *The Journals and Letters of Major John Owen*, 2:198–99.

10. *Native World Turned Inside Out*

1. Meikle, *Very Close to Trouble*, 72.
2. Owen, *The Journals and Letters of Major John Owen*, 1:216. Floods in the Hell Gate in June 1860 attest to heavy snows in the upper reaches as well. In mid-June

the Flathead camp remained in the Hell Gate Ronde and had not "gone to Bulls as they could not agree as to the route."

3. Owen, *The Journals and Letters of Major John Owen*, 2:203–4.
4. Owen, *The Journals and Letters of Major John Owen*, 2:214–16.
5. Owen, *The Journals and Letters of Major John Owen*, 2:225–26.
6. Owen, *The Journals and Letters of Major John Owen*, 2:238–39.
7. Owen, *The Journals and Letters of Major John Owen*, 2:239.
8. Louis Vercruysse to Pierre-Jean De Smet, February 13 and August 25, 1861, De Smetiana Series, Record Group IX, A, JARC. Owen, *The Journals and Letters of Major John Owen*, 1:236n and 2:234–35, 238–39, 262.
9. Quoted in Capps, "Leadership in Eastern Salish Communities," IN 19.2.
10. Chittenden and Richardson, *Life, Letters and Travels of Father Pierre-Jean De Smet, S.J.*, 4:1485.
11. Stone, *Following Old Trails*, 129–36.
12. Koelbel, *Missoula the Way It Was*, 17.
13. Hamilton wrote an autobiography titled *My Sixty Years on the Plains*, published in 1905. His personal view of his life story is at odds with the sketchy and unimpressive record of his life left by others.
14. Stuart, *The Montana Frontier*, 178–79. A plew was a French Canadian term for a skin.
15. Stuart, *The Montana Frontier*, 186.
16. For a man who boasted of his accomplishments in his autobiography as Hamilton did, it is notable that John Owen never mentioned him in his journals.
17. Owen, *The Journals and Letters of Major John Owen*, 2:265.
18. Stuart, *The Montana Frontier*, 200. Also see Owen, *The Journals and Letters of Major John Owen*, 1:253.
19. Raczka, *Winter Count*.
20. Owen, *The Journals and Letters of Major John Owen*, 1:244.
21. Owen, *The Journals and Letters of Major John Owen*, 1:245.
22. Stuart, *The Montana Frontier*, 244.
23. Owen, *The Journals and Letters of Major John Owen*, 1:246.
24. Owen, *The Journals and Letters of Major John Owen*, 1:245.
25. Owen, *The Journals and Letters of Major John Owen*, 1:245–56.
26. Owen, *The Journals and Letters of Major John Owen*, 1:247.
27. Stuart, *The Montana Frontier*, 197. This "Eneas" was likely a younger Pend d'Oreille man rather than Little Eneas the Iroquois who had helped introduce De Smet to the Salish.
28. Stuart, *The Montana Frontier*, 200.
29. Stuart, *The Montana Frontier*, 205.
30. Stuart, *The Montana Frontier*, 203–4.

31. Stuart, *The Montana Frontier*, 252.
32. Owen, *The Journals and Letters of Major John Owen*, 1:253. After Crawling Mountain was baptized and then became second chief, he appears as Moise in the vast majority of historical references.
33. Owen, *The Journals and Letters of Major John Owen*, 1:254.
34. Chittenden and Richardson, *Life, Letters and Travels of Father Pierre-Jean De Smet, S.J.*, 3:837.
35. Greeley, *Overland Journey*, Letter 13, "Lo! The Poor Indian!"
36. St. Louis's population in 1840 was just over 35,000 residents, and Portland's population in 1859 was around 2,500 white residents.
37. Stuart, *The Montana Frontier*, 214–15.
38. Stuart, *The Montana Frontier*, 214–15. Thomas Harris, an employee at Fort Owen, by 1860 saw "seven white women and a baby" at Captain Mullan's camp in the "Hell Gate Ronde." Weisel, *Men and Trade*, 115.
39. President Lincoln kept time available for the public to see him. All one had to do was make an appointment. De Smet's visit was just after the Battle of Bull Run.
40. Owen, *The Journals and Letters of Major John Owen*, 1:262.
41. Owen, *The Journals and Letters of Major John Owen*, 1:259–60.
42. Capps, "Leadership in Eastern Salish Communities," IN 35; Point, "Notes Biographiques," in "Souvenirs des Montagnes Rocheuses," 33–34, Nicolas Point, S.J., Fonds, Archive of the Jesuits in Canada.
43. Wilson, *Northern Paiutes of the Malheur*.
44. Stuart, *The Montana Frontier*, 226.
45. Owen, *The Journals and Letters of Major John Owen*, 1:262.
46. Owen, *The Journals and Letters of Major John Owen*, 1:279.

11. Disillusionment and Despair

1. See Farr, "'When We Were First Paid.'"
2. Alex White Plume, former president and leader of the Oglala Sioux tribe, interview by Sally Thompson, 2004.
3. Owen, *The Journals and Letters of Major John Owen*, 1:323.
4. Owen, *The Journals and Letters of Major John Owen*, 1:325–26.
5. Bigart and McDonald, *"Sometimes My People Get Mad,"* 247–48.
6. Quoted in Fahey, *The Flathead Indians*, 121, from report written December 24, 1864.
7. Owen, *The Journals and Letters of Major John Owen*, 1:330.
8. Thomas Harris quoted in Owen, *The Journals and Letters of Major John Owen*, 1:302.
9. Owen, *The Journals and Letters of Major John Owen*, 1:333.
10. Owen, *The Journals and Letters of Major John Owen*, 1:338.
11. Owen, *The Journals and Letters of Major John Owen*, 2:8.

12. Stuart, *The Montana Frontier*, 1:163.
13. Salish Kootenai College, *Challenge to Survive*, 3:18–19, 24; Bigart and McDonald, *"Sometimes My People Get Mad,"* 263.
14. Meagher, "Rides through Montana," 583.
15. Owen, *The Journals and Letters of Major John Owen*, 2:20.
16. Owen, *The Journals and Letters of Major John Owen*, 2:27–29. Alexander died on September 23, 1866. (See Capps, "Leadership in Eastern Salish Communities," IN 14.)
17. Owen, *The Journals and Letters of Major John Owen*, 2:30.
18. Fahey, *The Flathead Indians*, 124–26.
19. Owen, *The Journals and Letters of Major John Owen*, 2:42.
20. Owen, *The Journals and Letters of Major John Owen*, 2:47–48, 50.
21. Owen, *The Journals and Letters of Major John Owen*, 2:55.
22. Red Cloud was a Lakota warrior who led the Lakotas, Cheyennes, and Arapahos in their fight against the U.S. intrusion into their treaty-guaranteed lands. One strategy was to attack travelers on the Bozeman Trail.
23. Owen, *The Journals and Letters of Major John Owen*, 2:55–56.
24. Fahey, *The Flathead Indians*, 125–26.
25. As described by Edward Huggins at Fort Nisqually in 1855, quoted in Partoll, "Angus McDonald," 142.
26. Partoll, "Angus McDonald," 144.
27. Owen, *The Journals and Letters of Major John Owen*, 2:58.
28. Fahey, *The Flathead Indians*, 143. "Tyee" is a Chinook jargon word for chief.
29. Fahey, *The Flathead Indians*, 126, 143.
30. Fahey, *The Flathead Indians*, 143.
31. Sherman to President Grant, December 28, 1866, in Simon, *The Papers of Ulysses S. Grant*, 16:422.
32. Owen, *The Journals and Letters of Major John Owen*, 2:59.
33. Fahey, *The Flathead Indians*, 144, citing the records of W. J. McCormick, who was appointed as a temporary special agent.
34. Seifried, "Early Administration of the Flathead Indian Reservation," 57.
35. Seifried, "Early Administration of the Flathead Indian Reservation," 56.
36. Owen, *The Journals and Letters of Major John Owen*, 2:68
37. Owen, *The Journals and Letters of Major John Owen*, 2:69.
38. Owen, *The Journals and Letters of Major John Owen*, 2:83.
39. Owen, *The Journals and Letters of Major John Owen*, 2:89
40. Owen, *The Journals and Letters of Major John Owen*, 2:89–90.
41. Owen, *The Journals and Letters of Major John Owen*, 2:91.
42. Owen, *The Journals and Letters of Major John Owen*, 2:93.
43. Owen, *The Journals and Letters of Major John Owen*, 2:94.
44. Owen, *The Journals and Letters of Major John Owen*, 2:95.

45. Owen, *The Journals and Letters of Major John Owen*, 2:96.
46. Owen, *The Journals and Letters of Major John Owen*, 2:101–2.
47. Quoted in *Congressional Globe*, 2638.
48. Seifried, "Early Administration of the Flathead Indian Reservation," 65.
49. The commission had received and approved a petition from Bitterroot Valley residents on May 6, 1868, that a county road be laid out and built from Missoula City to the upper end of the Bitterroot Valley at S'kalkaho. Missoula County Commissioner records, Missoula.
50. Owen, *The Journals and Letters of Major John Owen*, 2:121.
51. Fahey, *The Flathead Indians*, 148.
52. Owen, *The Journals and Letters of Major John Owen*, 2:126.
53. Owen, *The Journals and Letters of Major John Owen*, 2:135.
54. Fahey, *The Flathead Indians*, 151–52.
55. Fahey, *The Flathead Indians*, 150.
56. Quoted in Fahey, *The Flathead Indians*, 151–52.
57. *New North-West*, August 13, 1869.

12. *The Shrinking World*

1. *New North-West*, August 27, 1869.
2. Quoted in *New North-West*, September 24, 1869. The same letter was sent to Territorial Governor James Ashley, James M. Cavanaugh, and the Helena paper, the *Helena Daily Herald*.
3. Quoted in *New North-West*, September 24, 1869, 2.
4. *New North-West*, September 24, 1869, 2.
5. Weisel, *Men and Trade*, 98.
6. *New North-West*, October 1, 1869.
7. Bigart, *Life and Death at St. Mary's Mission, Montana*, 128.
8. Owen, *The Journals and Letters of Major John Owen*, 2:143.
9. Fahey, *The Flathead Indians*, 150.
10. *New North-West*, October 22, 1869.
11. *Helena Daily Herald*, October 27, 1869.
12. *New North-West*, October 29, 1869.
13. *New North-West*, November 12, 1869.
14. Owen, *The Journals and Letters of Major John Owen*, 2:146.
15. Letter from Sherman to Sheridan, May 10, 1868, in Phippen, "Kill Every Buffalo You Can!"
16. Quoted in *New North-West*, January 28, 1870.
17. Wylie, *Blood on the Marias*.
18. *New North-West*, January 20, 1870.
19. Cited in Dwight Radford, "History of Montana," https://wiki.rootsweb.com/wiki/index.php/Montana_Family_History_Research.

20. *New North-West,* June 10, 1870.
21. Just before he died, Victor told his family to give his old gray war horse to his old friend Angus McDonald, and the family did. *Missoula and Cedar Creek Pioneer,* November 3, 1870, 3. Also see Curtis, *The North American Indian,* 7:1911.
22. Quotes from Mullan in this and the next two paragraphs are in *New North-West,* September 23, 1870.
23. *Missoula and Cedar Creek Pioneer,* October 20, 1870.
24. P. Ronan, *Historical Sketch of the Flathead Indian Nation,* 72.
25. *Missoula and Cedar Creek Pioneer,* November 10, 1870.
26. Fahey, *The Flathead Indians,* 158.
27. *Missoula and Cedar Creek Pioneer,* January 26, 1871.
28. Fahey, *The Flathead Indians,* 159n21. The others were Francis (not Saxa) and Laurence (Indian name unknown).
29. Petition quoted in Fahey, *The Flathead Indians,* 159; Seifried, "Early Administration of the Flathead Indian Reservation," 79.
30. *Report of the Commissioner of Indian Affairs, 1868,* House Exec. Doc. #49, Serial Set 1366.
31. *Missoula and Cedar Creek Pioneer,* June 1, 1871, 3.
32. *Missoula and Cedar Creek Pioneer,* June 1, 1871, 3.
33. *Missoula and Cedar Creek Pioneer,* August 17, 1871, 3.
34. *Missoula and Cedar Creek Pioneer,* August 17, 1871, 3.
35. *Missoula and Cedar Creek Pioneer,* August 17, 1871, 3.
36. See Merritt, "Fort Owen," 166–68.

13. Shadows Abound

1. Seifried, "Early Administration of the Flathead Indian Reservation," 80.
2. Fahey, *The Flathead Indians,* 160.
3. *Missoula and Cedar Creek Pioneer,* March 23, 1872, 2.
4. *Missoula and Cedar Creek Pioneer,* February 24, 1872.
5. *Missoula and Cedar Creek Pioneer,* March 9, 1872, 3.
6. Quotes in this and the next several paragraphs are from "Report of Hon. James A. Garfield, Commissioner for the Removal of the Flathead Tribe of Indians from the Bitter Root Valley, in Montana Territory, to the Jocko Reservation, in Said Territory, with Accompanying Papers. Washington DC, November 15, 1872," Annual Report of the Commissioner of Indian Affairs 1872, U.S. Department of Indian Affairs (USDIA), 109–18 (cited hereafter as Garfield Report, November 15, 1872). Also "Papers Accompanying the Report of the Commissioner of Indian Affairs, 1872—A Report of Hon. James A. Garfield, Commissioner for the Removal of the Flathead Tribe of Indians from the Bitter Root Valley, in Montana Territory, to the Jocko Reservation, in Said Territory, with Accompanying Papers," Annual Report of the Commissioner of Indian Affairs to

the Secretary of the Interior for the Year 1872, https://digitalcollections.lib.washington.edu/digital/collection/lctext/id/3498.

7. Garfield to Comm. Walker, in Garfield Report, November 15, 1872.
8. Fahey, *The Flathead Indians*, 163.
9. J. V. Sanders in the *Anaconda Standard*, May 24, 1908, part 2, p. 7.
10. Garfield Report, November 15, 1872.
11. Fourth Annual Report of the Board of Indian Commissioners, Def. Ex. 6, p. 172, USDIA.
12. Garfield Report, November 15, 1872.
13. Fahey concludes that the priest was Father Ravalli (*The Flathead Indians*, 164). Father Jerome D'Aste was another priest with whom the Indians confided.
14. Garfield Report, November 15, 1872; also see Fahey, *The Flathead Indians*, 164.
15. Garfield Report, November 15, 1872.
16. Garfield Report, November 15, 1872.
17. J. V. Sanders in the *Anaconda Standard*, May 24, 1908, part 2, p. 7.
18. Seifried, "Early Administration of the Flathead Indian Reservation," 109.
19. Garfield, "Diary of a Trip to Montana in 1872."
20. Quoted in Walter, *More Montana Campfire Tales*, 62–63. Charlo's name is spelled variably as Charlot, Charlos, Carlos, and Charles.
21. Quoted in Walter, *More Montana Campfire Tales*, 63.
22. Fahey, *The Flathead Indians*, 164–65.
23. *Weekly Missoulian*, March 7, 1873.
24. *Weekly Missoulian*, April 25, 1873.
25. Jasper Viall had been removed from office after the Treasury Department established that Viall had manipulated $16,000 in department funds to his advantage (Seifried, "Early Administration of the Flathead Indian Reservation," 91).
26. *Weekly Missoulian*, May 23, 1873, 2.
27. *Weekly Missoulian*, May 9, 1873, 3.
28. *Weekly Missoulian*, June 6, 1873, 3.
29. *Weekly Missoulian*, June 13, 1873.
30. *Weekly Missoulian*, August 1, 1873. According to Missoula naturalist Paul Hendricks in a personal communication, "Sharp-tailed grouse were the only open-country grouse that were in the area. Ruffed grouse and blue [dusky] grouse inhabited the riparian areas and forests. . . . It is also possible they were lumping all the grouse together and calling all of them chickens."
31. *New North-West*, October 11, 1873.
32. *Weekly Missoulian*, October 24, 1873, 3.
33. *New North-West*, October 25, 1873.
34. *New North-West*, November 1, 1873.
35. *Weekly Missoulian*, March 12, 1874, 3.

36. Quotes in this and the following paragraph are from *Weekly Missoulian*, March 14, 1874.
37. *Weekly Missoulian*, June 4, 1874.
38. *Weekly Missoulian*, September 16, 1874.
39. *Weekly Missoulian*, January 13, 1875, 2.
40. Phippen, "Kill Every Buffalo You Can!"
41. *Weekly Missoulian*, January 13, 1875, 2.
42. *New North-West*, April 9, 1875.
43. *Weekly Missoulian*, May 12, 1875, 3.
44. *Weekly Missoulian*, August 15, 1875.
45. Agent Medary to commissioner, September 13, 1875, in Bigart and McDonald, *"You Seem to Like Your Money,"* 20–25.
46. Agent Medary to Commissioner Smith, February 11, 1876, in Bigart and McDonald, *"You Seem to Like Your Money,"* 33–36.
47. Quotes from Charlo's speech in this and the next several paragraphs are in *Weekly Missoulian*, April 26, 1876, reprinted in Bigart and McDonald, *"You Seem to Like Your Money,"* 37–40.
48. The *Weekly Missoulian* article is the only record of Chief Charlo's brutally honest speech. Unfortunately, no matter how good the translation, the reporter's shorthand could not have grasped all that was said that day by the chief or by others. We have no real way of knowing what we don't know. I have done my best to read between the lines.
49. Seifried, "Early Administration of the Flathead Indian Reservation," 135–36.
50. Fahey, *The Flathead Indians*, 199. Palladino to Ronan, August 15 and 18, 1877, USDIA.
51. P. Ronan, *Historical Sketch of the Flathead Indian Nation*, 204.
52. From the *Montana Herald*, printed in the *Weekly Missoulian*, October 26, 1877. Water rights to this hot spring complex along Ten-Mile Creek had been given in 1874 to Charles Broadwater, who was interested in developing the spring's medicinal properties.
53. *New North-West*, July 20, 1877; Seifried, "Early Administration of the Flathead Indian Reservation," 140. Since the days when only Fort Benton served as a place of protection for non-Indians, nine military forts had been added on the east side of the mountains by the end of 1877.
54. *New North-West*, November 2, 1877.
55. Seifried, "Early Administration of the Flathead Indian Reservation," 141.
56. *Weekly Missoulian*, April 5, 1878, from the *Husbandman*, March 28, 1878.
57. Seifried, "Early Administration of the Flathead Indian Reservation," 148.
58. Seifried, "Early Administration of the Flathead Indian Reservation," 147, from Legis. Assembly to Pres. Hayes, February 5, 1879, USDIA.
59. *Weekly Missoulian*, March 19, 1880.

14. *Charlo's Lament*

1. Granville Stuart, letter to *Helena Independent*, January 27, 1882, published February 8, 1882, italics in original.
2. *Helena Independent*, February 8, 1882.
3. *Weekly Missoulian*, December 15, 1882.
4. Fahey, *The Flathead Indians*, 225.
5. *Weekly Missoulian*, September 28, 1883.
6. Will Sutherlin, "West Side of the Bitter Root—Sweat House Farmers," *Rocky Mountain Husbandman*, August 16, 1877, p. 2, col. 2–3.
7. Words of Indian Commissioner Hiram Price in 1882, quoted in Fahey, *The Flathead Indians*, 227.
8. Quoted in Fahey, *The Flathead Indians*, 228–29.
9. Fahey, *The Flathead Indians*, 228–29.
10. Father Ravalli, who had been extremely ill during Senator Vest's visit, died in October 1884 at the age of seventy-two.
11. Quoted in Palladino, *Indian and White in the Northwest*, 88–89.
12. D. J. Smith, "Procuring a Right-of-Way," 10.
13. Quoted in *Helena Independent*, September 13, 1883, 5; *Weekly Missoulian*, September 28, 1883.
14. Quoted in *Helena Independent*, September 13, 1883, 5.
15. Quoted in *Helena Independent*, September 13, 1883, 5.
16. Quoted in *Helena Independent*, September 13, 1883, 5.
17. Quoted in Fahey, *The Flathead Indians*, 235–36.
18. Fahey, *The Flathead Indians*, 234–35; Selis-Ql'ispe Culture Committee, "Beartracks Bridge."
19. *Tacoma Daily Ledger*, June 3, 1884.
20. *Weekly Missoulian*, April 26, 1876, reprinted in Bigart and McDonald, *"You Seem to Like Your Money,"* 37–40.
21. *Weekly Missoulian*, December 14 and 21, 1883, and March 14, 1884. "Poor Lo" is a takeoff from "Lo, the poor Indian," an eighteenth-century poem by Alexander Pope.
22. *Weekly Missoulian*, October 3, 1884, p. 3, col. 2.
23. *Weekly Missoulian*, March 12, 1886, from the *Rocky Mountain Husbandman*.
24. Ferris, *Life in the Rocky Mountains*, 107.
25. Olson, *Up the Creek*, 3.
26. See Bigart, "'Charlot Loves His People,'" for discussion.
27. Fahey, *The Flathead Indians*, 247, based on Carrington manuscript, "Exodus of the Flatheads," Carrington Papers (Mss 147), Maureen and Mike Mansfield Archives and Special Collections, University of Montana, Missoula.
28. Fahey, *The Flathead Indians*, 248–49.

29. Fahey, *The Flathead Indians*, 247–48.
30. Fahey, *The Flathead Indians*, 248–49.
31. Bigart, "'Charlot Loves His People,'" 30.
32. Fahey, *The Flathead Indians*, 249.
33. Bigart, "'Charlot Loves His People,'" 25n2.
34. Fahey, *The Flathead Indians*, 250.
35. *Missoula Gazette*, May 15, 1889.
36. Bigart, "'Charlot Loves His People,'" 35; Fahey, *The Flathead Indians*, 252–53.
37. Bigart, "'Charlot Loves His People,'" 35.
38. In this and the next several paragraphs Rickman is quoted in Fahey, *The Flathead Indians*, 314. Fahey notes that Rickman's account is not confirmed elsewhere. Neither was it ever negated. The Baptist pastor held positions in western Montana, including Helena, for many years, with a good reputation.
39. Quoted in Bigart, "'Charlot Loves His People,'" 38.
40. Information about McLaren is from a family history prepared by Jenny Saad, June 15, 2004, posted on Ancestry.com.
41. *Weekly Missoulian*, January 7, 1906. Original article is from the *Bozeman Chronicle* documenting the graduation address of Rev. M. L. Rickman on May 24, 1905.
42. Selis-Ql'ispe Culture Committee, "Beartracks Bridge," 9; Richard Malouf in Bigart, *Life and Death at St. Mary's Mission, Montana*, 242.
43. Bigart, "'Charlot Loves His People,'" 40.
44. *Weekly Missoulian*, December 22, 1903, 1.
45. Carrington, "Exodus of the Flatheads," ch. 12, p. 2, cited in Seifried, "Early Administration of the Flathead Indian Reservation," 167.
46. Stone, *Following Old Trails*, 29; Teit, "The Salishan Tribes," 364; P. Ronan, *Historical Sketch of the Flathead Indian Nation*, 77–78.
47. Fahey, *The Flathead Indians*, 255.
48. Ronan and Ronan, *Girl from the Gulches*, 214.
49. *Missoula Weekly Gazette*, October 21, 1891, 1.
50. Quoted in Selis-Ql'ispe Culture Committee, "Beartracks Bridge."
51. Selis-Ql'ispe Culture Committee, "Beartracks Bridge."
52. Fahey, *The Flathead Indians*, 270.
53. Fahey, *The Flathead Indians*, 270.
54. Menager, "Reminiscences of a Missionary Sister," 59–61.
55. Fahey, *The Flathead Indians*, 300.
56. Seifried, "Early Administration of the Flathead Indian Reservation," 147, from Legis. Assembly to Pres. Hayes, February 5, 1879, USDIA.
57. Fahey, *The Flathead Indians*, 297.
58. *Weekly Missoulian*, March 18, 1905.
59. *Weekly Missoulian*, March 18, 1905.
60. Fahey, *The Flathead Indians*, 280.

61. *Weekly Missoulian*, July 5, 1907, 3.
62. Myrna Dumontier (great-granddaughter of Louise Vanderburg), personal communication, January 11, 2022.
63. *Anaconda Standard*, May 20, 1908, 10.
64. Ronan and Ronan, *Girl from the Gulches*.

Epilogue

1. *Weekly Missoulian*, April 26, 1876, reprinted in Bigart and McDonald, "*You Seem to Like Your Money,*" 37–40.
2. Arlee, "The Gift of the Bitterroot."
3. Brown, *Transformation beyond Greed*, 47.

Bibliography

Archives and Manuscript Materials

Adrian Hoecken Papers, 1:11. Jesuit Oregon Provincial Archives, Gonzaga University, Spokane WA.

Archivum Romanum Societatis Iesu (ARSI), Rome.

Capps, George. "Leadership in Eastern Salish Communities, 1781–1850." August 2022. Manuscript in possession of the author.

Carrington Papers. Maureen and Mike Mansfield Archives and Special Collections, University of Montana, Missoula.

Cassily, Francis. "The Old Jesuit Mission in Council Bluffs." Council Bluffs Public Library.

Chouteau Collection. Missouri Historical Society.

Claude E. Schaeffer Fonds. Glenbow Museum, University of Calgary, Calgary AB.

Cox, Mildred C. "Gabriel Prudhomme Estate." 1956. Missouri Valley Special Collections, Kansas City Public Library, Kansas City MO.

Edward S. Curtis Papers. Seaver Center for Western History Research, Natural History Museum of Los Angeles County, Los Angeles CA.

Hilmo, Glen "Dusty." "The Rocky Fork of the Clark Fork." Manuscript in possession of the author.

Jesuit Archives and Research Center (JARC), St. Louis MO.

Davis Papers.

Missouri Province Collection, De Smetiana Series, Record Group IX.

National Archives and Records Administration (NARA).

Nicolas Point, S.J., Fonds. Archive of the Jesuits in Canada/Archives des jésuites au Canada, Montreal QC.

Pacific Northwest Tribes Missions Collection of the Oregon Province Archives of the Society of Jesus. Gonzaga University, Spokane WA.

Pambrun, Andrew D. "The Story of His Life as He Tells It." Typescript. MS-181. Eastern Washington University, Cheney.

Sir Henry James Warre Fond. Public Archives of Canada.

Siria, C. H. "Rock Creek, Past and Present." Manuscript in possession of the author.

Sperlin, O. B. "The Story of Grand Eneas (Big Ignace): An Account Given by His Son, Francois Saxa, to the Author and Recorded in a Letter to T. S. [*sic*] Elliott." Unpublished typescript, April 22, 1917. Missoula Public Library, Missoula MT.

Thomas Adams Papers, 1852–1859. Princeton University Library.

Published Works

Akers, Donna. "Native Nations in an Age of Western Expansion, 1820–80." In *American Indians/American Presidents: A History*, edited by Clifford E. Trafzer. New York: HarperCollins, 2009.

Anderson, William Marshall. *The Rocky Mountain Journals of William Marshall Anderson: The West in 1834*. Edited by Dale L. Morgan and Eleanor Towles Harris. Lincoln: University of Nebraska Press, 1987.

Arlee, Johnny. "The Gift of the Bitterroot." PDF. Salish Kootenai College: Npustin Press, 2008.

Ball, John, Kate Ball Powers, Flora Ball Hopkins, and Lucy Ball. *Autobiography of John Ball*. Grand Rapids MI: Dean-Hicks, 1925.

Bancroft, Hubert Howe. *The Works of Hubert Howe Bancroft*. Vol. 32, *History of British Columbia, 1792–1887*. San Francisco: History Company, 1887.

Baumler, Ellen. "A Cross in the Wilderness: St. Mary's Mission Celebrates 175 Years." *Montana: The Magazine of Western History* 66, no. 1 (Spring 2016): 18–38.

Bigart, Robert J., ed. "'Charlot Loves His People': The Defeat of Bitterroot Salish Aspirations for an Independent Bitterroot Valley Community." *Montana: The Magazine of Western History* 60, no. 1 (Spring 2010): 24–44, 92–94.

———, ed. *Crossroad of Cultures: Sacramental Records at St. John the Baptist Catholic Church, Frenchtown, Montana, 1866–1899*. Translated by Anita O. Scott and James M. Scott. Pablo MT: Salish Kootenai College Press, 2009.

———. *Getting Good Crops: Economic and Diplomatic Survival Strategies of the Montana Bitterroot Salish Indians, 1870–1891*. Norman: University of Oklahoma Press, 2010.

———, ed. *Life and Death at St. Mary's Mission, Montana: Births, Marriages, Deaths, and Survival among the Bitterroot Salish Indians, 1866–1891*. Pablo MT: Salish Kootenai College Press, 2005.

Bigart, Robert, and Clarence Woodcock, eds. *In the Name of the Salish and Kootenai Nation: The 1855 Hell Gate Treaty and the Origin of the Flathead Indian Reservation*. Pablo MT: Salish Kootenai College Press, 1996.

Bigart, Robert, and Joseph McDonald. *Duncan McDonald: Flathead Indian Reservation Leader and Cultural Broker, 1849–1937*. Pablo MT: Salish Kootenai College Press, 2016.

———, eds. *"Sometimes My People Get Mad When the Blackfeet Kill Us": A Documentary History of the Salish and Pend d'Oreille Indians, 1845–1874*. Pablo MT: Salish Kootenai College Press, 2019.

———, eds. *"You Seem to Like Your Money, and We Like Our Country": A Documentary History of the Salish, Pend d'Oreille and Kootenai Indians, 1875–1889*. Pablo MT: Salish Kootenai College Press, 2019.

Binnema, Theodore. *Common and Contested Ground: A Human and Environmental History of the Northwestern Plains*. Norman: University of Oklahoma Press, 2001.

Bright, William. *Native American Placenames of the United States*. Norman: University of Oklahoma Press, 2004.

Brown, Sidney Stone. *Transformation beyond Greed: Native Self-Actualization*. Self-published, 2014.

Buckley, Cornelius M. *Nicolas Point, S.J.: His Life and Northwest Indian Chronicles*. Chicago: Loyola University Press, 1989.

Buckley, Jay H. *William Clark: Indian Diplomat*. Norman: University of Oklahoma Press, 2008.

Burns, Robert Ignatius. "A Jesuit at the Hell Gate Treaty of 1855." In Bigart and Woodcock, *In the Name of the Salish and Kootenai Nation*, 121–48.

Cappon, Lester J., ed. *Adams-Jefferson Letters: The Complete Correspondence between Thomas Jefferson and Abigail and John Adams*. Chapel Hill: Omohundro Institute and University of North Carolina Press, 1988.

Capps, George. "Blackfeet Peacemaker: The Search for Nicholas the Small Robe." *Rocky Mountain Fur Trade Journal* 9 (2015): 86–109.

———. "Grand Ignace: 'Apostle of the Flatheads.'" *Rocky Mountain Fur Trade Journal* 15 (2021): 40–81.

Carriker, Robert C. *Father Peter John De Smet, S.J.: Jesuit in the West*. Norman: University of Oklahoma Press, 1995.

Cebula, Larry. *Plateau Indians and the Quest for Spiritual Power, 1700–1850*. Lincoln: University of Nebraska Press, 2003.

Charles, Robert, and Soong-Chan Rah. *Unsettling Truths: The Ongoing, Dehumanizing Legacy of the Doctrine of Discovery*. Westmont IL: InterVarsity Press, 2019.

Charlevoix, Pierre-François-Xavier de. *History and General Description of New France*. Vol. 1. Translated by John Gilmary Shea. New York: John Gilmary Shea, 1866.

Chittenden, Hiram Martin, and Alfred Talbot Richardson, eds. *Life, Letters and Travels of Father Pierre-Jean De Smet, S.J., 1801–1873*. 4 vols. New York: Francis P. Harper, 1905.

Clark, Ella. *Indian Legends from the Northern Rockies*. Norman: University of Oklahoma Press. 1966.

Clement, Priscilla Ferguson. "The Philadelphia Welfare Crisis of the 1820s." *Pennsylvania Magazine of History and Biography* 105, no. 2 (1981).

Clifton James A. "Billy Caldwell's Exile in Early Chicago." *Chicago History Magazine*, Winter 1977–78, 218–28.

The Congressional Globe: Containing the Debates and Proceedings of the Second Session, Fortieth Congress. Washington DC: Office of the Congressional Globe, 1868.

Crosby, Donald F., S.J. "Jesuits Go Home: The Anti-Jesuit Movement in the United States, 1830–1860." *Woodstock Letters* 97, no. 2 (1968).

Curtis, Edward S. *The North American Indian*. Vol. 7. Edited by Frederick Webb Hodge. Cambridge: Cambridge University Press, 1911.

Davis, William L. *A History of St. Ignatius Mission*. Spokane WA: C. W. Hill, 1954.

———. "Peter John De Smet: The Years of Preparation 1801–1837." *Pacific Northwest Quarterly* 32 (April 1941).

———. "Peter John De Smet: The Journey of 1840." *Pacific Northwest Quarterly* 35, no. 1 (January 1944): 29–43.

De Smet, Pierre-Jean. *De Smet's Oregon Missions and Travels over the Rocky Mountains in 1845–46*. In *Early Western Travels, 1748–1846*, vol. 29, edited by Reuben Gold Thwaites, 108–424. Cleveland OH: Arthur H. Clark, 1906.

———. *Letters and Sketches: With a Narrative of a Year's Residence among the Indian Tribes of the Rocky Mountains*. In *Early Western Travels, 1748–1846*, vol. 27, edited by Reuben Gold Thwaites, 123–411. Cleveland OH: Arthur H. Clark, 1906.

———. *New Indian Sketches*. New York: Sadler, 1863. Reprint, Fairfield WA: Ye Galleon Press, 1985.

———. *Origin, Progress, and Prospects of the Catholic Mission to the Rocky Mountains*. Fairfield WA: Ye Galleon Press, 1967, 1972, 1986.

———. *Western Missions and Missionaries: A Series of Letters*. New York: James B. Kirker, 1868.

Devitt, Edward I., S.J. "History of the Maryland–New York Province, VII." *Woodstock Letters* 62, no. 3 (1933).

Doty, James. *Journal of Operations of Governor Isaac Ingalls Stevens of Washington Territory in 1855*. Edited by Edward J. Kowrach. Fairfield WA: Ye Galleon Press, 1978.

Elliott, T. C. *Peter Skene Ogden, Fur Trader*. Portland OR: Ivy Press, 1910.

Evans, Lucylle H. *St. Mary's in the Rocky Mountains: A History of the Cradle of Montana's Culture*. Rev. ed. Stevensville: Montana Creative Consultants, 1976.

Ewers, John C. "Gustavus Sohon's Portraits of Flathead and Pend d'Oreille Indians, 1854." Washington DC: Smithsonian Institution, 1948. Smithsonian Miscellaneous Collections 110, no. 7.

Fahey, John. *The Flathead Indians*. Norman: University of Oklahoma Press, 1974.

———. *The Kalispel Indians*. Norman: University of Oklahoma Press, 1986.

Farr, William. "Going to Buffalo: Indian Hunting Migrations across the Rocky Mountains. Part 1: Making Meat and Taking Robes." *Montana: The Magazine of Western History* 53 (Winter 2003): 2–21.

———. "Going to Buffalo: Indian Hunting Migrations across the Rocky Mountains. Part 2: Civilian Permits, Army Escorts." *Montana: The Magazine of Western History* 54 (Spring 2004): 26–44.

———. "'When We Were First Paid': The Blackfoot Treaty, the Western Tribes, and the Creation of the Common Hunting Ground." *Great Plains Quarterly* 21, no. 2 (Spring 2001): 131–54.

"Father Mengarini." *Woodstock Letters* 16, no. 1 (1887): 93–97.

Ferris, Warren Angus. *Life in the Rocky Mountains: A Diary of Wanderings on the Sources of the Rivers Missouri, Columbia, and Colorado, 1830–1835*. Edited by Leroy R. Hafen. New rev. ed. Denver: Old West, 1983.

Flathead Culture Committee. *A Brief History of the Flathead Tribes*. Rev. ed. St. Ignatius MT: Flathead Culture Committee of the Confederated Salish and Kootenai Tribes, 1993.

Full Blood Flathead Indian Montana Study Group. *Full Blood Flathead Indian Montana Study Group, Arlee, Montana: Minutes of Meetings*. Missoula: Montana State University, Montana Study, 1947.

Fuller, E. O. "The Confederated Salish and Kutenai Tribes of the Flathead Reservation." In Horr, *Interior Salish and Eastern Washington Indians*, 3:25–168.

Garfield, James A. "Diary of a Trip to Montana in 1872." Edited by Oliver W. Holmes. *Frontier and Midland* 15, no. 2 (1934): 159–68.

Garraghan, Gilbert J. *The Jesuits of the Middle United States*. 3 vols. New York: America Press, 1938.

Genovese, Michael A., and Alyssa Landry. *US Presidents and the Destruction of the Native American Nations*. London: Palgrave McMillan, 2021.

Greeley, Horace. *Overland Journey from New York to San Francisco in 1859*. New York: C. M. Saxton, Barker, 1860.

Hamilton, William T. "A Trading Expedition amongst the Indians in 1858." *Contributions to the Historical Society of Montana* 3 (1900): 33–123.

Hanley, Philip M. *History of the Catholic Ladder*. Fairfield WA: Ye Galleon Press, 1993.

Harden, Blaine. *Murder at the Mission*. Lincoln: University of Nebraska Press, 2021.

Hoig, Stan. *Beyond the Frontier: Exploring the Indian Country*. Norman: University of Oklahoma Press, 1998.

Holterman, Jack. *Shining Shirt*. West Glacier MT: Glacier Natural History Association, 1991.

Horr, David Agee, ed. *Interior Salish and Eastern Washington Indians*. 3 vols. New York: Garland Publishing, 1974.

Jaenike, William F. *Black Robes in Paraguay: The Success of the Guarani Missions Hastened the Abolition of the Jesuits*. Minneapolis: Kirk House Publishers, 2008.

Jefferson, Thomas. *Notes on the State of Virginia, 1781*. Reprint, Harlow, England: Penguin Books, Penguin Classics, 1998.

Johnson, Olga Weydemeyer. *Flathead and Kootenay: The Rivers, the Tribes and the Region's Traders*. Glendale CA: Arthur H. Clark, 1969.

Jones, Landon Y. "Iron Will." *Smithsonian Magazine*, August 2002.

Josephy, Alvin M., Jr. *The Nez Perce Indians and the Opening of the Northwest*. Boston: Houghton Mifflin, 1997.

Juneau, Linda Matt. "Small Robe Band of Blackfeet: Ethnogenesis by Social and Religious Transformation." Master's thesis, University of Montana, 2007.

Karamanski, Theodore J. "The Iroquois of the Fur Trade of the Far West." *Beaver* 312, no. 4 (Spring 1982): 4–13.

Keyser, James D. *The Five Crows Ledger: Biographic Warrior Art of the Flathead Indians*. Salt Lake City: University of Utah Press, 2000.

Koelbel, Lenora. *Missoula the Way It Was*. Missoula MT: Gateway Printing and Litho, 1972.

Larpenteur, Chas. *Forty Years a Fur Trader on the Upper Missouri*. 2 vols. Edited by Elliott Coues. New York: Francis P. Harper, 1898. Reprint, Lincoln: University of Nebraska Press, 1989.

Lathrop, A. "Famous Indian Foot Race: Trader Secures Good Will of Band of Flatheads." *Contributions to the Historical Society of Montana* 6 (1907): 479–81.

Laveille, Eugene, S.J. *The Life of Father De Smet*. Chicago: Loyola University Press, 1981.

Maillet, Louis R., and W. F. Wheeler. "Historical Sketch of Louis R. Maillet." *Contributions to the Historical Society of Montana* 4 (1903): 197–228.

Malouf, Carling. "Economy and Land Use by the Indians of Western Montana, U.S.A." In Horr, *Interior Salish and Eastern Washington Indians*, 2:117–78.

Malouf, Carling, and Paul C. Phillips. "Flathead, Kutenai, and Upper Pend d'Oreille Genealogies." In Horr, *Interior Salish and Eastern Washington Indians*, 3:307–28.

Malouf, Richard T. "Family Histories." In Bigart, *Life and Death at St. Mary's Mission, Montana*, 225–331, 336–50.

Mann, Charles. *1491: New Revelations of the Americas before Columbus*. New York: Vintage Books, 2005.

Mather, Increase. *A Brief History of the War with the Indians in New-England*. 1676. Electronic edition. Edited by Paul Royster. https://digitalcommons.unl.edu/libraryscience/31/.

McNutt, Charles H., and Ryan M. Parish, eds. *Cahokia in Context: Hegemony and Diaspora*. Gainesville: University of Florida Press. 2020.

Meagher, T. F. "Rides through Montana." *Harper's New Monthly Magazine*, no. 209 (October 1867).

Meikle, Lyndel. *Very Close to Trouble: The Johnny Grant Memoir*. Pullman: Washington State University Press, 1996.

Mellis, John C. "Coyote People and the Black Robes: Indigenous Roots of Salish Christianity." PhD dissertation, Saint Louis University, 1992.

———. "Ignace Partui: Iroquois Evangelist to the Salish, ca. 1780–1837." *International Bulletin of Missionary Research* 33, no. 4 (October 2009): 212–15. University Microfilms International no. 9233816.

Menager, Gabriel M., S.J. "Reminiscences of a Missionary Sister." *Indian Sentinel* 22, no. 4 (April 1942): 59–61.

Mengarini, Gregory. *Mengarini's Narrative of the Rockies: Memoirs of Old Oregon, 1841–1850, and St. Mary's Mission*. Edited by Albert J. Partoll. Sources of Northwest History 25. Missoula: Montana State University, 1938.

———. *Recollections of the Flathead Mission: Containing Brief Observations Both Ancient and Contemporary Concerning This Particular Nation*. Translated and edited by Gloria Ricci Lothrop. Glendale CA: Arthur H. Clark, 1977.

———. "The Rocky Mountains: Memoirs of Fr. Gregory Mengarini." *Woodstock Letters* 17, no. 3 (1888): 298–309.
———. "The Rocky Mountains: Memoirs of Fr. Gregory Mengarini (Continued)." *Woodstock Letters* 18, no. 1 (1889): 25–43.
———. "The Rocky Mountains: Memoirs of Fr. Gregory Mengarini (Concluded)." *Woodstock Letters* 18, no. 2 (1889): 142–52.
Merriam, Alan P. *Ethnomusicology of the Flathead Indians*. New York: Wenner-Gren Foundation for Anthropological Research, 1967.
Merritt, Donald Roy. "Fort Owen: The History and Archaeology of a Contact Period Site in Western Montana." Master's thesis, University of Montana, 2020.
Miller, Robert J. *Discovering Indigenous Lands: The Doctrine of Discovery in the English Colonies*. New York: Oxford University Press, 2010.
Morgan, Dale. *Jedediah Smith and the Opening of the West*. Lincoln: University of Nebraska Press, 1964.
Mullan, John. *Report on the Construction of a Military Road from Fort Walla-Walla to Fort Benton*. Washington DC: Government Printing Office, 1863.
Mullen, Frank. "Father De Smet and the Pottawattamie Indian Mission." *Iowa Journal of History and Politics* 23 (1925): 192–216.
Nicandri, David L. *Northwest Chiefs: Gustav Sohon's Views of the 1855 Stevens Treaty Councils*. Tacoma: Washington State Historical Society, 1986.
Oakley, Robert D. *The Philipsburg Story: The History of the Philipsburg Ranger District, 1905–1980*. Butte MT: USDA Northern Region, Deerlodge National Forest, 1980.
[Ogden, Peter Skene.] *Traits of American-Indian Life and Character*. London: Smith, Elder, 1853.
Olson, Darlene. *Up the Creek: History of Early Settlers on Rock Creek, Bonita, and Quigley*. Clinton MT: Valley Publishing, 1990.
Owen, John. *The Journals and Letters of Major John Owen*. 2 vols. Edited by Seymour Dunbar and Paul C. Phillips. New York: Edward Eberstadt, 1927.
Palladino, Lawrence Benedict. *Indian and White in the Northwest: A History of Catholicity in Montana, 1831 to 1891*. 2nd ed. Lancaster PA: Wickersham, 1922.
Partoll, Albert J. "Angus McDonald, Frontier Fur Trader." *Pacific Northwest Quarterly* 42, no. 2 (April 1951): 138–46.
———, ed. *The Blackfoot Indian Peace Council: A Document of the Official Proceedings of the Treaty between the Blackfoot Nation and Other Indians and the United States, in October, 1855*. Sources of Northwest History 3. Missoula: Montana State University, 1937.
———. "Fort Connah: A Frontier Trading Post, 1847–1871." *Pacific Northwest Quarterly* 30, no. 4 (October 1939): 399–415.
Peterson, Jacqueline. *Sacred Encounters: Father De Smet and the Indians of the Rocky Mountains West*. Norman: University of Oklahoma Press, 1993.

Pierre, Eneas. "When the Buffalo Were First Seen Passing through the Bitterroot." In *The Buffalo of the Flatheads*, edited by Clarence Woodcock, Tony Incashola, Dolly Linsebigler, and Pete Finley, 12–26. Portland OR: Pacific Northwest Indian Reading and Language Development Program, 1981.

Phillips, Paul C. "History of the Confederated Salish and Kootenai Tribes of the Flathead Reservation, Montana." In Horr, *Interior Salish and Eastern Washington Indians*, 3:233–305.

Phippen, J. Weston. "Kill Every Buffalo You Can! Every Buffalo Dead Is an Indian Gone." *The Atlantic*, May 13, 2016.

Point, Nicolas. *Wilderness Kingdom: Indian Life in the Rocky Mountains, 1840–1847*. Translated by Joseph P. Donnelly. New York: Holt, Rinehart and Winston, 1967.

Prucha, Francis Paul. *Americanizing the American Indian: Writings by the "Friends of the Indian," 1880–1900*. Cambridge: Harvard University Press, 1973.

Raczka, P. M. *Winter Count: A History of the Blackfoot People*. Calgary: Friesen Printers for Oldman River Culture Center, 1979.

Radford, Dwight A. "History of Montana." In *Red Book: American State, County and Town Sources*, edited by Alice Eichholz. Lehi UT: Ancestry Publishing, 2004.

Rappagliosi, Philip. *Letters from the Rocky Mountain Indian Missions*. Edited by Robert Bigart. Translated by Anthony Mattina, Lisa Moore Nardini, and Ulrich Stengel. Lincoln: University of Nebraska Press, 2003.

Reid, John Phillip. *Contested Empire: Peter Skene Ogden and the Snake River Expeditions*. Norman: University of Oklahoma Press, 2002.

Robbins, William G. *Landscapes of Promise: The Oregon Story, 1800–1940*. Seattle: University of Washington Press, 1997.

Rockwell, David, compiler. *The Lower Flathead River, Flathead Indian Reservation: A Cultural, Historical, and Scientific Resource*. Tribal History Project. Pablo MT: Salish Kootenai College Press, 2008.

Ronan, Mary, and Margaret Ronan. *Girl from the Gulches: The Story of Mary Ronan*. Edited by Ellen Baumler. Helena: Montana Historical Society Press, 2003.

Ronan, Peter. *"A Great Many of Us Have Good Farms": Agent Peter Ronan Reports on the Flathead Indian Reservation, Montana, 1877–1887*. Edited by Robert J. Bigart. Pablo MT: Salish Kootenai College Press, 2014.

———. *Historical Sketch of the Flathead Indian Nation from the Year 1813 to 1890*. Helena MT: Journal Publishing, 1890.

———. *Justice to Be Accorded to the Indians: Agent Peter Ronan Reports on the Flathead Indian Reservation, Montana, 1888–1893*. Edited by Robert J. Bigart. Pablo MT: Salish Kootenai College Press, 2014.

Salish Kootenai College. *Challenge to Survive: History of the Salish Tribes of the Flathead Indian Reservation*. 4 vols. Tribal History Project. Pablo MT: Salish Kootenai College Press, 2008–11.

Salish–Pend d'Oreille Culture Committee. *The Salish People and the Lewis and Clark Expedition*. Lincoln: University of Nebraska Press, 2005.
Salish–Pend d'Oreille Culture Committee and Elders Cultural Advisory Council, CSKT. "The Swan Valley Massacre of 1908, a Brief History." 2008.
Sangiovanni, G. G. R. "Overland Trips across the American Deseret." *Young Woman's Journal* 23. Reprinted in *Deseret News* (Salt Lake City), 1912.
Seifried, Richard. "Early Administration of the Flathead Indian Reservation 1855 to 1893." Master's thesis, University of Montana, 1968.
Selis-Ql'ispe Culture Committee. "Beartracks Bridge." Historical background pamphlet. Pablo MT: Confederated Salish and Kootenai Tribes, 2022.
Simon, John Y. *The Papers of Ulysses S. Grant*. Vol. 16. Carbondale: Southern Illinois University Press, 1988. https://www.usgrantlibrary.org/collections/digital.
Sleeper-Smith, Susan. *Indigenous Prosperity and American Conquest: Indian Women of the Ohio River Valley, 1690–1792*. Chapel Hill: University of North Carolina Press, 2018.
Smith, Dennis J. "Procuring a Right-of-Way: James J. Hill and Indian Reservations, 1886–1888." Master's thesis, University of Montana, 1983.
Smith, Sarah Gilbert White, and Asa Bowen Smith. *The Mountains We Have Crossed: Diaries and Letters of the Oregon Mission, 1838*. Edited by Clifford Merrill Drury. Lincoln: University of Nebraska Press, 1999.
Stephens, Kyle Massey. *To the Indian Removal Act, 1814–1830*. PhD dissertation, University of Tennessee, 2013. http://trace.tennessee.edu/utk_graddiss/2487.
Stevens, Isaac I. "Narrative and Final Report of Explorations for a Route for a Pacific Railroad, near the Forty-Seventh and Forty-Ninth Parallels of North Latitude, from St. Paul to Puget Sound." In *Reports of Explorations and Surveys, to Ascertain the Most Practicable and Economical Route for a Railroad from the Mississippi River to the Pacific Ocean*, vol. 12, book 1. Washington DC: Thomas H. Ford, 1860.
———. "Report of Explorations for a Route for the Pacific Railroad, near the Forty-Seventh and Forty-Ninth Parallels of North Latitude, from St. Paul to Puget Sound." In *Reports of Explorations and Surveys, to Ascertain the Most Practicable and Economical Route for a Railroad from the Mississippi River to the Pacific Ocean*, vol. 12. Washington DC: Beverley Tucker, 1855.
Stone, Arthur L. *Following Old Trails*. Missoula MT: Morton John Elrod, 1913.
Stuart, Granville. *Forty Years on the Frontier*. 2 vols. Edited by Paul C. Phillips. Cleveland: Arthur H. Clark Co., 1925.
———. *The Montana Frontier, 1852–1864*. Edited by Paul C. Phillips. Lincoln: University of Nebraska Press, 1977. (Reprint of volume 2 of *Forty Years on the Frontier*.)
Teit, James A. "The Salishan Tribes of the Western Plateaus." Edited by Franz Boas. In *Forty-Fifth Annual Report of the Bureau of American Ethnology, 1927–1928*, 23–396. Washington DC: Government Printing Office, 1930.

Thompson, David. *Columbia Journals*. Edited by Barbara Belyea. Montreal: McGill–Queen's University Press, 1994.

Thompson, M. Terry, and Steven M. Egesdal. *Salish Myths and Legends: One People's Stories*. Lincoln: University of Nebraska Press, 2008.

Thompson, Sally. *Disturbing the Sleeping Buffalo: 23 Unexpected Stories That Awaken Montana's Past*. Helena MT: Farcountry Press, 2024.

Thompson, Sally, with Kootenai Culture Committee and Pikunni Traditional Association. *People before the Park: The Kootenai and Blackfeet before Glacier National Park*. Helena: Montana Historical Society Press, 2015.

Thwaites, Reuben G., ed. *The Jesuit Relations and Allied Documents*. 73 vols. Cleveland: Burrows Brothers, 1896–1900.

Tolan, Providencia. *A Shining from the Mountains*. Montreal: Sisters of Providence, 1980.

Turney-High, Harry Holbert. *The Flathead Indians of Montana*. Memoirs of the American Anthropological Association 48. Menasha WI: American Anthropological Association, 1937.

Victor, Frances Fuller. *The River of the West: The Adventures of Joe Meek*. 2 vols. Edited by Winfred Blevins. Missoula MT: Mountain Press, 1983.

Walter, Dave. *More Montana Campfire Tales: Fifteen Historical Narratives*. Helena MT: Farcountry Press, 2002.

Weisel, George, ed. *Men and Trade on the Northwest Frontier as Shown by the Fort Owen Ledger*. Missoula: Montana State University, 1955.

Whealdon, Ben I., and the Montana Writers Project. *"I Will Be Meat for My Salish": The Montana Writers Project and the Buffalo of the Flathead Indian Reservation*. Edited by Robert Bigart. Pablo MT: Salish Kootenai College Press, 2001.

Wheeler, Olin D. *The Trail of Lewis and Clark, 1804–1904*. New ed. 2 vols. New York: G. P. Putnam's Sons, 1924.

Whitaker, William E. "Pierre-Jean De Smet's Remarkable Map of the Missouri River Valley, 1839: What Did He See in Iowa?" *Journal of the Iowa Archeological Society* 55 (2008): 1–13.

White, Catherine M., ed. *David Thompson's Journals Relating to Montana and Adjacent Regions, 1808–1812*. Missoula: Montana State University Press, 1950.

White, Kris A., and Janice St. Laurent. "Mysterious Journey: The Catholic Ladder of 1840." *Oregon Historical Quarterly* 97, no. 1 (1996): 70–88.

Wilson, David H., Jr. *Northern Paiutes of the Malheur: High Desert Reckoning in Oregon Country*. Lincoln: University of Nebraska Press, 2022.

Winthrop, John. "Generall Considerations for the Plantation in New England." London, 1629. In *The Winthrop Papers*, vol. 2, edited by Allyn B. Forbes. Boston: Massachusetts Historical Society, 1927–47.

Woodcock, Clarence. "Salish Tradition." *Oregon History Magazine* 39, nos. 3–4 (1996): 8–9.

Woody, F. H. "A Sketch of the Early History of Western Montana." *Contributions to the Historical Society of Montana* 2 (1896): 88–106.
Wunder, John R., ed. *Native American Sovereignty*. Abingdon, Oxfordshire, England: Routledge, 1999.
Wylie, Paul R. *Blood on the Marias: The Baker Massacre*. Norman: University of Oklahoma Press, 2016.

Index

Page numbers in italics refer to illustrations.